Jimi Hendrix FAQ

Series Editor: Robert Rodriguez

Jimi Hendrix FAQ

All That's Left to Know About the Voodoo Child

Gary J. Jucha

Backbeat
Books

An Imprint of Hal Leonard Corporation

Published in 2013 by Backbeat Books
An Imprint of Hal Leonard Corporation
7777 West Bluemound Road
Milwaukee, WI 53213

Trade Book Division Editorial Offices
33 Plymouth St., Montclair, NJ 07042

The FAQ series was conceived by Robert Rodriguez and developed with Stuart Shea.

Printed in the United States of America

Book design by Snow Creative Services

Library of Congress Cataloging-in-Publication Data

Jucha, Gary J.
  Jimi Hendrix FAQ : all that's left to know about the Voodoo Child / Gary J. Jucha.
    p. cm.
  Includes bibliographical references and index.
  ISBN 978-1-61713-095-3
1. Hendrix, Jimi. 2. Rock musicians—United States—Biography. I. Title. II. Title:
Jimi Hendrix frequently asked questions.
  ML410.H476J83 2013
  787.87'166092—dc23
  [B]
                                                                    2012040963

www.backbeatbooks.com

For the young man
wearing his Jimi Hendrix T-shirt
on the 27 bus in Madrid, Spain,
on July 9, 2011

Contents

Foreword

He was like no other guitarist, and ever will be. In musical expanse and ambition, showmanship, songwriting abilities, overwhelming technique, flash, and charisma, Jimi Hendrix is revered as the most incandescent guitar player of the twentieth century, the century of the guitar. His sonic fretprints gathered all the earthen streams of popular music—the rock & roll, the rhythm & blues, the surf & turf— and propelled them into our future, where they await us today, a howl of feedback like a loop of returning comet.

That he accomplished all this body of work by the age of twenty-seven, in a career that only flourished within a five year span, makes his tale upon this earth even more fantastical. Once you saw him, you never forgot him. I witnessed Hendrix for the first time early in his lifeline, in August of 1966, at the moment when he was about to claim his destiny. He had been playing at the Café Wha? in Greenwich Village on MacDougal Street, with a back-up band known as the Blue Flames. He was calling himself Jimmy James then, having done his duty as a sideman with the Isley Brothers and Little Richard, where he was inevitably fired for stealing the show. This is what he proceeded to do that night, around the corner on Bleecker where the Café Au Go Go was having a Blues Bash. Richie Havens was on the bill, as was John Hammond Jr. with his Nighthawks; and sometime during the latter's set, John called up Jimi/Jimmy to sit in. I don't remember what he played, only how he played it: hammering on the guitar from back of his head, gnawing at the strings with his teeth, taking those 12-bar blues and elasticizing them in the same way Robert Johnson, or John Lee Hooker, or Buddy Guy might've, and then some.

It was during this merging of time and space that he was discovered by ex-Animal Chas Chandler and brought to England to become who he was meant to be. Wisely, Chandler not only encouraged the outré pyrotechnics of Jimi's guitar playing, but understood that, to truly realize his potential, Jimi needed to be more than an instrumentalist. Bracing him with a band that gave him enough latitude to wail at will—Mitch Mitchell's jazz-inflected drums, Noel Redding's guitar-like bass—Jimi partook of the dreamscape that was sixties psychedelia, enhanced by Eddie Kramer's sonic adventurism in the studio, and the willingness of the newly-empowered "progressive" rock audience to explore the interstellar reaches of his virtuosic talent.

There are iconic moments that have been seared into memory. On his knees at Monterey Pop, coaxing flames from his Stratocaster; the spangled stars of Woodstock, reconfiguring the National Anthem so it spoke to a generation anew; machine-gunning the Fillmore as the last moment of the sixties crossroaded at midnight into a new decade. He had high hopes for the seventies, when, in the cozy underground labyrinths of Electric Lady, his recording studio only a few blocks from where I first saw him, he mused about the universal language of music, and how to incorporate all these streams into its own tongue. If this was not in the cards, then his noble attempt, spread over a body of work that roams the spaceways even more so today than when Jimi lit the fuse on his interstellar rocket, stands as man's quest for leaving this Earth and venturing beyond.

He lived the myth of the rock star, when rock stars walked tall about the firmament, jamming into the afterhours dawn surrounded by all manner of temptation, fueling the adrenal stimulation that is creation at its highest. Garbed as some Inca chieftain, his shows—of immolation and human sacrifice—combined ritual and magick. Sometimes, though, the trappings got to him. One night, dressed in my own love beads and sandals and Nehru shirt, I went to see him at the old Symphony Theater in Newark. Martin Luther King had just been assassinated. Jimi looked out at his audience, who seemed to ignore what had transpired, waiting instead for that moment when Jimi would dismantle his instrument. He felt the weight of the gift he had been given and wondered if it was all worth it.

His death-by-misadventure came at an inopportune moment, when he was beginning to move his music to a newer, even more inclusive level that presaged his maturing musical grasp. The many what-if's are left to the imagination, even if he did predict the future in "1983 . . . (A Merman I Should Turn to Be)." One can imagine collaborations, productions, performances that simplified even as they reached further inside him, heading toward the core of his being like a planet falling into the sun.

He's fun to play, to emulate his spidery fingers accessing new shapes and chordal relationships on the guitar neck; he's fun to effect, given his volume and tonal palette, and lends well to overloading an amplifier; and he's fun to swagger, because he has a great sense of humor amidst his need to express the deep of emotionals. If I revere him as a guitar player, it's the songwriter who I sing along to: "Purple Haze," "Up from the Stars," and the divine "Little Wing," one of the most beautiful love odes ever written.

His flamboyant arc and life-lived to eleven are legend. There are as many questions as answers, and these frequency responses, like recording waves of sound, etch their imprint on the noise he would wrench from his instrument. Behind each musician's music is the musician, the essence of our relationship with sound and the making.

Lenny Kaye
December 2012

Lenny Kaye has been Patti Smith's guitarist since her band's inception. As a record producer and writer, he has worked with such artists as Suzanne Vega, Soul Asylum, Allen Ginsberg, and Waylon Jennings. His 1972 compilation of garage-rock, *Nuggets*, has long been regarded as defining a genre and was chosen by *Rolling Stone* as one of the most important rock albums of all time.

Acknowledgments

Jimi had his Catherina and I have my Kimarie: you are the love of my life and truly "the measure of my dreams," as the seemingly immortal Shane MacGowan sang.

For my two creative children—Zachary and Calla—let this be proof that it is never too late to succeed creatively.

For my younger brother Brian who is always there for me and to whom I owe a depth of gratitude for caring for our mother over the last thirteen months of her life.

For the Noones (Gerry, Kara, Eilish, and Megan): you mean more to me than words can ever express.

For Jim Epperly who helped guide me through perhaps the darkest period of my life, one that coincided with the writing of these pages.

This book would not exist if it weren't for Victor Marinelli (or Hellbomb Vic, and HBV, as he was known for eighteen months). Who says men can't make friends in their fifties? Bored one Thanksgiving weekend, HBV created a blog called *Hellbomb* that was supposed to be about motorcycles but changed direction after he asked me if I'd contribute. *Hellbomb* soon focused in on MusicArtThis&That, and for eighteen months or so, we posted positive reviews and articles and interviews that shed light on artists whose work we loved and wanted to shout about from hilltops (but settled for a blog).

We didn't do *Hellbomb* all by ourselves, of course, and so I do need to acknowledge the other writers who kept contributing even though we couldn't pay them a penny. It was a labor of love on their part. Thanks then to Kirsten "Boom Boom" Lee, "Ersatz Erik" Wuttke, PJ Owen, and "Anthony Kaboom" Kibort for everything they suggested and provided. (Extra thanks goes out to Anthony for reading over a few drafts of the chapters in this book.) Everything we wrote about is still available at Hellbombinc.com. You should check *Hellbomb* out. There's some wonderfully intelligent writing, and you might discover a new artist who will change the course of your life . . . like Titus Andronicus or Carla Bozulich or Roberto Bolaño.

If it hadn't been for *Hellbomb*, Robert Rodriguez would not have seen my Rockers Galore feature about the Clash's 16 Tons tour and would not have asked me if I was interested in contributing to his FAQ Series. The original request to do a book on the Clash morphed into this contribution on Jimi

Hendrix. (Hopefully something on the Clash or Joe Strummer materializes farther on down the road.) I appreciate Robert and publisher John Cerullo giving me an opportunity to share my thoughts on "King Guitar" (this sobriquet for Jimi was coined by a British journalist and has stuck with me over the years).

At Backbeat Books, I need to thank Gary Morris for editing my manuscript, and my Associate Editor Bernadette Malavarca, who walked me through the process of publishing my first book. Believe me: Bernadette has the patience of a saint.

And last I have to thank Lenny Kaye for providing the foreword. When I was beginning my research for this book, I stumbled across Lenny's *Rolling Stone* review of Jimi's first posthumous recording *The Cry of Love* and thought how cool it'd be if I could get Lenny to do the foreword for my book. We've never met, but as a Patti Smith aficionado, I've crossed paths with Lenny at a distance as far back as the Patti Smith Group's appearance at Avery Fisher Hall on March 24, 1976. I've seen Patti and her guitarist over sixty times since then, and so it's a real honor having Lenny contribute the foreword.

Introduction

I clearly recall the day *after* Jimi Hendrix died.

I was riding a Q44 West Farms–bound MTA bus that was crossing the Hudson River via the Whitestone Bridge. I had been attending Saint Helena's High School for only a few weeks, and since my stop was the second stop after the bus entered the Bronx, I was zipping up my bag full of school books and comics when a *New York Times* headline caught my eye: "Jimi Hendrix, Rock Star, Is Dead in London at 27."

I'd like to say I was already a big fan, but, remember, I was only a high school freshman. My five bucks allowance was spent every weekend at King Karol or Korvette's building up my burgeoning record collection with Beatles and Rolling Stones and—yes, I admit it—Monkees albums. Any left-over change was spent on rock magazines. According to those magazines, either Jimi Hendrix or Eric Clapton was King Guitar—the greatest guitarist in the world—but that summed up all I knew about Jimi Hendrix.

My total exposure, up until then, to the man who "played it left hand" (as Bowie said of Ziggy Stardust) had been a short clip of the Jimi Hendrix Experience on David Steinberg's *Music Scene*, a forty-five minute show the comedian hosted on Monday nights.

Now why would I remember a forty-five-second clip—if that—on a forty-five-minute show?

Because where else had a baseball fan like me ever seen a guitarist bat an amplifier?! I watched as Hendrix's scrawny bassist Noel Redding picked up a small amplifier and threw it toward Hendrix, who—grinning widely—swung his Fender Stratocaster and hit the amplifier, shattering the guitar as so many bats do nowadays. The amplifier flew a few feet before crashing to the concert stage. I had never seen anything like it.

The Saturday following the guitarist's death, I raced out to buy something by the Jimi Hendrix Experience. There were three studio albums prominently displayed among other Hendrix recordings on the shelf lining the right side of King Karol Records. I asked the intimidating, thin man behind the counter what was the best Jimi Hendrix record; cryptically, he said all three. I'm sure I looked confused. Finally, he pointed at the Hindu-looking cover and said that was the one to buy, but I was already gravitating toward the one that seemed aflame.

I picked it up. Back then those 12-inch albums seemed to me stuffed with the answers to the mysteries of the universe. I flipped the album jacket over. The back cover photo of the Experience—Hendrix wearing his Gypsy Eyes jacket and sitting and flanked by Redding and Mitchell, his massive hands crossed at the wrists pointing to his sidemen—has been a favorite ever since. I wanted it, only *Electric Ladyland* was a double album costing more money than I had. The other two Experience albums were within my price range, but being unable to get the Experience record I wanted, I spent the money on something else. (Probably Grand Funk Railroad because they were my favorite band now that the Beatles had disbanded.)

Fast-forward another year. I'm now a high school sophomore accompanying my friend Albert Hue into Manhattan to act as a front so he could meet his white girlfriend. Her parents objected to their relationship because he was a Chinese American, so I had to call for her at her apartment and bring her to Albert waiting on a nearby street corner downstairs. I don't remember her name but do remember that the young couple thought of "Alone Again (Naturally)"—the then hit record by Gilbert O'Sullivan—as being "their" song, so let's call her "Gilbertine."

Albert and Gilbertine and I headed downtown to Greenwich Village, where I had never been. I hadn't been in Manhattan much either. We wandered into a record store where I saw *Are You Experienced* in the window. I still did not own anything by Jimi Hendrix and said I always wanted to get one of his records. "He's supposed to be the best guitarist ever!" I told Albert, holding and inspecting the psychedelic cover. "I'll buy it for you," Albert said. "You sure?" "You're doing me a favor. Let me return it." And so that's how I acquired my first Jimi Hendrix record. I like to imagine that I was in Village Oldies and that Lenny Kaye, later of Patti Smith Group fame, sold it to me, but I know that's pure daydreaming. What I do know is that it was the first move in a long relationship with the music of Jimi Hendrix and the man himself.

I was soon buying everything Hendrix related that I could find. My first T-shirt was a Jimi Hendrix T-shirt bought at a head shop: it was yellow, with the same image of Jimi in blue that adorns the *Crash Landing* cover. I bought the first posthumous albums released by Michael Jeffery and the unfairly maligned albums overseen by Alan Douglas. I bought black light posters, too, got stoned at midnight screenings of *Jimi Hendrix* (recommended) and *Rainbow Bridge* (not), and now own every legally released recording and then some. Well, I exaggerate a little. I do not own the 7″ single of "Voodoo Child (Slight Return)" b/w "No Such Animal" and some of the Dagger releases.

And I'll admit to trading in some of the inferior Ed Chalpin–released recordings after I realized what an insult they are to Hendrix.

I've heard many of the bootlegs, seen most of the filmed performances, read most of the books. There are a lot of tall tales in them; some told by Jimi to hide a shabby childhood and some told by associates to cover their tracks because, you see, the story of Jimi Hendrix's life and music is one of a redemption song. You could say he was sold to the merchant ships. His was a life that spun out of control but has been salvaged by the one thing he cared for most deeply: his music. From the boxes and boxes of unreleased studio and live recordings he left behind, he has been redeemed. I'd like to share some of my expertise, acquired knowledge, and maybe a few original insights with you about his life and his work that keeps on beating decades after his death. The most amazing thing about Jimi Hendrix is not that he was King Guitar but how the great expectations he had for the music he wrote, recorded, and produced to affect the world have been met.

I'm Wondering If They Don't Want Me Around

At Last the Beginning

Belly Button Window" was selected by coproducers Eddie Kramer and Mitch Mitchell to close out *The Cry of Love*, the first of many posthumous Jimi Hendrix releases. Recorded by Hendrix alone on August 22, 1970, at his new Electric Lady Studios, it was sung from the perspective of an unborn and unwanted child in his mother's womb. He "can see a lot of frowns," and he wonders "if they want me around." In a little over two and a third years, the Supreme Court would hand down *Roe v. Wade* legalizing abortion, the act that the parents of the boy in "Belly Button Window" seem to be illegally contemplating.

I mention this because in the intervening years, *Roe v. Wade* has polarized the electorate and placed the largely liberal "Freedom to Choose" advocates against the largely conservative "Right to Life" movement. It is these same conservatives who argue against honoring Jimi Hendrix by issuing a stamp in his honor because they say it would glorify drug use. But if the "Right to Life" movement really knew anything about Jimi Hendrix's childhood, they'd understand he is their ideal poster child; that Jimi Hendrix overcame the odds of being an unwanted and uncared for black boy in a racist society to personally persevere and triumph as one of the twentieth century's most influential musicians is the most persuasive argument against abortion I have ever heard.

A fast-forward backward glance at Jimi Hendrix's life reveals that his seventeen-year-old mother Lucille gave birth to Johnny Allen Hendrix at 10:15 a.m. on November 27, 1942, at King County Hospital in Seattle, Washington.

His father, James Allen (Al) Hendrix, was serving in the U.S. Army in the Pacific theater during World War II and would not see his son until

December 1945 when he went to Berkeley, California. There he reclaimed Johnny from Mrs. Champ, a church friend of Clarice Lawson Jeter (Lucille's mother), who had been raising Johnny ever since Lucille's beating by John Page, a man Lucille had been living with. Although uncertain if the boy was indeed his son and not John Page's, Al had the boy's name legally changed to James Marshall Hendrix on November 11, 1946. The middle name mirrored that of Al's brother, Leon Marshall.

With her son back in Seattle and John Page serving five years in prison for beating her, Lucille moved back in with Al for what would be remembered as the best months of their marriage. Al and Lucille went out a lot—their first date was a Fats Waller concert—but they also drank and fought a lot as Al was often jealous of the men Lucille met. Hendrix's brother Leon was born. Then there was another boy (Joseph Allen), unfortunately born with defects: the source of more fighting between Hendrix's parents. With Al unable to find well-paying employment, the family moved frequently and finally the children were sent to live with Al's mother, Nora, in Vancouver, British Columbia, where she entertained young Jimmy with tales of his Cherokee ancestors.

Hendrix's Cherokee heritage through Grandma Nora *and* his maternal grandmother Clarice Lawson Jeter made a lasting impression on Jimmy, and he would forever after speak of his Indian heritage. (Actually, as recounted in William Saunders's *Jimi Hendrix London*, one of Jimi's funniest comments was his saying, when shown the cover artwork featuring a modified Hindu devotional painting that Track Records planned for *Axis: Bold as Love*: "I ain't that kind of Indian.") It was Hendrix's embrace of his Indian blood, and not his black blood, that went a long way toward making him seem colorless, and, therefore, not a threat to the white rock 'n' rollers who, in turn, embraced him and his music.

Jimmy returned to live with his parents in Seattle in October 1949. In fall of the following year a sister was born, but Kathy Ira was blind and made a ward of the state. Another sister named Pamela was born in October 1950, but she was placed in foster care. Al Hendrix's unwillingness to pay for the operation that would correct Joseph Allen's birth defect led to Lucille leaving him in fall of 1951, and, in her absence, Jimmy was more or less raised by his grandmothers, an Aunt Delores, and friends and neighbors who felt pity for Jimmy and his brother Leon, who were often left alone while Al tuned out with his vices.

Lucille had much in common with another famous rock 'n' roll mother: John Lennon's Julia. They were two party girls who married too young, liked to have a good time, and were more like an older sister or hip aunt than a mother to their sons. Still, the Hendrix boys preferred Lucille to Al.

To biographer Charles R. Cross, Leon said that he and Jimmy "used to get into trouble on purpose so we could go visit our mother. My dad made this our punishment—'You gotta stay the weekend at your mama's if you're bad!' That was what we wanted!"

Lucille was married to her second husband, William Mitchell, for just one month when she died on February 2, 1958, and so her brick grave marker in Greenwood Memorial Park in Renton, Washington, bore his surname and not that of Hendrix. Her son was buried in the same cemetery twelve years later. (It is interesting how certain surnames from Jimmy Hendrix's childhood reappear during the height of his stardom. His middle name Marshall was the same name as his favored amplifier, and Mitchell, of course, is shared by the man who would be his favored drummer.)

Lucille's death was determined to be the result of splenic rupture and hemorrhage. But while Lucille literally passed way, she also figuratively passed into myth. His brother Leon remembered Jimmy telling him his mother was an angel. The reason she was able to assume this mythic role to Jimmy in death was because, while publicly respectful to him—and despite a "photoshopping" of the past in interviews and his book *My Son Jimi*—Jimmy's father was a miserly, distant figure who favored Leon (until he was suspiciously written out of Al Hendrix's will in the 1990s and bequeathed only one gold album).

Al told his two sons to take their mother's death like a man, and each "man" drank a shot of Seagram's 7. Al did not allow his sons to attend their mother's funeral. Hendrix's relationship with his father—while never previously close—never recovered. And you can see in this childhood—the absent mother and father and shuffling around between relatives—the source of Hendrix's inability to form deep, meaningful relationships with other kids in the neighborhood and, when older, with women and even his fellow musicians and producers.

Believe it or not, brooms are an inanimate object that figure largely in recollections of Hendrix's youth. And once one is aware of this, the "Wind Cries Mary" lyric that "A broom is drearily sweeping up the broken pieces of yesterday's life" becomes more revealing. It was one of the first lyrics Hendrix incorporated autobiography into that was not related to life on the road.

Shirley Harding (daughter of family friend Dorothy Harding) would tell bedtime stories to children, including young Jimmy. The stories featured three characters, including Roy, the Sweeping Boy (based on Jimmy because he was always sweeping the Harding kitchen), who was one day going to be "rich and famous because of his broom guitar," as recalled by Ebony Harding for author Charles R. Cross.

This may seem like an odd detail, but ever since sometime in 1953, Jimmy had been holding brooms and strumming along to songs on the radio. His brother remembered Jimmy taking the broom to school with him. One school counselor even urged school authorities to find the money to buy Jimmy a guitar, thinking it would make him a better student. (Look at concert photos of Hendrix, and the guitar necks are held like broom handles.)

Hang onto your dragonfly now while I take you on a quick trip from Seattle to New York City, a trip through Jimmy's earliest gear and the bands he played it in. I'm sure Hendrix wouldn't mind seeing as he was usually losing or pawning them. His first "guitar" was a ukulele and then a 1-string acoustic guitar bought for him for five dollars by family friend Ernestine Benson when Al would not. (This lends further credence to Keith Richards's advice in *Life* that children should be given an acoustic guitar as their first guitar because it's better for learning finger coordination.) Jimmy would walk around with the acoustic guitar slung downwards across his back like the hero in *Johnny Guitar*, a Nicholas Ray flick Jimmy had seen.

Jimi Hendrix got credit on Little Richard's 45s only after his death.
Courtesy of Robert Rodriguez

Jimmy listened to any guitarists he could—Ole Grand Opry performers on the radio, Ernestine Benson's blues recordings, Duane Eddy—and had seen Elvis Presley (from his perch on a hilltop overlooking Sicks' Stadium) and Little Richard—and knew he needed an electric guitar. Again it was Ernestine Benson who came to the rescue as she hounded Jimmy's father to buy a white Supra Ozark from Myer's Music for his son. He didn't have an amplifier and he didn't have a case, but Jimmy had his first electric guitar.

The first song Jimmy Hendrix learned to play was the Fabulous Wailers' "Tall Cool One," maybe because, with his electric guitar, he felt taller and cooler. But as fate would have it, the Supra was stolen when he left it backstage at Birdland, a Seattle club that Jimmy's second band, the Rocking Kings, played at.

Some think he left his guitar at the club because he was afraid what his father would do to it. Sammy Drain, a school friend, told author Sharon Lawrence that "Al sometimes called it devil's music," referring to the music Jimmy played. Jimmy's father wasn't about to immediately reward his son's foolishness with another guitar, so Jimmy was without a guitar until members of the Rocking Kings chipped in to buy his second electric guitar: a white Silvertone Danelectro. This guitar came along with a Silvertone amplifier, too.

Jimmy soon painted the Danelectro red with the name Betty Jean in white lettering along the base of the body for his second girlfriend Betty Jean Morgan, not his first as is commonly reported. Hendrix played the only guitar he would name for a girl with the Rocking Kings, Thomas and the Tomcats, and the King Kasuals, by which time he was a soldier with the 101st Airborne Division in Campbell, Kentucky, and already plotting his early discharge. As soon as that came through, he traded in his Danelectro for a red Epiphone Wilshire, sort of a poor man's Gibson SG. It was cosigned for by Army buddy and fellow King Kasual bassist Billy Cox, of whom we will talk more in later chapters.

Jimmy painted the black scratch plate white to make it more visually striking. He took the Wilshire back with him to Vancouver, where he avoided his father and Betty Jean Morgan in Seattle by living with his grandmother Nora and played with the Vancouvers in December 1963. Springtime, however, found him back in Tennessee, playing the chitlin' circuit for the first time either with the King Kasuals or supporting the likes of Solomon Burke, Otis Redding (later to be paired with Jimi Hendrix on a live recording issued by Reprise Records of the Monterey International Pop Festival), and the Marvelettes. By this time the Epiphone Wilshire had been traded in for a Wilshire Coronet, yet again a poor man's version of another Gibson guitar: the Les Paul Junior.

Lured by the promise of work that never materialized, Jimmy headed for New York City in December of 1963. A pattern also began around this time of pawning his guitar to make ends meet and getting money from his latest flame or band leader to get the guitar out of hock, which is where it was in February 1964 when singer Kelly Isley—seeking a guitarist for the Isley Brothers' upcoming tour—was told of this amazing guitarist, who he sought out.

Jimmy knew the Isley Brothers' material, which was a definite advantage, but when asked to play something, he admitted his guitar was in a pawn shop. Kelly Isley paid to get it out of hock only to find the guitar had no strings, so he had to get some for Jimmy's guitar as well. In no time the guitar was in tune and Jimmy was in the Isley Brothers.

In his nine months with the group, Jimmy toured regularly, was given more freedom than normally offered sidemen, made his first studio recordings, and acquired a blond Fender Duo-Sonic. This is also the guitar Hendrix probably used for the Don Covay sessions that resulted in the first Top 40 single Hendrix performed on: "Mercy, Mercy" (now readily available on the *West Coast Seattle Boy* box set). Jimmy quit the Isley Brothers when one of their tours took them through Nashville. There he joined up with Gorgeous George Odell, got stranded in Kansas City, and made his way to Atlanta, where Little Richard hired him to be a member of his Upsetters.

A new band for Jimmy usually meant a new guitar, and so it is with his stint with the Upsetters where photos show Hendrix playing a sunburst Fender Jazzmaster. Little Richard, since 1962, had been attempting a comeback after turning his back on rock 'n' roll at the height of his commercial success to be a preacher. (Hendrix and his brother Leon attended one of Little Richard's sermons in Seattle in the summer of 1957.) When his attempts at cashing in on a rock 'n' roll revival didn't pan out, he tried R&B, with even less success.

Though Jimmy's stint in the band lasted approximately nine months and did include some studio time, it was not as rewarding a period as the nine months with the Isley Brothers. Little Richard allowed his backup band little freedom and was visibly upset when others tried to upstage him by dress or stage antics, something that led to confrontations with, and fines for, Maurice James, Jimmy's professional name at this time. Little Richard's lack of success also meant the band was not paid as promised. All Hendrix got out of his time with Little Richard was apparently a good imitation, as Jimi Hendrix was known in later years to be a gifted mimic.

Stranded in New York City in the summer of 1965, Hendrix tried to find work as a session musician. He signed a two-year contract with Sue Records owner Juggy Murray, but that is the last they saw of each other. Of much

Jimi may look happy backing Wilson Pickett, but his days as a sideman would soon be over.   *Photo by William "PoPsie" Randolph*

more long-term consequence was a meeting with Curtis Knight in the lobby of the Hotel America, located in Times Square on Forty-Seventh Street. Hendrix by this time had pawned the Jazzmaster, so when Knight offered Hendrix a job in his band the Squires, Knight also loaned him a Danelectro.

With Knight, Hendrix was also offered more musical freedom and recording sessions, including one that took place the following day. The PPX studio this session was held in was owned by Ed Chalpin, who, upon hearing the guitarist, signed Hendrix to a one dollar contract with PPX that followed Hendrix around like a bad penny for the rest of his life.

At PPX studios, Hendrix participated in many sessions for Curtis Knight (and one for Jayne Mansfield, the buxom B-movie actress) that seem destined to be continually reissued as inferior posthumous Hendrix recordings until the end of time.

During this busy time period, he also did some session work and gigs with the Isley Brothers, toured with Joey Dee and the Starliters of "Peppermint

Twist" fame, and joined King Curtis's All Stars for six months. The King Curtis stint culminated in performing as the house band for an Atlantic Records Showcase in May 1966 that featured the likes of Wilson Pickett, whose "In the Midnight Hour" was a favorite of Jimmy's.

May 1966, however, also found Jimmy playing a sunburst Fender Duo-Sonic with Curtis Knight's Squires, which had a flexible lineup, including saxophonist Lonnie Youngblood, the other primary source of inferior prefame posthumous recordings. Jimmy finally quit the Squires on May 20, 1966.

Knight's guitar was traded in for a white Fender Stratocaster—the difference paid by his first white girlfriend Carol Shiroky—and this was the guitar he unplugged on June 3, 1966, after playing as one of Carl Holmes's Commanders and was overheard to say: "That's the last time I play this shit."

For almost four years Jimmy Hendrix had played on package tours with the likes of legends Sam Cooke and Curtis Mayfield and backed a who's who of rhythm and blues stars including Otis Redding, Ike and Tina Turner, and a past-his-prime Little Richard. Poorly paid and often abandoned by the side of some dirt road, he figured he could starve as well as a front man as he could as a sideman. Despite inhibitions about his vocal ability, Jimmy Hendrix was ready to lead a group.

Where Do I Purchase My Ticket?

The Early Haze

C has Chandler said it wasn't until he heard Jimi Hendrix performing "Like a Rolling Stone" with the Blue Flames in Greenwich Village's Café Wha? that he understood Bob Dylan's lyrics. This is because Jimi Hendrix had an uncanny knack for inhabiting the cover songs he performed. Dylan may have written the lyrics, but Hendrix had lived them and knew what it was to be a rolling stone. Coming from Jimi's lips, Dylan's lyrics were more than clever wordplay; they were profound. It wasn't the last time Hendrix would out-Dylan Dylan.

A long way from the Seattle hometown that never was a home to him and touring as a chitlin' circuit sideman to both upcoming and down-on-their-luck frontmen, Hendrix knew what it was to scrounge for a meal, knew how it felt to be without a home, and had gotten used to living on the street. By the end of this chapter, he will be in London, the starting point of his ascension, but his girlfriend Kathy Etchingham said that success did not break his habit of walking around with a dollar in his shoe in case he found himself in desperate straits again. As he told her, he knew what it was like to eat rattlesnake. He knew what it was like to have nothing to lose, which is why he went to London, which he'd never visited, with a wannabe manager who said he would make him a star.

The Blue Flames

Not long after becoming a fixture at the Café Wha? on MacDougal Street—one door down from Minetta Lane—Hendrix tried convincing saxophonist Lonnie Youngblood to follow him downtown. Youngblood told author Charles R. Cross that Hendrix said the two of them could "own the Café Wha?"

But even though Youngblood respected Hendrix's abilities enough to invite him to sit in on June 1966 recording sessions, he could not hear what

Hendrix heard. Hendrix's new songs "were weird," and, with a wife and child to provide for and the mortgage on a house to pay off, he reasoned following his fellow musician downtown was impractical.

During a weeklong gig in late May as a Commander in Carl Holmes's band, Hendrix had been sighted by folk singer and guitarist Ritchie Havens, who urged him to find gigs in the Village. Seeing something of himself in Hendrix—in temperament if not musical style—Havens thought the Village, then—as almost always in the twentieth century—a melting pot of American bohemians: the folkies, poets, and abstract artists could find room for a black musician not finding acceptance in black musical circles. Havens told Hendrix he could arrange an audition with Manny Roth, manager of the Café Wha? (and uncle of Van Halen's original vocalist David Lee Roth).

Hendrix was well acquainted with Bob Dylan's albums by 1966 (the first Dylan album he is known to have owned is *The Freewheelin' Bob Dylan* and Hendrix's Harlem girlfriend Fayne Pridgeon often told the story of how Hendrix once spent his last five dollars on *Highway 61 Revisited*), but it is not known if he was aware that Dylan played at the Café Wha? the first night he came to Manhattan in 1962. If he did know this, he might have thought it auspicious that the same club of his hero's New York City debut was being recommended to him. Whatever the reason, Hendrix showed up one June night, white Fender Strat in hand, and introduced himself to Roth, who told him to take his shot when the house band took a break that evening.

Playing a slow blues solo, Hendrix was soon joined by Tommy "Regi" Butler, the house bassist. The two hit it off—Hendrix even showing Butler a riff to jam on—and soon they had a trio with Chas Matthews on drums: Jimi Hendrix's first trio, the blueprint for the Jimi Hendrix Experience. Hendrix called them the Blue Flames. (Contrary to what you'll read elsewhere, there is no record that this musical outfit was ever advertised as Jimmy James and the Blue Flames, even if Jimmy James was his then-current stage name. The "James" surname was in honor of bluesman Elmore James who shared Hendrix's affinity for loud amplification. Hendrix would go on to often record and perform James's "Bleeding Heart"—sometimes credited as "Blues in C#" and "People, People, Peoples" on Hendrix's recordings, official and otherwise—while use of "the Blue Flames" honored another bluesman: Memphis singer Junior Parker.) When not performing at Café Wha?, they used the Rainflowers for a band name as well as others.

Around this time, Hendrix met Randy Wolfe at the infamous Manny's Music on Forty-Eighth Street in Manhattan (closed and converted in June 2009 into part of a Sam Ash guitar shop). All of fifteen years of age, Wolfe had just relocated from California with his mother and stepfather and was shopping for a guitar when he saw Hendrix playing a guitar—"I think it was a Telecaster" he told *Guitar World* in 1985—and asked if he could try it out.

Wolfe was into the Delta blues, as was Hendrix, who must've been impressed by Wolfe's playing because "he told me his name was Jimmy James, and invited me down to the club that night, the Café Wha?, to play with him." Not before long Wolfe—rechristened by Hendrix as Randy California (the stage name he would keep as a founding member of the influential California-based rock band Spirit and until his death January 2, 1997, while surfing)—was playing rhythm to Jimmy James's lead.

Randy Wolfe became Randy California because there was already another Randy in the Blue Flames on bass. Despite his initial enthusiasm, "Regi" Butler had since been replaced occasionally by Manny's employee Jeff "Skunk" Baxter (later well known for his work with Steely Dan and the Doobie Brothers) and more often by Randy Palmer, a Texan, who was soon dubbed Randy Texas by Hendrix so he could differentiate between the two Randys. (Got to say this for Hendrix as a leader: he sure knew how to pick them. The Blue Flames were the only band Hendrix led prior to the formation of the Experience, and two of his Blue Flames went on to become noteworthy musicians in their own right.) Danny Casey had by this time replaced Matthews on drums.

The Blue Flames' repertoire chiefly consisted of covers. Given the source of their name, it is not surprising that they played several Junior Walker numbers, including "Driving Wheel," "In the Dark," "Annie Get Your Yo-Yo," and the 1965 hit "Shotgun" (although Walker recorded "Shotgun" with the All Stars and not the Blue Flames). They played a number of other hits from the mid-'60s: Don Covay's "Mercy, Mercy" (a session date Hendrix had contributed to), the Animals' "House of the Rising Sun," and the McCoys' "Hang On Sloopy."

They are rumored to have done the Beatles' "Rain," which was released as the B-side to "Paperback Writer" the same month of the Blue Flames founding. Hendrix is said to even have attempted mimicking John Lennon's backwards-taped vocals. Given Hendrix's fascination with, and later mastery of, backwards tape recordings, this sounds entirely plausible.

The Blue Flames also covered three songs Hendrix would perform infamously with the Experience: Bob Dylan's "Like a Rolling Stone," the Troggs' "Wild Thing," and a little song of jealousy and murder called "Hey Joe." According to Randy California, they worked up four originals, one of which was "Mr. Bad Luck" (later recorded by the Experience as "Look over Yonder"). Depending on who you believe, "Foxy Lady," "Remember," and "3rd Stone from the Sun" may have been the others. But while "Red

House" was in the works during this period, it was not attempted by the Blue Flames.

(Please note that when referencing titles, I will be using the original spelling. "Foxey Lady" and "Third Stone from the Sun" were how the song titles appeared on the American version of *Are You Experienced*, which—by the way—did not have a "?" on either album cover, although the American song title did.)

One final significant thing happened during this four-month period leading up to his signing by Chas Chandler: Jimmy James changed his name to Jimi James. Carol Shiroky remembers seeing Jimi James's name advertising the guitarist within the Café Wha? shortly before their breakup over Jimi James's interest in Linda Keith, Keith Richards's girlfriend, who had taken an excessive interest in the left-handed guitarist she saw as a bluesman who had more than paid his dues.

In August, Linda Keith persuaded the Animals' bassist Chas Chandler to check Hendrix out. Impressed by Hendrix's versions of "Hey Joe" and "Like a Rolling Stone," Chandler said he was interested in taking Hendrix back to England and producing him but that it would have to wait until the Animals' tour of America was over in September, by which time Hendrix was nowhere to be found, having already checked out of his Broadway hotel. Record producers had made empty promises to Hendrix before. With Linda Keith back in England, it took Chandler four frantic days to locate the musician he wanted to make a star.

Only Hendrix was noncommittal now about going to England. On the one hand he had just played a weeklong stand as a member of lineup fronted by John Hammond Jr. called the Screaming Nighthawks at Café Au Go Go, an upscale club in Greenwich Village. Hammond was a white bluesman of some repute who had recorded an album called *So Many Roads* in 1965 with musicians who would go on to support Bob Dylan and form the Band. His father, John Hammond, founded the careers of musicians who practically set the course for American pop music throughout the twentieth century. He helped further the careers of Benny Goodman, guitarist Charlie Christian, Billie Holiday, Bob Dylan, Aretha Franklin, and Bruce Springsteen. John Hammond Jr. had even convinced his father to give Hendrix a listen. With these gigs and John Hammond's interest, Hendrix might have felt he was on the cusp of making a breakthrough in his home country.

On the other hand, he felt he owed something to the other Blue Flames and tried to recruit his band members into going overseas with him. But as Randy California put it "Chas wasn't interested in me at all," a sentiment confirmed by Chandler's comment in *Ultimate Hendrix* that . . . "all

(California) wanted to do was play the blues and I didn't think that just playing blues was the way to make a hit with Jimi Hendrix."

And so, as California remembered it: "One day I arrived to find that Jimmy'd split for England. That was the end of (the Blue Flames)."

Linda Keith

With her boyfriend playing the Manning Bowl in Lynn, Massachusetts, English-born fashion model Linda Keith decided to hit the town with two local friends: Roberta Goldstein and Mark Kaufman. It was June 24, 1966, and one of the clubs they hit was an empty Cheetah with its two stages. Despite leading the Blue Flames, Hendrix was playing "this shit" with Curtis Knight and the Squires again. The money the Blue Flames was making at Café Wha? was seven bucks a night for the whole band, and so Hendrix occasionally picked up sideman jobs for the money.

Initially the band didn't interest Keith, but then she saw Hendrix "playing quite discreetly in the back row" as Tony Brown, Hendrix's first historian, quotes her in *Jimi Hendrix—A Visual Documentary*. (Possibly because he found it embarrassing to find himself a Squire once again.) Keith found she was watching his hands. Mesmerized, she cajoled Kaufman into inviting the guitarist to their table for a drink and afterwards back to her friends' apartment that was known as the Red House for its red velvet walls. Hendrix did two things for the first time that night: dropped acid and, back at Richards's Hilton Hotel room, heard Dylan's newest album *Blonde on Blonde*, playing along with it on guitar.

Whether or not Keith and Hendrix were lovers depends on your point of view. Carol Shiroky thought so. Hendrix's friend from the village Paul Caruso certainly thought so. The first two music industry executives Keith showcased Hendrix to thought so too.

Seeing a bluesman extraordinaire in Hendrix, Keith made it her mission that summer to have him noticed before she went back to London when the thirty-date 1966 Rolling Stones American tour was over on August 28th. Keith persuaded Rolling Stones manager Andrew Loog Oldham to drop by the Café Au Go Go, where the Blue Flames were playing (probably as the Rainflowers), and give Hendrix a listen. Keith had even "borrowed" Keith Richards's white Fender Stratocaster and given it to Hendrix to replace the pawned guitar Shiroky had bought him.

Oldham passed on representing Hendrix partially because Hendrix's type of music didn't appeal to him but primarily because he was concerned with how Keith Richards was going to react when he found out his girlfriend was running around with a black American musician speaking to her from the Café Au Go Go stage.

Seymour Stein also noticed the close relationship between Hendrix and Keith both times he saw Hendrix play, and it made him apprehensive as well about managing the "amazing guitar player." During Stein's first visit, the interracial couple argued when Hendrix roughly handled and damaged Richards's white Stratocaster. Stein would go on to found Sire Records, future home of the Ramones, Talking Heads, and the Undertones, but not Jimi Hendrix.

Linda Keith insists, "I was not his girlfriend; I was still dating Keith Richards," and the fact that she persuaded all of the Rolling Stones to attend a Hendrix gig at Ondine's on July 2nd after their appearance at Forest Hills Tennis Stadium in Queens, New York, leads one to believe that the relationship was platonic . . . at this point anyway. Only Bill Wyman was impressed by Hendrix on this occasion, but there was little the Rolling Stones' bassist could do for the guitarist as the Rolling Stones' tour moved on to the Asbury Park Convention Hall in Asbury Park, New Jersey, the following night.

Keith had played her best cards and come up empty. On August 2nd she bumped into Chas Chandler, also in Ondine's. The Animals had been touring with Herman's Hermits since July 1st but were not part of the bill for three August gigs in Atlantic City. After a show in West Hyannis, Massachusetts, the Animals had flown back to New York City. When Chandler mentioned he was leaving the Animals at the tour's end and looking for someone to produce, Keith, as related in John McDermott's *Setting the Record Straight*, told Chandler there's "this guy in the Village that [Chandler] had to see." The Animals were playing Wollman Skating Rink in Central Park as part of the summer Rheingold Festival the next night, but Chandler made plans to meet Keith down at the Café Wha? before the show.

"The first song Jimi played on stage that afternoon was 'Hey Joe,' " said Chandler in a *Guitar World* interview. "He had it all. You just sat there and thought to yourself, 'This is ridiculous—why hasn't anybody signed this guy up?' " (Of course a few had. See Chapter 12 for more details.)

Having made good on her promise to get Hendrix a manager but having broken up with Keith Richards, Keith continued to attend Jimi James's concerts through August. Returning to England, Keith was around when Hendrix arrived in London in late September. While she would figure in a few wild stories, including a bar fight and stealing back Keith Richards's Strat, for the most part she disappeared from Hendrix's life after 1966.

Near the end of his life, however, Linda Keith was often on Hendrix's mind again. He recorded a new song called "Send My Love to Linda" that he said was an ode for the woman that got him a manager. During his performance of "Red House" at the Isle of Wight Festival on August 30, 1970, he ad-libbed the lyrics saying it was Linda—not his baby—who "doesn't live here anymore." And, during the last week of his life, he met her at London's Speakeasy and not by accident. He handed her a guitar case with a new Stratocaster, saying that he owed her it for giving him one when they first met in New York City in 1966. It's only when she got home that she discovered the letters she wrote him that summer were in the case with the guitar.

The Animals

Chandler and Hendrix did not fly off to London on August 4, 1966. Chandler had to be in Fort Wayne, Indiana, because the Animals were still in the middle of their American tour supporting Herman's Hermits, a tour that wouldn't end until September 5th with a weeklong appearance at the Steel Pier Resort in Atlantic City, New Jersey. Even with Chandler's departure and the intention to build the New Animals around singer Eric Burdon when the band got back to England, the 1966 summer tour of America could not be classified as a farewell tour because founding member Alan Price had already left and so the touring band was not the original lineup that produced a myriad of hits, including "We Gotta Get out of This Place," "Don't Let Me Be Misunderstood," and "House of the Rising Sun."

Any self-respecting retelling of Jimi Hendrix's rise and fall should include a few words on the Animals. Not because the band was inducted into the Rock and Roll Hall of Fame in 1994, but because it was the Animals' organization—its management team and roadies—that abetted Hendrix's ascension during his early days in London. The Animals were the de facto launching pad for the Jimi Hendrix Experience.

For example, when unable to locate his birth certificate because, unbeknownst to him, the name on his birth certificate was Johnny Allen not James Marshall, it was the Animals' U.S. representative and attorney Leon Dicker who handled the paperwork resulting in U.S. passport, no. G1044108, for Hendrix. When arriving at Heathrow Airport on September 24, 1966, it was Terry McVay, the Animals' roadie, who carried Keith Richards's purloined guitar because Hendrix didn't have a work permit. When the Animals' manager became Hendrix's comanager, their Bermuda tax dodge became the Experience's tax dodge. So a retelling of the Animals' history is warranted.

It begins with Alan Price, who formed the Alan Price Rhythm and Blues Combo, a jazz-flavored trio with a fluid lineup that eventually expanded to include Hilton Valentine on guitar, Chandler on bass, John Steel on drums and an R&B enthusiast named Eric Burdon on vocals. The combo played clubs in Newcastle-upon-Tyne, including the Downbeat Club and Club-A-Go-Go, both owned by Michael Jeffery, who signed the fivesome with insurance money received after one of his nightclubs mysteriously burnt down like a scene out of *Goodfellas*. The Animals were the first band Jeffery would manage.

An unusual scheme was concocted whereby the Animals would play Yardbirds gigs and vice versa. Jeffery came up with many unusual schemes, but this one was brainstormed by Giorgio Gomelsky, the Yardbirds' manager. In London, playing for the Yardbirds, the combo

The Animals in 1964 were bigger than the Rolling Stones.

Courtesy of Robert Rodriguez

enjoyed easy success and soon changed their name, allegedly because one night in Club-A-Go-Go Alan Price had overheard a patron saying, "The animals are playing tonight." If Price did indeed relate this to his bandmates, he came to regret it, as he was not in favor of changing his band's name.

In a similar position as when Chandler found Hendrix, Mickey Most was a musician looking to make a career change but remained in the industry when he attended an Animals concert at Club-A-Go-Go and told them he was interested in producing them. (He would go on to hold a producer chair for Herman's Hermits, Donovan, the Jeff Beck Group, and others. He specialized in producing hit singles; his demise in the late 1960s was greased when he continued to champion the three-minute song and failed to understand the change the long-playing album was bringing to the industry.) The Animals would go on to release ten studio albums, five EPs, and twenty-two singles (not including compilations and reissues).

Price and Burdon often butted heads, and this as well as a fear of flying led to Price leaving and being replaced with Mick Gallagher (later one of the Blockheads supporting Ian Drury and touring member and session player for the Clash) and then Dave Rowberry. Drummer John Steel was soon to leave as well.

Following the 1966 American tour, the New Animals quickly became Eric Burdon and the Animals with a completely new lineup except for Burdon and Barry Jenkins, the drummer who had replaced Steel. This lineup embraced psychedelia and the Summer of Love and relocated to California. The albums were more experimental, reflecting the era, but failed to connect with the generation they were supposedly representing. There were more lineup changes, including a stint by Andy Summers, later of Police fame, but Eric Burdon and the New Animals never matched the chart success of the Animals. They disbanded in February 1969.

Reunions followed as well as legal disputes as to who owned the rights to the Animals' name. In England it was awarded to original drummer John Steel.

Chas Chandler

When Jimi Hendrix met Chandler in August 1966, it was the third time the two crossed paths. The first occasion was on a multiact bill that included the Isley Brothers and the Animals at New York City's Paramount Theatre in September of 1964. The second time was at the same venue in April 1965, while Hendrix was supporting Little Richard. Being a sideman in someone else's band, Hendrix did not make an impression on Chandler, understandably so since the Animals were at the height of their popularity as part of the British Invasion and riding a series of Mickey Most–produced hit singles.

Bryan James "Chas" Chandler was born in Newcastle-upon-Tyne, England, on December 18, 1938. Known as Newcastle to the rest of the world, it is a workingman's town, a fate Chandler escaped by becoming a musician. Being 6′4″ tall, Chandler looked every bit the bassist playing his Gibson EB-2 in the Animals. Best known for his descending bass riff in the Animals' hit "Don't Let Me Be Misunderstood," it was revealed by John McDermott in 2009's *Ultimate Hendrix* that it was Chandler, not Noel Redding, playing the striding bassline in "Hey Joe." Redding, a guitarist, was still getting acquainted with playing bass during the "Hey Joe" sessions, so Chandler overdubbed the bassline without Redding's knowledge. It was the only Hendrix track that Chandler played on.

Few musicians in the '50s and early '60s considered playing in a rock band as a lifelong career. Ringo Starr even said he was sending money to his aunt so he'd be able to open a hair salon once Beatlemania subsided. By all accounts members of the Animals fared even worse than most musicians, and when Chandler departed at the end of the summer of 1966, all he is reported to have had for his five years involvement were £1,000 and five bass guitars. No doubt Chandler had seen how Jeffery was the one member of the Animals entourage with money.

Not only did he have an eye out for an act, but he knew he wanted "Hey Joe" for that act's first single. The Leaves had had a minor hit in America with Billy Roberts's song and Chandler thought with the right production it could be a hit in England. In his autobiography *Life*, Keith Richards says Linda Keith says she played Tim Rose's demo for Hendrix and that's why he favored the slower arrangement. It is likely that Chandler in Ondine's had mentioned to Keith he was looking for an act to record "Hey Joe" because when Chandler walked down the stairs and into Café Wha? "It just so happened the first song Hendrix played that afternoon was 'Hey Joe,'" as he says in Bill Smeaton's *Jimi Hendrix: Live at Monterey*.

It is not an understatement to say without Chas Chandler, there would have been no Jimi Hendrix Experience. In the early days in Swinging London Hendrix was soon to be representative of, he and Chandler were thick as thieves. Living together in cramped quarters with their lovers as well, the two played with risk, both figuratively and literally. Risk!, the American board game, was a favorite game to be played while the musician and manager competed and plotted Hendrix's rise. Chandler constantly reassured Hendrix that his singing voice was more than adequate, encouraged him to write his own songs, and pointed out promising riffs such as the one that would be recognized by the world as "Purple Haze."

Not only did Chandler use his connections to create a buzz around Hendrix, not only did he hock his bass guitars to finance recording sessions and an important press party, not only did he produce the majority of the Experience's recordings, he also knew when to let go of his original idea of his first act leading a soul revue.

Chas Chandler looks as if he has more on his mind than bass lines. *Courtesy of Robert Rodriguez*

Fulfilling a promise made in New York City (and looking to get London's musicians talking about the new black guitarist he was promoting), Chandler finagled an invitation from Eric Clapton to have Hendrix sit in at Cream's Regent Polytechnic appearance on October 1, 1966. It was Hendrix's jam with Cream on Howlin' Wolf's "Killing Floor" that convinced Hendrix that he wanted to lead a power trio, not the nine-piece band originally discussed. Chandler was smart enough to let him have his way. (Plus, it'd cut down on expenses!)

Are We Experienced?

If it was Chas Chandler who decided Jimi James should use his real surname and become Jimi Hendrix, it was Michael Jeffery who decided the act he was comanaging with Chandler would be called the Jimi Hendrix Experience. Hendrix at first rebelled, then relented. Management wanted the focus to be on the black, left-handed guitarist, perhaps with the contractual foresight of understanding that the Experience—the musicians supporting Hendrix—would only be hired hands.

Chandler and Hendrix worked quickly when rounding up musicians for the new band. On his fifth day in London, they plucked Noel Redding from the New Animals audition session for a guitarist and tabbed him as the Experience's bassist the following day; Redding's curly hair and memory for chords earned him easy entry.

Within two weeks of Hendrix's arrival in London, Mitch Mitchell was onboard, his offer having been decided on a coin toss. (The other drummer being considered was Aynsley Dunbar, then drumming with John

Mayall and the Bluesbreakers. Dunbar would go on to play with the second incarnation of Frank Zappa's Mothers of Invention and Journey. He also did session work with Lou Reed on *Berlin* and David Bowie on *Pin-Ups* and *Diamond Dogs,* and even cowrote Black Sabbath's "Warning'" from their debut album.) The Experience experimented with Procol Harum's original bassist Dave Knights so that Redding—a guitarist by trade—could play rhythm guitar, but Hendrix, having already embraced the power trio concept, soon squelched the idea of the Experience being a foursome.

The Experience had to get its act together fast. Not only was Chandler short on funds, but he had secured a support slot on Johnny Hallyday's upcoming tour of France, his first in five years. It was Hallyday's father Lee who offered the spot after seeing Hendrix jam with the Brian Auger Trinity in Blaise's, a club in Kensington. Chandler quickly accepted. Johnny Hallyday was a French rock star in the Elvis Presley mold, so the shows were sure to be well attended. (He would go on to have eighteen platinum albums and sell over 100 million records!) Even better, it was an opportunity for the new band to road test their live act away from England's eyes.

It was only a fifteen-minute slot on a four-date tour of France. (Mitchell's *Inside the Experience* lists an additional show in Luxembourg on October 16, 1966.) Also on the package tour were Long Chris, the Blackbirds, and Hallyday. The Brian Auger Trinity was added onto the bill for the final show at L'Olympia in Paris. (Package tours were the custom of the day, something that the Jimi Hendrix Experience would play a significant role in ending as their stardom grew exponentially.)

The first concert was in the Novelty Theatre in Evreux, France (the town now has a plaque commemorating the occasion), and not only did Hendrix astound the audience, he astounded his bandmates. Neither Redding nor Mitchell had yet seen Hendrix on a stage. They had only rehearsed together, so Mitchell, as he remembered in his autobiography, knew Hendrix "had the chops, but I didn't know about the musicianship that went with it. It was like 'Whoosh! This man is really out front!'"

Still, Hendrix and Chandler were not averse to picking up pointers from a commensurate pro like Hallyday. In addition to analyzing the Experience's performance of the previous night, they would sit in with Hallyday's audience and look for what they could steal for their own act. Hendrix told Sharon Lawrence that he watched Hallyday's pacing of the show and the purpose behind his movements. Of Hallyday's stage presence, Chandler said in Harry Shapiro's *Electric Gypsy*: "He had that marvelous nerve of doing nothing at the right time except pose. The tricks became part of the Hendrix Experience."

The Jimi Hendrix Experience's performance at L'Olympia in Paris on October 18, 1966, was taped by French radio; all shows are. The raw, unbridled sound of Hendrix, Redding, and Mitchell can be heard in preserved performances of "Killing Floor," a pre-studio finessed "Hey Joe," and "Wild Thing": all covers because the band, less than two weeks old, had not worked up any original material yet. The performance was an unmitigated success, and Paris thereafter retained a special spot in the Experience's collective memory for the warm welcome the unknown band received.

Another part of the stage act that Hendrix became known for—the smashing of the guitar—did not occur in Paris and came about only through happenstance while playing the Big Apple in Munich on November 11, 1966. Pulled into the audience by German fans, Hendrix's guitar was inadvertently cracked when he tossed it back on the stage. Chandler said Hendrix "just went barmy and smashed everything in sight." Unexpectedly, the audience responded wildly, and smashing the guitar became part of the stage act (as did spearing the amplifiers) when events warranted or amplifiers malfunctioned. According to Noel Redding, the same guitar was saved expressly for this purpose throughout early tours. It would be played and smashed, reglued, played and smashed again, reglued, and so on.

The Experience and Chandler would confer regularly and analyze each performance. It was determined to play up Hendrix's exoticism for the press and to sell tickets. He would soon be known as "The Wild Man of Pop," "The Cassius Clay of Rock," and "The Black Elvis." He was told not to smile in early photographs. According to Noel Redding, Mitch Mitchell was to be "the bouncy type" and given a perm so his hair resembled the other members of the Experience. Redding's persona was to be very much like that of George Harrison, the serious one, which his eyeglasses helped put over. He was also instructed to minimize his stage movements so as not to upstage Hendrix, the star attraction.

The Experience had been crisscrossing England for three months, but their first official tour began when they joined the Walker Brothers' farewell package tour that began on March 31, 1967, at Finsbury Park, Astoria (later famously known as the Rainbow). The venue being in London and a guarantee of good press, Chandler was looking for something special to draw press attention to his act embedded in a formidable lineup that also included Englebert Humperdinck and Cat Stevens. Chandler wanted to ensure that Hendrix was not overshadowed.

New Musical Express journalist Keith Altham—an early Experience champion—was in the Finsbury Park dressing room, and Tony Brown quotes him as saying jokingly: "What would happen if he set fire to his guitar?" Next thing you know, Altham's idea had caught fire, roadie Gerry Stickells was dispatched to find lighter fluid, and Hendrix closed the Experience's five-song set with "Fire" and the burning of his Fender Stratocaster. Hendrix's most infamous stunt was only repeated twice more, but, thanks to the Monterey International Pop Festival footage, it dogged the rest of his career as he began to feel people were coming to his concerts for the spectacle and not his music.

One of the great "known unknowns" of Jimi Hendrix's career—to use a term coined by George W. Bush's Secretary of Defense Donald Rumsfeld—is why he grew disenchanted with flashy stage antics he was so insistent on making when backing the likes of Little Richard. Who cared if some fans were drawn to the concert for the wrong reasons? That's been going on forever. But it was as Jeff Beck told *New Musical Express*: "Jimi's only trouble will come about when he wants to get off the nail he hung himself on. The public will want something different and Jimi has so established himself in one bag that he'll find it difficult to get anyone to accept him in another."

3

You Will See a Few Minds Being Blown

Hendrix and Contemporary British Lead Guitarists

Although the theory of "exceptionalism" is typically applied to nations, it can be applied to certain musicians as well, musicians such as Keith Moon and Jimi Hendrix. They were musicians "quite distinct from, and often superior to, (other musicians) in vital ways" as exceptionalism is defined at dictionary.com.

Michael Bloomfield was a gifted guitarist in his own right, ranked #22 in *Rolling Stone*'s "100 Greatest Guitarists of All Time," a poll from 2002. In 1966, Bloomfield's star was already rising when he was told to check out a guitarist playing at the Café Au Go Go with John Hammond Jr. This was during Hendrix's weeklong stint while Chandler wrapped up his Animals commitments. "In front of my eyes, he burned me to death," which would've been very pleasing for Hendrix to hear because while Bloomfield may not have known who this guitarist was, Hendrix was well acquainted with Bloomfield's work on Bob Dylan's *Highway 61 Revisited*.

Hendrix was a very generous guitarist—giving away new guitars when success came his way; playing bass at jams while Noel Redding, his frustrated bassist, played electric guitar; giving opening slots on his bills to blues heroes such as Albert King. But he also had a competitive side that wanted others to know he was the best there was; how else to explain Jimi shaming Eric Clapton, Pete Townshend, Mike Bloomfield, and others when they first met or when the stakes were high. Once he'd asserted himself with a rival, however, Hendrix became friendly and encouraging.

This almost athletic competitiveness was an aspect of the rough-and-tumble chitlin' circuit. On his way up the ladder, Hendrix had been "burned to death" similarly by the Imperials' Johnny Jones. Junior Wells once invited Hendrix up onstage, which Muddy Waters's harp player soon vacated to the guitarist's bewilderment and eventual shame when Wells returned cursing Hendrix out and accusing him of hijacking his band.

The impressive list of Bloomfield's achievements before his death in 1981 includes being a member of the Paul Butterfield Blues Band and leader of the Electric Flag. (Drumming for the Flag was Buddy Miles, who would go on to be one of the two drummers identified with Hendrix.) Electric Flag's influence greatly outlasted the Chicago-born band whose lineup on their first album was together for barely a year. Bloomfield went on to work with Al Kooper (on the hugely successful jam album *Super Session*), Janis Joplin, John Cale, and Dr. John.

Bloomfield's career may have been cut short by insomnia problems and heroin addiction (he overdosed at a party, and, like the scene out of Lou Reed's "Street Hassle," his lifeless body was moved to be found elsewhere), but everyone—journalists, fellow musicians—has attested to his command of the electric guitar. And yet Bloomfield immediately grasped Hendrix's exceptionalism when watching him in Café Au Go Go. As quoted by Jerry Hopkins in *The Jimi Hendrix Experience*, Bloomfield said: "He was getting every sound I was ever to hear him get right there in that room with a Stratocaster, a Twin (amplifier), a Maestro fuzztone and that was all; he was doing it mainly through extreme volume. How he did this, I wish I understood. He just got right up in my face with that axe and I didn't even want to pick up a guitar for the next year."

Bloomfield's reaction was one that Swinging London's leading lead guitarists soon empathized with.

Jeff Beck

When Jeff "Beckson"—as Hendrix nicknamed him—bumped into Pete Townshend while storming out of Blaise's Club at 121 Queens Gate, Kensington, in East London on December 21, 1966, he told the Who's guitarist: "He's banging his guitar against the amp. You'll have to tell him that's your thing." Also recorded in Andrew Neill and Matthew Kent's recommended *Anyway, Anyhow, Anywhere*, their chronicle of the Who, according to Curtis Knight, Townshend told him that he went into [Blaise's with Eric Clapton] and found Hendrix "was doing a lot of the things I used to do, like banging his guitar around, and he was using lots of high feedback. But he was also playing in a way that I couldn't hope to approach."

It was, however, as Chas Chandler told Chris Welch: "Jimi didn't get it from Pete Townshend. The only guitarists he had heard before he came to England were Eric Clapton and Jeff Beck. He wasn't really aware of what Pete was doing with feedback because the Who hadn't made it big

Mike Bloomfield was a member of the Paul Butterfield Blues Band.

Author's collection

Jimi around the time he was turning the heads of Eric Clapton, Pete Townshend, and Jeff Beck.

Author's collection

in America at that time." The British guitarist whose playing affected Hendrix's own playing the most while still in America was Jeff Beck. This may explain Beck's initial reaction: Hendrix was hitting too close to home, and Beck's self-defense mechanisms attributed Hendrix's technique to another guitar player.

Hendrix had admitted as much to Mike Bloomfield when discussing their craft. Hendrix had always played loud, had said he wanted to get out of his guitar the same sound he heard when parachuting out of U.S. Army airplanes while with the 101st Airborne. When he busted an amp's speaker through sheer volume, he was fascinated with the fuzzy tone the amp now made. When he heard the Yardbirds' Jeff Beck on the singles "I'm a Man" and "Shapes of Things," Hendrix had found another guitarist out there plowing the same sonic fields and must've felt what Jeff Beck felt when he first saw Hendrix. As Beck told the *Daily Telegraph* in a 2010 interview, "He hit me like an earthquake when he arrived. I had to think long and hard about what I did next." That's completely understandable seeing as Beck had just decided to go solo and signed with Micky Most. "The wounds were quite deep, actually, and I had to lick them on my own. I was constantly looking for other things to do on the guitar, new places to take it."

While Hendrix and Beck jammed after hours and at benefits, they never shared a stage the way Hendrix did with Clapton or engage in Battle of the Bands as the Experience and the Who did on two memorable occasions. (They did both appear on the same episode of *Top of the Pops* once, however.) But the two guitarists did become quite friendly. When the basset hound named Ethel Floon that Kathy Etchingham gave Hendrix as a twenty-fifth birthday gift grew too big and barked too loud, it was Jeff Beck who took her in.

Beck was even closer to the Experience's bassist. Redding and Beck played together on the Lord Sutch and Heavy Friends albums; almost played in a band together (this is the band Redding was supposedly joining when it was announced that he would *not* be rejoining the Experience for what became the *Cry of Love* weekend tours in the spring of 1970); and Redding was invited to try out with Beck and Carmine Appice to form the band that would become Beck Bogert and Appice, although I suppose it would've been Beck Redding & Appice. Beck also used Redding's kitchen to make himself the bacon sandwiches he couldn't make at home because his wife was vegetarian.

Hendrix continued to be fond of Beck's music; he liked to listen to *Truth* ("Beck's Bolero" perhaps inspiring Hendrix to tackle his own "Bolero," an instrumental intended as a lead-in to "Hey Baby" that wasn't released until 2010) and cited *Beck-Ola* as a favorite album. The riff from the posthumously released recording "In from the Storm" is inspired by "Rice Pudding" from that same album.

After Hendrix's death, Beck pioneered rock fusion, which, to my ears anyway, sounds an awful lot like Jimi's jams like "Jam 292" that surfaced on official and bootlegged recordings after Hendrix's death. Jeff Beck continues to be complimentary to Hendrix in interviews and even was one of the fifteen acts that participated in Patti Smith's *Songs of Experience*, held as part of the Meltdown Festival Smith curated in London in June 2005.

Songs of Experience was an evening devoted to the music of Jimi Hendrix. Jeff Beck was saved for last. According to *The Independent*: "Smith announced 'the jewel in our crown,' Jeff Beck—the only man present that night who'd taught Hendrix anything. Beck and his group played five numbers, the highlights being a stunning exhibition of relaxed Beck blues guitar on 'Red House' and a riotously jubilant workout on 'Manic Depression.' Exit Beck to tumultuous acclaim, all of it deserved."

Pete Townshend

Keith Moon called Hendrix a "savage," and Townshend admitted his future rival did look "scruffy" the first time they met inside IBC Sound where the Who was recording. They talked amplifiers. Ostensibly the idea was for Hendrix to find out from one of England's best electric guitarists what type of amp to purchase, but it was also Chandler's way of making other note-worthy musicians aware of Hendrix. When Townshend said he used Sound

City but a Marshall might be better for Hendrix, Hendrix told Chandler he wanted both. Hendrix's reserved nature and "lukewarm handshake" did not prepare Townshend for Hendrix's stage performance.

Townshend has said he saw all of the Experience's earliest London appearances. His version of bumping into Beck barging out of Blaise's differs from Curtis Knight's retelling. As included in Johnny Black's oral history of Jimi Hendrix: "Eric Clapton called me and suggested we check him out. It was kind of keeping the eye on the competition. We arrived at the show a little late as I was stuck in the studio and, just as we arrived, Jeff Beck was walking out. I asked Jeff, 'What's the matter, mate? Is he that bad?' Beck could only roll his eyes upward and say 'No, Pete, he's that good!' When Eric and I saw his show we knew what Jeff meant."

(I include both versions since they are equally colorful and also as evidence of how evasive truth is when digging through Hendrix's past. Curtis Knight was a slippery character, so any statement attributed to him has to be carefully weighed; yet in his version Beck sounds like Beck, combative personality and all. But if you do the research, Townshend's recollection seems faulty too. The Who played two shows at the Upper Cut the same evening that the Jimi Hendrix Experience played Blaise's. Upper Cut showtimes were advertised as 7:30 and 11:30, so it's likely that Townshend hopped in a cab after the Who's 11:30 seven-song set and went to Blaise's where shows were held from 10 p.m. to 4 a.m. [Chris Welch, who penned an oft-printed review of the Experience's Blaise's performance, had also seen the Who that night.] Maybe he met up with Clapton outside the club.)

The Who's second album, *A Quick One*, had just been released to rave reviews, and yet here was their guitarist feeling deflated and that "I hadn't the emotional equipment, really, the physical equipment, the natural psychic genius of somebody like Jimi," as Pete Townshend told Matt Resnicoff in a 1989 *Guitar Player* interview. "I realized that what I had was a bunch of gimmicks which he had come and taken away from me. He attached them not only to the black R&B from which they came, but also added a whole new dimension. I felt stripped, and I took refuge in my writing." That's an interesting conclusion for Townshend to come to, but the right one: if there's one thing differentiating Hendrix and Townshend from Beck and Clapton, it's that they were superior songwriters.

On January 29, 1967, the Experience and the Who went head-to-head at Beatles manager Brian Epstein's Saville Theatre. Both bands being on the same bill was the handiwork of the Who's manager Kit Lambert, who had just signed the Experience to Track Records, the record company he was trying to get off the ground. The Who were the headliners. (The Koobas and Thoughts were also on the bill).

The Who would hold their own against the Experience at Monterey later in the year, and definitely bested Hendrix's Gypsy Sun and Rainbows lineup at Woodstock in 1969 and the under rehearsed Cry of Love Band at the Isle of Wight in 1970 (when the Who performed *Tommy* in its entirety; all that writing Townshend did paid off). But on that January night in the Saville Theatre, Townshend said, when the Who came out, he "just stood and strummed."

Eric Clapton

Clapton had been present for the Saville Theatre's advertised "battle of London's most explosive bands," and when he said the Experience's "gig was just blinding," he hadn't been surprised. He had seen it all before.

Ignorant of Townshend's "auto-destruction" but probably wary of Beck's way with feedback, Hendrix had flown into London gunning for Eric Clapton. It has often been repeated how Hendrix only agreed to accompany Chandler across the Atlantic when the Animals' former bassist promised an introduction to the blues guitarist known via local graffiti as "God."

Chandler quickly made good on his word, and slightly over a week after his London arrival, Hendrix was standing onstage at Regent Polytechnic College jamming with Cream. Drummer Ginger Baker was against the idea of having an American interloper jam with Cream's rhythm section, but, having learned that both Clapton and bassist Jack Bruce had already agreed, he gave up the argument. Baker insisted, however, that his lead guitarist stay on the stage, which is why Clapton was standing off to the side lighting a cigarette as Hendrix tore into Howling Wolf's "Killing Floor." Clapton retreated backstage, which is where Chandler found his friend. Clapton's cigarette was still unlit.

Cream's rhythm section was comprised of jazz musicians trying to apply some of the Ornette Coleman Trio's ensemble conceptions to rock music. Clapton was an Englishman who had made the electric guitar into a virtuoso's instrument but at heart was a bluesman. To play as well as *the* Delta bluesman Robert Johnson was his deepest aspiration. He immediately knew the song Hendrix was playing. He also immediately knew Hendrix had mastered a song he never could. It's estimated that Hendrix shared Cream's stage for only eight minutes, but he left it having proven he could better Britain's best. Or as Clapton was later to put it on ITV's *South Bank TV Show: Jimi Hendrix*: "He walked off and my life was never the same again, really."

Hendrix's girlfriend of a week—Kathy Etchingham (previously linked romantically with both Keith Moon and Brian Jones)—said afterwards of her new boyfriend: "He walked off stage with this smirk. He knew exactly what he was doing." Not knowing they were to become friends, Hendrix later regretted showing up Clapton at Cream's own gig and praised Clapton as his "favorite" of Britain's leading lead guitarists and saying positive things about Cream's "Strange Brew" when reviewing it for *Melody Maker*.

What was initially a strained relationship blossomed into friendship as the two leading blues guitarists of their generation jammed at the Speakeasy in London and at the Scene and elsewhere in New York City in the coming years. If Clapton's version of conflicting reports is true, he had made plans to meet Hendrix at London's Lyceum where Sly and the Family Stone were playing the night of Hendrix's death. Clapton had a surprise for Hendrix: a left-handed Fender Stratocaster that he intended to give his friend as a birthday gift. Only Hendrix never showed up.

Eric Clapton was the most affected by Hendrix's death of the British contemporaries, and is probably the unnamed musician who cried during unused interviews for Joe Boyd's documentary *Jimi Hendrix*. Robin Turner, a newspaperman who ditched newsprint to handle press relations, told Chris Welch: "Clapton cried for three days after his death. He said, 'How can he go, and leave me?' He saw it as Robert Johnson all over again. Eric wanted to do a Robert Johnson—a few good years and then go.'"

There's that name again: Robert Johnson. Johnson is the father of twentieth-century delta blues. Only two photographs of him survive, but that is not why Johnson is mythic, the stuff of inspiration: first to other rural, Southern blacks and a generation later to middle-class British whites. Legend is Johnson met the devil at a crossroads in Clarksdale, Mississippi, and sold his soul so he could be the world's best blues musician. The devil kept his part of the bargain. Johnson was soon playing better than those who mentored him—outstanding bluesmen such as Son House—but after only twenty-nine recorded songs (forty-one takes), Johnson was dead and buried in an unmarked grave at twenty-seven: either the victim of a jealous husband who poisoned him or the devil who came collecting if you're into myths.

Hendrix was also dead at twenty-seven. He had his few good years and was gone. Johnson and Hendrix are members of the 27 Club. Clapton was enamored with Robert Johnson, and prior to September 18, 1970, he had already recorded Johnson's "Cross Road Blues" twice. For a guitarist who often thought Hendrix bested him at every turn (for example, he was devastated when *Are You Experienced* was everything that Cream's *Disraeli Gears* was supposed to be), the final indignity was to have Hendrix pull a Johnson. One can only speculate on the role this had in Clapton's collapse into drug addiction the following year.

4

Everybody Knows It's the Same Old Story

Rhythm and Blues Reconfigured

The Hendrixian legacy is manipulated for reasons pro and con by journalists, sensationalists, and conservatives. The musician, the flamboyant sex symbol, the figurehead of a drug generation who reaped what he sowed—these are all Jimi Hendrixes the world knows today. Having died pretty, he remains marketable and cutting edge and can be used to sell musical products and laptops. Having died young due to drugs, he becomes a cautionary tale.

What gets lost are his multifaceted musical innovations. He elongated the recording studio's stretch at capturing sound; his music was a lab where rock and blues and jazz collided and created heavy metal, fusion, and the roots of rap; he redefined the concert experience.

What has also been lost in the rainy day shuffle of time is the staying power of Hendrix's own deeply personal, yet universal lyrics, and his uncanny ability to make comprehensible other lyricists' song lyrics, most notably Bob Dylan's. The majority of late 1960s lyrics have not aged well, but Hendrix's have, and this is because they fall into four categories that remain relevant:

1. Rhythm and blues
2. Science fiction and fantasy
3. Realism
4. Classical elements

We'll take a look at each of these corners of Hendrix's oeuvre beginning with the rhythm and blues.

It's only natural that when faced with Chas Chandler's demands that he write his own material, Hendrix would reach for what he knew best: the couplets of the thousands of rhythm and blues songs he played as a backup musician on during tours through the chitlin' circuit and in recording studios between 1963 and 1966. Prior to playing with Cream and getting

Jimi's early songs with the Experience relied on rhythm and blues imagery.
Author's collection

the notion that he might want to lead a trio, Hendrix ideally envisioned leading a nine-piece rhythm and blues revue. And when it came time for him to write his own compositions, rhythm and blues is what he initially turned to for inspiration.

The best evidence of Hendrix's education is on Disc One of *West Coast Seattle Boy*, a four-disc anthology issued by Sony Legacy in 2010. This disc gathers together examples of Hendrix's recorded work as a session man for other rhythm and blues singers and recording acts such as the Isley Brothers, Don Covay, Little Richard, and King Curtis. Sort of the soundtrack for *Jackie Brown* that director Quentin Tarantino never thought of, this time capsule in CD form lets you hear where the lyrical idea for "Foxy Lady" may have come from (the Icemen's "(My Girl) She's a Fox") or how the Isley Brothers' "Have You Ever Been Disappointed" (also without the question mark!) led Hendrix to ask the same of his listeners when it came to Electric Ladyland.

(But since this is probably the only spot in this book where I will touch upon this unique disc in the Hendrix catalog, this period also lays the ground for his 6-string breakthroughs. The fan will quickly hear how Hendrix's session work informed his own recordings just a few years later.

Ray Sharpe's "Help Me" has a rhythm similar to the Experience's version of "Gloria"; the guitar sound of Jimmy Norman's "That Little Old Groove Maker" looks toward "Come On (Part 1)"; and in Hendrix's playing on the aforementioned "Have You Ever Been Disappointed," you can clearly make out the melody to "Drifting.")

In this chapter we'll explore how Jimi Hendrix reconfigured rhythm and blues. By using established song structures, encouragement from a manager to play guitar like himself, and the addition of autobiographical lyrical touches, he personalized a very tried and true musical branch originally known as race music.

"Stone Free"

When Chas Chandler was satisfied with "Hey Joe" ("that cowboy song," as Hendrix referred to it), his thoughts turned to the B-side of the Jimi Hendrix Experience's first single. Hendrix wanted to go with another musician's composition and suggested Don Covay's "Mercy, Mercy" or Howlin' Wolf's "Killing Floor" (that had left Clapton on the figurative floor a few months earlier) or even "Land of 1,000 Dances," a song recently popularized by Wilson Pickett. The Experience was already familiar with that latter 1966 hit, having rehearsed it at their initial jams when feeling each other out and Hendrix recruiting his sidemen.

Chandler would not hear of it. Having not made even a dime of song-writing royalty from the many covers that his previous band the Animals had recorded definitive versions of, he knew the real money for the musician (and manager) was in recording your own compositions. Chandler was quite adamant about it: the B-side had to be an original Hendrix composition.

So Hendrix wrote "Stone Free" at the Hyde Park Towers Hotel flat he was staying at, and following rehearsals at clubs around town and Aberbach Publishing House, Jeff Beck's favorite Hendrix song was recorded and mixed at De Lane Lea Studios on November 2, 1966. The recording features the Experience playing live in the studio with minimal overdubs: percussion, Hendrix's harmony vocals, and a second guitar track.

For his first musical composition, Hendrix drew upon his life as a rhythm and blues musician and sings of the freedom that only a touring musician can enjoy. His lifestyle is carefree: every day he is on the move, the townspeople pointing him out, women unable to tie him down. The language is quite brutal. He's compared to a dog and sounds like one the way he moves on before being caught. He brags of being "Stone free, to ride the breeze!" and of "goin' down the highway" like the Highway Chile he will sing of in the B-side to his third single.

This freedom is also conveyed in the Experience's sound, which is why it was a revelation when the listener flipped over the "Hey Joe" 45 and played it. For all of his unfamiliarity with the instrument, Redding's bass playing on early recordings was forceful, pushing the tempo, and works with Mitchell riding the cowbell to suggest the forward motion of the song's protagonist.

"Can You See Me"

One thing that the Experience's earliest engineers have made quite clear is that, although he was hurting for money, Chandler did not let that dictate the goings-on at recording sessions. "Can You See Me" was demoed at the same session that produced "Stone Free" and then revisited at CBS and Olympic studios. To Americans this seems to be an obscure cut—and maybe even a B-side since its inclusion on *Smash Hits*, the greatest hits package released by Reprise in July 1969 when the fourth Experience album was never nearing completion (and never would)—but it does hail from the UK version of the Experience's debut album.

The song features Hendrix talking to some girl he is leaving and setting her straight about his return: never gonna happen. Lyrically it has the standard rhythm and blues structure, which is known as the AAB pattern. (Hendrix uses it frequently in songs as disparate as "Red House," "Lover Man," and "In from the Storm.") What the AAB pattern consists of is a first line (A) that is then repeated with minimum, yet significant, alteration (A) and then completed with a punch line (B).

The punch lines in the "Red House" verses are wittier, which may be why Hendrix resorts to a boomeranging guitar note to help finish off the punch lines in "Can You See Me": the guitar note being the song's most memorable attribute. Hendrix will ask if the girl can hear him crying over her, will ask again, and then he says: "If you can hear me doing that/you can hear a freight train coming from a thousand miles." Bwang!

"Remember"

There's no "bwang" in "Remember" or little else to identify this as a Jimi Hendrix Experience number. Of all of the songs recorded by Hendrix, this is the most derivative. It sounds like a Stax soul number and only stands out on the UK version of *Are You Experienced* because it is sandwiched between a sci-fi spectacular ("3rd Stone from the Sun") and a trippy masterpiece ("Are You Experienced").

This is the type of soul song that Otis Redding was known for, not Jimi Hendrix. Singing of a mockingbird that is no longer singing "since my baby left," this is one of the few songs where Hendrix is pleading for his baby to come back home. And with bluebirds and honey bees, it's a very rural scene to find him in.

Among the memorable performances turned in at the Monterey International Pop Festival was the one Otis Redding closed the Saturday night concert with. Known for his version of the Rolling Stones' "(I Can't Get No) Satisfaction" as well as his own "Sitting by the Dock of the Bay," a curfew forced Redding to shorten his set to five songs, all of which were released on Side Two of an album that presented the first, albeit edited, version of the Experience's Monterey performance to be issued.

Historic Performances Recorded at the Monterey International Pop Festival was released August 26, 1970, and no one could have foreseen Hendrix's death the following month. Otis Redding, too, was gone, having died December 10, 1967, in a plane crash.

"Up from the Skies"

You wouldn't expect a song told from the perspective of space people to have such an earthy sound, but with Hendrix's guitar wah-wahing and Mitchell using brushes instead of drumsticks, any listener in 1967 would've known that *Axis: Bold as Love* was going to be a very different palette from the Experience's previous LP. The first song proper—after all, "EXP" is really modulated dialogue with a feedback coda—has a laid-back, jazzy vibe (*Rolling Stone* compared it to the work of Mose Allison) and lacks the sonic thrust of "Foxy Lady" or ballsy riff of "Purple Haze" that respectively open the UK and USA versions of *Are You Experienced*.

No hippie himself, Hendrix's song nonetheless implies a "new age" plea to save the earth. The space person narrator is actually a returning visitor who lived on earth before the ice age and is dismayed with what he has found on his return. He finds people "living in cages tall and cold" and "the smell of a world that's burned." As Sheila Whitley wrote in *Popular Music* in 1990, the song's "upward moving figures suggest flight and disorientation." And still the returning visitor wants to buy himself a ticket and stay and see what will happen to this planet he once knew.

Hendrix himself saw "Up from the Skies" as an effort to make people see that new ways of treating Mother Earth and living your life were possible. "These buildings ain't goin' to be here for all that long," he said in *Rock: A World As Bold as Love*, "so why be like that?"

Rarely played live, this little number was released in the United States as a single on February 26, 1968, backed with "One Rainy Wish." It peaked at #82 and only spent four weeks on the chart. Considered a chart failure, what is even more perplexing is why such an obvious album track was considered as a suitable single in the first place.

"Wait Until Tomorrow"

Guns pop up regularly in the work of Jimi Hendrix. In "Hey Joe," Joe's going somewhere with a gun in his hand, a very vivid image. In "Machine Gun," soldiers are shooting the farmers caught up in a war zone. In "Freedom," the singer's bringing his lead. And in "Wait Until Tomorrow," an eloping groom is shot dead by the gun-toting father.

Despite the violent ending, "Wait Until Tomorrow" is something of a comedy, a notion confirmed by Chas Chandler, who said "it was originally written as a put on. When (Hendrix) was first experimenting with it, we saw it as a joke, a comedy song almost." Noel Redding even aurally plays the love interest in drag, using a falsetto for elopee Dolly Mae's comments

"Have You Ever Been (to Electric Ladyland)"

Among the guitarists whose styles Hendrix absorbed was Curtis Mayfield, but Mayfield was such a singular vocalist and guitarist in his own right that his influence on certain Hendrix recordings was never completely diminished.

Mayfield was born the same year as Hendrix but achieved mainstream success much earlier with his band the Impressions, which had their first hit in 1958 with "For Your Precious Love" when Jerry Butler led them. The first hit featuring Mayfield's falsetto lead vocals was "Gypsy Woman" in 1961. The falsetto was one of Mayfield's signatures. The other was his guitar, which was uniquely tuned to a piano's black keys.

Hendrix and Mayfield crossed paths on the chitlin' circuit during the first half of the 1960s, and on one occasion when Hendrix borrowed Mayfield's amplifier without permission he damaged it due to his excessive use of volume, which led to Hendrix being sacked from the tour. So it's with some irony then that what he absorbed from Mayfield for his own recordings was the softer style heard in *Electric Ladyland*'s title track and "Little Wing."

Mayfield left the Impressions to pursue a solo career, and, like many recording artists circa 1970, his music became more socially conscious. By this time Mayfield was listening to Hendrix and would be familiar with the Band of Gypsys songbook that was more confrontational than that of the Experience.

Of Hendrix, Mayfield told Chuck Philips of the *Los Angeles Times* in 1989 that "Jimi's approach to music transcends racial barriers. His imagination spoke to people on a deeper level than that. With the psychedelics and what have you, he was almost like a scientist, studying the effects."

That is a perfect understanding of "Have You Ever Been (to Electric Ladyland)." Like "Up from the Skies," on the previous LP, the first song proper on *Electric Ladyland* mentions flight: Hendrix points to the magic carpet he wants to "ride you with sounds and motions," a notion he harkened back to in interviews. When he wants the listener to see "Good and evil lay side by side while electric love penetrates the sky," he is trying to bust those racial barriers Mayfield spoke of.

An advertisement for the *Historic Performances* album.
Author's collection

"Who Knows"

Call and response is a music pattern as old as the hills and the seas, too, as you can find examples of it in songs sung by slaves as they worked the fields and sea shanties. That it is commonly found in African American musical forms such as gospel, blues, and rhythm and blues, makes its usage in one of the dozen or so original songs recorded by Hendrix's all-black three-piece Band of Gypsys unsurprising.

The call and response routine of this song by Hendrix and drummer Buddy Miles on this recording from *Band of Gypsys* disguises the fact that its roots lay in the negative side of Hendrix's relationship with Devon Wilson. Almost all of his songs about relationships from the 1969–1970 period center on this troubled relationship, which he was trying to extract himself from up until the time of his death. In "Who Knows," the "Stone Free" musician has returned from the road only to not find his baby waiting for him. The tables have been turned, and it is his girl who is sleeping around and the musician who has "chains attached to [his] head."

This live recording from the first show on New Year's Day 1970 at the Fillmore East is, according to Charles Shaar Murray in *Crosstown Traffic*, "a brand new funk (Hendrix) never attained with any other combination." It was sampled nearly twenty years later and put to good use by Digital Underground on *Sex Packets*' second track "The Way We Swing," which introduced many hip-hoppers to the music of Jimi Hendrix.

"(Here He Comes) Lover Man"

Of all of Hendrix's compositions, none seems more troubled than that of "Lover Man." Derived from B. B. King's "Rock Me Baby," which the Experience played at the Monterey International Pop Festival, a recording was first attempted on April 4, 1967, at Olympic Studios. Despite the energetic take put to tape, the song did not make the final cut for inclusion on *Are You Experienced*.

What it did make is countless set lists throughout the Experience's career. In fact, it was played by every lineup that Hendrix led post-stardom. According to the seminal Hendrix recording bible *From the Benjamin Franklin Studios* by Gary Geldeart and Steve Rodham, as of 2008, forty-eight versions were available of this song that never was released in Hendrix's lifetime.

It's the typical AAB rhythm and blues vocal pattern, and there's nothing much to the lyrics except for the puzzling concept that if the narrator is "your lover man," why is he getting his "head from this pillow" or asking to have his running shoes handed to him. It's really an excuse for some exciting guitar work that apparently never lived up to Jimi's standards to be released.

5

She's Trying to Put My Body in Her Brain

Girlfriends and Groupies

Jimi Hendrix certainly liked his ladies—electric and otherwise. And yet, while he usually idealized women in his songs, his behavior toward them in real life was cavalier. He was known to pick up the worst-looking or craziest-acting women on the road before sleeping with them and then tossing them out of his room.

There is a laundry list of women mentioned in his biographies. His teenage girlfriends in Seattle were Carmen Goody and Betty Jean Morgan when he was extremely introverted, penniless, and only interested in his guitar. In Nashville, there was Joyce Lucas, a beautician who owned Joyce's House of Glamour, and barmaid Verdell Barlow. In New York City, there was Harlem groupie Lithofayne "Fayne" Pridgeon and Carol Shiroky. In London, his relationship with Kathy Etchingham was largely monogamous except when he was on the road. (And then both were promiscuous.)

Hendrix often expressed his disdain for marriage in interviews and lyrics of his songs such as "51st Anniversary" with its descriptions of the institution's bad side outweighing the good and "Castles Made of Sand" where a married couple argues in the street, the man moaning: "What happened to the sweet love you and me had?" Marriage was a chain Hendrix was going to be wise enough not to wrap himself in. Nor did he seem to think the marriage vows of others were of his concern, as he was known to have slept with a number of musician's wives and girlfriends, including those of Eric Burdon and Dallas Taylor, who drummed on Crosby, Stills, Nash, and Young's *Déjà Vu* and was a member of their touring band.

After his return to America, he had serious relationships with Devon Wilson and Playboy bunny Carmen Borrero. And toward the end of his life, two paternity suits had been filed that have been acknowledged as having validity. Hendrix had a son with a Swedish woman named Eva Sundquist, and before that (even before his fame) he had a daughter with a New York City prostitute named Diana Carpenter that he befriended.

All of these women had been drawn by Hendrix's gentle nature and soft-spokenness. Once he was a traveling musician, his guitar playing and maturing sexuality also lured them in. He is said to have been nicknamed "Buttons" by a band of women in Nashville because they were always mending what little clothing he owned. The women he met between 1963 and 1966 often paid to get his guitar back from the pawnbroker.

So for all the women he flirted and partied and slept with, the two women who claimed he proposed to them in the weeks before his death, even "Bil of some English town in England" to whom he partially dedicated *Electric Ladyland*, Hendrix was only seriously close to three women in his life, the first two of whom offered Hendrix a different future.

Betty Jean Morgan

The fact that Hendrix only once named a guitar after a woman, going so far as to paint "Betty Jean" in large white lettering on his red Silvertone Danelectro, means he was serious about Betty Jean Morgan, his Seattle sweetheart. They met at Garfield High School in autumn 1958. For all his bravado to his childhood friend Jimmy Williams, the relationship was hardly sexual. They were both shy Seattle teenagers, and due to Hendrix being from an impoverished family, they mostly spent their time walking in nearby Leschi Park. Hendrix would also come over for family-cooked meals at the Morgans—Hendrix got on as well with Betty Jean's mother as he would later with the "mums" of Noel Redding and Kathy Etchingham—and try to woo Betty Jean by playing his guitar on her porch afterwards.

Hendrix dated Betty Jean throughout his high school years, which were shorter than most since he dropped out in October of his senior year. They still continued seeing one another while he played in local bands at night while doing gardening jobs with his father. He later said it was his father's decision to have his oldest son drop out of school; Hendrix was uninterested in school anyway, but he complained that his father pocketed all of the money they made gardening.

Within the span of four days in May 1961, Hendrix was arrested twice for joy-riding in stolen cars. He would later tell interviewers he enlisted to avoid being drafted and sent to Vietnam but this is one of Hendrix's tall tales accepted as fact in the earlier Hendrix biographies. It is possible that he informed his assigned public defender of his interest in enlisting in order to avoid potential imprisonment.

Hendrix even stated his desire to become a paratrooper in the famed 101st Airborne stationed in Nashville, Kentucky, a persuasive detail that must have made him sound even more serious about enlisting. Hendrix knew of the U.S. Army's paratrooper division because Fred Rollins, the leader of his first band the Rocking Kings, had already enlisted, and everyone was impressed by Rollins's Screaming Eagle patch when he visited Seattle on furlough. The fact that paratroopers were also better paid than other military personnel also appealed to the perennially penurious Hendrix.

Having signed his name on the dotted line of the enlistment papers, Hendrix was instructed to report to Fort Ord, near Salinas, California, and arrived on May 31st. (Fort Ord was approximately twenty miles away from Monterey, the city where in just over six years the Jimi Hendrix Experience would make its legendary debut at the city's equally legendary international pop festival.) Before his arrival Hendrix made good on an earlier marriage proposal and gave Betty Jean an inexpensive rhinestone ring after his final appearance with the Velvetones in Seattle. He also left his guitar with her, certain it was safer with Betty Jean than with his father.

From all accounts, Hendrix was not spared the "distance makes the heart grow fonder" syndrome, and he corresponded frequently with Betty Jean and other members of her family, and even his father, who he asked to retrieve and mail him Betty Jean—his guitar, not fiancée—two months after arriving at boot camp. He was homesick and the letters exchanged many. Betty Jean's letters were emotional and full of jealousy, and according to Harry Shapiro's biography she warned her boyfriend to "leave those sapphires alone." What prompted Betty Jean to make such comments is unknown.

Despite the engagement ring and the many emotional letters, the teenage couple rarely saw one another after Hendrix's enlistment. From all accounts he only visited Seattle once on furlough before being transferred to Fort Campbell in Kentucky. The letter writing continued from Kentucky.

When Hendrix managed to finagle an early discharge from the U.S. Army—for psychological reasons feigned to a military psychiatrist and not the broken ankle often spoken of to journalists—his immediate plans were to catch a Greyhound bus in Clarksville, Kentucky, and head back to Betty Jean, where marriage and the prospects of manual labor awaited him.

With $400 in his pockets, he stopped in a bar and spent freely. As a forerunner of those days when he'd foot the bill for all of his hangers-on, he bought drinks and lent money until he only had $14 left, $26 short of the $40 needed for the one-way bus ticket to Seattle. Fearful of admitting to his father how he'd squandered his cash, he decided to try his luck at making a buck with his guitar, which he retrieved or stole (it isn't entirely clear) from the serviceman he'd sold it to. Fellow soldier Billy Cox was soon to be discharged, and Hendrix hoped to form a band with him.

Though genuinely in love with Betty Jean, Hendrix later confided to UPI journalist Sharon Lawrence that Betty Jean "didn't really like to hear it when I talked of going to places like Los Angeles and New York one day." What awaited Hendrix with the first of the three women he was serious about was the very real prospect that Betty Jean would make the same demands as his father: forget all the guitar foolishness and forever forsake any notion of being a musician, a calling that even Betty Jean had noticed had become more important to him over the course of his letters. Perhaps Hendrix, in his evasive way, knew exactly what he was doing when he squandered his money in Clarksville.

Kathy Etchingham

Of Kathy Etchingham, Jimi Hendrix told a London newspaperman in early 1969: "Kathy is my past girlfriend, my present girlfriend, and probably my future girlfriend. My mother, my sister and all that bit. My Yoko Ono from Chester." Kathy Etchingham had come a long way from the girlfriend manager Chas Chandler had wanted to hide away, or even better hoped would go away, two years earlier. Now it was Chandler who had gone away, and while she was happy not to be hidden away in the cupboard of the flat they shared on Brook Street, Etchingham was a practical girl at heart, and she thought Hendrix was being "soppy" to the newspaperman. A blue plaque now adorns the façade of 23 Brook Street. It was put there largely through the efforts of Etchingham in 1996, who did not know as Hendrix was being interviewed that their relationship was winding down.

They had met the day of Hendrix's arrival in London. At night actually, as Etchingham, then a twenty-year-old party girl, was sleeping off the previous night's activities when Ronnie Money, wife of bandleader Zoot, came upstairs to Etchingham's flat and told her she had to come down and check out the "Wild Man from Borneo" jamming with her husband's band. Too tired to make the effort to get up and see a musician—even if he was from America—Etchingham said she'd catch up with them at the Scotch of St. James later on. What could be so special about this musician, even if he was from America?

The St. James was where London's hottest musicians and youngest aristocrats mingled. The clientele were mostly ego-driven, self-absorbed youths, which is why Etchingham was surprised to find the club so quiet upon her entrance with the Moneys and her girlfriend Angie (who would briefly marry Eric Burdon). Everyone was listening to a black guitarist playing his electric guitar unaccompanied until Chandler interrupted him because he was concerned that Hendrix was playing a club and only had a seven-day visa. The last thing Chandler needed was his discovery being deported over any infraction. It was this same caution on Chandler's part that threw Etchingham and Hendrix together for almost three years.

They were already flirting when a violent fight broke out between jilted model Linda Keith and Mrs. Money, a Glaswegian who knew how to handle the broken whiskey bottle she was holding against the model's throat. At Chandler's urging, Etchingham taxied Hendrix safely to the Hyde Park Towers Hotel where Hendrix explained away Linda Keith over drinks while they waited for the other members of their party. They quickly found they had unpleasant childhoods in common and understood where each was coming from, if not going. Etchingham moved in with Hendrix and Chandler and his fiancée Lotte that evening, and the two couples would share three flats over the course of the next twenty-two months.

The foursome formed the original basis of Hendrix's inner London circle that made him. Etchingham and Lotte attended Experience auditions to judge the musicians' appearance. Etchingham attended the "Hey Joe" sessions and then made the round of music shops buying up copies of "Hey Joe" at Chandler's request, thereby insuring that the Experience's first single would chart. She toured with the Experience throughout northern England between the Hallyday and Walker Brothers tours. It wasn't catching Hendrix in a ladies' room latrine in Manchester with another woman that persuaded her to stay in London but the boredom of life on the road.

Before Hendrix's fame escalated, the two loved shopping together, visiting friends, even skating, which Hendrix soon became good at. Hendrix could eat anything except for Etchingham's cooking, and this led to not only most of their rows but the composition of "The Wind Cries Mary," Hendrix's third hit single that is somewhat unsung nowadays. After arguing and breaking dishes and staying at a friend's flat overnight, she returned to find he had written the song using her middle name. Etchingham was not mollified. She was—as Michael Jeffery's personal assistant Trixie Sullivan said—"the only one who ever stood her own ground" with Hendrix.

Nor was "The Wind Cries Mary" the only song Etchingham influenced. The line in "1983 . . . (A Merman I Should Turn to Be)" about the narrator's "love, Catherina" refers to Etchingham, who was lying in bed beside Hendrix when he wrote the lyrics. Once again, she was not amused. Nor does she seem to approve of the recorded version, the centerpiece of *Electric Ladyland* and arguably the fullest fusion of Hendrix's disparate interests. According to Etchingham's *Through Gypsy Eyes*, the song has "this strange rushing, buzzing sound you hear when you are tripping."

It was Chandler's decision to sell his management stake in Hendrix to Jeffery in late September 1968 that led to Etchingham finding a flat above Mr. Love, a restaurant. The bitter Chandler had checked Etchingham and Hendrix's things—he was back in America—into a decrepit hotel as payback for Hendrix's ingratitude. This was how Jimi Hendrix came to move next door to where Frederick Handel, another expatriate musician, had lived a little over a quarter century from 1723 until 1759.

Perhaps the first sign of the irrevocable damage Hendrix's inner New York City circle would cause was the wedge they drove between Hendrix and Etchingham when she crossed the Atlantic to join him in mid-March 1969. She checked into the Pierre Hotel on Fifth Avenue, not far from the Central Park Zoo. And a zoo is not far from what she thought she found herself in when Hendrix arrived with the entourage of pimps and groupies feeding off of her lover man.

Sizing up the situation, Etchingham was aware that although they both had come from similarly neglected childhoods, they came away with different lessons. Everything for Hendrix was transitory. The gold watch Bill Graham gave him, the gold Dunhill cigarette lighter, the expensive guitars slipped through his fingers. The lesson Hendrix took was that nothing lasts, whereas Etchingham was a survivor.

The final straw was, when a Columbo-looking drug dealer entered her hotel room carrying a bag full of drugs and a gun, she promptly checked out and returned to London, even though it took several days and other eyebrow-raising incidents that are recounted in Etchingham's enjoyable biography, *Through Gypsy Eyes*. (A well-recommended paperback if you can find a reasonably priced copy, it contains straightforward observations about Swinging London and its denizens, such as the fact that John Lennon was "too domineering to be likeable." Turns out those that knew them had favorite Beatles as well, and Etchingham's was Paul.)

Back in London, Etchingham fell in love and married a man named Ray—his surname is not available but he was apparently not Eric Clapton's

The Jimi Hendrix Experience's third single "The Wind Cries Mary" was written for Kathy Mary Etchingham after a terrible argument.   *Courtesy of Robert Rodriguez*

chauffer as mentioned in Hendrix's earlier biographies—without informing Hendrix, who was still stateside. In fact, almost a year had lapsed since Etchingham's return to London when someone informed Hendrix of her marriage. A sudden phone call led to a sudden flight back to London for Hendrix. Etchingham was shocked to find that Hendrix still thought they were a couple. She booked him a room at the Londonderry Hotel because the flat that would one day adorn a blue plaque with his name was not his to share any longer.

Regrouping, Hendrix participated in separate recording sessions with Stephen Stills and Love's Arthur Lee and discussed a joint tour with Emerson, Lake, and Palmer before jetting back to New York City on March 19, 1970.

Etchingham and Hendrix met several times during his final weeks in London, with Hendrix asking her to contact him at his hotel. She never did. Like Jake Barnes and Lady Brett Ashley at the conclusion of Hemingway's *The Sun Also Rises*, it's pretty to think that Hendrix might not have died when he did if she had contacted him. The survivor carried on with her life and rebounded from the bad marriage with Ray to embark on a successful one with Nick Page, a medical practitioner. While raising two sons and enjoying success as a realtor, Etchingham also found time to joust with Monika Dannemann, the Queen of Libel; reopen the inquest into the circumstances surrounding Hendrix's death; and have the blue plaque affixed, not only as a tribute to her lover man, but as a tribute too to her other friends that died far too young: Brian Jones, Keith Moon, John Lennon, and Chas Chandler.

Devon Wilson

One need go no further than Hendrix's compositions to discern the difference in his relationships with Etchingham and Devon Wilson, a former teenage prostitute who had ditched the name Ida Mae for Devon and parlayed her sexual talents into becoming a black super groupie who would exert enormous influence over Hendrix in America.

Etchingham inspired lovely ballads; Wilson is remembered through turgid rockers such as "Dolly Dagger," "Crash Landing," "Freedom," and "Stepping Stone." (She also sparked "Steppin' in Her I. Miller Shoes" from Betty Davis's eponymous debut album.) You could attribute the cause to the divergent lifestyles Hendrix led in London and New York City, but as he sang in "Highway Chile": "It goes a little deeper than that."

Equally well researched—and recent—biographies honestly disagree on the date that Hendrix first met Wilson. I'll cite December 1965. It was Emmaretta Marks, an original cast member of the 1968 Broadway production of *Hair*, who made the introduction. (Marks would later provide the Merry Claytonesque backing vocals on "In from the Storm.")

Coming off of the Monterey International Pop Festival triumph that reverberates to this day, Hendrix and Wilson were reintroduced to one another in Laurel Canyon by Electric Flag's Buddy Miles, and by the time the Experience booked Houston Studios in Los Angeles to record their fourth single, Wilson was on hand and can be heard on the underrated "The Stars That Play with Laughing Sam's Dice," which—with its allusion to drugs (i.e., STP with LSD)—could be said to be Hendrix's "Lucy in the Sky with Diamonds."

In the go-getter groupie from Milwaukee, Hendrix found a kindred spirit—they traded stories of groupies he had scored and rock stars Wilson had slept with—and Wilson quickly established herself as Hendrix's personal assistant and social secretary. (That's what Kathy Etchingham underestimated her as being the summer she visited New York City: an assistant who brought them tea.) Wilson procured drugs and women for Hendrix. She decided who could attend studio sessions. She found the Twelfth Street apartment in New York City that Hendrix invited her to share.

But she was also like those women in Woody Allen movies who warn that they're "trouble" and then go on to prove it. She feuded with the Record Plant's owner Gary Kellgren. She not only introduced Hendrix to Chuck Wein (the filmmaker behind the *Rainbow Bridge* debacle) but also Collette Mimram and Stella Douglas, wife of producer Alan Douglas, who was to go on to become caretaker of Hendrix's tapes for two decades. She possibly spiked Hendrix's drink before Band of Gypsys' disastrous appearance at Madison Square Garden in February 1970. Various sources suggest that she introduced Hendrix to snorting heroin.

According to the *New York Post*'s Al Aronwitz: "Whenever a rock hero came to New York, the chances were you'd find Devon in his hotel room." Rock stars Wilson is known to have slept with include Arthur Lee, Eric Clapton, and Brian Jones. For Mick Jagger, making his move on Wilson was a bit of payback for Hendrix making moves on Marianne Faithfull; Jagger had greater success. Because of this dalliance between Jagger and Wilson, Hendrix was forced to spend his twenty-seventh (and final) birthday attending a Rolling Stones concert at Madison Square Garden.

Film footage survives of Hendrix, dressed in black, sitting unobtrusively in the Stones' dressing room corner much like he is said to have sat at parties during his first months in London. Keith Richards chats him up a bit, Jagger walks by cagily, new lead guitarist Mick Taylor is the friendliest, perhaps a little starstruck, and together they talk shop and Hendrix is even seen playing Taylor's guitar upside down. During the concert, Hendrix could be sighted onstage standing behind Richards's amplifiers.

After the concert, Jagger attended the surprise twenty-seventh birthday party Wilson threw for Hendrix at Monte Kay's apartment. (Monte Kay was a figure of the New York City jazz scene in the 1940s and '50s, but by the time of Hendrix's birthday party, he was better known as producer of Flip Wilson's television show on NBC.) According to an interview in *Rags* magazine, Wilson said "Mick came in an out-of-sight black and white checkered Zoot suit and a Mafia sized ruby ring on his little finger." Other Stones attended too. This was the party where Wilson allegedly licked blood off of Jagger's pricked finger (the source of the "Dolly Dagger" line that "she drinks her blood from a jagged edge"), and despite rumors that Hendrix and Jagger disappeared and fought over Wilson, Sharon Lawrence reports in her book that what really happened was that Jagger offered words of encouragement to a fellow rocker who was facing jail time for heroin possession in Canada. This did not, however, prevent Jagger from leaving the party with Wilson.

The *Rags* interview described Wilson as being "posed on harem pillows" in Hendrix's Twelfth Street apartment and wearing "a tasty Ossie Clark hostess gown." The interview was mostly about Jagger. (It's no accident that Hendrix's song about Wilson is about Dolly Dagger (as in rhymes with!). No wonder Hendrix was biding his time in his bedroom while Wilson held court. The interview concluded with Wilson saying: "So what do I do for an encore? I don't know, probably marry Jimi . . . Will you publish my wedding photos?"

But within nine months of the magazine's street date, both Hendrix and Wilson were dead. I wonder if *Rags* published photos from Hendrix's funeral that was attended by Stella and Alan Douglas and Devon Wilson, who—like the mother in the scene of Laura Palmer's burial in *Twin Peaks*— tried to throw herself into Hendrix's open grave.

Devon was more successful on February 2, 1971, when she threw herself from her Chelsea Hotel room. (The Chelsea, on Manhattan's Twenty-Third Street, is known for artists and a number of infamous deaths, including Sid Vicious's stabbing of Nancy Spungen, another rock groupie, on October 12, 1978. Sid Vicious, by the way, died eight years after Wilson on February 2, 1979.) I'm being flippant. There are really few firm facts surrounding Wilson's death. Her drug use, which was already worsening throughout 1970 (and was referenced in Hendrix's lyrics), spun out of control following his death, and so no one knows if she jumped, accidentally fell, or was pushed from one of the Chelsea's upper floors. Those who are into conspiracy theories believe she was murdered to keep her quiet about Hendrix's murder by Michael Jeffery.

Electric Ladies

By 1968, groupies were an integral part of Hendrix's own experiences, but when talking of these women he said, "I prefer the term 'Electric Ladies.'" And when it came time to name his third album, he paid these ladies of the road a compliment by incorporating his nickname for groupies in the title.

In our predominantly conservative society, the definition of a "groupie" has taken on inappropriate connotations by stressing the sexual gratification aspect of the relationship only available to celebrities and overlooking the emotional benefits. Songs about groupies swing both ways. There are the positive (e.g., Steppenwolf's "Hey, Lawdy Mama") and negative (e.g., Michael Jackson's "Dirty Diana"). Groupies as subject matter was explored at length by Frank Zappa over the course of two albums by the second incarnation of the Mothers of Invention: *Fillmore East—June 1971* and *200 Motels*, which is the soundtrack for the movie of the same name. The former may be Zappa's best live album.

It's more of an American phenomenon to this day if one is to believe Kid Rock, who is quoted as allegedly saying, "Europeans don't seem to have the groupie mentality." As Hendrix biographer Harry Shapiro put it, the London "groupie scene was restricted to a hardcore dozen or so." In America, however, there was a dozen or so at every show in every American town. And often the dozen or so could be found in Hendrix's bed. Reading stories of the Experience on the road recalls John Lennon's comparison of Beatles tours to *Satyricon*. For example, by late summer 1968, according to Noel Redding (who should know), the Experience was "no longer welcome at the Waldorf-Astoria because one night, in order to get into the orgy in Jimi's room, one had to undress in the busy hallway."

Mitch Mitchell and Noel Redding also attracted their share of the spoils, partially because they looked every inch the skinny, long-haired, pale British rocker with the exotic accent. Redding also appears to have been a groupie favorite. Where super groupie and author Pamela Des Barres was intimidated by Hendrix's sexuality, she pursued Redding without regret. As she wrote in her book *I'm with the Band:* "I was totally under his control. He put me in a hundred positions and did stupendous things! It's doubtful that anybody could surpass his proism. It was like being caught in a web, unable to free myself—wanting to get more tangled . . . Noel said, 'That, my dear, is what you call a fuck.'"

Redding did not rise as well to the occasion on February 25, 1968. The Experience was booked to do two shows at the Chicago Opera House, one of which was a 3 p.m. matinée. Returning to the Conrad Hilton between shows, three groupies accosted the three band members. They were known as the Plaster Casters, because, going further than just sleeping with rock stars and writing about it afterwards in their diaries, they wanted to preserve for posterity the occasion by making a mold of the musician's hard-on. Hendrix and Redding were game, while Mitchell demurred.

The Plaster Casters consisted of Cynthia (their leader), Dianne, and Marilyn, who did not engage in any sexual activity but took notes for what was actually the first time any rock star had agreed to the Plaster Casters' unusual proposition. It was Dianne's role to get the rock star erect, according to Cynthia: "I didn't see any nervousness on her face. I think she was just concentrating on shoving the whole thing in her mouth." Of Hendrix she wrote in her diary: "He has got just about the biggest rig I've ever seen!" Of the mold, she wrote: "I was really anxious to see the finished product, and I accidentally cracked the mold open and it crumpled into pieces. But I very carefully folded it back together again, and it came out fairly intact. It's fairly huge, very thick and rather long."

They also encountered problems with Redding's contribution. As he put it in his autobiography: "My offering was unusual—a corkscrewed rendition—the result of a combination of bad timing of the rate the plaster would set and (road manager) Stickells's surprise entry into my room at the crucial moment."

The Story of the Lost Sex Tape

In what could be termed the revenge of *The Goodbye Girls*, an 8mm stag film—to use the vernacular of the era—was found in 2006 in a trunk bought at auction. The film canister was labeled "Black Man," and when the winning bidder watched the film he quickly suspected that the black man being serviced by two white girls with '60s hairdos was Jimi Hendrix. In order to confirm this theory, the two groupies referenced above were brought together and asked to attend a "screening" of the film. Now middle-aged, the two women were being asked to authenticate the buyer's theory.

If you will recall, Des Barres never actually bedded Hendrix—she revealed in her book that she was underage when propositioned—and instead was Redding's "girlfriend" when the Experience came to her California town a tour or two later. So it was really up to Cynthia Plaster Caster, who actually saw Hendrix's "Hampton Wick" as she called Hendrix's penis, to verify based on memory and her mold made that day in Chicago. Known as #00004 O (which, as Plaster Caster commented, was made on George Harrison's birthday), it has come to be known as the Penis de Milo.

And so that is largely what this porno DVD consists of: Des Barres and Plaster Caster viewing and commenting on the 8mm stag film. Neither doubt the thin black man wearing only a bandana and rings is Hendrix. The few grainy facial shots—one of the man reclining and the other giving fellatio—seem to confirm this. Plaster Caster also remembers the color of the thighs as being like Hendrix's and believes the member matches the Penis de Milo.

Des Barres says that Kathy Etchingham told her Hendrix liked being filmed having sex with a succession of partners. Hendrix is known to have created a series of films of girls waving goodbye after they spent the night with him. Shot from his hotel window, he called the films *The Goodbye Girls* and would show the silent films to friends and mimic the girls and make rude comments.

I wouldn't recommend the DVD to anyone. It's padded with footage of Haight-Ashbury in 1967 and hippie concerts, has a horrendous soundtrack of someone imitating Hendrix playing guitar, and when they finally do show the 8mm film, it's censored like a Japanese S&M movie. This is a shame because "Black Man," from what you can see of it, is erotic, especially when the two women kiss. It's erotic because they aren't acting.

The two groupies are of the opinion that the women are Scandinavian. This adds up because Hendrix often toured Scandinavia, and the region was known for its sexual liberation. Anyone who remembers the Swedish magazines Iggy Pop sang of in "Five Foot One" will know what I mean. Des Barres goes on to say in the DVD: "Doesn't look like a hotel room. It looks like he picked these two girls at a club and they took him home like two very wise girls."

6

Can You See Me?

Hendrix on Film

n Universal City, there are streets named after not only film stars (Jimmy Stewart) and directors (Alfred Hitchcock), but musicians: Muddy Waters, Buddy Holly, and Jimi Hendrix. And even though Hendrix never made a film for Universal, this is totally appropriate considering the role his music played in several notable films.

For example, the soundtrack to *Easy Rider* featured the Experience's anti-establishment credo "If 6 Was 9," and it was this album's commercial success that led to the now common practice of scoring films entirely with contemporary music. And it's hard to imagine two of the best rock concert movies—*Monterey Pop* and *Woodstock*—without Jimi Hendrix. It's no accident that both of these concert performances have since been released by Experience Hendrix on DVD. Those films have helped promote the Hendrix legend to subsequent generations just as Hendrix has helped promote the magic of film.

Here then, chronologically, are the concert DVDs you should seek out. The less said about the movie *Rainbow Bridge* and DVD *Blue Wild Angel*, the better.

BBC and European Television Appearances

The Jimi Hendrix Experience's first appearance on television on BBC-TV's *Top of the Pops* included a live performance of their first single, "Hey Joe," which had been issued thirteen days earlier. This performance is lost, but fortunately many of the Experience's 1967 television appearances in the United Kingdom, France, and Sweden survive and are available on bootleg DVDs. The quality varies and the performances are a mixture of live and lip-synching (a practice Hendrix abhorred) but still worth seeing, especially live performances of "Purple Haze" pruned for television scheduling. You also see a band that is still coming to grips with the musical powers they are striving to master, sort of like Clark Kent and his superpowers when he was Superboy or Harry Potter and his magic throughout J. K. Rowling's novels.

The songs are always A- and B-sides of the Experience's first four singles, which is to be expected, and so you'll get multiple renditions of "Hey Joe," "Stone Free," "Purple Haze," "The Wind Cries Mary," and "Burning of the Midnight Lamp." Earliest footage shows the pre-permed hairdo of Mitch Mitchell, and you get to see how the Experience's wardrobe gets more and more psychedelic throughout the year. A special treat is seeing Hendrix performing in his legendary Royal Veterinary Corps jacket and footage of the Experience walking around town and clowning in a very Monkee-esque manner that exhibits the camaraderie the threesome had initially.

Monterey Pop

Jimi Hendrix wrote the lyrics to "Little Wing" while at the Monterey International Pop Festival, and D. A. Pennebaker's 1968 film *Monterey Pop* perfectly mirrors Hendrix's paean to the festival. Along with *Woodstock* it has to be happiest festival ever documented, and its importance cannot be overstated. It captures the hippie era in full bloom as well as several career-defining performances (Janis Joplin, Otis Redding) in addition to that of the Experience. The stunned look on faces after Hendrix burns his guitar and leaves the stage is not to be missed. (Nor is Mama Cass Elliot getting off on Joplin's performance of Big Mama Thornton's "Ball and Chain" that afterwards was no longer Big Mama Thornton's just as "Wild Thing" no longer belonged to the Troggs once the Experience were done with it.)

It is a varied musical reflection of the times. Unlike *Woodstock*, which is rebelliously electric, *Monterey Pop* casts a wider net, and so you have Top 40 acts (the Mamas and the Papas, Scott McKenzie), soul performers (Lou Rawls, Otis Redding), folk acts (Simon and Garfunkel), and international artists (Hugh Masekela, Ravi Shankar). It gets even more varied with the *Complete Monterey Pop Festival* box set that was released by Criterion in 2002, including short films on Otis Redding, who died within six months of the festival, and the Jimi Hendrix Experience.

Jimi Plays Monterey

As a Hendrix fan, you do not want to miss *Jimi Plays Monterey* by Pennebaker and Chris Hegedus. "As remembered by John Phillips," this short documentary presents the majority of the Experience's performance. Former Papa and festival organizer Phillips sets the stage over film clips of the pre-festival Experience and London (including shots from the Beatles' "A Day in the Life" video).

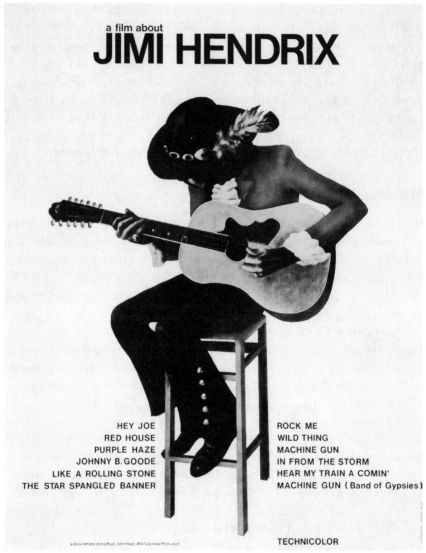

Advertisement for the first documentary on Jimi Hendrix. It would not be the last.

Courtesy of Robert Rodriguez

More importantly, there is footage of the Experience and the pimp-hatted Hendrix playing "Sgt. Pepper's Lonely Hearts Club Band" and a truncated "Wild Thing" with a Christmas-themed feedback intro from the *Christmas on Earth, Continued* concert filmed on December 22, 1967, at L'Olympia in Paris. (Also on the bill were Pink Floyd and the Who: now those were the days.)

Eric Burdon's "Monterey" is then used as a soundtrack to present film clips of the festival audience and performers, including the Who, Jefferson Airplane, and the Grateful Dead.

Of special interest are Brian Jones's introduction of the Experience, critic Charles Shaar Murray's audio commentary, and an excerpt of a 1987 Pete Townshend interview where he recalls Monterey and the classic Who-Experience rivalry as to who would follow whom. Kudos also to David Fricke's booklet notes that correctly identify both Otis Redding and Hendrix as "R&B classicists."

By the way, the "soundtrack" CD differs from the Hendrix estate version issued in 2007: the introduction is longer and the mix is by Joe Gastwirt. I'm not saying it's better than Eddie Kramer's 2007 mix—it's not—it's just different.

The Jimi Hendrix Experience: Live at Monterey

Experience Hendrix LLC issued *The Jimi Hendrix Experience: Live at Monterey* in October 2007. Although it includes the original concert footage directed by D. A. Pennebaker, this film is directed by Bob Smeaton, who reedited the footage.

There is a good overview of how Hendrix was discovered fleshed out with rare footage and interviews by Chas Chandler, Animals tour manager Tappy Wright, Experience Makers Mitchell and Redding, Chris Stamp, Andrew Loog Oldham, and Dave Mason of Traffic.

There's a lengthy setting up of the scene as key participants John Phillips, Michelle Phillips, Derek Taylor, and others describe how the festival came about and how after the headliners (the Mamas and the Papas, Simon & Garfunkel, and Otis Redding) were booked, the organizers branched out to invite exotic and/or unknown musical acts, including the Jimi Hendrix Experience.

The Experience's entire June 18, 1967, performance is presented in the correct order sans "Can You See Me," regrettably not filmed because the camera crew had to swap out film to continue shooting. (It is regrettable because there is no known footage of this song, one of the Experience's earliest.) After decades of hearing Bob Dylan's "Like a Rolling Stone" and B. B. King's "Rock Me Baby," it was a joy to finally see the performances. You get to see Jimi wearing his Gypsy Eyes jacket during the first number and toward the end chewing on his guitar pick while playing the combined British and America national anthem during the intro to "Wild Thing."

The estate did a fine job with this DVD, and of all the DVDs devoted exclusively to Jimi Hendrix it is one of the two you must own. The colors of the concert footage are vibrant, practically psychedelic, and the audio soundtracks feature new 5.1 and 2.0 stereo mixes by Eddie Kramer. The accompanying booklet has notes by Mitch Mitchell and John McDermott and photos of Jimi before (shopping, watching Electric Flag, rehearsing) and during his performance. Unfortunately there's only one group shot of the Experience.

In addition to Smeaton's film, the DVD contains the following bonus features:

- *American Landing*—Documents Hendrix rise from Greenwich Village unknown to "overnight" star and includes interviews with Chandler, Mitchell, and Redding.
- *A Second Look*—The Experience's Monterey Pop performance seen from normally unseen camera angles.
- *Never Before Released Live Performances*—Black-and-white footage of the Experience's earliest known live concert to be filmed: February 25, 1967, in Chelmsford, England, featuring the rarely filmed "Like a Rolling Stone" and "Stone Free."
- *Music, Love & Flowers*—Reminiscences of the legendary festival by cofounder Lou Adler.

The Lulu Show

When Elvis Costello and the Attractions abruptly stopped playing "Less Than Zero" and switched gears (or the dial) for the antimedia "Radio, Radio" on *Saturday Night Live* on December 17, 1977 (an act that got Costello banned from the show for twelve years), they were copying what the Jimi Hendrix Experience had done on BBC-TV's *The Lulu Show* on January 4, 1969.

This was a historic performance culturally and musically. First off, you've got the Experience playing "Voodoo Child (Slight Return)," one of their noisiest rockers that will please even the die-hardest fan. The fact that *Electric Ladyland*'s closing track wasn't even a single, however, did not mollify Hendrix's attitude about being asked to also sing "the song that absolutely made them"—as Lulu introduced "Hey Joe"—next. By 1969 Hendrix had tired of the song formerly associated with Tim Rose and did not want to play it.

The tremolo-barred intro throws Hendrix's Strat's tuning out of whack, but after turning and grinning to his fellow Experience Makers, he soldiers on, singing a verse or two (while quoting the Beatles' "I Feel Fine" on guitar), and playing a tuneful solo before signaling to Mitchell and Redding to stop playing. Announcing to the television studio audience that "we'd like to stop playing this rubbish and dedicate a song to the Cream, regardless of what kind of group they may be in," he then takes the Experience off on a spirited, if shortened instrumental rendition of "Sunshine of Your Love." It was shortened because it was unplanned, and by playing a third number, the Experience had exceeded their allotted time limit, and now Lulu, a singer best known in America for the hit single "To Sir with Love," could not perform her closing number.

It's another performance you should really make an effort to view if only to see the Experience lined up differently onstage, with Mitchell up-front stage right like a guitarist, Redding center stage and standing on a drummer's platform, and Hendrix stage left.

Woodstock

"Lincoln at Gettysburg. Hendrix at Woodstock. Pujols at Arlington. The performance of a lifetime," is how sports columnist Tom Verducci summed up Albert Pujols's three-homer performance in the third game of the 2011 World Series between the St. Louis Cardinals and the Texas Rangers. Hendrix's performance at Woodstock was so legendary that sports reporters know jocks are aware of it.

Only Hendrix's performance wasn't legendary. It was in flashes, and one of those flashes is what is captured in Michael Wadleigh's 1970 movie: Hendrix's historic interpretation of "Star Spangled Banner." And for this reason alone you have to see the movie. But it isn't the only reason.

Brilliantly edited by Martin Scorsese, Thelma Schoonmaker (she's edited every Scorsese movie since *Raging Bull*), and others, the film captured "half a million kids [having] three days of fun and music" (as farmer Max Yasgur described the free festival held on his land). Crosby, Stills, and Nash's "Long Time Gone" and "Wooden Ships" sandwich Canned Heat's "Going up the Country" as the stage is erected and the audience arrives. And then the fun begins.

There is nary a bad nor boring performance, but the highlights are Santana's "Soul Sacrifice," Ten Years After's "I'm Going Home," and Sly and the Family Stone's medley of "Dance to the Music," "Music Lover," and "I Want to Take You Higher." And then comes Hendrix playing the national anthem and "Purple Haze." As the crowd picks up and goes home, Hendrix's instrumental "Villanova Junction" provides a poignant backdrop.

Although this performance is also included on *Jimi Hendrix: Live at Woodstock*, you have to view Wadleigh's film in order to see the properly edited performance as the camera moves from perfectly framed shots of Hendrix's head to dramatic images of his hands playing guitar. Just don't watch the bloated Director's Cut, which ruins the original film by not adding one iota of good film.

Jimi Hendrix: Live at Woodstock

The Hendrix estate's release of Jimi Hendrix's Woodstock performance is not as bad as once feared and even very enjoyable if you have reasonable expectations. This is the complete 140-minute set that Gypsy Sun and Rainbows played that August Monday morning except for the Impressions medley; "Mastermind," which rhythm guitarist Larry Lee sang; and Hendrix's "Hear My Train A Comin'" (but that blues number is shown on *A Second Look*, a second disc of the [almost] complete concert featuring black-and-white video and alternate color angles).

The Rainbows and others describe the rehearsals, the concert, and its aftermath, but the highlight is the concert itself. Although there are some obscure songs in the set, nine of the fourteen songs had been played previously at Experience concerts. The set really caught fire toward the end during "Voodoo Child (Slight Return)," "The Star Spangled Banner" (not written down on Hendrix's original set list), and "Purple Haze," but that doesn't mean there weren't any highlights before. True, "Red House" is cut short when Hendrix breaks a guitar string, but from the surviving footage you can see the crowd really was into "Jam Back at the House" (aka "Beginnings") and "Fire."

The booklet featuring John McDermott's insights on director Michael Wadleigh's filming of the festival as well as background on the black-and-white videotape made by Albert Goldman, a Bard College student majoring in drama, is invaluable. There's other DVD bonuses too, including a Jimi Hendrix press conference two weeks after the festival, Eddie Kramer's recollections of recording the concert (and not only Hendrix's performances but every act's), and Billy Cox and Larry Lee talking about meeting Hendrix and playing with him on the chitlin' circuit.

Jimi Hendrix: The Dick Cavett Show

Jimi Hendrix only made three appearances on American television. The July 10, 1969, appearance on Johnny Carson's *The Tonight Show* appears to be lost to posterity (although the audio recording remains). Black comedian Flip Wilson was the substitute host as Carson was either ill or absent because he didn't want to be seen hosting a show with a controversial black rock 'n' roller. The appearance appears to have been a disaster, with Hendrix nervously chewing gum, Wilson playing up black stereotypes for Carson's white audience, and Hendrix's amplifier blowing up during a performance of "Lover Man" dedicated to Brian Jones, the recently drowned Rolling Stone. The appearance is of special note as it was Billy Cox's first public performance as Hendrix's bassist.

Earlier that same month, on July 7, 1969, Hendrix made the first of two appearances on *The Dick Cavett Show*. (Former comedian Cavett was not yet one of Carson's rivals for the late-night throne, and so Hendrix's appearance was aired prime time, albeit summertime.) He also appeared on September 9, 1969. Both of these appearances can be found on the DVD *Jimi Hendrix: The Dick Cavett Show*.

The DVD is not a must-view experience, but if you can find it used, by all means grab it. The documentary and Hendrix's handwritten notes for a Cavett assistant are not essential, but it is fun seeing Hendrix sitting with other guests such as Broadway stars Gwen Verdon and Robert Downey and for someone like me who remembers *Marcus Welby, MD*, it's a hoot to see actor Robert Young smiling on benevolently as Hendrix defends his controversial arrangement of "The Star Spangled Banner" played at Woodstock weeks earlier. Hendrix also shows off his self-deprecating humor several times. (For example, he says he's "the best guitarist in this chair" when Cavett describes him as the best guitarist in the world.)

The real reasons to watch this DVD are the three songs Hendrix plays:

1. "Hear My Train A Comin'"—Backed by the Dick Cavett Show Band, Hendrix's second-best blues number has a jaunty feel and clocks in at 2:24. The guitar is low in the mix, but this is worth seeing because you get to see Hendrix in front of an American television audience. More importantly it's worth hearing because this is the closest Hendrix ever came to performing with a big band.

2. "Izabella"—The September appearance included Mitch Mitchell on drums, Billy Cox on bass, and Juma Sultan on percussion, so it wasn't "the inimitable Jimi Hendrix Experience" as Cavett incorrectly introduced the band. "Izabella" was a love song from a soldier to his love back home and reflected the direction toward realism that Hendrix's lyrics were moving during the war torn summer of 1969.

3. "Machine Gun"—This is why you need to see the *Dick Cavett Show* DVD: the debut performance of one of Hendrix's signature numbers. Like "Hear My Train A Comin'" back in July, "Machine Gun" too gets a shortened performance (2:32), but it is worth hearing in its pre-Band of Gypsys form. Mitchell's drumming lacks the machine gun volleys of Buddy Miles but is more tribal, and Billy Cox's brooding bassline is magnificent.

Band of Gypsys

One of the best rock DVDs and the blueprint for how all rock documentaries should be presented, so if there are any budding documentarians out there, please take note. Rather than interspersing talking heads with frustratingly clipped live performances, director Bill Smeaton lets the talking heads set the stage and then permits Band of Gypsys to play a full musical number before cutting back to the talking heads. This is so much more satisfying because, after all, while we *might* be interested in hearing what the talking head is saying, we are *definitely* interested in hearing what the band is playing.

This film documents the Band of Gypsys' four appearances at Bill Graham's Fillmore East on December 31, 1969, and January 1, 1970. Released in 1999, it began the process of reassessing the band nearly 30 years after the concerts and made fans see there was lot more to Band of Gypsys' songbook than "Machine Gun."

Hendrix had revealed to *New York Post* reporter Alan Arkonwitz, in a piece that ran on January 2, 1970, that he had arranged to have some performances recorded on videotape, a then unheard-of medium. And then probably due to the Gypsys' sudden demise and Hendrix's death, the filmed performances disappeared.

An impressive array of talking heads is lined up—music industry insiders (Don Cornelius, Frankie Crocker), Jeffery business associates (Trixie Sullivan, Gerry Stickells), latter-era musicians (Slash, Vernon Reid), Experience Makers (Mitch Mitchell, Noel Redding), even Hendrix's fellow Gypsys (Buddy Miles, Billy Cox). There are conflicting memories, but everyone is given a chance to be heard, and even Buddy and Billy can be seen playing along with their younger selves.

The highlight are the eight filmed performances, even if they are in black-and-white, which can also be viewed separately. Only "Earth Blues" is incomplete.

Jimi Plays Berkeley

Jimi Plays Berkeley was the first film featuring extended concert footage of Jimi Hendrix to be released. A composite of two concerts shot at the Berkeley Community Theatre on May 30, 1970, during the *Cry of Love* tour, if you want to call it a tour, as the band was only playing weekends so Hendrix could record during the week. The film has several exquisite performances and demonstrates that on occasion the lineup of Hendrix, Mitchell, and Cox could ascend to incredible musical heights.

Jimi Plays Berkeley features some of the best Hendrix live performances caught on film, but this poster uses footage from the Maui Hawaii performance featured in *Rainbow Bridge.* *Courtesy of Robert Rodriguez*

The proof is in the very first number: Chuck Berry's "Johnny B. Goode." At one time played by every rock band in every garage in America, Hendrix dusts off the by-then-tired cover and gives it a spirited romp at a breakneck tempo that I bet Berry never played it at. The highlight is the cinematic guitar solo that, like Hendrix's "All Along the Watchtower" solo, is broken into distinct parts, each upping the ante. And then he does it again during the outro before diving into a bath of feedback.

Other highlights include the finest version of "Hear My Train A Comin'" that Hendrix ever recorded (unfortunately edited but thankfully—and I do mean fully—available on *Jimi Hendrix: Blues*), the rarely filmed "I Don't Live Today," and "Voodoo Child (Slight Return)" (a song one never tires of), where Jimi plays his guitar between his legs, flirts with two girls standing in front of him, and prolongs the final verse.

Shot by Peter Pilafian at Michael Jeffery's behest, it is a padded film with unnecessary generation clashes (about the Woodstock movie of all things) and war and riot footage, but it is worth seeing even if it is forty-nine minutes in length. This is compensated for somewhat by the DVD version

The live rendition of "Johnny B. Goode" is not only one of the highlights of *Jimi Plays Berkeley,* it is one of the highlights of Jimi's live catalog.   *Courtesy of Robert Rodriguez*

released in 2003 including an audio-only version of the complete second set that runs sixty-seven minutes. The 2012 edition adds more than fifteen minutes of footage, including more screen time for "Hear My Train A Comin'" and "Machine Gun" as well as crowd interviews and more riot scene. The audio is also improved.

7

Here I Come to Save the Day

The Debut Album: *Are You Experienced*

With the question mark-less question it asks, the Jimi Hendrix Experience's debut album *Are You Experienced* guaranteed itself a longevity that eludes the other seminal albums in that musically seminal year of 1967 because as each generation comes of age and discovers the album, the listeners ask themselves if they are experienced. And we all know that when we are teens we want to be experienced.

When Michael Jeffery had his brainstorm and said Hendrix's group would be called the Jimi Hendrix Experience, Hendrix balked. It's a daunting concept to fulfill. "Experience" is sort of like what Prince said about "life" during the "Let's Go Crazy" intro: it's an electric word; one that Hendrix during that Pan Am flight over the Atlantic to London had to wonder if he could fulfill. When Hendrix asks "Are you experienced?" on the title track released eight months later and then intones "I am," much is answered about how his confidence had grown in that short time span.

The Recording Sessions

The recording sessions for what would be named *Are You Experienced* began on November 2, 1966, with the "Can You See Me" demo (another question mark-less title!) and concluded in the wee hours of April 25, 1967, a span of 176 days during which the Experience also released three singles. The album was recorded at three London studios (De Lane Lea, CBS, and Olympic), where the boards were manned by five different engineers. The sessions were tightly managed and produced by Chas Chandler.

De Lane Lea Studios Sessions

Olympic Studios and Eddie Kramer would become Hendrix's recording studio and engineer of choice, but the bulk of *Are You Experienced* was actually recorded at De Lane Lea Music Ltd. at 129 Kingsway, Kingsway, London WC2, on the edge of London's business district and engineered by Dave Siddle.

The "Can You See Me" demo was recorded at the end of the session that produced "Stone Free" and laid the blueprint for how songs were developed during the first six months of the band's existence. It was an effective blueprint and one that Hendrix would regrettably stray from once he conquered America and made New York City his center of operations in 1968.

With Hendrix sharing his living space with Chandler, the manager and client would craft songs in the apartment at Hyde Park Towers Hotel. Together may be too strong a word for it, and Chandler never received any songwriting credits, but with Hendrix using a small Vox amplifier and tinkering on Keith Richards's white Fender Stratocaster, Chandler would champion certain riffs or rhythmic forays and urge Hendrix to further develop them.

When a song's basic structure was defined and the lyrics came into focus, Chandler booked the Experience into a rehearsal space, and this is where Redding and Mitchell would acquaint themselves with the material worked up by Hendrix and Chandler.

CBS Studios Sessions

CBS Studios at 73 New Bond Street, London, might have become Hendrix's favorite London studio if not for bickering over unpaid bills between Chandler and Jake Levy, one of the brothers who owned the studio. Kit Lambert, the Who's manager, recommended CBS Studios when Chandler expressed displeasure with De Lane Lea. Chandler thought the sound left something to be desired but was still looking for something that fit his practically nonexistent budget. Yes, he had signed a contract with Lambert and Chris Stamp for the Experience's recordings to be issued by the fledgling Track Records, but money was still tight. Yes, the "Hey Joe" b/w "Stone Free" single was in the can but wouldn't be released until three days after the first CBS sessions.

Mike Ross was the recording engineer for the Experience's only two sessions on December 13 and 15, 1966, at CBS. Far better known as Mike Ross-Trevor, he went on to become an orchestral engineer and has been behind the technical end of many well-known film scores, including *Medicine Man,* *Hoosiers,* and *Tombstone.* But back in 1966, CBS had owned the former Levy Sound Studios for only one year, and Mike Ross was the studio's only employee. In addition to the Who, Ross had engineered Donovan's "Wear Your Love Like Heaven" prior to the Experience sessions at CBS.

It's just happenstance, but the first song tackled at CBS was "Foxy Lady," the song that would open the UK version of *Are You Experienced*. Mitchell arrived uncharacteristically early, and, being the only one in the studio besides Ross, persuaded the engineer to mike the tom-toms as had been done at Landsdowne Studios at a session Mitchell had contributed to with another recording artist. It was the first time Ross employed multiple microphones when recording percussion.

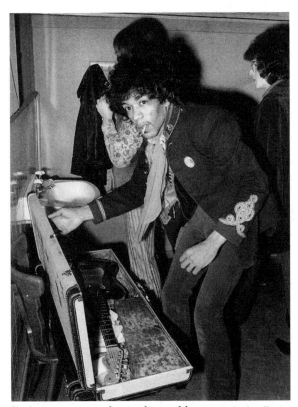

Jimi prepares to wake up the world.   *Author's collection*

Hendrix, Redding, and Chandler popped in around 4 o'clock. Hendrix had with him his standard stage gear because he liked recording loud. Ross was perturbed about what sort of mix they'd get, but, as he states in Sean Egan's *Not Necessarily Stoned, but Beautiful*, Hendrix's instruction to "just put a microphone about twelve feet away on the other side of the studio" did the trick. What Ross remembers chiefly from the recording was "the sheer power of everything. Just how loud everything was. I'd never heard anything like it in my life."

After the band laid down the foundation for the "Foxy Lady" version used for the album, they also ran through and recorded multiple takes of "Can You See Me," "3rd Stone from the Sun," and "Red House," their first stab at the blues number that would become a concert staple. Live vocals were not recorded when the backing tracks were being laid down, and Hendrix's guitar playing was so spontaneously revolutionary—leaping from rhythm to lead, fiddling with Marshall knobs while Mitchell played a drum fill—that Ross was flabbergasted when Chandler mentioned adding lyrics. Ross thought he was recording an instrumental band!

Chandler apparently was a big proponent of editing tapes to achieve the best recording, which came in handy two days later when Mitchell missed the session and the time was used instead to mix monaural all of the songs except for "Can You See Me."

Ross thought Chandler acquitted himself well in the studio. As John McDermott relates in *Ultimate Hendrix*: "He would actually go out on the floor and direct. He would work individually with Jim and Noel and show Mitch what to play and what drums to hit." Ross regretted only working two days with the Experience. As he told Sean Egan: "I'd never recorded anything up to that point that sounded that good, so I remember going home on a high . . . ."

Unfortunately, Jake Levy wouldn't allow Chandler to book more time until the previous hours had been paid for. Finances were tight and so Chandler promised payment as soon as the album was released. Levy was unyielding. The ever-battling Chandler was taken aback. This was not how he was accustomed to previously paying for recordings with the Animals. He eventually scrounged up the money because he needed the tapes, but the Experience never recorded at CBS Studios or with Ross again.

The CBS Studios sessions may have been of short duration, but they had lasting impact. Recorded and mixed in two sessions that the public knows so well from *Are You Experienced* was the basic track for "Foxy Lady" and remixed versions of "Can You See Me" and "Red House." (The CBS Studios version of "3rd Stone from the Sun" was completely scrapped and erased.)

Are You Experienced is not the only album of note that was recorded at CBS Studios. It is not only even the only debut album of note as the Clash's eponymously named aural onslaught was recorded there over three weekends in February 1977. Iggy and the Stooges also recorded *Raw Power* at CBS Studios with David Bowie behind the boards in 1973.

CBS Studios would be renamed Whitfield Street Studios when Sony Corporation acquired CBS in 1989. It was called the Hit Factory for a spell and then finally after the street it was on (31-37 Whitfield Street, London, "because generally"—as Ross-Trevor stated in a 2000 interview with Dirk Wickenden—"studios named after the street that they're on usually works [for example, Abbey Road]. . . . "

De Lane Lea Studios Sessions (Slight Return)

Lack of funds forced the Experience back to De Lane Lea Studios on December 21, 1966. And, even after the chart success of "Hey Joe" opened Polydor's coffers (Polydor was distributing Track Records' releases, including those of the Jimi Hendrix Experience), lack of available studio time at Olympic Studios kept them going back sporadically through March 29, 1967.

During these De Lane Lea Studios sessions, the Experience revisited "Red House" and began work on "Remember," "Fire," "I Don't Live Today," and "Manic Depression." They also recorded and mixed the two songs that would comprise the band's second single ("Purple Haze" b/w "51st Anniversary") and third single A-side ("The Wind Cries Mary"). All three of the Experience singles that charted in the United Kingdom and fueled their rise were recorded at De Lane Lea Studios.

Olympic Studios Sessions

The Jimi Hendrix Experience's first recording session at Olympic Studios was on February 3, 1967. Hendrix had already visited the studio on November 16, 1966, for the Rolling Stones recording session for "Title X," a Richards/Jones composition that you know as "Ruby Tuesday," which was about Linda Keith: Keith Richards's old flame, Jimi Hendrix's facilitator, and Brian Jones's girl after Anita Pallenberg left him. And so it's no surprise that both Brian Jones and Bill Wyman, the Rolling Stones most supportive of Hendrix, had encouraged both Chandler and Hendrix to record at Olympic, an independently owned studio that had opened the previous year.

The move to Olympic at 117 Church Street, Barnes, SW London, was indicative of the Experience's progress. In a little over five months, they had released a hit single, wowed and/or intimidated the elite rock musicians of Britain, and were garnering exploitative headlines in the British press ("The Wild Man of Borneo" is how *Disc and Music Echo* described Hendrix, a derogatory and racist term that would catch on.) They were challenging the Stones' claim to the title of bad boys of London. Chandler had words with Polydor's brass. The smash success of "Hey Joe" had convinced them that Hendrix had earning potential and so they opened an account for Chandler at Olympic so he could finish recording the Experience's first album.

As good as Dave Siddle and Mike Ross had been behind the sound-boards, along with Olympic Studios came Edwin (Eddie) Kramer, the engineer most clearly associated with Hendrix's recordings and the engineer who continues to mix Hendrix's recordings for Legacy Hendrix at the time of this writing in 2012. With the admittance of Kramer, the triumvirate recording team was now in place that would record, mix, and produce the bulk of *Are You Experienced*, all of *Axis: Bold as Love*, and a larger portion of *Electric Ladyland* than they are given credit for.

Second engineer George Chkiantz believes it was Kramer's appreciation of avant-garde jazz that made him the ideal engineer for Hendrix, who was playing louder in the studio than anyone else and introducing new devices that more staid engineers would only see as gimmicks. With Kramer, Hendrix found someone he could bounce ideas off of. Hendrix heard the sounds he wanted but didn't always know how to achieve them. With Kramer he had a willing cohort.

Kramer introduced valuable technique changes to the way the Experience recorded. He introduced Hendrix to close-micing and the use of all four tracks to record the Experience's basic backing tracks: Hendrix's guitar

Jimi's unorthodox stage movements won him many fans.   *Author's collection*

on one track, Redding's bass on another, and Mitchell's drums on the remaining two. As George Martin also did with Beatles recordings, Kramer would then "bounce down," a mixing process where tracks are moved (or bounced) on subsequent tape generations in order to create space for vocal and instrumental overdubs, new instrumentation, sound effects, and so on.

This method appealed to both Chandler—who was more old school and concerned about losing basic tracks—and Hendrix, who was clearly new school. He was one of the first musicians to understand the possibilities of tape manipulation.

The first Olympic recording session was actually an overdubbing session for adding "Purple Haze's" evocative sounds. They used the Octavia, a box designed by electronics wizard Roger Mayer, to color Hendrix's guitar notes on February 3rd, and on February 7th they added background vocals and background noise, which, as Kramer told McDermott in *Ultimate Hendrix*, is actually "a recording being fed back into the studio through the headphones held around a microphone, moving them in and out to create a weird echo."

With the second single in the can, work resumed on *Are You Experienced*. Although Olympic became the only studio the Experience would use for future recording in England, no more than three *Are You Experienced* tracks were actually cut in their entirety there. These are "May This Be Love" (initially entitled "Waterfall"), "Are You Experienced," and "3rd Stone from the Sun" and in that order at sessions held in April 1967.

Chandler had agreed to let Polydor hear the Experience's new album on April 25, 1967, at 11 a.m., and it took an all-night mixing session to accomplish this. Chandler, Hendrix, and Kramer hunkered down to make mono and stereo mixes for eight of the eleven songs earmarked for *Are You Experienced*. Only the title track, "Can You See Me," and "Red House" were already considered finished.

Chandler was nervous as he watched Polydor's head of A&R, Horst Schmaltze, place the lacquer on the turntable. Nobody outside of Hendrix's inner circle had heard what the Experience had been recording, rerecording, overdubbing, fixing, and mixing for five months in three London studios. Chandler knew it was different and original, but was it too different and original? He needn't have worried. Schmaltze said, "This is brilliant. This is the greatest thing I ever heard," Chandler recounted in *Ultimate Hendrix*. "From that point on we had a crusader for us within the Polydor establishment."

Delayed by technical glitches, the UK version of *Are You Experienced* was released on Track Records 612 001 on May 12, 1967, just in time for the weekend. The length was 40:12. Track Records' first LP entered the charts on May 25th and stayed there for thirty-three weeks. Its highest position was #2. It never could dislodge the Beatles' *Sgt. Pepper's Lonely Hearts Club Band* from the top slot.

UK Version Versus USA Version

Unsurprisingly given the time period, there are two versions of *Are You Experienced*. Typically in the 1960s, different labels in the United Kingdom and America issued the recordings domestically, and usually the American label felt justified in tailoring content for commercial sales and profit. For example, when the Rolling Stones issued their fourth full-length LP *Aftermath* in the United Kingdom in 1966, it was their sixth full length in America. London Records (an American label despite the name) had been omitting blues tracks, adding singles, and creating new product to keep the public interested. The same was true of the Beatles catalog as well as other

Jimi thought the British cover of *Are You Experienced* made him look like a "fairy."

Courtesy of Robert Rodriguez

well-known British artists. So what label was going to think twice about doctoring the debut album of an unknown black American guitarist and his British group?

As a result, the UK and USA versions offer very different interpretations of the "experience" that Jimi Hendrix asks whether you have or not. In the UK version, the experience is overtly more sexual and physical, whereas in the USA version it is more druggy and cerebral.

For example, the UK version opens with the sexy "Foxy Lady." Excuse this metaphor, but the loudening feedback swells like an erection until it is a turgid riff. (It's never been said, but I suspect the intent was to duplicate the Experience's entrance—during its fourth-ever concert appearance, before the Parisian audience in L'Olympia—Hendrix's guitar could be heard offstage feeding back and rising ominously.) In the USA, *Are You Experienced* opens with the druggy "Purple Haze."

Cover Art (UK Versus USA)

The chief contribution of Track Records' dynamic duo of Kit Lambert and Chris Stamp to Jimi Hendrix's rise and lasting fame was their handling of his image on the album and 45 sleeves in the United Kingdom. Although sometimes controversial, many of the images they selected have become iconic.

It's no surprise that the "Hey Joe" 45 had no artwork since it was rush released on Polydor and the Jimi Hendrix Experience was virtually unknown. "Purple Haze," however, features purple, brown, and orange hues with lettering on the top and bottom of and horizontal oval photo of an unsmiling Jimi Hendrix Experience. (Hendrix was instructed by Chas Chandler not to smile in early photos.) And by the time of "The Wind Cries Mary" release (only a week earlier than *Are You Experienced* to Chandler's consternation), the focus was on Hendrix himself as a kaleidoscopic triad of the same monochromatic Hendrix was used. (And again he is not smiling!) The move was on to focus on Hendrix and not his sidemen.

The cover shoot for the UK album was shot on February 27, 1967, and so all three members of the Experience appear in what is generally accepted as an underwhelming photo that in no way captures the spirit of the album within the sleeve. It is something of family portrait as it shows the Experience pre-stardom and speaks to how the members interrelated while they gained their musical bearings. Mitchell's hair is not even permed yet to match the locks of Hendrix and Redding.

It was actually Chandler who recruited the photographer, Bruce Fleming. Chandler was a fan of Fleming's work with the Hollies, Lulu, and Chandler's previous band the Animals. Fleming attended recording sessions and Experience performances before the photo shoot, which was held on a single day and not two as sometimes reported. Despite this, the photographer did not specify what the band members should wear, and this is why it is to me something of a family shoot.

I say this mostly because of Hendrix's flowered shirt and cape. The black shirt with red roses was a present to him from his girlfriend Kathy Etchingham. And while the cape was a clothing attribute he would soon lose, it was the epitome of early London Jimi and the reason why this was the image that the Experience wanted to use, even if it was Fleming's concept. I can see it as being an inside joke to the band. Because of the cape,

Hendrix was nicknamed "The Bat" by those close to him after his first days in London, and that is why he was pictured standing above Mitchell and Redding. (The photo made it look like Hendrix was standing on a box, but Fleming has insisted that, if anything, it was Mitchell and Redding on boxes but kneeling.)

Fleming wanted this pose because he felt that the band's music suggested flight and that a photo of Hendrix with his arms outstretched wearing the cape would make him look winged and suggest the album's airborne music. After the photo was developed, Fleming cropped the photo to allow Alan Aldridge to do the album title lettering flanking Hendrix's head. Sometimes compared to half-moons, the titles look more like eyes to me. The band's name does not appear. Track Records had final say on the artwork, but decades later Stamp was unhappy with it. As Sean Egan wrote in *Not Necessarily Stoned, but Beautiful*: "The contrast between the vitality of the album and its cover's staidness is striking." This is not a problem that the USA cover shares.

Michael Jeffery had signed a deal with Warner Brothers records for Jimi Hendrix's albums to be released on their Reprise subsidiary, far better known at the time as Frank Sinatra's label. The cover of the USA version is credited to Reprise's artistic director Ed Thrasher, but this is incorrect, and Hendrix apologized personally to Karl Ferris, the psychedelic photographer who actually designed the cover for USA and future international releases at Hendrix's behest.

Hendrix was decidedly not pleased with the UK cover. According to Ferris in an online article for *Rock Pop Gallery*, Hendrix thought the UK cover "made him look like a fairy." He wanted an image to match the music inside and, while he objected to having it classified as "psychedelic," told Ferris that he was "the only photographer that is doing with photography what I am doing with music—knocking down barriers and going beyond limits."

Karl Ferris played a significant role in shaping the look associated with psychedelic music in the 1960s. He was a photographer for teen and fashion magazines when a chance meeting with *Rubber Soul* photographer Robert Freeman led to Ferris experimenting with the work of fashion designer Marijke Koger. Exposure of these photos in the London *Times* was a revelation and led to album cover assignments.

Ferris had been present at the Experience's since-infamous Bag O' Nails show held on January 11, 1967, the one attended by a who's who of rock stars, including members of the Beatles, the Rolling Stones, and the Hollies. It was Ferris's design for the Hollies' *Evolution* released in May 1967 that made Hendrix ask Chandler—who knew Ferris from photos he had done for the Animals—to reach out and see if Ferris would do one for the Experience.

Ferris was as impressed by Hendrix as London's top rockers and eagerly accepted the assignment but said he'd need to "absorb [Hendrix's] music for inspiration. [Hendrix] said that I should accompany him to Olympic studios, where he was recording his next LP."

He too thought the Experience was bringing "unworldly space music to earth" and wanted to somehow capture this photographically. He settled upon using an infrared technique he had invented along with Nikon's "fisheye" lens that gives the approved image its apartment door peephole effect. And unlike Fleming's session, Ferris selected the clothing each band member would wear and went so far as to go through Hendrix's clothing in his apartment where he found the painted jacket he wanted Hendrix to wear, what Hendrix called his "Gypsy Eyes" jacket.

What is little known is that the Experience's permed hairstyle that all three members wore on the front and back covers of *Are You Experienced* was Ferris's suggestion. He saw Hendrix step out of a shower one night and was "amazed to see his hair all knapped out, as he would normally wear it like the English guys." He encouraged Hendrix to wear it that way—"it looks unique and spacy—just what we need for the cover!"—and Kathy Etchingham shaped it. When Redding and Mitchell saw Hendrix's new look the next day, Ferris encouraged them to follow suit.

The photo shoot in Kew Botanical Gardens was held on four occasions between June 6th and 10th, but the approved shot came from the very first roll taken. When Hendrix saw the photos, he suggested that Ferris also design the album cover. He originally created a "spheres flying through space concept" suitable for a gatefold cover but had to go back to the drawing board when Chandler informed him Reprise Records had not approved the expense for a gatefold.

So returning to "the approved fisheye shot," he added gold leaf matte and "purple filigree psychedelic lettering printed on gold metallic matte, which would make the lettering also seem metallic," but Reprise again chose to be economical and printed everything in one layer, which is how Reprise's artistic director received credit for the finished product.

Ferris's photography would contribute to all three Experience albums. When Track Records decided to go with the Hindu poster design for *Axis: Bold as Love*, they came to Ferris "to use (a) head shot of the group as an illustration to replace the Hindu god heads."

And in America, another Ferris shot of the threesome was used for the back cover of *Electric Ladyland*. Interestingly, Hendrix is wearing once again the Gypsy Eyes jacket that adorns the front cover of *Are You Experienced*. It is also similar to Fleming's disavowed cover in that Hendrix is seated and positioned above Redding and Mitchell, his large hands resting on his knees and crossed at the wrists seemingly pointing at his fellow musicians. Still glaring, still unsmiling.

The USA version of *Are You Experienced* was released on September 1, 1967, on Reprise RS 6261. It entered the charts at #190 and eventually rose to #5. It was on the charts for a little over two years: 106 weeks.

Core Identity

Both the UK and USA versions contain eleven tracks. In the USA, "Red House," "Can You See Me," and "Remember" were swapped out for the three UK hit singles ("Hey Joe," "Purple Haze," and "The Wind Cries Mary"). Of the eight tracks appearing on both versions, the four that held their spot in the sequencing give *Are You Experienced* its core identity.

"Manic Depression"

Occupying the second slot, the whiplash intro ideally followed the fade-out of the opening cut (i.e., "Foxy Lady" in the UK and "Purple Haze" in the USA). Saying the body of the song is 9/8 won't mean much to most; suffice it to say it was a fast waltz that made doubting Thomases believers because the performances of all three musicians on "Manic Depression" were top-notch.

There's Hendrix, of course, but Mitchell's spherical drumming was the first hint that jazz fit comfortably within the Experience's musical worldview. And then, as if that was not enough, Redding's riff anchored the rhythm and revealed the bass instrument's true role in Experience compositions and concerts: timekeeper. A regular electric guitarist by trade, Redding's notes rang out—they did not rumble—and allowed his guitarist and drummer to soar around him. Redding was quite proud of this performance and rightly so.

Hendrix wrote the lyrics shortly after Chandler critiqued one of his interviews by saying he sounded like a manic-depressive. The band cut the track the following day, March 29, 1967, at their final session at De Lane Lea Studios. Mitch Mitchell claimed "Manic Depression" was captured in a single take, but three have since surfaced on the indispensable, but somewhat costly, twenty-two-CD bootleg collection *Moonbeams and Fairytales*.

"I Don't Live Today"

Often prefaced in concert with a dedication to Native Americans (and less often other minorities), "I Don't Live Today," with Mitchell's tribal drumming, concluded Side One powerfully by dousing any sense of escapism that the other psychedelic, trippy tracks encouraged. Hendrix reminded the listener that even in the Summer of Love, there were people not feeling that love who should not be ignored.

Hendrix's grandma Nora on his father's side was of Cherokee, making Jimi one-sixteenth Cherokee, and the aspect of his ancestry he embraced the most. With his rootless, motherfucker musician lifestyle, Jimi spoke more frequently about his Cherokee heritage than being African American. But while the song's subject matter may have its root in the plight of the American Indian heard of firsthand at his grandma's knee, it touched on a universality that extends to this day, ironically capturing more forcefully a manic-depressive mood than the Hendrix composition bearing that title.

Let's recall where this song was coming from. It was the latter part of the mid-'60s. War was raging in Vietnam, a generation gap was never more significantly felt, riots were occurring across the home of the brave. Hendrix may be trying to be the voice of the American Indian, but many Americans in 1967 did not feel alive, and the song captured that angst. That's the unsatisfying, suffering part of the "experience" that *Are You Experienced* asked you about. The song even concluded after a guitar freak-out with Hendrix telling the listener to "Get experienced. Get experienced. Get experienced." It's as if Hendrix was telling the public what so many philosophers and artists have concluded elsewhere: it is only through suffering and disappointment that we really grow spiritually, because while the song's protagonist is not living today, his life may improve, and he may live tomorrow.

Sessions for "I Don't Live Today" began on February 20, 1967, at De Lane Lea Studios. After the basic backing track was captured, Hendrix worked on perfecting his guitar parts, including the descending seven-note riff introducing each line of the verse, bracing notes ringing out with alarm during the chorus, and the only feedback-laden solo on the album epitomizing the lyrics' violent despair. There are multiple guitar tracks, and Hendrix even employed the use of a hand-controlled wah-wah device. (Hendrix would not come across the foot-operated wah-wah pedal until attending a Mothers of Invention concert in June 1967.) The lead vocal was added at Olympic, where the song was also mixed.

"3rd Stone from the Sun"

"Purple Haze" was the earliest Hendrix composition said to have been influenced by Chas Chandler's collection of science fiction, but "3rd Stone from the Sun" overtly mentions the flying saucers and space people that will inhabit "Up from the Skies" and "House Burning Down" on latter albums. Hendrix was not pleased when reviewers tried classifying his music by calling it "space rock" (one journalist even called it "Science Fiction Rock"), but the few performers merged the realistic with science fiction as well as Hendrix without seeming a little ridiculous and/or adolescent.

This mostly instrumental number was the centerpiece of Side Two, and at a length of 6:50 (on the UK version; the USA version is ten seconds shorter), it was easily the longest song on *Are You Experienced*. It is another number that made serious musicians take notice of Hendrix. An embryonic version dated back to Hendrix's New York City days pre-Chandler according to Random Blues guitarist Bob Kulick. This was confirmed by the fact that, though ultimately unused, a version was recorded on December 13, 1966, at CBS Studios as one of the Experience's first songs.

Anchored again by Redding's bass, Hendrix and Mitchell spiraled off like a couple of sonic saucers, encouraging each other to go out further and further, aided by Kramer's final mix where Mitchell's cymbals were featured prominently as were the whooshing and spaceship noises courtesy of Hendrix's mouth and his playing with headphones.

For an instrumental, the track was somewhat overshadowed by the voices of Hendrix and Chandler engaging in what was labeled "Wild Chat." With Chandler unable to say his lines and Hendrix cracking up in laughter and talking about a "superior cackling hen"—perhaps this is where neo-psychedelic rocker Robyn Hitchcock's fascination with hens in his lyrics was hatched!—the takes were then edited to create a dialogue between spacecraft's pilot and Space Command. Words were slowed down, but one phrase of Hendrix's stood out: "May you never hear surf music again."

Those seven words stood out because they seemingly summed up Hendrix's musical philosophy. After the musical breakthroughs heard throughout *Are You Experienced*, how could surf music hold up? (It wasn't until the 2000 box set that Hendrix was heard saying that his own statement "sounds like a lie to me!")

Interestingly, surf bands embraced "3rd Stone from the Sun," and surf guitarist Dick Dale even recorded a version.

"Are You Experienced"

Are You Experienced is an album whose importance is not just verified by some pop magazine best-of issue but by being permanently preserved in the United States Library of Congress, the nation's oldest federal cultural institution. This is the same institution that protects a draft of the Declaration of Independence; when you consider it, *Are You Experienced* was a declaration of independence of sorts.

The title track is a march of backwards-played guitar parts propelled by a processional rhythm, the drums reminding listeners of the drum and bugle corps seen in parades. Created in a single day (April 3, 1967) at Olympic Studios, with everything seemingly backward, one almost didn't hear the guitar. Something stringy rang out, but it was so slippery as to defy identification. This was because after doing six takes to achieve the basic arrangement across four tracks, tracks were bounced down so another track featuring guitar, bass, and drums could be recorded with the intention of then playing the track backwards in the final mix.

This had been done before on the Beatles' "Tomorrow Never Knows," but Hendrix took the concept to another level. He frequently played personal tapes backward on his reel-to-reel tape machine, and this

Jimi was much happier with the artwork that Karl Ferris created for *Are You Experienced*.   *Courtesy of Robert Rodriguez*

familiarity enabled him to play his guitar forwards and yet carry a tune when played backwards. Ever the perfectionist, he also expected Mitch Mitchell to do the same, which led to some tense moments in the studio when Mitchell was unable to play drum rhythms "backward" upon request.

Hendrix's backwards guitar was strategically placed. The chorus featured his treated voice asking the listener if they are experienced in the second person, which makes it more personal and confidential. I know every time I hear his voice, I feel as if he's in the room asking me the question directly. After asking if you've ever been experienced during the second chorus (very similar to his question two albums later when he asks if you've ever been to Electric Ladyland) and saying that he has, he says "Let me prove it to you," and substantiates this claim by playing backwards and hitting all the right notes.

A 1966 poem of Hendrix's served as the basis of the third verse. This is where he talked about the trumpets and violins calling. Many critics have critiqued "Are You Experienced" as being about sex or drugs or even a paean to date rape. Most think he's addressing a woman. I've never thought that. He clearly states that he wants to watch sunrise from the bottom of the sea, a notion similar to "1983 . . . (A Merman I Should Turn to Be)." What does that have to do with sexual assault? By taking hold of the minds of his listeners at the end to chiming piano notes and militaristic drumbeats, he wasn't trying to get in anyone's pants, he was trying to give us inner knowledge.

Are You Sergeant Pepper?

The two psychedelic albums to have the greatest resonance in the banner year of 1967 for rock recordings were the Beatles' *Sgt. Pepper's Lonely Hearts Club Band* and the Experience's *Are You Experienced*. And you can make the argument that Hendrix's album has greater relevance today; whereas the Beatles' magnum opus defined a period, it was a musical cul-de-sac that even the Beatles soon drove away from.

Neil Young himself has commented of *Pepper*: "In the long run it had a negative effect, 'cause it made all of us into record producers and geniuses and we really should've just been in a band playing." Isn't this confirmed by what happened to the Rolling Stones? When their *Pepper, Their Satanic Majesties Request*, tanked, they quickly regrouped, reverted to just being "a band playing," and righted themselves by abandoning strings and orchestration for the rock and country rhythms of *Beggar's Banquet*, their first important album.

But of *Are You Experienced*, a dispirited Eric Clapton commented, ". . . that was all anyone wanted to listen to. He kicked everybody into touch, really, and was not just the flavor of the month but of the year." It was Cream that was supposed to make 1967's resounding masterpiece, but *Disraeli Gears* had been upstaged by the work of a trio Cream probably provided the impetus for.

Clapton again: "I was angry. Because he'd come to here to England and we'd gone to America and made *Disraeli Gears* and came back to deliver it. And nobody wanted to know. You'd go to a club and they'd say 'Have you heard Jimi's album?'—Yeah, it's fine, great. I mean what the fuck's going on here?"

But Hendrix knew what was going on. Even if he couldn't dislodge *Pepper* from the #1 spot on the UK charts, he knew he had made the more forward-looking album. He showed this at an Experience performance at Brian Epstein's Saville Theatre on June 4, 1967. It was the Beatles' weekend. *Pepper* had just been released, reviews were breathtaking, and it was being played everywhere. Members of the Beatles sat satisfied in the theater waiting to see the Experience.

Noel Redding wrote in his autobiography that Hendrix walked into the Saville Theatre dressing room clutching his copy of *Sgt. Pepper's Lonely Hearts Club Band* and played the title track a couple of times while excitedly telling his bemused bandmates that he wanted to open the evening's show with it. Soon they'd worked up an arrangement with Hendrix's feedbacking guitar notes making everyone forget the horny Beatles version only four days old.

According to British critic Hugh Nolan: "[Hendrix] started the night with a driving version of 'Sergeant Pepper's,'" an experience that Paul McCartney said was "the single biggest tribute for me." Once again Hendrix picked the right song for the right moment. But it wasn't homage. It was like when Hendrix upstaged Clapton at Polytechnic Central or Pete Townshend later at Monterey. Hendrix's competitiveness was in full display, and he wanted to show he could play "Sgt. Pepper's Lonely Hearts Club Band" better than the Beatles.

Again according to Hugh Nolan, the set concluded with a smashing, ear-splitting "'Are You Experienced.' Jimi was handed a guitar from the wings—a guitar he'd painted in glorious swirling colors and written a poem on the back dedicated to Britain and its audience—and, bathed in flickering strobe light, crashed the guitar about the stage and hurled what was left to eager souvenir hunters."

It was as if Hendrix was daring the Beatles—who weren't even playing live anymore—to try and top that!

8

Guaranteed to Raise a Smile

Jimi Hendrix Meets the Beatles

There are eighteen known recorded versions of Jimi Hendrix playing the Beatles' "Sgt. Pepper's Lonely Hearts Club Band," none of which is the infamous Saville Theatre performance in front of the Beatles themselves. All except two feature the Experience, although the most often heard version—the opening number of Hendrix's ill-fated performance at the Isle of Wight Festival—features the *Cry of Love* lineup of Mitchell and Cox. When it was played, it was always the opening number.

Nor is "Sgt. Pepper's Lonely Hearts Club Band" the only song in the Beatles catalog of which known Hendrix versions exist. The most commonly known is the version of "Day Tripper" on *BBC Sessions*, a collection of BBC radio (mostly) and television appearances that were originally recorded between February 18, 1967, and December 15, 1967, as well as the three songs played on *The Lulu Show* on January 4, 1969. All feature the Jimi Hendrix Experience, which makes it indispensable in any collection.

BBC performances of the Experience often featured the unexpected and otherwise unreleased. Blues numbers such as Muddy Water's "Catfish Blues" or Howlin' Wolf's "Killing Floor" or Hendrix's own "Hear My Train A Comin'" were aired. Unless they saw him perform live, the general public did not have access to this favored side of Hendrix.

This extended to pop hits such as Elvis Presley's "Hound Dog" (complete with a barking chorus), and "Day Tripper." "Day Tripper" was recorded for *Top Gear* by Bernie Andrews on December 15, 1967, and broadcast on Christmas Eve of that year. For decades this spirited version of "Day Tripper" was bootlegged and marketed as featuring John Lennon on background vocals, which were, in fact, courtesy of Noel Redding. According to Redding it was just another example of the band ad-libbing in the studio.

If this is so, it's a case of Hendrix reaching back to his New York City days with Curtis Knight and the Squires, because a live version recorded in Hackensack, New Jersey, dating back to December 26, 1965, exists. Multiple

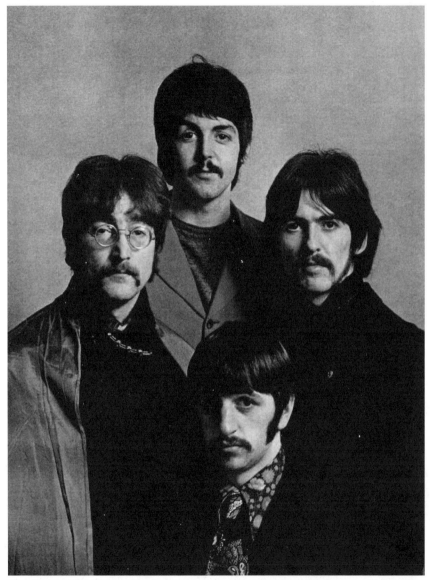

The *Sergeant Pepper*–era Beatles around the time that Paul McCartney was pulling strings to help Jimi Hendrix.   *Courtesy of Robert Rodriguez*

versions from the regrettable 1967 session with Knight and Ed Chalpin also exist (see Chapter 12), and these feature Hendrix on an 8-string Hagstrom bass guitar.

Another Beatles cover with Hendrix on guitar is available on a bootleg recording known as *Woke Up This Morning and Found Myself Dead*, perhaps because it featured two rock musicians who did just that: Jim Morrison and Jimi Hendrix. It is part of a jam session featuring a clearly intoxicated Morrison that was recorded in March 1968 at the Scene Club, one of Hendrix's favorite after-midnight haunts in New York City.

Being a virtuoso jammer, Hendrix was fond of quoting or referencing other songs during his solos. Most familiar is probably his allusion to Frank Sinatra's "Strangers in the Night" during the Monterey performance of the Troggs' "Wild Thing." He was also known to quote the "Tomorrow Never Knows" theme in May and June 1969 performances.

And last, but not least, there is Hendrix's ironic usage of the Beatles' "I Feel Fine" during "Hey Joe" that can be heard during the Experience's January 4, 1969, appearance on *The Lulu Show* found on the *BBC Sessions*.

Paul McCartney

The Beatles, however, never returned the favor. They never played any of Jimi Hendrix's songs. Paul McCartney did at the 2010 Isle of Wight festival—thirty years after Hendrix's own ill-fated appearance at the same festival—play "Foxy Lady." It is apparently a favorite of Hendrix's contemporaries to play as Mick Jagger also performed "Foxy Lady" during his solo tour in 1988.

Of the Beatles, it is Paul McCartney who comes across as having had the friendliest relationship with Hendrix. In biographies you'll find McCartney buying Hendrix a pint or handing him a joint after a fantastic Experience performance or dropping acid together. (McCartney also apparently shared an afternoon in bed with Hendrix's "bird" Kathy Etchingham.)

Paulie was the Beatle who went out of his way to offer a helping hand to a musician whose talent should be made known to the world. In the February 23, 1967, issue of *Melody Maker* he heaped praise upon the Experience's second single "Purple Haze": "You can't stop it. I really don't know if it's as commercial as 'Hey Joe' or 'Stone Free.' I bet it is though. Probably will be. Fingers Hendrix. An absolute ace on the guitar. This is yet another incredible record from Twinkle Teeth Hendrix!" McCartney's last statement is obviously a reference to seeing Hendrix play his guitar with his teeth at London clubs.

Shortly thereafter, McCartney offered the still relatively unknown Experience a spot on the McCartney concept that was to become the Beatles' worst trip: the *Magical Mystery Tour* television show that the Beatles made and was aired BBC-TV to resoundingly negative reviews.

It was also Paul McCartney who insisted to the promoters of the Monterey International Pop Festival, of which McCartney (and Mick Jagger) had agreed to serve on the Board of Governors when the Beatles (and Rolling Stones) declined to appear, that the Experience had to be invited. To McCartney the weekend festival would not live up to the "International" part of its name without Jimi Hendrix's participation.

Later, when Hendrix was firmly established and regularly winning awards such as the Melody Maker Top World Musician on September 26, 1967, the left-handed guitarist returned the favor by appearing at the launch party for McCartney protégé Mary Hopkins's album *Postcard* and lending his talents to *McGough and McGear,* an album McCartney produced in 1968.

McGough and McGear was no ordinary project in that the McGear in the album title was Mike McGear, Paul McCartney's brother, who was also a musician. McGear had formed a band called Scaffold with McGough and John Gorman, and *McGough and McGear* was a side project that led to Hendrix returning to De Lane Lea Studios, where he had laid down so many tracks for *Are You Experienced.*

The date was January 20, 1968, and "Hendrix turned up at the recording studios, on his own, carrying a small guitar case," according to Mike McCartney's *The Macs: Mike McCartney's Family Album.* He was not the only famous musician that McCartney had lured into the studio. Also participating in the sessions were the Experience's rhythm section, Spencer Davis, Traffic's Dave Mason, John Mayall, and the Hollies' Graham Nash. When the now hard-to-find *McGough and McGear* was finally released by Parlophone Records, an uncredited Hendrix graced two tracks: "So Much" and "Ex-Art Student." (An unused track called "Oh to Be a Child" that featured Hendrix and other London rockers on toy instruments was not heard until 1992, when it was released on a Scaffold greatest hits collection.)

John Lennon

Given John Lennon's interest in backwards taping and backmasking (he originally wanted "Rain" in its entirety to be played backwards, but producer George Martin and Paul McCartney persuaded him to save the unique sound for the song's final thirty seconds), it's surprising there aren't more stories of the two backwards tape masters being together, but then Lennon was something of a loner musically.

Lennon, like McCartney, first appeared in Hendrix's history as a member of the audience. He was in attendance at the Experience's Bag O' Nails performance in January 1967. A blistering forty-minute set left Lennon saying that the band's version of "Wild Thing" was "amazingly cool," according to Sharon Lawrence. Later in the dressing room bassist

Noel Redding was flabbergasted to watch Lennon enter and tell him the show had been "Fuckin' grand."

The other half of the Lennon/McCartney songwriting team also tried his hand at helping Hendrix out, but Lennon could not convince his American label to offer the Jimi Hendrix Experience a contract stateside.

Hendrix's girlfriend Kathy Etchingham is at the center of the better of Lennon stories, although not all involve Hendrix. But if you accept Etchingham is Hendrix as Lennon is Hendrix as Lennon is Etchingham (and they are all together!), then Etchingham's stories form part of Lennon's interaction with Hendrix.

Etchingham met Jimi Hendrix his first night in London at the Scotch of St. James in Mayfair. It is likely that this was where Etchingham also first met John Lennon, as the Beatles had a private booth reserved for them at London's "in place" for London's "in musicians." He certainly knew Etchingham by the time Lennon took the phone Hendrix was waving around in a heated argument with her out of the guitarist's hand. Like many men, the philandering Hendrix didn't believe this "right" extended to girlfriends, and he was extremely possessive and jealous whenever she showed an interest in another member of the opposite sex, and on the night in question, he thought she had been flirting with someone over the phone.

Etchingham's 1998 autobiography *Through Gypsy Eyes* tells several Lennon-related stories: of getting high with Lennon in his Rolls-Royce and being mortified when Lennon told his chauffeur to stop so he could take a piss in one of London's red telephone kiosks or how the Beatles' rhythm guitarist used to drop by the flat Etchingham shared with Hendrix when Hendrix was out of town so he could trip and crash. Etchingham admits that Paul was her favorite Beatle, not John.

The other Lennon-Hendrix connection is when Hendrix's drummer Mitch Mitchell formed part of the all-star band playing with Lennon on the Rolling Stones' *Rock and Roll Circus* television program that was to be as much of an albatross to the Stones as *Magical Mystery Tour* had been for the Beatles, except the Stones wisely never aired it and saved it for a DVD-only release twenty-eight years later, by which time it was the stuff of legend and exempt from criticism.

The Dirty Mac—Lennon's assemblage for the occasion—consisted of Lennon on vocals and rhythm guitar, Eric Clapton on lead guitar, Keith Richards on bass guitar, and Mitchell behind the kit. Recorded on December 11, 1968, Lennon led them in their rendition of the Beatles' "Yer Blues" from *The Beatles* (aka *The White Album.*)

Mitchell says in his autobiography *Inside the Experience* that it was Mick Jagger who invited him to form part of the Dirty Mac: "Though I was a long-time admirer, this was the first time I'd played with Lennon, who really delivered the goods. Great voice, great rhythm guitar—I hope he enjoyed it as much as I did."

After "Yer Blues," Yoko Ono led the Dirty Mac through a shriekfest known as "Whole Lotta Yoko," a title that could only have been thought up many years later.

George Harrison

George Harrison was in the Saville Theatre audience with his wife Patti Boyd when the Jimi Hendrix Experience audaciously opened with the title track from *Sgt. Pepper's Lonely Hearts Club Band.*

Ringo Starr

Ringo Starr owned several pieces of property in London, including 34 Montagu Square, which became Jimi Hendrix's second residence/address in London. Not far from Hyde Park, Montagu Square is your typical square in London, where a row of connected buildings line the city block but are divided into private houses and not apartments.

Having little money to afford living at Hyde Park Towers, Chas Chandler jumped at the offer to rent Starr's private house. Chandler and his fiancée got the carpeted bedroom, and Hendrix and Etchingham got the basement with an old fireplace. It was still better than what either was accustomed to. Ringo's neighbors were not accustomed to having a rock musician and producer living in their midst, and Hendrix, Chandler, and girlfriends were forced to vacate within several months, a move eased by a clause in the lease that said blacks were not allowed.

Linda Eastman

Before she was Linda McCartney, Linda Eastman was an entertainment lawyer's daughter who discovered a passion for photography at the University of Arizona. Her natural style allowed her to disarm the famous rock musicians she photographed. Following a successful photo shoot of the Rolling Stones aboard a yacht, she was soon a regular contributor to *Rolling Stone*, and, prior to marrying Paul McCartney, photographed many '60s musicians at the height of their fame, including the Doors, Simon and Garfunkel, and the Jimi Hendrix Experience, who she first photographed at their outdoor concert at Central Park's Wollman Skating Rink in July 1967.

Her photo of the Experience with children on the Alice In Wonderland statue in that same park was the image chosen by Hendrix for the *Electric Ladyland* cover in America. According to Linda in Johnny Black's oral history: "[Hendrix] said, 'I really want you to take this album cover on the Alice In Wonderland sculpture in Central Park. In fact, I want it to be a little black boy and two little white boys.' And I thought, Oh, lovely, That'd be Jimi, a little black boy . . . ."

The Warner Brothers art department, however, ignored Hendrix's handwritten instructions when designing the album sleeve. Hendrix had insisted that Eastman's photo be used for the cover. Warner Brothers did at least use Linda's photos along the inner border of the gatefold to frame Hendrix's "Letter to the Room Full of Mirrors," including the Alice photo, maybe because his instructions did say: "Please use all the pictures."

9

If My Daddy Could See Me Now

Conquering America

Returning to America on June 13, 1967, as the leader of England's fastest-rising rock group, Jimi Hendrix made no effort to contact his father, with whom he had an estranged and strange relationship. According to Kathy Etchingham's autobiography *Through Gypsy Eyes*, when he had previously contacted his father, Al Hendrix, to let him know about his success, his father did not believe him. Then, when Etchingham's English accent did convince Al that his son was across the Atlantic, he told her to tell his son "to write me. I ain't paying for no collect calls!" The son was not too prodigal and put off seeing his daddy until February 12, 1968.

Monterey International Pop Festival

When Papa John Phillips called Chas Chandler offering the Experience a slot on the Monterey International Pop Festival bill, it was Rolling Stone Brian Jones who answered the telephone. As Chandler explained on the *South Bank Show: Jimi Hendrix*, which aired on ITV on October 1, 1989: "Because Brian answered the phone we said, 'Yeah, Brian will do the announcing . . . ,' and Brian went out with us and announced Jimi on-stage." ("A bit over-dressed," Mick Jagger bitchily told rock author Stanley Booth afterwards.)

The TWA flight over the Atlantic for the Monterey appearance was a memorable experience for Experience bassist Noel Redding. It was his first transatlantic flight, and in his autobiography he recalled "flying first class to New York, seated next to Brian Jones, who had taken me under his wing, and cruising on a tab of purple Owsley." Three nights later, Jones was still seemingly tripping when he stood in front of the festival crowd and said, "I'd like to introduce a very good friend, a fellow countryman of yours . . . he's the most exciting performer I've ever heard—the Jimi Hendrix Experience," before yielding the stage to Hendrix's career-making performance.

Jimi on the grounds of the Monterey International Pop Festival.   *Author's collection*

You have to feel somewhat bad for Cyrus Faryer's the Group with No Name that appeared fourth on the ten-act bill that illustrious Sunday that concluded the festival. Every other act is still known four decades later even if it's only a hit single like Scott McKenzie's "San Francisco." Preceding the Jimi Hendrix Experience onstage that day had been Ravi Shankar, Janis Joplin's career-making performance with Big Brother and Holding Company, the Buffalo Springfield (with both Stephen Stills and Neil Young), the Who, and the Grateful Dead.

The Dead were strategically scheduled and acted as a buffer between the Who and Experience sets since the British acts seemed so superficially similar. After all, both bands featured guitarists known for the destruction of their instruments. Having shared the Saville Theatre stage previously in January, neither band wanted to follow the other.

One of the best interview clips in Joe Boyd's documentary *Jimi Hendrix* is that of Pete Townshend recollecting Hendrix's reaction to the coin toss's outcome:

> Before the show at Monterey we were starting to talk about the running of it. But more for Brian Jones, who was introducing us, I think, and Eric Burdon, who was introducing him or vice versa. I can't remember. And they wanted to know what was gonna come first and we couldn't really decide. So I said to Jimi, "Fuck it, we're not gonna follow you on." So he said, "I'm not gonna follow you on." So I said, "Listen, we are not gonna follow you on and that is it. As far as I'm concerned, you know, we're ready to go on now, our gig's gonna be there, that's the end of it."
>
> And, there was a certain look up in his eye. He got on a chair and he played some amazing guitar just standing on a chair in the dressing room. Janis Joplin was there . . . Brian Jones . . . Eric and me, and a few other people just standing around. And then he got down off the chair and just said . . . turned to me and said: "If I'm gonna follow you, I'm gonna pull out all the stops."

The Experience's performance at Monterey was captured on film by D. A. Pennebaker and released in 1968. That movie and the Experience's performance are discussed in Chapter 6, but this is the right spot for comparing the Who and Experience performances that evening. Both bands kicked ass. Both guitarists destroyed their guitars. Hendrix's destruction is more renowned and the stuff of legend, but there's more to it than Jimi setting his guitar aflame and Townshend not. The key is actually in a line from Bush's most famous song, "Everything Zen": "There's no sex in your violence."

Jimi Hendrix did not smash his guitar every night and only did so when a surly mood called for it. Pete Townshend, however, did smash his guitar at every concert, much to money man (and singer) Roger Daltry's chagrin. (The cost of the guitars was even budgeted.) He justified this destruction of instruments by crediting stateless artist Gustav Metzger and his concept of auto-destruction.

In 1959 in protest of nuclear weaponry, Metzger, a German Jew who had been displaced by World War II, created acid-based images that he sprayed onto nylon that would self-destruct. It was an act of creativity that auto-destructed. And that's how Townshend saw the smashing of his guitar during "My Generation," the Who's set closer: the music he was creatively making auto-destructed.

Hendrix, however, never relied on a "concept" for justifying the smashing of his guitar. It was a spontaneous act and rarely calculated, although the destruction at Monterey certainly was. The hard-to-put-a-finger-on-it element that sets Hendrix's destruction apart from Townshend's was the "sex in his violence." The Who have always appealed more to males. Townshend's destruction is like that of a young man's temper tantrum. Hendrix's violence is sexier. When he knelt over his guitar at Monterey and sprayed lighter fluid on his Fender Stratocaster especially painted and made up for the occasion, he was like a lover in the final throes of passion.

Days after Monterey, the Jimi Hendrix Experience played a free concert in Golden Gate Park.

Author's collection

Nico—model, Velvet Underground vocalist on that group's eponymous debut album, icon—gave Hendrix a kiss as he left the feedbacking stage, and she spoke of Hendrix's innate sexuality in his performances: "He was the most sexual man I ever saw on stage. Even Mick Jagger said so. It was not all the vulgar things he did with his guitar, though I enjoyed when he burned his guitar at the festival. It was his presence. He was like a cat. He moved elegantly for a man. He was suave."

Hey Hey, It's the Monkees!

The Jimi Hendrix Experience's booking as the Monkees' opening act was a direct result of the Monterey International Pop Festival, but as friends of more respectable rock musicians the Monkees were aware of the Experience well before. The green ski-capped guitarist Mike Nesmith tells of hanging out in London in late 1966 eating with, amongst others, John Lennon

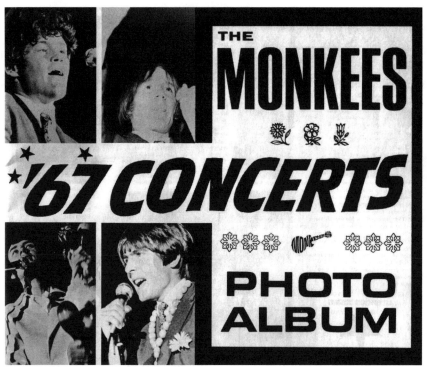

The Monkees hired the Jimi Hendrix Experience to open their 1967 concerts so they could stand in the wings and watch their favorite musician.

Courtesy of Robert Rodriguez

and Eric Clapton when Lennon asked the restaurant to turn off whatever music they were playing so he could play "Hey Joe." According to Nesmith, in a March 1988 *Guitar World* article: "Everybody was reverential . . . like everybody said 'Gee. If we could play like that, we would!'"

Unfairly slighted by history, I think Peter Tork was right when he told *Rolling Stone* that "with all due modesty, since I had little to do with it, the Monkees' songbook is one of the better songbooks in pop history. Certainly in the top five in terms of breadth and depth." (To Tork's songwriting credit, he did write "For Pete's Sake," the closing theme to the Monkees' second season of shows.) The Monkees not only recorded some of pop music's finest songs (e.g., "(I'm Not Your) Stepping Stone," "Pleasant Valley Sunday," and "Daydream Believer"), but during the Summer of Love they were at the height of their fame and had the record sales to prove it. The Monkees had four #1 records within one year and were moving more units than the Beatles or the Rolling Stones

It is commonly thought that the Experience's invitation to open for the Monkees was Peter Tork's idea because Tork—who got his gig as the

Monkees' bassist when his friend Stephen Stills declined but recommended him; the producers chose Tork based on his resemblance to Stills— befriended Hendrix at Monterey, but it was drummer Micky Dolenz's brainchild. Both were at Monterey, and Tork says it was "Mickey [who] picked up on it."

According to Dolenz: "It just so happened that we were due to begin our summer tour in a couple of weeks, and we still needed another opening act. When we got back to L.A., I mentioned Hendrix and his impressive theatrics to [our producers]. The Monkees was very theatrical in my eyes and so was the Jimi Hendrix Experience. It would make the perfect union."

Hendrix's people turned out to be manager Michael Jeffery, who, up until Monterey, had taken a backseat in the management of the Jimi Hendrix Experience to Chas Chandler, handling the minutiae of music management such as securing Hendrix's passport or buying out contracts Hendrix had signed before Chandler "discovered" Hendrix or negotiating the American distribution rights with Reprise Records.

The Jimi Hendrix Experience had flown into California for the Monterey appearance without any other shows lined up. That soon changed. Bill Graham offered the Experience a six-night stand at the Fillmore West for $500 per night opening for local heroes Jefferson Airplane. After a single night, the Jefferson Airplane was going on before the Experience. Like the Who, there was no way they were gonna follow the Experience's act.

So imagine Chandler's shock when Jeffery called Chandler and informed him he had completed negotiations with *American Bandstand* host Dick Clark and that the Jimi Hendrix Experience were booked to play July 8th in Jacksonville, Florida, supporting the biggest act in America. Chandler said he "dropped the fucking phone" when he heard just what act the Experience was supporting.

It was a disaster from the get-go. A black man leading a white band in the still racially charged south opening for a teenybopper band in front of adolescent girls could only lead to trouble and poor press.

(I must say, however, that while Hendrix's innuendo-laden performances did not go over well with the teenyboppers in the audience waiting for the Monkees, audience clips such as those included in Bill Smeaton's documentary *Jimi Hendrix: Voodoo Child* clearly show that "the little girls' Aunts understood," if I may paraphrase Jim Morrison singing Willie Dixon's "Backdoor Man." The documentary is available as part of the box set version of 2010's *West Coast Seattle Boy*.)

The Experience's slot on the bill was just before the Monkees, and Peter Tork said Hendrix was booed off the stage that first night in Jacksonville. When journalists asked why the Monkees had booked the Experience on the tour, Tork said he was trying to provide the band with work: "Nobody thought, 'This is screaming, scaring-the-balls-off-your-daddy music compared with the Monkees,' you know? It didn't cross anybody's mind that it wasn't gonna fly."

But Tommy Boyce, who cowrote some of the Monkees' greatest hits such as "Last Train to Clarksville" said it was self-indulgence on the part of the Monkees, who just wanted to stand in the wings and watch the Jimi Hendrix Experience: "It was a personal trip. They wanted to watch Jimi Hendrix every night, they didn't care if he fit in." This is confirmed by Nesmith, who said he heard "some of the best music I've heard in my life."

Nesmith also offered the most vivid image of Hendrix from what turned out after eight dates to be a short-lived tour for the Jimi Hendrix Experience. Both bands were staying at some southern hotel in North Carolina, when Nesmith sighted the Experience in a hallway: "Hendrix appeared in silhouette, with this light in back of him, and of course his hair was out to here . . . and he took a step forward, and it was like it [was] choreographed. Noel and Mitch both came up on either side of him, and they made the perfect trio. It looked like the cover of *Axis*."

The reception of the Experience's twenty- to twenty-five minute sets picked up somewhat after their slot on the bill was moved up, and they opened the show and appeared before the Sundowners and Lynn Randall, an Australian singer, instead of performing right before the Monkees. Still, it was not a good situation, and Chandler—overruling Jeffery—sought a way to get the Experience off of the remaining tour dates and concocted a legendary rumor in order to do so.

The Daughters of the American Revolution is an organization comprised entirely of women whose ancestors contributed to that war's successful resolution, including combatants and signers of the Declaration of Independence. There are chapters in every state (and a few foreign countries as well, despite their motto being "God, Home, and Country.") If you believed a press release that was issued in July 1967, these Daughters were upset by the erotic nature of Hendrix's act undermining America's morals.

Not true. The Daughters' protest was invented by Chas Chandler partially to shield Hendrix and partially to generate publicity stateside. The actual press release was written up by Lillian Roxon, a music critic, whose *Rock Encyclopedia* published in 1968 was one of the first books to take rock seriously as an art form.

Via telephone Hendrix inadvertently admitted the press release was a hoax by explaining the Monkees mess to the *New Musical Express*. In an interview that was published on July 29, 1967, he said: "Some parents who brought their kids complained that our act was too vulgar. We decided it was just the wrong audience. I think they're replacing me with Mickey Mouse."

Less than a year later on March 19, 1968, it was the Monkees who were scheduled as the opening act for the Jimi Hendrix Experience in Ottawa, Canada. They canceled.

The Fourth (and Best) Single

The Jimi Hendrix Experience was one of the rock bands that killed the 45 single and established the album as the preferred forum for the presentation of a band's work. Thanks to the Experience, by 1969 bands such as Black Sabbath and Led Zeppelin could ignore the 45 format entirely and still achieve rock stardom and mega-success. It wasn't until the punk era that the 45 regained importance and that chiefly because of the DIY punk ethic as kids went around the record companies and took back their art form.

This explains why the Jimi Hendrix Experience only released four singles proper in less than one year: between December 16, 1966, and August 19, 1967 (all dates are that of UK release). By proper I mean songs that were recorded purposely to be released as singles and not for inclusion on albums. Any singles released thereafter were just music label decisions (with the exception of the hastily withdrawn "Izabella" b/w "Stepping Stone" in April 1970, and that wasn't an Experience effort anyway).

Recording of the fourth single's A-side, "Burning of the Midnight Lamp," actually began on May 9, 1967, when Hendrix, inspired by his discovery of a harpsichord in Olympic Studios' cavernous Studio A, led the Experience through four takes.

Work resumed at Houston Studios in Los Angeles on June 30th, but the studio did not live up to expectations, so the female vocal overdubs they had intended to do went undone and the Experience used the booked time to fine tune "Burning of the Midnight Lamp." Redding later said that he added the song's distinctive 12-string wah-wahed guitar to the introduction, although that has been disputed.

It was at this session that "The Stars That Play with Laughing Sam's Dice" was attempted for the first time. As Mitch Mitchell said in his autobiography: "(It) was a deliberate joke, you know? STP and LSD."

Tom Wilson was a black producer who gained his greatest fame producing some of the best white recording artists of the 1960s, including Bob Dylan, Simon and Garfunkel, the Velvet Underground, and the Mothers of Invention. Looking for a studio to record in while in America, Wilson recommended Mayfair Recording Studios in New York City to Chas Chandler, and that's where the recording of "Burning of the Midnight Lamp" resumed on July 6, 1967, at 4 p.m. According to Chandler, "Jimi found the solution to the song in America, and we decided to just do it there."

Engineered by Gary Kellgren, over the course of the next six hours and two reels of tape, it took the Experience thirty takes before they had perfected the song to Hendrix's satisfaction. (The background vocal talents of the Sweet Inspirations, gospel singers who had backed Aretha Franklin, were also added at this session.) Little did the musicians involved know it was a hint of things to come when recording with Hendrix, who was becoming increasingly perfectionist in trying a catch on tape what he heard in his head. Redding, like Chandler, did not approve of all the time wasted tweaking "Burning of the Midnight Lamp" and wrote in his autobiography that it "took forty-two hours to record . . . while 'The Wind Cries Mary' had taken six minutes." Redding's point being that a hit record ("Mary") was recorded in much less time than a flop ("Lamp").

Further work on the single was interrupted by the Monkees tour, which the Experience hopped off of after three shows at the Forest Hills Tennis Stadium in Queens, New York City. The band moved from the Waldorf-Astoria Hotel to the Gorham Hotel and proceeded to get their groove back by returning to Mayfair Recording Studios on July 19th to record twenty-one takes of "The Stars That Play with Laughing Sam's Dice." Overdubs were added the following night after the Experience played the Salvation Club. The song was mixed as well.

"Burning of the Midnight Lamp" was a personal favorite of Hendrix's possibly because it marks a Dylanesque turn in his lyrics. While it's true that there are autobiographical elements in "Highway Chile" and "The Wind Cries Mary," "Burning of the Midnight Lamp" was the first song where Hendrix achieved "tangible obscurity," to employ a description used by Hendrix's Greenwich Village friend and sometime harp accompanist Paul Caruso in a letter published in the June 22, 1968, issue of *Rolling Stone*.

Hendrix himself said he wrote the words during the flight from Los Angeles back to New York City and admitted the song's personal nature but quickly added: "I think everyone can understand the feeling when you're traveling alone." The central theme of the song is loneliness; even the use of a wah-wah pedal reveals the composer's intention. According to Hendrix: "The wah-wah pedal . . . feels like that, not depression, but that loneliness and that frustration and yearning for something. Like something is reaching out."

The Jimi Hendrix Experience's fourth single peaked at #18 and departed the British charts after nine weeks. Bruce Johnston of the Beach Boys reviewed it negatively in *Melody Maker*: "The best passages . . . are when the

Despite its lack of chart success, "Burning of the Midnight Lamp" was a personal favorite of Jimi's.   *Courtesy of Robert Rodriguez*

drums are rock steady and Jimi and his guitar are cooking. But there is a great deal of record time devoted to jew's harp noises and other extraneous effects."

Hendrix did not let the lack of chart success diminish his enthusiasm for "Burning of the Midnight Lamp," attributing its poor reception to the "recording technique," which may explain why Mayfair Studios was not used again by Hendrix although engineer Gary Kellgren was.

"You couldn't hear the words so good," explained Hendrix. "That's probably what [the problem] was." He thought the mono mix undermined the song and called it "the best one we ever made." He thought so highly of "Burning of the Midnight Lamp" that he included it on *Electric Ladyland*, where it originally closed Side Two: further testament of Hendrix's faith in his composition.

Janis Joplin

When the Jimi Hendrix Experience arrived in June 1967 to play Monterey, they had one date lined up: the festival itself. Less than nine months later, the first tour of America in 1968 crisscrossed sixty cities in sixty-six days. The 1968 tour was a spectacle, or, to borrow a line from "Burning of the Midnight Lamp": "a circus in a wishing well." And as always happens when the circus comes to town, the press lapped it up. Whereas in 1967 rock critic Robert Christgau had dismissed Hendrix's Monterey performance by calling him an Uncle Tom, in 1968, the *New York Times* asked if Hendrix was the black Elvis: high praise for a boy who once stood atop a hill so he could see Elvis Presley in concert.

The 1968 tour began at the Fillmore West in San Francisco on February 1st. The next night the Experience topped the Fillmore West bill that also included John Mayall and the Bluesbreakers, left-handed blues guitarist Albert King, and the Soft Machine. Then, having outgrown Bill Graham's original San Francisco venue, they moved to Winterland, the larger venue that Graham operated, for three shows. The same bands were on the bill but Janis Joplin, with whom Hendrix was romantically linked, and her inferior backing band Big Brother and Holding Company were added the final night.

There's a newfound photo of Hendrix greeting Janis and an unidentified friend. He is holding her hand backstage at this concert. This is only the second photo I've come across of the two of them together. The photo that was more readily available in the '70s and '80s is nowhere to be found on the Internet. It is as I recollect a photo of Jimi Hendrix backstage (at what I assumed was Monterey) with a film camera in hand. He is standing and Joplin sitting. I remember her holding a bottle of Southern Comfort, but that is probably a wishful memory. Only now I seem to remember Hendrix wearing this same hat, and any image of Hendrix wearing the pimp hat dates the image as being from late '67 and '68.

For decades I had the misconception that these two members of the 27 Club who gained international fame at Monterey disliked one another. This could not be further from the truth. Both Hendrix and Joplin fully embraced the concept of the times—free love—and shared it with one another. That's right. Instead of hating one another, band stories abound of Jimi and Janis comingling in a bathroom backstage at the Fillmore West and doing much more than holding hands.

Since their untimely deaths within nine months of one another, the images of Hendrix and Joplin and Jim Morrison have often been used together by unimaginative illustrators to promote romanticized views of rock 'n' roll, but the artist rendering I want to see—and might even buy—would be that of an incident that occurred one night in a New York City club where the Chambers Brothers were headlining. Hendrix was jamming with the band when an obviously intoxicated Jim Morrison crawled over to Hendrix and propositioned him. Joplin was apparently in the club and, disgusted with Morrison's behavior, smashed a whiskey bottle to smithereens over the Doors singer's head. Now that's the artwork I want to see: Joplin smashing a bottle of Southern Comfort over the head of the crawling King Snake and the Voodoo Chile flashing his wide grin at the Kozmic Mama!

Unfortunately, given all their encounters at concert festivals and jam sessions, there never seems to have been a time when the voodoo blues guitarist and Texan blues belter shared a stage, not even at the Newport Pop Festival where Hendrix jammed with the Janis Joplin Revue, her backup band.

The last time these two musical giants crossed paths was at Sicks Stadium in Seattle, Washington, on July 26, 1970. Janis Joplin was the opening act the last time Hendrix played the hometown he said he'd come back and buy.

Come Back and Buy This Town

Robert Wyatt's Soft Machine was on the bill for approximately two-thirds of the first 1968 tour and typically warmed up the audience for the Experience, of whose sound Wyatt said in *UniVibes* magazine:

> was like a Science Fiction film where you were in an enormous place and you open a door and suddenly you are in a vortex . . . I didn't in fact identify immediately particular tunes or instruments . . . this was . . . a total group actually.
>
> (Mitch and Noel) both had their role. I always compare it with the John Coltrane Quartet—it is very important that the bass player and the pianist stepped into these very simple anchor points . . . Noel and Mitch, if anything, suffered in reputation 'cause they were so good at being that one sound, and allowing (Hendrix) to be the spectacle, the front of it . . .

Before the spectacle swung away from the West Coast during that 1968 tour, the Experience had one fateful date left at the Seattle Center Arena in Hendrix's hometown. He had not seen his father in seven years, nor his stepmother or siblings by birth or remarriage. He had only returned once since his enlistment, when his waiting at the train station sounds an awful lot like the situation he had been singing of in "Hear My Train A Comin'" since as far back as a BBC radio recording in mid-December 1967.

Seattle was added hastily to the tour, but with the "hometown boy does good" angle, the show sold out within a week. Hendrix's nervousness was palpable; Mitchell in his autobiography says, "he was probably a little apprehensive about it." While his rhythm section went off to their rooms at the Olympic Hotel, Hendrix went to his father's house to have bourbon and see and greet family and friends.

The set that night featured all his British hits, except "Burning of the Midnight Lamp," and later at an after-show party at the Olympic Hotel, Hendrix insisted his family order steak meals via room service. The following morning he attended an assembly in his honor at Garfield High School, the same school he had dropped out of.

It was an inauspicious event in front of a black student body unfamiliar with Hendrix, who, to them, looked like a hippie. Hendrix had not slept all night and unwisely appeared without his guitar. Nervously he said a few words, mentioned that "Purple Haze" was written with the Garfield High School colors of purple and white in mind, and stopped speaking. Seattle promoter Pat O'Day had accompanied him and, trying to alleviate the situation, asked if anyone had any questions. Hendrix answered the two questions put to him with obscure responses. He would return to Seattle but wisely never appear in front of the school assembly again.

10

Don't Let Your Imagination Take You by Surprise

Science Fiction and the Fantastic in Jimi Hendrix's Lyrics

The Experience's cauldron of sound defied easy classification, so the era's reviewers fell back on Hendrix's lyrics to make sense of it. And since the lyrics were increasingly referencing spaceships, they took to calling the music "space rock" and "science fiction rock."

The evolution of Hendrix's lyrics from standard rhythm and blues imagery began with Hendrix sharing living space with Chas Chandler's collection of science fiction. Hendrix's devouring of these books and magazines during his first few months in England when money was tight and there wasn't much to do besides play Risk and read led to the presence of spaceships and dragonflies you could fly in his songs. Science fiction and fantastic images began crowding out the humdrum world of rhythm and blues, and soon the highway chile of fact was jettisoned for the voodoo chile of lore.

"Purple Haze"

Although generally accepted by the public as a paean to LSD, which it is not, "Purple Haze" was actually a love song of sorts with a ballsy riff; you could also characterize it as the first "cock rock" song, the type that Led Zeppelin would be more noted for.

"Purple Haze" was also lyrically Jimi Hendrix's first foray into science fiction imagery, although by the time the original lyrics were pared down to fit a three-minute single release, all the science fiction had been obliterated as effectively as if flying saucers had shot it up with space rays. The lyrics were written on December 26, 1966, in the Upper Cut Club's dressing room in Forest Gate, London, before one of the Experience's earliest appearances. The first draft began with "Purple Haze—Jesus saves." (You have to wonder if Courtney Love was aware of this when penning the lyrics to one of Hole's best songs: "Old Age.")

Hendrix claimed that the song originally "had a thousand words," and to *International Times* interviewer Jane Mendelssohn he said the lyrics to "Purple Haze" and "The Wind Cries Mary" "were about ten pages long, but then were restricted to a certain time limit . . . so once I'd broken the songs down, I didn't know whether they were going to be understood or not. Maybe some of the meanings got lost, by breaking them down, which I never do any more."

Keith Altham in an *NME* article said it "was written about a dream Jimi had that he was able to walk about under the sea," which links the lyrics to "Are You Experienced" and the epic "1983 . . . (A Merman I Should Turn to Be)."

The dream was influenced by Philip José Farmer's *Night of Light: Day of Dreams*, which was in Chandler's science fiction collection. According to Roby and Schreiber's *Becoming Jimi Hendrix*: "The 'purplish haze' Farmer wrote about was caused by sunspots that had a disorienting effect on a distant planet's inhabitants," which sounds like the spell the girl puts on Jimi.

"3rd Stone from the Sun"

The Experience's most daring number had been in the works for almost five months when Jimi Hendrix and Chas Chandler added the "Wild Chat" on April 10, 1967, at Olympic Studios to the almost seven-minute instrumental. The "Wild Chat"—an imagined dialogue between "Star Fleet" and the pilot of a scout ship—was the first overt usage of science fiction imagery in one of Hendrix's compositions. (And the first spaceship to make an entrance, too!)

By all accounts the five takes were apparently a lot of fun for the participants, perhaps mostly for Hendrix, who did not have to sing on the track. Chandler was the voice of the Star Fleet Commander and Hendrix the scout ship pilot orbiting around the third stone from the sun, which he confirms is earth before entering the atmosphere for a closer look (as will the spaceman in "Up from the Skies").

With sped-up voices that were then slowed down to induce disorientation in the listener, the pilot is tantalized by earth's natural beauty but confused by the behavior of earth's people and decides to attack and destroy the third stone from the sun. Hendrix must have enjoyed using dialogue because he reused the technique for the opening of "EXP," *Axis: Bold as Love*'s first cut, where once again he plays a spaceman answering questions, only this time from an interviewer portrayed by Mitch Mitchell.

It is also entirely appropriate that the song about space exploration on *Are You Experienced* should also be the one that is about music exploration. This is the track that even tantalized jazz bassist Jaco Pastorius, who, when discussing "3rd Stone from the Sun" in a 1982 issue of *Downbeat*, said that "for anyone who doesn't know about that by now, they should've checked Jimi out a lot earlier." The song structure is very controlled, and the first third has been compared to a Shadows instrumental, but after the scout ship pilot lands his "kinky machine," the music ironically takes off for the outer reaches of the musical universe.

One of the stranger images in all of Hendrix's lyrics is the "superior cackling hen" in the final verse that has led some to surmise that a plotline in a Donald Duck comic from 1968 was influenced by the Experience's "3rd Stone from the Sun." Issue #126 of *Donald Duck* contains a story by Carl Barks that is called "Officer for a Day," and within it, Donald Duck is a substitute policeman who encounters many strange incidents including that of space visitors who are convinced that only chickens are intelligent enough to talk to.

The mono mix of the original UK version of *Are You Experienced* was considered the definitive mix as stereo was considered a passing fad at first by industry insiders, and the mono mix of "3rd Stone from the Sun" contains a line stricken from subsequent versions that ties in with the alien's destruction of the third stone from the sun: "War must be war."

According to Chandler it was another book in his collection—*Earth Abides* by George R. Stewart—that shaped the lyrical content of "3rd Stone from the Sun."

"Spanish Castle Magic"

Noticeably absent in Jimi Hendrix's singing is the histrionics of singers of the fantastic such as Genesis's Peter Gabriel or Yes's Jon Anderson, which is why listeners do not question the more questionable goings-on in his songs. Take, for example, "Spanish Castle Magic," one of the few *Axis* compositions to become a concert staple (and often a concert opener at that). Hendrix's vocal delivery was so natural that when he sings of flying dragonflies, the listener reaches for his hand.

The "Spanish Castle" in the title is a biographical reference to the Spanish Castle Club in Seattle—hence the line that "It's not in Spain"— where Hendrix got his start playing in bands. It was just about the only realistic detail in this fantastic love song of magic where Hendrix the magician conjures up a floating woman among low-lying clouds overflowing with cotton candy. Just about the only other realistic element are the "battle grounds red and brown," but Jimi is reassuring and says that everything is going to be alright.

"Voodoo Chile"

Jimi Hendrix's final residence in England may have been next door to that of George Frederick Handel, but he was much more taken by *The Planets*, English classical composer Gustav Holst's seven-movement orchestral suite. He felt a kinship with the subject matter, and so it is not surprising that several compositions from *Electric Ladyland* reference the planets, including the mythmaking "Voodoo Chile," or what Charles Shaar Murray in *Crosstown Traffic* calls "part of a long, long line of supernatural brag songs."

Both Sides One and Three of the original vinyl release featured lengthy compositions but that was where the similarity ended. Whereas "1983 . . . (A Merman I Should Turn to Be)" is about life underwater and carefully assembled in the studio with myriad overdubs and the result of an epic mixing session, "Voodoo Chile" is about flight and the result of a blues jam recorded after hours, actually early morning as recording began at the Record Plant at 7:30 a.m.

After recording "Three Little Bears" on May 2, 1968, Hendrix had spent the night at the nearby Scene Club, one of his favorite haunts in Manhattan. And after that club closed, he returned to the Record Plant with friends and musicians to record a blues number that had its roots in "Catfish Blues"—a Muddy Waters medley of sorts—that Hendrix had been developing privately for a couple of months, including a demo made in his hotel in April 1968.

Finally ready for studio recording, Hendrix recruited the talents of Jefferson Airplane bassist Jack Casady and Traffic organist Steve Winwood along with Experience drummer Mitch Mitchell. (Jazz guitarist Larry Coryell was also present and invited to participate but declined, feeling there was no role in the song for him.) Basic recording took three takes. The first take allowed Hendrix to show the other musicians the song's structure, and the second take was marred when one of Hendrix's strings broke. (These two takes were later edited to create "Voodoo Chile Blues," which graces *Jimi Hendrix: Blues*.)

The barroom voices were added after the third take was in the can and later mixed in to recreate a bar scene. The puzzled voice saying "The bar is closed?" at the very end is that of Jeannette Jacobs.

I stand up next to a mountain and chop it down with the ledge of my hand...

I'm a Voodoo Chile...

Even advertisers get the two voodoo songs mixed up.   *Author's collection*

"1983 . . . (A Merman I Should Turn to Be)"

Freed from Chas Chandler's hit record mentality, Hendrix was able to finally record a song that he had written a thousand words for. I exaggerate, but "1983 . . . (A Merman I Should Turn to Be)" was the chief Experience Maker's second-longest studio recording and the song where he was most able to fully realize a fantastic vision. (Originally, the last two verses following the long instrumental interlude were credited in songbooks to "Moon, Turn the Tides . . . Gently, Gently Away," but that is no longer the case.)

As in the mono version of "3rd Stone from the Sun" there is a war, except this time it is manmade. There's a machine that other earthlings mock—much like Kryptonians mocked Superman's father Jor-El—that Hendrix and his love Catherina use to flee and live underwater with mermaids in Atlantis. There is no doubt that "1983" is—according to Charles Shaar Murray in *Crosstown Traffic*, his groundbreaking analysis of Hendrix's effect on music post-Hendrix—"rock's premier work of science fiction; Hendrix was the music's first and funkiest cyberpunk."

There's a funny story in Kathy Etchingham's autobiography *Through Gypsy Eyes* where Hendrix, so visibly proud of "1983," read her the lyrics, only to be told that his "Catherina" wasn't coming along and he could "go to the bottom of the sea by yourself."

Hendrix laughed but was not to be put off, and the first recording of what was to become "1983" was as of March 13, 1968, named "Angel Catarina."

"House Burning Down"

At first glance, Hendrix's commentary on the riots inflaming America's urban ghettoes—particularly those following the assassination of Martin Luther King Jr.—seems coldly realistic. There's a hellfire red sky, black smoke, a house is burning, and family members are crying. Hendrix offers the rioters some common sense and tells them to "try to learn instead of burn."

But how is Hendrix getting around this dismal scene? He is riding a chariot and standing on his horse's back. In "House Burning Down," realistic elements bang up against fantastic and science fiction imagery, none weirder than the "giant boat from space" that "has taken all the dead away." (It is also chronologically the final appearance of a spaceship in Hendrix's songs.)

This is one of Hendrix's most powerful songs, and while it seems odd that only four versions have been released either officially or bootlegged, all the recording was done at two sessions, the first of which only included Hendrix and Mitchell as Noel Redding was feeling increasingly marginalized during the *Electric Ladyland* sessions in New York City and prone to disappearance. Much has been written of his effort at recreating an oceanic scene for "1983 . . . (A Merman I Should Turn to Be)," but the same is true of "House Burning Down," where Hendrix and engineer Eddie Kramer went through multiple takes before achieving a guitar tone that mimicked the fire burning the house down.

"Angel"

As if in counterpoint to the women who wanted to put him in a "plastic cage," several songs by Jimi Hendrix feature a fantastic female figure offering freedom. She's found in "Little Wing" and "Hey Baby (New Rising Sun)" to name a few. She often rescues Hendrix from an otherwise bleak existence that could be caused by a childhood's poverty, racism's oppression, or the unreasonable demands of superstardom.

The most famous of this type of lyrical content is "Angel," a demo of which dates as far back as the 1967 *Axis* sessions, but only saw the light of day as part of *The Cry of Love*, the first posthumous release in 1971. While *The Cry of Love* was a huge success and reached #3 in America, it was Rod Stewart's 1972 hit recording of "Angel" that finally brought one of Hendrix's most beautiful compositions the attention it deserved.

Drenched in fluid imagery, like the reassuring figure in "Hey Baby (New Rising Sun)," this angel takes Hendrix away with her to a better world just as Hendrix takes the listener to a better world in "(Have You Ever Been to) Electric Ladyland." It is a recurrent theme of Hendrix's that his music can take you to a better place, which is maybe why family friend Fannie Mae Gautier chose to read the lyrics of "Angel" at Hendrix's funeral. He had finally been rescued.

It's Too Bad Our Friends Can't Be with Us Today

The London Entourage

At the time of Jimi Hendrix's untimely death in London in September 1970, he was speaking of no longer centering himself from New York City, his base of operations since the *Electric Ladyland* sessions began in April 1968. He was extracting himself from the clutches of Devon "Dolly Dagger" Wilson, talking of dumping manager Michael Jeffery, and revealing to British interviewers his desire to relocate to London.

Most significantly he was attempting to persuade Chas Chandler to return as his record producer. He invited Chandler to his new studio in New York City to wrap production on a double album nearing completion. Chandler showed interest, but when he balked at flying to New York City because he was about to become a father, Hendrix made arrangements to have the album's tapes sent from Electric Lady Studios to London.

It was Hendrix's admission that things had gone awry with his triumphant return to America, and a return to London and his British friends and colleagues would serve him better than remaining with the hangers-on feeding off of him. He was coming to terms with the fact that the men who comprised his London entourage had fed him and, perhaps more importantly, had fed his music.

Roger Mayer

You cannot imagine "Purple Haze" without its Octavia-based guitar solo after Hendrix excuses himself to kiss the sky. But the Octavia wasn't a foot pedal that was available in any London music store. (And even if it was, at the time of recording the Experience's second A-side he couldn't have afforded it.) Jimi Hendrix did not find the Octvaia, it found him. Or rather, its inventor, Roger Mayer, a member of the Royal Naval Scientific Service, found Jimi Hendrix.

With the Royal Naval Scientific Service, Mayer was employed by day at a Teddington research laboratory analyzing noises in order to make the Royal Navy's ships quieter. At night and during his off-hours, Mayer was applying this research to music and was at the forefront of the development of the foot pedals on those pedalboards that you now see every electric guitarist toting around.

This is not as strange as it sounds because Mayer, before joining the Royal Navy, had been a guitarist, but playing gigs and the adversity of touring did not appeal to him.

More importantly to his ultimate contribution to Jimi Hendrix's recordings was his friendship to his childhood neighbors Jeff Beck and Jimmy Page. These young guitarists were willing to use and popularize Mayer's experimental devices such as early fuzzboxes. Page's work as a session guitarist is well known; less known is that it was Mayer's fuzzbox that Page played on two of the hit singles American songwriter-singer P. J. Proby had in the United Kingdom: "Hold On" (#3) and "Together" (#8).

(Even less known is that the studio session band Jimmy Page had rounded up for what became Proby's album *Three Week Hero* would go on to become Led Zeppelin! *Three Week Hero* is Led Zeppelin's earliest recording, although they were still known as the New Yardbirds at the time. Robert Plant, however, does not sing on Proby's album. His contribution is limited to harmonica playing.)

It was at the Experience's Bag O' Nails concert that Mayer, like so many others, first experienced Jimi Hendrix. Mayer knew many of the Animals, and it was through this connection that he was able to introduce himself to the American guitarist. During the conversation that ensued, Mayer divulged to Hendrix the sonic nature of his inventions. Hendrix, whose instinctual knowledge of guitar-related electronics is often ignored, was intrigued and invited Mayer to the Experience's gig at Chislehurst Caves on January 27, 1967.

Mayer showed Hendrix the latest version of the fuzzboxes he was working on and the Octavia, a pedal that "produces a sound that is an octave higher than the note" being played by a guitarist. Despite Mayer's childhood friendships with other electric guitarists of high caliber, it was Hendrix who innately understood the true possibilities of Mayer's inventions, and Mayer was soon developing gadgets solely for the head Experience Maker. He would also perfect third-party units such as wah-wah pedals and Fuzzfaces to suit Hendrix's needs.

Mayer's Octavia was used by Hendrix on many studio ("Fire," "Little Miss Lover") and live recordings ("Who Knows"), but its presence on "Purple Haze" is the one most are familiar with (even if they don't know it). Those high notes you hear just after Hendrix accuses the girl of putting a spell on him (the first mention of voodoo in Hendrix's work) demonstrates Mayer's Octavia evoking the spell's effect. It's used again during the outro.

Hendrix considered Mayer so integral circa 1967 that during an interview he went so far as to say "the secret of my sound is largely the electronic genius of our tame boffin who is known as Roger the Valve," and according to Kathy Etchingham, a friend of Hendrix's despite his day job. He would drop by the guitarist's flat or hang out in clubs talking shop. He also attended recording sessions to ensure his devices were working properly and to Hendrix's satisfaction.

Mayer did not follow Hendrix to New York City, so he had little impact on the recording of *Electric Ladyland*, an album Mayer considers a little overbaked. His favorite Jimi Hendrix Experience album is *Axis: Bold as Love*.

An interesting side note: Mayer worked decades later with the seminal shoegazer band My Bloody Valentine.

Eddie Kramer

Unlike Roger the Valve—referred to as such so that he'd never be accidentally identified to his superiors at the Royal Naval Scientific Service—engineer Eddie Kramer was not an intimate friend of Jimi Hendrix's as Kathy Etchingham made clear in her autobiography. They did not socialize; theirs was a working relationship. But we all have coworkers we consider friends even if we do not socialize with them, so it is on these terms that I include Kramer in Hendrix's circle of friends.

When Kramer met Hendrix at Olympic Studios on February 3, 1967, to help complete "Purple Haze," it was the beginning of a working friendship that extends to over four decades after Hendrix's death as—at the time of this writing—Kramer continues to engineer (and coproduce with Janie Hendrix and John McDermott) releases issued and reissued by Experience Hendrix, L.L.C., Hendrix's estate. In September 2011, he contributed to the remastered, extended, and replacement version of *Hendrix in the West*, and the *Winterland* box set, which is explored in detail in the discussion of the elusive fourth Experience album in Chapter 18.

What Eddie Kramer had in common with Roger the Valve was the willingness to help musicians achieve the sounds in their heads. Hendrix, like John Lennon, often described the sounds he sought in colors, and Kramer often found himself using his mixing board like a box of Crayola crayons; with his love and knowledge of avant-garde jazz musicians and recordings, he was able to coax out of Hendrix the sounds Hendrix heard.

Kramer's first contribution was the introduction of reduction mixing to the process of creating Hendrix's compositions. He would record the Experience live in the studio on four tracks with the drummer getting two of the four tracks. Afterwards the four tracks were mixed down to two tracks, thereby "finding" two unused tracks for Hendrix and the Experience (and later guest musicians and friends) to add guitar leads, vocals, overdubs, and additional instrumentation. This approach appealed to Hendrix who was already familiar with 8-track recording back in the States.

When Hendrix saw an upright piano at Olympic Studios and instinctively wanted to use it, Kramer showed him some basic piano chords. This led to the out-of-tune piano heard tolling in the background during the outro of the Experience's title track to *Are You Experienced*.

Axis: Bold as Love is the only Experience or Hendrix album that Kramer exclusively engineered, and, as we will explore in Chapter 36, it is the favorite of the majority of Hendrix's London entourage. By the time of the *Electric Ladyland* sessions—figuratively a double album in its own right if you catch my drift—Kramer was sharing engineering duties with Gary Kellgren, who had migrated from Mayfair Studios to the Record Plant, where *Electric Ladyland* was largely recorded.

The epic "1983 . . . (A Merman I Should Turn to Be)" is the pinnacle of the mixes he made with Hendrix. This 13:39 masterpiece—the second-longest Experience song (though neither it nor "Voodoo Chile" can truly be said to be Experience recordings since Noel Redding is not on either, which means that "3rd Stone from the Sun" is truly the Experience's longest completed track)—was the result of three sessions, including the final mixing session that, according to Kramer, went on "for about 18 hours straight. We mixed the entire thing in one go with no interruption, so it was a complete piece. With all the panning, all the effects, we would rehearse it numerous times obviously. But it was like a performance . . . ."

As challenging as an eighteen-hour mixing session may have been, more daunting for Kramer was shaping *The Cry of Love*, Hendrix's first posthumous album. Manager Michael Jeffery asked Kramer and Mitch Mitchell to produce it because he felt they were the two men who best understood the music Hendrix had been readying for release. Mitchell was Hendrix's drummer of choice throughout the summer of 1970, and Kramer had played a large role in the development of Electric Lady Studios.

The space that would become Electric Lady Studios was first conceived as part club, part studio, and architect John Storyk was commissioned to come up with a floor plan. Kramer was whisked over from London to help Storyk design the studio section, but he thought too little space was being set aside. Audits of Hendrix's expenses at Record Plant then came in and revealed the enormous sums he was spending recording, and so the club was jettisoned and the premises redesigned to strictly hold a studio.

Kramer helped with the design and stayed on to acquire the equipment for Hendrix's state-of-the-universe studio. Then he stayed on to engineer Hendrix's fourth album, a double album called many titles by Hendrix over the years, but *First Rays of the New Rising Sun* is the title the estate has settled on using.

It is more accurate to describe Kramer as coming back to engineer Hendrix's recordings because in the studio Kramer was all business. He did not socialize with Hendrix, and their working relationship had been strained when he objected to all of the hangers-on cluttering the Record Plant during recording sessions. The work the two did during the summer of 1970 was an attempt to mend their working relationship, and Hendrix allowed Kramer to vet to some extent who attended the sessions in Studio A at Electric Lady.

Kramer and Mitchell wanted to put out an honorable album, a recording that would honor Hendrix's intentions. This should have meant the release of a double album, but without Hendrix around, Jeffery could get the single album he had been advising his act to release. Kramer was worried at the time that "there's all kinds of unscrupulous people in the business, who shall remain nameless, that will release tapes of Jimi now. We'll have to do our best with Warner Brothers to stop it."

That Warner Brothers was in possession of some of the better unreleased recordings, according to Mitchell in his autobiography, steepened the challenge they rose to meet as *The Cry of Love* remains one of the finer posthumous studio albums released in the 1970s; only *Rainbow Bridge*, which Kramer and Mitchell also produced along with John Jansen, betters it. You can cobble both albums together from box sets and other CDs since released, but it is a shame that Reprise discontinued both albums in the wake of *Crash Landing*'s commercial success in 1975.

The director of engineering at Electric Lady Studios from 1970 through 1974, Kramer has engineered a who's who of recording artists, including Traffic, Led Zeppelin, the Rolling Stones, Derek and the Dominoes, David Bowie, Curtis Mayfield, and Santana. His production credits are less impressive but range widely: NRBQ, Peter Frampton, Buddy Guy, John McLaughlin, and Kiss. We'll forgive him for Kiss.

Gerry Stickells

It was Noel Redding who arranged Gerry Stickells's entrance into the Jimi Hendrix entourage, and Stickells remained a member till the very end, outlasting the friend who had recommended him. It was Stickells who accompanied Hendrix's body from London to Seattle after the autopsy.

He was the Experience's driver, van mechanic, and organizer during the early tours of England and Europe; the only tour he wasn't part of was the initial tour of France. He supervised the mega-tours of America that came in the wake of Hendrix's stardom while still driving the band to concert venues from their hotel, including the infamous final Experience show at the Denver Pop Festival, where his resourcefulness saved the band members from being mauled by fans or worse.

Redding's feelings were already ruffled before the show because a journalist upon sighting him wondered what he was doing at the concert. He thought Hendrix had said in an interview that Redding was being replaced. For the umpteenth time, Redding quit. He would carry on as leader of Fat Mattress. The Jimi Hendrix Experience went out, and even Redding, who was often critical of Experience concerts in 1969, wrote in his biography that the band reached incendiary heights that final night. They were so good that the audience began jumping onstage to be with their heroes.

The police panicked and resorted to tear gas to subdue a crowd of over 30,000. The Experience kept playing, hoping everything would subside, but the windy weather conditions pushed the tear gas toward the stage. The band members could not breathe, let alone play, and found themselves surrounded by their fans.

Saving the day, Stickells backed his van against the stage and guided the Experience to safety. He told Chris Welch in his biography of Hendrix that he had to "lock the group in the back." The van was covered with banging fans, and since it was windowless, the band members had no idea how bad things were outside. Inside it sounded horrible. Redding rolled a joint, lit it, and passed it around as Stickells somehow got in the driver's seat and slowly drove the van with clinging fans back to the hotel. "It was murder," he told Welch, "but there was no other way out, and they squashed the roof of the truck flat."

"I was a friend—he knew I wasn't over-enthusiastic about his music, but that didn't stop us from being friends. I'm not a great fan of loud of rock and roll music." Nor did that prevent Stickells from parlaying the experience he garnered supporting Hendrix into a successful career. After working a spell at Electric Lady Studios, he went on to organize and supervise tours for Three Dog Night, Queen, Michael Jackson, and Madonna.

Eric Barrett

If you're a fan who follows a band from town to town, you usually get to recognizing their roadies: tattooed guys who haul and set up the equipment and serve as de facto butlers throughout a performance, ensuring that everything is in its right place. Fulfilling these roles for Jimi Hendrix were Gerry Stickells behind the wheel and Glaswegian Eric Barrett behind the amplifiers. You can actually see Barrett in footage from various concerts such as the Royal Albert Hall bracing himself behind Hendrix's stacks of Marshall amps and preventing them from toppling over as the guitarist jousted or rubbed himself up against them.

To say Barrett is rarely interviewed is an understatement. He is only on record in Chris Welch's 1972 biography of Hendrix and thereafter must have decided to keep Hendrix's stories and secrets to himself. What little we do know of Barrett is that he was a roadie for the Koobas at the show they played opening for the Who and the Jimi Hendrix Experience. Approximately fifteen months later, in May 1968, he was invited to roadie for the Experience during their upcoming tour of Italy. Once again, it was Noel Redding who brought Barrett into Hendrix's inner circle. "After five days in Italy I loved (Jimi)," Barrett told Welch, "and realized what he was trying to do."

Barrett remained in Hendrix's employ, caring for the guitarist's equipment until his death, which may explain how he came into possession of Hendrix's black Gibson Flying Arrow that was played during the *Cry of Love* tour and at the Isle of Wight concert and is now owned by the Hard Rock Café in London.

According to Tony Brown in *Hendrix: The Final Days*, Barrett "relocated to Los Angeles where he set up a very successful independent production company to advise rock bands on their equipment and lighting requirements." Tours he is known to have worked on include David Bowie's *Station to Station* tour in 1976 and Madonna's world tours.

He also has served in various producer roles for films and videos, including those of Sheryl Crow and the Red Hot Chili Peppers.

12

Go to Hell with Your Hustling Ways

Business Problems

imi Hendrix's fall was as meteoric as his rise. Less than two years after release of his third magnum opus he was resting in his burial plot. The cast of characters contributing to this fall are many and include Devon Wilson, Monika Dannemann, even Hendrix himself, whose evasiveness when dealing with Michael Jeffery and Edward Chalpin—the men whose contracts he signed—was probably the single heaviest contributing factor to his early demise. Chalpin hounded Hendrix to his grave with international lawsuits, and Jeffery has even been suspected by some of murdering his client. It is one thing to sign a bad contract as many a musician has been guilty of; it's another thing to sign a contract that was tantamount to signing your own death warrant.

Michael Jeffery

The rarely photographed Michael Jeffery can rightly be described as the anti-Chandler of Hendrix's stardom: he was the manager who handled the business side of Hendrix's affairs. But the diverging comparison goes deeper than that. Whereas Chandler nurtured Hendrix until the rocker's overindulgent lifestyle forced Chandler to wash his hands of his protégé, Jeffery continually schemed and connived to legally snare Hendrix, his goose that was laying the golden eggs.

It was through his discovery of the Animals that Michael Jeffery became Jimi Hendrix's manager. The Animals enjoyed a string of successes in the first half of the 1960s, but, unlike fellow rhythm and blues artists the Rolling Stones, their success stalled due to lack of original material. When the Animals' bassist expressed his interest in trying his hand at managing, Jeffery, citing Chandler's signed contract with him, offered to comanage any acts he signed.

Chandler returned from his final tour with the Animals with the newly dubbed Jimi Hendrix. Jeffery helped resolve passport issues and arrange contract signings, but his focus initially was in finding Animals singer Eric Burdon the musicians that would comprise the New Animals. It was only after Chandler got the Experience signed to Track Records and "Hey Joe" was released that Jeffery took a more active interest. He gave Kathy Etchingham money to buy copies of the 45 in stores to drive the record up the charts.

"Mike Jefferies," as Etchingham said everyone called Jeffery (a fact confirmed in the index to Mitch Mitchell's book, where Jeffery's name is given as Mike Jefferys), was all things to all people. For example:

- "He was an incredibly talented man and could see talent in others."— Trixie Sullivan
- "He was the quintessential parasite manager who had struck lucky."— Lois Appleton
- "To Jimi and me, he seemed like someone we could look to for guidance, someone we could trust."—Kathy Etchingham
- "A real wheeler-dealer, he rarely let his left hand even know he had a right hand."—Noel Redding
- "He could certainly take care of business, but a lot of juggling was going on."—Mitch Mitchell
- "Jeffery wanted to put invisible chains around you."—Chas Chandler
- "I told Jeffery he was an out-an-out complete idiot and a fucking asshole to boot."—Buddy Miles
- "I understood he was a dangerous fellow."—Sharon Lawrence

Initially Jeffery contributed little to Jimi Hendrix's success. It was Chandler who had signed him with Track and gotten him exposure on television. This changed in a big way in 1967 when Jeffery signed distribution rights with Barclay Records in France and negotiated with Warner Brothers for the American rights to the Experience's recordings for $150,000, which then was an unheard-of amount of money for an unknown recording artist.

It was also Jeffery who sensed before anybody what a goldmine America would be for a touring band. After December 22, 1967, Jimi Hendrix only played three concerts in the United Kingdom and less than a month's worth in Europe. Every other concert took place in an American state because that was where the money was, as drummer Mitch Mitchell stated to the British press when asked about the Experience's absence from the local concert scene.

It was also Jeffery, with help from publicist Mike Goldstein and tour manager Gerry Stickells, who revolutionized the rock concert experience as thoroughly as Desi Arnaz institutionalized the multiple-camera filming of live comedies. Before Jimi Hendrix, rock concerts were package tours with each band getting a short set. We have seen this with the Experience's tour with the Walker Brothers and the Monkees and even the 1968 tours of America that showcased bands that Jeffery managed in addition to Hendrix (e.g., Soft Machine).

But the Soft Machine's support never hardened, and Eric Burdon's career stalled, and so Jeffery moved, strengthening his stranglehold on Hendrix in two significant ways. First, he bought out Chas Chandler for $300,000 when Chandler found himself unable to steer the Experience Maker in the studio during the *Electric Ladyland* sessions. This meant Hendrix would no longer have a comanager who understood Hendrix's artistic needs. Second, by purchasing the Generation Club with Hendrix in hopes of turning it into a small studio as well as functioning club, Jeffery now had a business partnership that transcended the management contract; a not-so-invisible chain that bound him closer to Jeffery.

Jeffery's endless touring demands, filming schemes (e.g., entire tours would be filmed, the Royal Albert Hall concert would be released as a film, Hendrix would star in and record a soundtrack for Chuck Wein's *Rainbow Bridge*), band-aids to the Experience lineup, resistance to black musicians supporting Jimi, and absence of support during the Toronto drug trials and tribulations (even Chandler attended the trial as a character witness for Hendrix) all strained their relationship, and it is unlikely Hendrix would've renewed his management contract with Jeffery if he had not died in London on September 18, 1970.

And of course this has led to accusations that Hendrix was murdered by Jeffery, charges that have been leveled as recently as in May 2009 when, in an article in *The Independent*, former Animals tour manager Tappy Wright claimed Jeffery confessed to murdering his famous client and "killing him by stuffing pills into his mouth and washing them down with several bottles of red wine because he feared Hendrix intended to dump him for a new manager." After all, Hendrix was worth more to him dead than alive if the management contract was terminated.

Only there isn't any proof that Jeffery was in London at the time of Hendrix's death, and, in fact, his presence in Majorca, Spain, was confirmed by at least three eyewitnesses.

Jeffery's fear of flying is commented upon by just about anybody who writes of him at length, so it's ironic that he should have died in a plane crash. But that is just what happened on March 5, 1973. Hendrix's former manager was aboard an Iberia DC-9, one of two Spanish planes that crashed into one another over Nantes, France. Jeffery's body was identified through his watch and jewelry.

Ed Chalpin

During a lean period in October 1965, Hendrix was befriended by bandleader (and pimp) Curtis Knight when they met in the Hotel America lobby, a meeting with far-reaching consequences. Hendrix said he played guitar but had pawned his to pay the rent. When Curtis brought a sunburst Fender Duo-Sonic to Hendrix's room to see how well the guitarist played, he gave Hendrix the guitar as a gift, probably as a means of getting Hendrix to join his band the Squires.

Knight was recording singles at the time for Chalpin, who owned PPX Enterprises, and the first one Hendrix played on was a modified version of Dylan's "Like a Rolling Stone" that PPX released as "How Would You Feel," which is what Chalpin did: released cheap covers in international markets. Chalpin thought Hendrix had some talent and on October 15th signed him to an exclusive three-year, one-page contract for a one dollar advance. Never has a contract for one dollar proven to be so costly.

Hendrix played with Knight and recorded for Chalpin through May 1966. Over the course of those eight months, Hendrix played on what must be the most frequently repackaged thirty-three tracks ever recorded by a rock musician, because ever since the Experience struck it big, Chalpin has been re-releasing and re-producing those tracks and gotten away with it because Hendrix neglected to inform Chandler of the contract when asked. Other contracts were bought out, but not the one with PPX Enterprises.

Chalpin had already moved legally to prevent Experience recordings when Hendrix dined with Curtis Knight in August 1967. After all, Hendrix's three-year contract with PPX wasn't even two years old yet, and so Chalpin, as reported in the July 4, 1967, edition of the *Evening Standard*, had gone to court in England to prevent further recordings of Hendrix being issued by Track and Polydor in the United Kingdom. Hendrix was aware of the legal moves being played out and yet returned twice to the studio with both Chalpin and Knight that month as if they were his best friends. It wasn't until Capitol Records via Decca Records in England issued two singles credited to Hendrix and Curtis Knight from those August sessions that Hendrix finally understood that the two men were not to be trusted.

A larger insult came, however, when Decca and Capitol simultaneously released an album in the United Kingdom and America called *Get That Feeling* in December 1967, the same month as the Experience's *Axis: Bold as Love*. The cover featured a shot of Hendrix from his Monterey Pop

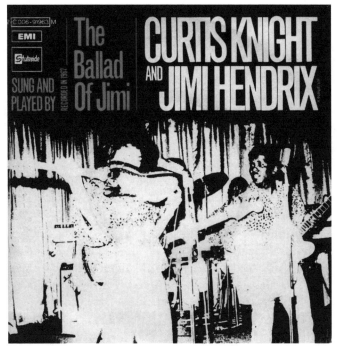

Ed Chalpin is responsible for many of the more inferior studio recordings in the Jimi Hendrix catalog, including this one: "The Ballad of Jimi" with the reprehensible Curtis Knight. Do yourself a favor and do not buy this.

Courtesy of Robert Rodriguez

appearance, and the music within was advertised as "Jimi Hendrix Plays and Curtis Knight Sings." It wasn't until March 1968 that a court ordered Decca to remove *Get That Feeling* from the market. No such order was forthcoming in America, although the cover was to be redesigned.

The American settlement of Hendrix's contract with PPX on June 24, 1968, was a generous agreement that gave Chalpin a percentage of the two Experience albums already on the market and the third currently being recorded. Complete ownership and profit of the fourth album released by the Jimi Hendrix Experience would be given to Chalpin, who could also market recordings of Hendrix and Knight as he wished. Warner Brothers also paid Chalpin a generous sum in the millions (the amount is disputed), and in exchange Chandler and Jeffery allowed Warner Brothers to sign Hendrix directly.

The fourth Experience record would be on the Capitol Records label, because they were now a partner in the PPX suit against Hendrix because of a court injunction preventing sale of the *Get That Feeling* LP.

Chalpin later balked when Hendrix and his management team proposed to fulfill the settlement with a live Band of Gypsys recording and not the Experience, which had disbanded. Capitol, however, was eager to get the album and overruled Chalpin, accepting the album because they felt the record's sales would not be affected if it was not the Experience. They reasoned it was Hendrix's presence, not the Experience, that would move units.

Unresolved was Chalpin's lawsuit against Hendrix and Track and Polydor in England and Barclay in France. The fact that depositions in the case were to be taken the day that Jimi Hendrix died cannot be understated. Hendrix was unhappy with the way the PPX contract was settled in America and felt that his management and that of Warner Brothers had not fought hard enough in court. The idea of losing again and perhaps owing Chalpin even more product weighed heavily on him during his final week on earth and may have contributed to his death.

And so Hendrix wasn't around to take some satisfaction when Chalpin's lawsuit was finally heard in England. Unlike Warner Brothers, Track and Polydor heavily contested Chalpin, perhaps because they were represented by Leo Branton, who also represented Hendrix's father Al Hendrix and the rights to Hendrix's estate were at stake. Out-of-court settlements prior to the hearings were rebuffed as Chalpin anticipated the court awarding a bigger piece of the voodoo pie. This time gambling didn't pay off, and it was Chalpin who was ordered to pay the court costs of $200,000.

Chalpin, in the end, did acquire the rights to additional music recorded by Jimi Hendrix with and without the Experience. Many of those bootleg CDs and box sets that you find on eBay are from recordings that Michael Jeffery owned the rights to. When Jeffery died, his estate went to his parents and, upon their death, was given to fourteen charities. That's when Chalpin stepped in and offered his services to the charities to ensure they were reaping the maximum benefit from the Jeffery estate's donation. They took him up on his offer.

13

The Dodgy Subject

Things Gone Wrong

People have been selling their souls for as long as there have been devils. And no one is more desperate to make this deal than a struggling musician. The most widespread myth in modern music is that of blues guitarist Robert Johnson meeting the devil by the crossroads of US 61 and US 49 in Clarksdale, Mississippi.

There is another myth—the Rosedale version reported by Rolf Potts that is based on a "vision" of bluesman Henry Goodman, a handwritten copy of which was handed to Potts by a waitress not far from the crossroads; it could be a scene out of a David Lynch movie.

Goodman's "vision" has Johnson walking in search of whiskey when at the crossroads, he encounters a man sitting on a log while a hairless hell-hound moans. The man stands up. Johnson digs the sound of the hound, says it's his sound and he's got to have it. The devil says it's the sound of the Delta blues. "Where does he sign?" asks Johnson. The devil tells Johnson there's nothing to sign, but if he takes one more step north into Rosedale, "my left hand will forever be wrapped around your soul."

The rest is the stuff of legend. Johnson is the Delta blues. His life was full of the whiskey and women that the devil promised him along with the blues. That is, until a jealous husband murdered him with strychnine-laced whiskey.

I'm surprised no similar myth has arisen for Jimi Hendrix, upon whose death Eric Clapton immediately thought the left-handed guitarist had pulled a Robert Johnson. Hendrix's overnight success from struggling Greenwich Village musician to London rock star has all the making of a deal with the devil that would go like this: Hendrix has met Chas Chandler, who has offered him success if he flies across the Atlantic to London. Hendrix has already agreed but harbors doubts. At a traffic light blue with sorrow he meets the devil amidst crosstown traffic. As with Johnson, there are no papers to be signed. If Jimi takes a step north, however, success will be his. Only don't ever come back to America, or the devil will be collecting.

Trashed Hotel Room in Sweden

The first hint that a fall would quickly follow Jimi Hendrix's rise was a trip to Sweden and Denmark for eight shows in January 1968. The Experience had only played one date in Gothenburg when Hendrix was arrested for trashing Room 623, Mitch Mitchell's hotel room. It was the first time other members of the Experience witnessed how whiskey brought out Hendrix's dark side, and it was alarming.

According to Mitchell, the fact that Swedes were not used to drinking regularly may have contributed to this incident because a lot of alcohol was consumed by the Experience and friends who had met them at the hotel as the band returned from Klubb Karl, a club where they had hung out after the show. According to Redding's autobiography, drunken conversation quickly led to a gay journalist suggesting some sort of unusual sexual arrangement.

It was not this suggestion that Hendrix objected to—he was even receptive to the idea of a foursome at first; hints of Hendrix being bisexual can be found throughout his biographies—but the night receptionist at the Opelan Hotel was contacted at approximately 4 a.m. by an irate guest complaining about the ruckus emanating from the room above him.

When Per Magnusson, the receptionist, went to investigate, he found a hotel room so utterly destroyed he could not believe it. According to legend, only the telephone was undamaged; even the window had been smashed by Hendrix, who was now lying on the bed with a bloody hand. Mitchell, who had stopped his guitarist's destruction of the room by sitting on him, was now sitting beside the bed.

Magnusson summoned the police, who took Hendrix to a hospital to have his hand treated, and thereafter he spent what remained of the morning in jail. Now sober, Hendrix sheepishly offered to pay all damages, although it was Chandler who actually did the paying. The hotel never did press charges but the press for the first time had something tangible to pin on their Wild Man of Borneo.

When Hendrix says "I just got out of a Scandinavian jail" in the posthumously released "My Friend," he is referencing this unpleasant incident.

Car Crashes

When French photographer Alain Dister took a cab to the Speakeasy on Valentine's Day 1967 with the Experience, little did he know that the car accident that was to happen was not a rare occurrence when you were in Jimi Hendrix's vicinity. Noel Redding and Mitch Mitchell knew otherwise;

they had already heard that not only had Hendrix crashed Chas Chandler's car in 1966, he had just walked away from the accident and left it embedded in a tree like George Bailey in Frank Capra's *It's a Wonderful Life*.

Car crashes were so common in the life of Jimi Hendrix that I have no doubt more than one person who knew him must've thought he died in a car accident when they first heard of his death.

Jimi Hendrix was at his peak in 1968, but, as this photo hints, all was not well in the year he produced *Electric Ladyland*.   *Author's collection*

In October 1968, he bought a Corvette Stingray in New York City and had Gerry Stickells drive it across America's mountains and prairies to Los Angeles, where the band was about to perform six shows at Winterland. Hendrix wrecked the car on October 7th—the first day he had it—and a second one on October 19th after seeing Cream play their farewell U.S. concert at Bill Graham's Fillmore West. According to Mitch Mitchell, after a party back at the house the band was renting, the drummer had just gone to sleep when he heard Hendrix say, "Guess what, I've just crashed my car." When Mitchell passed by the site of the accident the next day, he saw that Jimi had luckily crashed into some rocks; on the other side was a canyon drop.

Those who knew him attributed Hendrix's car accidents to the fact that although his eyesight was poor enough that he needed eyeglasses, he never wore them when driving. One friend even compared Hendrix's driving to that of Mr. Magoo, the nearsighted cartoon character voiced famously by Jim Backus.

Drug Bust in Toronto

Almost a decade before the Dudley Do-Rights busted Keith Richards in Toronto, they did the same to Jimi Hendrix on May 3, 1969. Flying in from Detroit, Michigan, he was detained when members of the Royal Canadian Mounties found a vial of heroin in the hand luggage he was carrying. That the Mounties and not customs agents found the vial immediately raised suspicion that someone had planted the drug on Hendrix—not linked at this time to heroin—and that the arrest was a setup at best, a warning at worst.

Each member of the Experience knew well enough not to carry drugs on them when entering a new country and passing through customs, but Mitch Mitchell recalled them being specifically warned by roadies about bringing drugs into Canada while at Detroit's Cobo Hall, site of the previous night's concert. Rumor had it that there were going to be problems for anyone not being careful. Mitchell was unconcerned: he often wore a suede suit with no pockets and wore no underwear when passing through customs in order to ensure authorities never planted anything on him. Hendrix should've followed his drummer's lead.

Which is not to say Hendrix disregarded the warnings he'd received; according to reports he was as shocked as anyone when Officer Marvin Wilson reached in Hendrix's hand luggage and showed him an Alka-Seltzer bottle containing three packets of white powder and a tube for smoking the powder. As if being made an example of, Hendrix was detained in full view of other travelers while waiting four hours for lab tests to determine the type of drug the Mounties had found.

Police harassment of musicians is as old as the times, and drug-related busts are common. In England in 1967 and 1968, the authorities found easy targets in Beatles and Rolling Stones, but none had been arrested for heroin, a more frowned-upon drug in the public consciousness. And so, as Hendrix was booked and released and checked into the Four Seasons hotel, his public relations manager Michael Goldstein worked frantically behind the scenes to ensure bad press did not derail the spring tour of America underway. Remarkably no major American paper picked up the story until *Rolling Stone* did in a sympathetic piece almost a month after the arrest.

The show, however, must go on. While he was incarcerated, concert promoters warned the Mounties that Maple Leaf Gardens would be a riot scene if Hendrix was not permitted to perform. The show was sold out, and there was too little time to cancel it. The Mounties, fearing the negative press of a riot would overshadow the positive press of busting a rock star, relented and even escorted the band to the concert.

Hendrix had an amazing ability to rally in concert, and so, despite the surreal events of the day, the Jimi Hendrix Experience gave a sublime

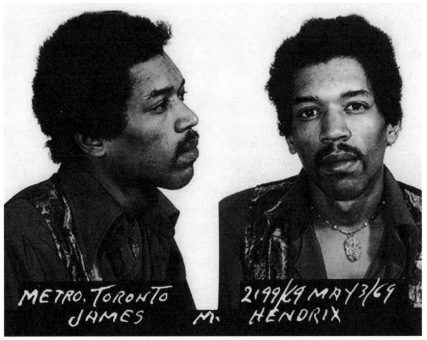

Jimi's mug shot after his bust in Toronto on trumped up charges.   *Author's collection*

performance in Toronto. Telling the audience that "We'll build our own little world right here . . . ," the band's set list contained some rarely aired material. "Spanish Castle Magic," the set's third song detoured into space with "3rd Stone from the Sun," a drum solo said to be one of Mitchell's finest, and "Little Miss Lover" a song the Experience had never played live before (or again), before returning to "Spanish Castle Magic."

The day's events were reflected, however. "Red House" contained the line "When I get out of jail, I'll come and see you." And "Room Full of Mirrors," getting its only second live airing since the February 24th Royal Albert Hall performance, featured ad-libbed lyrics and became an ironic warning about drug abuse. Leaving the Toronto stage, Hendrix told the audience to "remember what I tried to say to you."

Unfortunately, Hendrix could not just leave the drug bust behind like one of his smashed Corvette Stingrays. Two days later he was back in a Toronto courthouse, where a preliminary hearing was set for June 19th, the eve of the Experience's appearance at the three-day Newport Pop Festival. At this event, being staged in Northridge, California, the band was being paid $100,000, their largest paycheck ever, but small consolation to Jimi Hendrix, who, if convicted in Canada, faced ten years in prison.

On June 19th, a fully suited Jimi Hendrix learned that his trial date would be December 8th. He then flew to the festival, where he was harassed backstage by people who possibly had Black Panther connections. This harassment and the lingering uncertainty of how everything would resolve itself in Toronto led to Hendrix turning in a subpar performance after the Experience's 8 p.m. appearance was pushed back to 10:30 p.m. Noel Redding in his autobiography says his guitarist played for twenty minutes (and with his back to the audience), but the surviving ten-song set list indicates otherwise.

Still, to compensate for his poor performance, Hendrix did return on Sunday and made an unscheduled appearance jamming with the likes of Buddy Miles, Eric Burdon, Mother Earth, and members of Janis Joplin's Full Tilt Boogie Band.

It has never been determined exactly who set up the drug bust of Jimi Hendrix.

Was it the authorities? Customs officials at Toronto International Airport already had a reputation for giving rock bands a tough time when entering Canada, which increases the unlikelihood that Jimi Hendrix was foolish enough to leave heroin in his flight bag.

Sharon Lawrence, a journalist with UPI and personal friend of Hendrix, would testify at the trial and recounts in her personal history of Hendrix that she saw a hippie chick place a yellow-topped bottle in Hendrix's bag in the Los Angeles hotel room where she had interviewed Hendrix a few days before the bust.

Another rumor had it that a jilted gay groupie had planted the vial on the flight.

The most malicious rumor is that the planting was the handiwork of Michael Jeffery, Jimi Hendrix's own manager, in order to keep Hendrix dependent on him. This motive is immediately undermined by the fact that Michael Jeffery never left New York City to help bail out his biggest client. Nor was he likely to put at risk his cash cow, one that was about to be paid one hundred grand for a single performance. Even the manipulative Jeffery could see that the outcome of a trial in Toronto, where authorities were being tough on the hippie community, was a crap shoot that could backfire and have Hendrix behind bars for years.

Despite having been busted, the Jimi Hendrix Experience still turned in a fine performance at Maple Leaf Gardens. *Author's collection*

Still, the rumors persist that Jeffery had wanted to scare Hendrix—to put him in his place—and if Hendrix did go to jail, Jeffery would still be bringing in money from the recording studio under construction that he co-owned with Hendrix and the very unreleased tapes that would prove to be so posthumously lucrative. Maybe Jeffery knew what he was doing after all.

By the time Hendrix got back to Toronto in December, the Experience was no more, Woodstock had come and gone, and he'd even been kidnapped. He was arguably the biggest rock star in the world, but recording sessions for his next album were not going well; Gypsy Sun and Rainbows, his ragamuffin Woodstock band, had disbanded; and management was not enthused about his idea of forming an all-black band, thereby alienating his white fan base. Worse, Hendrix very seriously believed he was going to be made an example of and incarcerated for up to ten years in Canada.

Incredibly, Hendrix was detained again at Toronto International Airport on suspicion of drug possession as he arrived to attend his trial. Hendrix's lawyers' loyalty was being tested, but their faith in their client returned when the suspicious substance was too small to be identified. They still expected a guilty verdict on the original charges, but at least the guitarist had not sealed the case shut by hiding drugs in his acoustic guitar.

Five days later UPI wired the world that "a 12-man jury deliberated eight and a half hours before setting the 27-year-old singer free" and concluded with: "Hendrix thanked his young fans for sticking by him. Some remained in the courtroom for nearly 12 hours Wednesday." An accompanying photo of Hendrix, flanked by singer Jeanette Jacobs and an unidentified friend flashing peace signs, was also wired.

The Kidnapping

The kidnapping of Jimi Hendrix is among the most bizarre in the annals of rock history. It was first reported in David Henderson's 'Scuse Me While I Kiss the Sky, a biography so wildly inaccurate (and so biased that Hendrix's London entourage sued the author for libel) that you have to question its validity because the incident is only given a single paragraph and was based in Henderson's book on the hearsay of Juma Sultan, a percussionist Hendrix worked with in 1969 and 1970. Subsequent biographers have substantiated Sultan's basic premise of the kidnapping, but not the details.

Sultan was a member of Gypsy Sun and Rainbows, Hendrix's expanded lineup that had appeared at Woodstock, and was continuing to rehearse and had played two shows in September: a street festival in Harlem (September 5th) and the Salvation Club (September 10th).

The rehearsal sessions for this band were held at the house Hendrix was renting in Boiceville in Shokan in Ulster County in upstate New York. Sultan said he heard the story directly from Hendrix at Shokan, which means that the kidnapping incident probably occurred sometime after the Salvation Club appearance but before the end of September when Hendrix disbanded Gypsy Sun and Rainbows.

Hendrix said he had been abducted from his West Village apartment by four strange men who rang his doorbell, took him downstairs, and shoved him into the back of a car before blindfolding him. He was then driven to a building—presumably in New York City—bound and threatened but never physically harmed. After hearing frantic activity going on around him, the blindfold was removed and he found his manager Michael Jeffery and members of his staff standing around him. The rope tied around his wrists was removed, and Hendrix was returned to his apartment. One has to remember that by summer 1969 Hendrix's daily drug intake included several tabs of acid, which may explain some of the implausibility attending his version of things.

What appears to have happened is that Hendrix had often frequented the Salvation Club prior to the Gypsy Sun and Rainbows concert; in fact, that was why Hendrix agreed to play the club: as a personal favor to the owner, Bobby Woods, a former used car salesman who thought he could make a killing running a club downtown (and who would be murdered *Godfather*-style a few months after the Hendrix kidnapping).

The Salvation Club was initially a great success and attracted celebrities who liked the easy access to cocaine at the club. Woods, however, had never run a club before, and was fined for various infractions; and the celebrities stopped coming around but not members of the Mafia looking to put the squeeze on Woods for protection money. They eventually pressured Woods into hiring one of their own as manager and another as doorman.

Unlike other celebrities, Hendrix continued coming around for cocaine, was friendly with its providers, and one evening was persuaded to accompany them while they scored some of the white stuff. They then held Hendrix at gunpoint in a Little Italy apartment—not his—and he was forced to call Michael Jeffery and inform him that he was being held against his will. The ransom? Jeffery's management contract with Hendrix.

The kidnapping was never reported to authorities. Jeffery instead reached out to someone he knew with contacts to New York City's underworld. This person found out that Hendrix had indeed been kidnapped, but, when he went to the address where he said Hendrix would be, the kidnappers had fled with Hendrix. The kidnapping had not been sanctioned, and so they were not safe and had no place to hide the star they had stolen. Incredibly, they wound up at Hendrix's house in Shokan where the superstar was found, comfortably smoking joints without a care in the world.

14

Haven't I Seen You Somewhere in Hell?

The Difficult Bassist: Noel Redding

Noel Redding has never received his due as an electric bassist, which is unfortunate because within the Experience's live performances, Redding served as the axis for the improvisations of Hendrix and Mitchell. While Hendrix went where only Hendrix could go and Mitchell Elvin Jonesed himself, it was Redding picking away on his Fender Jazz Master who held the songs together. He stayed in the middle register, treble on full, and waited for his fellow Experience Makers to come back to the song's core, whether it be the nearly eight-minute version of "I Don't Live Today" (Stockholm, Sweden, January 9, 1969, second show) or a seventeen-minute version of "Voodoo Child (Slight Return)" (Oakland, California, April 17, 1969). He wasn't particularly pleased with this time-keeping role, but he was the musician in the band most concerned with being professional and giving the fans their money's worth.

So in some respects, it was Redding who was done the greatest service when Hendrix's best live album, *Hendrix in the West*, was reissued and expanded by Experience Hendrix LLC in 2011 because it's on the group's live recordings that convincing evidence exists of Redding's superb playing. You can quibble that the resequencing and/or substitution of certain tracks weakens the reissue, but for Redding's legacy it is a triumph.

For example, *Hendrix in the West* includes the finest readily available version "Red House." By spring 1969 Hendrix's signature blues number had quadrupled the length of the original studio recording thanks to fortissimo stretches where Redding, not Mitchell, pushes the pace in a way that Billy Cox never would. This was because it was as Hendrix said in a 1967 *Open City* interview: Redding was "in a rock bag." Hendrix was into the blues, Mitchell was applying jazz techniques to rock, and so it was Redding who was the Jimi Hendrix Experience's resident rock 'n' roller, and he gives this latter-era version of "Red House" its drive.

Another reason Redding's "bassic" contributions tend to be undervalued by posterity is that it is generally known that Hendrix regularly erased Redding's basslines and redid them himself on the Experience's second and third albums. The argument would seem to be along the lines of: "If the best bass solo on a Jimi Hendrix Experience record is the one Hendrix takes during *Electric Ladyland*'s "1983 . . . (A Merman I Should Turn to Be)," then it stands to reason Redding is not worthy of any consideration when debating bassists; even his own guitarist thought lowly of his bass playing."

But what most people do not know is that it wasn't Hendrix's dissatisfaction with Redding's bass playing that led to overdubs, but Hendrix's endless desire a la Glenn Gould to improve his recordings. If Redding hadn't gone to the nearest watering hole when fed up listening to Hendrix do take number forty of a guitar solo, Redding would've been called upon to play the bassline and would've performed it admirably.

Part of the problem stems from Redding himself. He spent the majority of his tenure in the Experience insisting he was a guitarist. And he was. His hiring as Hendrix's bassist was a quirk of fate; it was a case of being in the right place at the right time, although Redding wasn't so sure. Hendrix was well aware of his bassist's frustrations and concerned enough to encourage Redding to write his own compositions for the Experience, hoping this might alleviate some of his bassist's frustrations.

Hendrix recordings as a session man for Stephen Stills or Love are not worth seeking, but for Redding's songs released on Experience albums, Hendrix brought his "A" game. In interviews Hendrix even encouraged Redding's Fat Mattress project, although he resented their role on tour as the opening act. In all likelihood, it was Redding's frustrations with his role coupled with his constant carping to the British music press and erratic behavior that led to Redding's dismissal on the eve of Hendrix's American tour in spring of 1970. How was it that the man that manager Chas Chandler once described to Chris Welch as being "always the same happy little guy" wound up so estranged from the Jimi Hendrix Experience?

Relationship with Hendrix

The burr in Noel's Redding's relationship with Hendrix stems from the fact that he was a rock guitarist by trade. When he trained into London on September 29, 1966, he was responding to an audition notice in *Melody Maker* for a guitarist in Eric Burdon's New Animals, not the Jimi Hendrix Experience.

Riding the train into London for the audition, Redding was at the end of his rope. His previous band, the Loving Kind, had released three Pye singles with diminishing sales, and Redding had confessed to his mother, to whom he was to remain inordinately attached, that he was considering giving up his dream of being a rock musician. His "mum" urged him to give it one more go, and when he saw the ad for the Eric Burdon audition soon after, he thought it a promising sign. Burdon had once joined the Loving Kind for a few songs at London's Mayfair Room. Burdon was sure to remember him.

Redding had been told the previous day to show up at Birdland, literally a dive near Jermyn Street. Redding did a few blues numbers with Burdon, but it was more out of courtesy because the position had already been promised to Vic Briggs (a British guitarist whose skills Hendrix thought highly of).

But Burdon's former bassist was on hand scouring for backing musicians for Hendrix, and when Chas Chandler noticed that Redding "had the same haircut as Jimi's," he mentioned, "I got this guy in America that's looking for a bass player." The syntax of Chandler's recollection is a bit off as Hendrix was in a nearby room, not America, but having lent Redding his own bass, Chandler listened as the two ran through three numbers, including "Hey Joe" and "I Need Somebody to Love."

There was no sign of the friction that was to come later, and despite Redding's distaste for Hendrix's clothing—he was wearing out-of-style shoes, and who other than London bankers wore Burberry raincoats?—he accepted the position when offered the next day. Chandler and Etchingham agree he was given the bassist slot based on the curliness of his hair. Ironically, several years later Redding took to having his hair straightened because he was annoyed people thought he permed his hair to look like Hendrix. But that's several years away and let's let Noel and Jimi get along for a few paragraphs.

For example, Hendrix, who never had much of a family life, was invited by Redding to spend part of his 1966 holiday season in his hometown of Folkestone, England, approximately an hour's travel from north London and right across the Channel from Europe. Redding had persuaded (with difficulty) the proprietor to book the unknown Experience into Stan's Hillside Club for what would be the Experience's only New Year's Eve gig.

Afterwards, everybody brought in the New Year with Redding's family. Looking to warm himself at the fireplace, Hendrix asked Margaret Redding, Noel's "mum," "May I stand next to your fire?," and it is assumed by all that this was the origin of the key line in "Fire." Redding let Hendrix and Kathy Etchingham have his bed, and "he stayed up drinking in 1967."

The January calendar was full of London bookings as the Experience built up steam based on BBC television appearances, the chart success of "Hey Joe," and words out of musicians' mouths. The early days of success meant girls, however, not money, and Redding says in his autobiography, he "spent most of January in bed."

Jerry Hopkins's 1983 biography of Hendrix doesn't have much to recommend about it—basically it cobbles together the work of previous biographers and adds original details about Hendrix's kidnapping—but he does have one important insight. And it is one that gets at the heart of the Hendrix-Redding estrangement. The Experience, including management, was a well-functioning unit until they went to America. Then, after several months, Hopkins points out: "Consequently only Jimi was 'home' in the U.S., and the others around him were homesick." One of those who was homesick was Redding.

The deterioration of Hendrix's relationship with Redding mirrors that of manager Chas Chandler. Both wanted to go home to England to friends, family, and, in Chandler's case, a fiancée. This, coupled with Hendrix's growing confidence in the recording studio, alienated both men. Redding was annoyed with the endless takes as Hendrix pursued the perfect solo and often disappeared to drink and "pull a bird," as he would put it in his vernacular. Already displeased, Redding often returned to find that Hendrix had overdubbed new basslines, causing further alienation between the two musicians.

Redding, who was more frugal and more concerned with where the Experience's money was going than Hendrix or Mitchell, agreed with Chandler that all this studio time was a waste of money. Chandler told Chris Welch that "When I split from them, Noel had more money than the rest put together. . . . Noel would stay with the roadies and save."

Redding's penny-pinching ways and aloofness from the other Experience Makers is what led—more than anything—to Redding's eventual dismissal. When it came to money, Hendrix and Redding were direct opposites. Other than the dollar that Hendrix superstitiously kept in his shoe or hatband, he was never concerned about money (although he was worried about management not paying his taxes and winding up like impoverished heavyweight champion Joe Louis, a concern that bore fruit when it was determined after his death that Hendrix's management team had *not* paid Hendrix's U.S. taxes).

Big spenders (such as Hendrix) and spendthrifts (such as Redding) do not generally get along well even without the burden of sharing the same pie. Experience management may have only considered Redding to be a hired hand receiving a weekly wage, but Redding did not. (Neither did Mitchell.) He reasoned that he'd endured the same risks as Hendrix and so should share in the Experience's spoils. In fairness to Hendrix, he concurred with his sidemen and agreed orally—that's a key point—that Experience profits were to be divided on a 50-25-25 basis.

As for Redding's aloofness, Mitch Mitchell commented in his autobiography that when he and Hendrix went out to check out other musicians and bands: "Noel never wanted to come, preferring to stay in the hotel and listen to the Small Faces." This echoes Chandler's comment. It also contrasts with what I think is the most incredible sentence in Redding's autobiography, coauthored by Carol Appleby: "That was the main difference between us. Jimi wanted to be a star. I wanted to be a musician." And yet Redding would not hang out in clubs with Mitchell and Hendrix checking out other acts or jamming, resented musicians such as Buddy Miles or Jack Casady making guest appearances at concerts or recording sessions, and refused to hang around the studio as Hendrix strove to improve on what had been recorded.

Add to this tenuous atmosphere the familiar refrain of the frustrated songwriter, and you have the beginning of the unraveling of the Experience. Redding was growing aware of the money to be made in songwriting credits and started writing songs. In interviews Hendrix said he supported the other members' creativity, but Redding's view would be—to use an unfortunate cliché—that Hendrix didn't put his money where his mouth was. Although he got his one song per album on *Axis: Bold as Love* and *Electric Ladyland* (where "Little Miss Strange" led off the second side), the bassist felt "the star" wasn't interested in developing his other songs such as "Dream" and "Walking Through the Garden."

The incredible solution was thus "hatched for each of us to form his own band and regroup twice a year for an Experience tour with our own bands serving as opening acts," Redding wrote. Noel would form Fat Mattress, Mitch would lead Mind Octopus, and Hendrix's solo group would be the Band of Gypsys (the first mention of what would become Hendrix's all-black lineup). Although Hendrix in interviews also promoted this original concert concept, privately he did not. While he spoke of expanding the Experience lineup to include an organist or horns or even another guitarist, he did not want to disband the Experience in late 1968 as press reports were hinting.

Redding, however, was insistent and blackmailed Experience management into having Fat Mattress as one of the opening acts during the 1969 American tour: he would not make the tour unless his demands were met. According to Mitchell: "I always thought that was strange, him doing that, and Jimi resented it. Fat Mattress were just OK, but essentially they were a pretty lightweight band. Hendrix used to call them Thin Pillow."

Songs Written/Influenced for/with the Experience

Another way of measuring Redding's deteriorating relationship with Hendrix are the statements Redding and others made regarding the songs he wrote while in the Experience. The palpable enthusiasm within the trio while recording "She's So Fine" contrasts with the indifference accorded later tracks such as "Walking Through the Garden" or, even worse, "Noel's Tune," an instrumental that was run through at Olympic Studios on February 26, 1969, during what was the Experience's lowest ebb as a functioning unit before the final split in June.

"She's So Fine (She's in with Time)"

In spring of 1967, the Experience did not yet have access to a wide-open expense account—that wouldn't happen until they conquered America—and feeling the financial pinch, Redding tried his hand at writing a song, which turned out to be "She's So Fine (She's in with Time)." Redding said the song that would be the third track on Side Two of *Axis: Bold as Love* was "about hippies. I had seen some bloke walking about with an alarm around his neck, attached by a bit of string." (Sounds like Public Enemy's Flavor Flav!) "He must have figured it looked very avant-garde."

Redding had brought his acoustic guitar with him to "while away the time" while hanging around the television studio for a live performance on *Top of the Pops*. "We went into the studio that night and put it down." That night was May 4, 1967. Just one of five songs that the Experience worked on that night in Olympic Studios, everyone was fully focused on recording a version of Redding's composition that he was pleased with.

The third take was the first complete take, but twenty-two followed before Chandler told the band to have a listen in the control room. The fourth retake after that was designated as the master take. The camaraderie abounds. Chandler said, "Jimi was laughing when Noel was singing." Noel finally got to play guitar on an Experience recording (if you discount the "bass" track on the original recording of "Red House"), and Jimi "thought of the G solo in the middle," Redding said, "because I couldn't think of anything. I was overwhelmed that my song was being recorded."

Redding may have done some overdubbing on September 27, 1967, at Rye Muse Studios, but to what extent, if any, is unknown because neither of the other Experience Makers were present nor was his producer. Final production was done on October 1, 1967, at Olympic Studios as it was readied for inclusion on the Experience's sophomore album. Hendrix and Mitchell contributed "funny vocals in the background" at this session.

"She's So Fine" is the Experience at their Who-iest. Listen to the "previously unreleased alternate recording" on *Noel Redding: The Experience Sessions* without vocals, and if you didn't know better, it sounds like Townshend and Moon whaling away on electric guitar and drums, not Hendrix and Mitchell.

"Dream"

Although poppier than either Beatles song, Hendrix's bass playing in "Dream" is reminiscent of Paul McCartney's in "Rain" (and other *Revolver*-era recordings), while Redding singing "I'm only dreaming" can only bring to mind John Lennon singing "I'm Only Sleeping." The fact that Hendrix is on bass indicates how little attention this droney rocker received as Redding is on record as saying Hendrix usually played bass "when I introduced a song." Even if "Hendrix really liked 'Dream,'" it didn't get past the demo stage. Redding and Hendrix recorded their parts on December 20, 1967. Overdubs were made on December 30, 1967, including Mitchell's drumming. The 4-track master was then transferred to 8-track on February 24, 1968, and that's the last that was heard of it for over sixteen years when a stereo mix was released with additional guitar overdubs on July 20, 2004, as part of *Noel Redding: The Experience Sessions*.

Its unrelease in the 1960s is a significant disappointment because it's the best song Redding wrote with the Experience, if only for the lyrics. (Redding's correct when he said: "It was a good tune with a lot of validity.") Seeing as "Dream" was initially recorded December 20, 1967, in between albums it would've made a superb B-side to the unreleased fifth Experience single. (It doesn't fit in with what would become *Electric Ladyland*.) All the song lacks is a proper finish. Even at 2:19, the forced phase-out is unsatisfying. It should end with a snap like a rude awakening.

"Dance"

Another Redding original was demoed on December 20, 1967. "Dance" was a tune Redding offered as a Mitch Mitchell vehicle when Hendrix reiterated his previous offer to have his drummer sing a song on an Experience album just as his bassist had done. Nothing much came of the effort except bitterness when Redding heard Hendrix's "Ezy Ryder." As quoted in *Ultimate Hendrix*, "The riff to 'Dance' later came out as a tune credited to Hendrix." It was not the last time. According to Redding, what he referred to as "the Booker T. riff" became the basis for the "Midnight" riff. Redding also believed he deserved compositional credit for what he contributed to "Remember" and "My Friend" as well.

"Little Miss Strange"

Redding's second and last song to see an official release was begun on July 29, 1967, when he "tried recording the roots of 'Little Miss Strange.'" "I had a cash shortage and began to see that writing was a definite help." On March 13, 1968, "Little Miss Strange" was attempted for the first time in the studio. What really is strange is despite Redding's aversion to working with musicians outside of the Experience lineup, the fifteen takes on this occasion were performed by Redding on guitar, Stephen Stills on bass, and Buddy Miles on drums while Hendrix produced and directed the session from the control room.

By the time the band got around to recording "Little Miss Strange," band members were missing sessions. The April 20, 1968, session was only attended by Redding and Mitchell, but the third take was deemed good enough for a basic track. Redding added bass to go along with the acoustic guitar and drum parts. (The song was also known as "Lilacs for Captain Curry's Coffin" at this time for unknown reasons.) Redding added an electric guitar and double-tracked vocals the following day.

Hendrix's parts were added on April 24, 1968. According to engineer Eddie Kramer: "There was always this 'wink, wink' thing with Noel's songs, but Jimi was respectful and wanted to make sure Noel approved of whatever contributions he would make." Other overdubs were completed at this session, and Redding recorded a new vocal, which was bolstered by a Mitchell vocal track as well.

"Walking Through a Garden"

On May 5, 1968, Redding dropped by the Record Plant "and no one even turned up. That's when I did 'Little Miss Strange' just to fill the time." His recollection doesn't seem accurate as final mixes had already been made on April 28, 1968. What was recorded on May 5, 1968, however, were overdubs to the final Redding composition recorded by the Experience: "Walking Through the Garden."

Little is known about this song begun on April 24, 1968, but the preserved takes are promising. The lyrics are weak but Hendrix gives Redding's song a very "1983" production, and it is not difficult to imagine this song closing out Side Three of *Electric Ladyland* had Hendrix been so inclined.

ever felt the sound of the Jimi Hendrix Experience?

February 14, 1968 the Jimi Hendrix Experience experienced the sound of Sunn.
They now use Sunn amplifiers and sound systems exclusively. **sunn** 〔◉〕

This ad for Sunn amplifiers illustrates the classic stage set-up of the Jimi Hendrix Experience. Noel Redding, one of rock's underrated bassists, is seen at the far right.   *Courtesy of Robert Rodriguez*

This similarity is also derived from the flute playing of Chris Wood of Traffic (just as he does on "1983"), Hendrix playing bass (just as he does on "1983"), and Mitchell on drums (just as he does on "1983"). The unknown pianist is possibly Steve Winwood. (This supposition comes from the fact that Winwood was Wood's bandmate in Traffic, and Traffic were also in the Record Plant at the time recording with producer Jimmy Miller of Rolling Stones production fame and Hendrix's engineer Eddie Kramer.) Redding contributed guitar, bass and vocals.

Eventually unused by the Experience, "Walking Through the Garden" was added by Redding to Fat Mattress's repertoire.

Fat Mattress

As friction increased within the Experience, both Redding and Hendrix sought solace in old friends . . . pre-Experience friends. It's possible that Hendrix in this regard was influenced by Redding, who, feeling creatively stifled within the Experience—instructed by management not to even sway onstage, not being allowed to sing any of his Experience songs even when audience members called out for them—formed Fat Mattress with friends long before Hendrix contacted former army buddy Billy Cox still living in Nashville.

And so Fat Mattress—a band that "wasn't meant to be a band at all . . . just a one-off album allowing Noel to record his own songs and get back to playing guitar"—wound up signing contracts with enormous advances ($55,000 less management and legal fees in the UK and Ireland and $120,000 before percentages were deducted overseas). These were incredible advances for a band whose debut album was not yet finished and largely due ironically to Redding: his management (Chandler again) and record company contacts were a direct result of his being a member of the Experience. It was success through an association that Redding was trying to sever.

Fat Mattress was cofounded by singer Neil Landon (a stage name: his name at birth was Pat Cahill), who had played with Redding in his pre-Experience and even pre–Loving Kind days. Bassist Jim Leverton picked up where he had left off in the Loving Kind. The Mattress (as Redding referred to his escape route from the Experience) was squared off when Englebert Humperdinck's drummer Eric Dillon was recruited by Leverton. (Jethro Tull's best lead guitarist, Martin Barre, was briefly a member.)

According to Tony Brown's *Jimi Hendrix—A Visual Documentary*, Fat Mattress's first album was recorded in a single day at Pye Studios in London for £31, a figure that would've impressed Chas Chandler who believed according to Mitchell that because "House of the Rising Sun" "had cost like four quid to make . . . had the attitude . . . there was no need to piss around in the studio wasting time and money."

The eponymously named album contained two songs ("How Can I Live?" and "Walking Through the Garden") that at the very least were demoed at Experience sessions. Incredibly—albeit probably intentionally—both tracks were consigned to close Side Two as if Redding was trying to distance their songs from their Experience origin. (Leverton's liner notes to the expanded 2009 edition omits the participation of Hendrix, who played percussion on "How Can I Live?," but does mention that "All Night Drinker" "featured Mitch Mitchell on percussion." The discography in Harry Shapiro's *Electric Gypsy* also indicates Mitchell played on "Magic Forest.")

Other Experience-related participants included Traffic's Chris Wood on flute and engineering courtesy of George Chkiantz, who often engineered the Experience's Olympic Studio sessions.

Redding's reputation plus exposure at Experience concerts ensured moderate success for Fat Mattress, which is what they achieved. "Magic Forest" may have been a Netherlands hit, but Hendrix was correct in saying the band was "thin." Listened to decades after the album's release, the songs reflect the craftsmanship of the era, but none would merit inclusion on Lenny Kaye's *Nuggets* collections. The songs are marred by unexpected time signatures and Landon's vocals. He's one of those thousands of vocalists out there who can hit all the notes and never touch an emotion.

Disputing the perception that Fat Mattress was intended as the vehicle that would allow him to escape the Experience, Redding stated that "Fat Mattress was a writing outlet for me." So it's surprising that out of the debut album's ten tracks, only two are solely credited to Redding while another four are cowritten with Landon. This is a disservice to Redding, who was the band's strongest composer, at least musically. His "Everything's Blue" is the only Fat Mattress song that is marginally interesting decades later. Everything else sounds derivative. For example, "I Don't Mind," one of Redding's compositions with Landon, sounds like one of Michael Nesmith's country-flavored rockers such as "Just Might Be the One" that make the Monkees' six albums much more listenable and rewarding than anything recorded by Fat Mattress.

After opening for the Experience at the second Royal Albert Hall gig on February 24, 1969, and throughout the Experience's spring 1969 tour of America, Fat Mattress was finally touring in December on their own in support of the debut album, when, according to Redding's autobiography, the band formed of Redding's friends ironically broke up for the same reason that the Experience, a band formed of strangers, had disbanded: Redding's repugnance of non-band members joining Fat Mattress onstage. In this case it was a sax player that Leverton and Dillon invited onstage at the New Jersey Action House.

Redding, believing Fat Mattress was his band, threatened to sack both band members only, incredibly, to be sacked himself. "Gratitude, eh?" is how Mitchell succinctly puts it in his autobiography. Hendrix-related autobiographies are a cottage industry; if you knew or worked with Hendrix and lived long enough, a book deal always awaited you, and so Redding, in his autobiography, disputes Mitchell, saying the tour was "simply cancelled, and I took the blame via a press release which said I'd had a nervous breakdown."

All things considered, Mitchell's version holds more water. Redding may not have written Fat Mattress's "All Night Drinker" but the song title describes Redding as reflected in his own interviews and that of others. Kathy Etchingham in her autobiography—see what I mean?—says Fat Mattress's manager Chas Chandler berated Redding about the detrimental affect his drinking was having on his career and advised him to take stock of his situation.

Redding must've listened because he regrouped with Fat Mattress long enough to record a second album at the behest of Chandler, although this might have been due to recordings owed the record companies that had given Fat Mattress their unheard-of advances. An appearance on German television was a success, but Redding was disenchanted with his "writing outlet" by this time and soon tossed "the Mattress" out of his life.

The Denver Pop Festival

The Rolling Stones' December 1969 Altamont Speedway Free Festival has been immortalized in the Maysles Brothers' documentary *Gimme Shelter* and lionized as "a symbol for the death of the Woodstock nation" because one man was murdered, probably in self-defense, and the crowd unruly. But the truth is that violence at rock festivals was nothing new. As Mitch Mitchell put it in his autobiography, after Monterey "the spirit had gone out of those kind of events." The events of the three-day Denver Pop Festival held the weekend of June 27, 1969, are a prime example. They are also evidence that the spirit had long gone out of the Jimi Hendrix Experience.

The two Royal Albert Hall concerts four months earlier were supposed to be the final Experience concerts, which is why they were filmed by Jerry Goldstein and Steve Gold, two filmmakers from America that Hendrix denigrated by calling them "weekend hippies." In interviews, Hendrix said the band was going to take a break—what bands nowadays call an "indefinite hiatus"—leaving each Experience Maker free to pursue other interests; a generous bit of public relations from Hendrix that allowed Redding's promotion of his side project Fat Mattress and put a band-aid over the fact that the increasingly difficult bassist had already told the British music press in 1968 that he had quit. Redding was only coaxed back into the fold for an American tour when management met his demand that Fat Mattress be an opening act.

This meant that Redding was performing as many as four sets a day now that he was playing with Fat Mattress because management often booked two Experience concerts on a single date. In describing this tour in his autobiography Redding bitches about botched rehearsals and Hendrix's behavior and Experience performances. Only the Experience shows in Los Angeles, Oakland, and, surprisingly, the show immediately following Hendrix's drug bust in Toronto are favorably commented upon, so it comes as no surprise that Redding quit when an unidentified member of the press innocently asked him what he was doing at the band's final date of the tour in Denver. Apparently Jimi Hendrix had informed *Rolling Stone's* Jerry Hopkins earlier that month that Billy Cox was Redding's replacement, and word was spreading throughout the critical community even though the article wouldn't be published until July.

The Denver Pop Festival held at Mile High Stadium was publicized as the First Annual, but subsequent events involving gatecrashers, an overzealous police force, and tear gas put the kibosh on the Second Annual ever taking place. Promoter Barry Fey's lineup wasn't as ambitious as Woodstock would be less than two months later but did include Big Mama Thornton, Three Dog Night (who performed at the Friday and Sunday shows), the Mothers of Invention (legend has it that it was at this concert that Frank Zappa invented the "audience wave"), Joe Cocker, and Johnny Winter. The headliners were Iron Butterfly (Friday), Creedence Clearwater Revival (Saturday), and the Jimi Hendrix Experience (Sunday).

The Jimi Hendrix Experience's final set opened with "Tax Free," an instrumental by Swedish musicians Bo Hansson and Janne Karlsson that was often used as the opening number during the spring 1969 tour. (Live versions dwarf the studio version both in length and performance grade.) If management was demanding that Hendrix play his hits, this set doesn't reflect that. There's no "Hey Joe," no "All Along the Watchtower"; the only single performed was "Purple Haze."

Tension was in the air. Not only had Redding quit (so Hendrix knew that for better or worse his dalliance with recruiting Billy Cox on bass was about to become a reality and the Experience a thing of the past), but the police and a ticketless crowd in the parking lot had baited each other again. The police had used tear gas the previous night on an estimated crowd of 500 gate-crashers and had no qualms about doing so again.

Hendrix, having shared acid with a friend of his named Herbert Worthington, was in a combative mood. He told the audience that it was the Experience's final concert together, flew lyrics from "Hear My Train A Comin'" into "Voodoo Child (Slight Return)," and invited the audience to get closer to the stage, something the police did not want, when, as Redding puts it in his autobiography "the crowd started to move en masse towards (the Experience.) We didn't feel too calm about it either, but kept playing, hoping it would ease up. The police had tear gas, so they used it but forgot to check the wind direction first. Of course it was blowing towards the stage."

Pandemonium ensued and the members of the Experience had to flee the stage. It had come to this: the band that nobody wanted to book less than three years earlier could be at the center of riots and police altercations involving thousands. The band's head roadie, Gerry Stickells, came to the rescue when he commandeered a van, locked the band inside it, and waded through a mass of young people, many of whom were climbing atop the van.

Redding flew back to England the following day, and the Jimi Hendrix Experience never played together again. Redding focused on Fat Mattress but jumped at the chance to rejoin the Experience for the 1970 tour of

The Jimi Hendrix Experience around the time that Noel Redding (far right) became disenchanted with his role within the band.   *Courtesy of Robert Rodriguez*

America that had been discussed in the wake of Band of Gypsys' sudden dissolution detailed in Chapter 23. Equally sudden was an interview on February 4, 1970, with *Rolling Stone* announcing the re-formation of the Experience, an interview where even the Experience-friendly interviewer, John Burks, smelled something fishy. And he was right. Both Hendrix and Mitchell had reservations about touring again with Redding, and when the

Cry of Love tour of America did begin on April 25, 1970, at the Los Angeles Forum, Redding was not on the stage, Billy Cox was. Redding's name was bandied about as a replacement for Billy Cox—as was Ric Grech's—when Cox had a bad reaction to some acid someone spiked his drink with in Stockholm in September 1970, but the decision was made to cancel the tour's remaining dates.

Post-Experience Experiences

"Around 1969 we were so overwhelmed by money and the glamour of being so-called pop stars, we all forgot we were people. We made mistakes, but if we had just done that last tour in 1970 together we would have made it again," is what Redding said to Chris Welch during the course of an interview shortly after Hendrix's death. By then Redding had seen the errors of his ways and begun to appreciate what he had taken for granted. He went through a bitter divorce, had drug problems with Mantrax as well as alcohol, picked up the bass guitar again while in Los Angeles, and formed a trio called Road with ex-Rare Earth guitarist Rod Richards and drummer Leslie Sampson. After one album, they disbanded.

Other musical pursuits also failed to bear fruit, and much of his time afterward was consumed in lawsuits with lawyers representing record companies and the Hendrix estate. As expected, Hendrix's oral agreement to split everything "50-25-25" did not hold up in a court of law. Redding eventually signed away his rights to Warner Brothers/Reprise Records for a paltry $100,000. He had been persuaded there wasn't much more money to be made from a dead man's unreleased recordings. At the time, no one, including Redding, foresaw the money that would be made from repackaging and reissuing of the Experience's music via cassettes, 8-track tapes, CDs, mp3 files, and who knows what delivery format for music is around the corner.

Redding used a portion of his settlement money to purchase a house in Ireland. He formed the Noel Redding Band, which released albums on RCA and toured Europe several times and America once. The Noel Redding Band broke up over management issues. Redding also contributed to Traffic and Thin Lizzy recording sessions and appeared with Phish in 1993.

He met Carol Appleby and formed a deep partnership with her, which included performing in pubs together and Appleby whipping Redding's autobiography into shape. *Are You Experienced—The Inside Story of the Jimi Hendrix Experience* was turned down by several publishing houses mostly because it talks too much about the business side of the music business, the very thing that makes it invaluable, especially to young people in rock 'n' roll bands. It is one of the better autobiographies to be written by someone who entered Hendrix's orbit.

Noel Redding died on May 11, 2003, not long after his mother. He was found dead in his home in Ardfield, the small village on the southwest coast of County Cork, Ireland, where he lived. His autopsy report concluded that the Experience's bassist died due to "shock haemorrhage due to oesophageal varices in reaction to cirrhosis of the liver."

At the time of his death, Redding was preparing to sue the Hendrix estate for monies owed, which he estimated to be £3.26 million. Redding's son Nicholas from his only marriage inherited a settlement of $800,000.

15

I Wanna Ride You with Sounds and Emotions

Electric Ladyland

E lectric Ladyland is Jimi Hendrix's New York City album. There's crosstown traffic and rain falling in city parks and telephones screaming. There are hot summer nights and New York drowning and houses burning in the ghetto.

(And spaceships. Can't forget the spaceships. After the thunderous drumbeats that open the album foreshadowing the rain that will fall on Sides Three and Four, if you listen closely, you can hear the spaceships. Even producer Chas Chandler referred to that whirring sound as the sound of spaceships.)

Hendrix wasn't pleased with the final cutting of the record and wondered to music journalist Meatball Fulton how unimaginative recording engineers could take "such a beautiful sound" and "screw it up so bad." Explicit instructions on the cutting of *Electric Ladyland* were ignored. It was if they could not adhere to psychologist J. J. Gordon's maxim to "Trust things that are alien, and alienate things that are trusted."

Four decades after its release, *Electric Ladyland* with its sound modulation and elephantine blues and definitive cover tunes and sonic seascapes is still revolutionary, still sounds ahead of the times, but Hendrix was frustrated by the product the public was listening to. He envisioned "stereo where it goes . . . up . . . and behind and underneath . . . 'Cause all you can get now is just across and across . . . ."

Produced and Directed by Jimi Hendrix

Electric Ladyland is a Jimi Hendrix Experience album in name only. In this respect the gatefold sleeve for Track Records' No. 613 008/9 released on

October 25, 1968, got it right: the Experience is not photographed together. Instead, each sideman's much slighter portraits is below a huge photo of Hendrix (that was later used as a cover for *Experience Hendrix: The Best of Jimi Hendrix*, a 1998 release that is the greatest of the Jimi Hendrix greatest hit packages). After October 1968, the Experience was a band in terms and conditions of concert contracts only and largely because of the trials and tribulations of the *Electric Ladyland* sessions.

That *Electric Ladyland* is a Jimi Hendrix album is clear from the liner notes that claim the double album was "Produced and Directed by Jimi Hendrix." Masterfully plotted like an epic novel, themes and melodies appear and sink before bubbling to the surface again. The spaceship landing backdrop of " . . . And the Gods Made Love" is eerily similar to "Moon, Turn the Tides . . . Gently, Gently Away." The wah-wah solo that fades out "Rainy Day, Dream Away" opens "Still Raining, Still Dreaming." The riders in "Gypsy Eyes" and "House Burning Down" could be the same riders who appear in Hendrix's iconic take on Dylan's "All Along the Watchtower."

Chas Chandler's Contributions and Departure

The reasoning behind Jimi Hendrix's failure to give Chas Chandler his due for his contributions to *Electric Ladyland* has never been explained, nor does it appear to have been questioned during the artist's life. Shortly after Hendrix's death, Chandler told British journalist Chris Welch that he left the sessions because "there was a dreadful atmosphere in the studio, which was full of hangers-on. We did six tracks for the *Electric Ladyland* album and nobody was ready to compromise anymore. All I was doing was sitting there collecting a percentage. So I said, 'Let's call it a day.'"

Hendrix's New York City album was begun in Olympic Studios in London on December 20, 1967, a mere nineteen days after *Axis: Bold as Love* was issued on Track Records (No. 613 003). "Crosstown Traffic" was one of the "six" tracks that Chandler can be said to have produced, not Hendrix, at least initially. (The final approved mix can be credited to Hendrix.) Four that were begun in London prior to the sixty-six-date, two-month tour of America were:

1. "Burning of the Midnight Lamp"
2. " . . . And the Gods Made Love" (originally titled "At Last the Beginning")
3. "All Along the Watchtower"
4. "Tax Free" (unissued as part of *Electric Ladyland*)

Chandler-led sessions resumed at the Record Plant in New York City on April 18, 1968. Songs Chandler produced in New York City include:

1. "Long Hot Summer Night"
2. "Little Miss Strange"
3. "South Saturn Delta" (unissued as part of *Electric Ladyland*)
4. "Three Little Bears" (unissued as part of *Electric Ladyland*)
5. "1983 . . . (A Merman I Should Turn to Be)"
6. "Gypsy Eyes"
7. "Tax Free" (an entirely different version and also unissued as part of *Electric Ladyland*)
8. "House Burning Down"
9. "Voodoo Child (Slight Return)"

So when Chas Chandler removed himself from the helm of the third Jimi Hendrix Experience album on May 8, 1968, you can see he had been present for the production of nine, not six, of the album's sixteen tracks. The liner notes of the 2010 reissue still do not recognize the true extent of Chandler's contributions.

Jimi Hendrix, Bassist

Chandler left for many of the same reasons why Noel Redding is often in absentia on *Electric Ladyland*. Chandler even advised Redding to quit the Experience as he was walking out the door and catching a (likely) BOAC flight back to Britain. As the manager who had signed and nurtured Hendrix, you could say Chandler was the fourth member of the Experience, and his absence would be a death blow not only to the band but literally to Hendrix. It is easy to imagine a scenario where Hendrix would not have died in London in September 1970 if only Chandler had not left due to exhaustion and frustration, the same frustration that Redding felt.

If you accept Chandler as the fourth member, then the Experience had splintered into two camps by 1968 in terms of how studio sessions should be managed. And attended. By the time sessions resumed at the Record Plant, Hendrix was a bona fide star in his home country and was surrounded by a large entourage led by Devon Wilson that felt recording studios were just another place to party.

Chandler and Redding were dismayed at how these "friends" of Hendrix's cluttered the studio and prolonged the proceedings with drug-addled distractions. Redding complains in his autobiography that one of Hendrix's hangers-on had the audacity to question whether Redding had any right to be present at the session. He certainly had. He was, after all, only the band's bassist.

But in name only because Hendrix had taken to erasing Redding's basslines and replacing them with his own with alarming regularity. There are several reasons for Hendrix doing this, and some have to be laid at Redding's fingertips. Redding wasn't interested in acquiring a "studio tan" (as Frank Zappa named one of his instrumental albums from the 1970s). This is why you can hear Hendrix playing bass on several tracks on Noel Redding's favorite Experience album *Axis: Bold as Love*. Not only does Hendrix play on the title track, "Spanish Castle Magic" features him playing an 8-string Hagstrom bass through Roger Mayer's Octavia to individualize the bass sound.

An ideal example of this failure to communicate between the Experience Makers—to use a catchphrase of the era popularized in *Cool Hand Luke* starring Paul Newman—is the version of Bob Dylan's "All Along the Watchtower" that would go on to be Hendrix's biggest hit in America. Hendrix had long planned on the inclusion of one of Dylan's skeletal recordings from the recently released *John Wesley Harding* on the third Jimi Hendrix Experience album and on January 21, 1968, with the Rolling Stones' Brian Jones and Traffic's Dave Mason in the studio, he made his virgin attempt.

That there were an unknown number of rehearsal run-throughs before the twenty-four takes committed to tape must've been trying for Redding, who had words with Hendrix and retreated to a pub long before the final take. Guitarist Dave Mason was no slouch on bass guitar, and so he played bass on some takes.

Near the end of the session, Hendrix, who was very comfortable playing right-handed electric and bass guitars, picked up a bass guitar that Rolling Stone Bill Wyman had given Glyn Johns—then a house producer at Olympic Studios—and overdubbed the bassline that one hears in the final mix that was completed the following evening. And so the recording that was mixed the following evening and issued as the centerpiece of Side Four of *Electric Ladyland* does not have Experience bassist Noel Redding playing bass on it.

This work habit of Hendrix carrying on in the absence of the Experience's bassist led to Hendrix playing bass on five other tracks on *Electric Ladyland*, including, in album order:

1. "Have You Ever Been (to Electric Ladyland)"
2. "Long Hot Summer Night"
3. "Gypsy Eyes"
4. "1983 . . . (A Merman I Should Turn to Be)"
5. "House Burning Down."

Side A: 1. And the Gods made love/ 2. Electric Ladyland/ 3. Crosstown traffic/ 4. Voodoo Chile
Side B: 1. Little Miss Strange/ 2. Long Hot Summer Night/
3. Come on/ 4. Gipsy eyes/ 5. Burning of the Midnight Lamp
Side C: 1. Rainy day, dream away/ 2. 1983 (A Merman I should turn to be)
3. Moon, turn the tides . . . gently gently away
Side D: 1. Still Raining Still Dreaming/ 2. House burning down/ 3. All along the Watchtower/
4. Voodoo Chile (slight return)
Produced and directed by Jimi Hendrix
Photographs by David Montgomery. Cover by David King

The inner artwork for *Electric Ladyland* clearly illustrates how management viewed the contributions of Noel Redding and Mitch Mitchell.   *Author's collection*

This means that Redding does not play the most famous bass solo in the Experience canon. This bass solo, actually a lead, begins at the 9:40 mark during "1983 . . . (A Merman I Should Turn to Be)." Played through a delay effect, this lead is based on dyads; two-note chords can clearly be heard. As was reported in issue #21 of *UniVibes* (February 1996), "it is a simple motif brought alive by Jimi's rhythmic playing." It is also a mournful passage that signals the end of the long, controversial instrumental interlude and opens onto the song's closing verses where Atlantis is full of cheer.

That Hendrix should be so adept at bass guitar came as no surprise to his contemporaries. He often played bass during late-night jam sessions at clubs worldwide with performers Georgie Fame (Mitch Mitchell's former band leader!), Ben E. King, Jeff Beck, and others. There are even a few surviving studio recordings, including many with Curtis Knight and a Robert Wyatt demo called "Slow Walkin' Talk."

The most extended studio example of Hendrix's bass playing to be found is "Live and Let Live" on Side One of Timothy Leary's 1970 album *You Can Be Anyone This Time Around*. In addition to Hendrix, this track clocking in at 14:12 features Stephen Stills on guitar, John Sebastian on harmonica, and Buddy Miles on drums and was later adorned with Leary talking about things like marijuana. It is a jam on Joni Mitchell's "Woodstock," which she had just written. Stills also played organ on the second of the day's five takes.

The recording stemmed from a jam session at the Record Plant on September 30, 1969, that Hendrix turned up at. Of particular relevance to the Hendrix history, it was the first session overseen by producer Alan Douglas that Hendrix attended. When he heard that Stills was participating on guitar, Hendrix offered to play bass, and once again he had to resort to using a right-handed bass. No one ever expected the session to be used for anything, and when the album was released, no credit was given to the musicians.

That Jimi Hendrix was a more than competent bassist is also reflected in the recognition given to him posthumously by other bassists. There is, of course, the Jimi Hendrix tattoo on Flea's left bicep. But long before the Red Hot Chili Peppers' bassist hit the scene, Weather Report's Jaco Pastorius played a medley of "Purple Haze" and "3rd Stone from the Sun" in concert. Other bassists who have acknowledged Hendrix include Stanley Clarke, Michael Manning, Paul McCartney, Phil Lynott, even Jim Lee of Slade, the band that Chas Chandler managed after selling his stake in the Jimi Hendrix Experience.

Jeannette Jacobs

It's odd that Jeanette Jacobs has been airbrushed out of Jimi Hendrix's biography. Yet she's the voice heard asking "The bar's closed?" at the end of "Voodoo Chile," is rumored to have sung backing vocals on select *Electric Ladyland* tracks (not so far-fetched considering she was a member of the 1960s girl group the Cake before touring with Dr. John and joining Ginger Baker's Air Force), and claimed in an interview with British music journalist Chris Welch to be one of the four women Jimi Hendrix loved.

There is some evidence of this close relationship. She was photographed with Hendrix flashing a peace sign following his acquittal for drug possession in Toronto on December 10, 1969; accompanied him on tours; witnessed firsthand his excitement at having nailed the Curtis Mayfield-like vocals on "Have You Ever Been (to Electric Ladyland)"; and she said he was jumping around while listening to Eddie Kramer play the track back and saying "I can sing, I can sing!"

Jacobs saw Hendrix the day before his death and suffered a nervous breakdown soon after. Befitting one of Hendrix's lovers, her early death at age thirty-two is surrounded by mystery. Rumors say it was a drug overdose that did her in, but in all likelihood it was an epileptic fit on January 1, 1982.

Signature Tracks

Selecting standout tracks on *Electric Ladyland* is an impossibility. Every track stands out. Even "Burning of the Midnight Lamp" has been unfairly maligned. I agree with Chris Welch, who wrote that the Experience's fourth single has ". . . a variety of sounds and feeling of grandeur that would have done credit to Phil Spector." The following then lists *Electric Ladyland*'s signature tracks, those that give the album its character.

". . . And the Gods Made Love"

". . . And it starts with a ninety-second sound painting of the heavens. I know it's the thing people will jump on to criticize so we're putting it right at the beginning to get it over with. I don't say it's great, but it's the Experience." This is how Jimi Hendrix described *Electric Ladyland*'s opening track to *Melody Maker*'s Alan Walsh.

So many of the studio techniques used to create " . . . And the Gods Made Love"—panning, tape loops, modulated voices—were so uncommon in 1968 that *Rolling Stone* in its album review had to go to the trouble of educating the reading public. Phasing was so rare then that the reviewer referenced the Small Faces' hit single "Itchycoo Park" to find common ground on which to discuss the track.

It's an ominous track that nurtured the likes of Chrome and the Butthole Surfers—it's hard to imagine "Jimi" from *Hairway to Steven* without it—so it is disappointing to learn what Hendrix's slowed-down voice is actually saying is: "for a second . . . yeah something like that . . . OK one more time . . . ."

"Voodoo Chile"

Tony Glover's *Rolling Stone* review of *Electric Ladyland* rightly characterizes "Voodoo Chile" as (mostly) "a live cut, which sounds as though it was recorded late at night in a small club, at one of the jamming sessions Hendrix is known for." It is not the put-down that John Perry in his 33 1/3 exploration of *Electric Ladyland* makes it out to be. Glover instead mentions the participating guest musicians (Steve Winwood on organ and Jack Casady on bass) and identifies the traces of John Lee Hooker and Muddy Waters that can be found in the Experience's longest studio track. Because it is a studio track. The audience applause, the plea from someone to "Turn that damn guitar down!" when Hendrix's feedback cuts a little too close, the concluding chatter were all tacked on to the third take to simulate a live setting.

Jimi Hendrix recorded so often at the Record Plant that the recording studio featured the Experience in an advertisement. *Author's collection*

"Voodoo Chile" is an outgrowth of the Experience playing Muddy Waters's "Catfish Blues" in concert and on BBC Radio broadcasts. By the time of the late winter, early spring tour of America in 1968, the performance had morphed into a medley as Waters's "Two Trains Running" was also played, although it's difficult to notice a difference other than in the lyrics. The best readily available version of this arrangement can be found on *Paris 1967/San Francisco 1968*. It can also be found on a five-track bonus disc that was issued with the 2011 *Winterland* box set. (Some bootlegs give "Experiencing the Blues" as a title for this medley because that's what Hendrix called it.) And just as B. B. King's "Rock Me, Baby" was the impetus for "Lover Man," this live arrangement spawned "Voodoo Chile," which Hendrix demoed in his hotel room in April 1968.

Keith Chadwick in *Jimi Hendrix: Musician* is on the money when he points out that while the instrument lineup in "Voodoo Chile" (electric guitar, organ, bass, and drums) was identical to that of Blind Faith that Winwood played in with Eric Clapton, the result was vastly different. Ironically, it is Blind Faith's debut album that sounds like jams and not "Voodoo Chile." This was due partly to the fact that Mitchell and Hendrix knew this arrangement inside out, knew where the spaces were for jamming, knew where Mitchell would solo, which is important as "Voodoo Chile" features one of Mitchell's best studio solos.

Take 1 was used to sketch out the song's structure to Winwood and Casady, who thought he was just in the studio for a jam. Take 2 was not used because a broken string hampered Hendrix's performance, and Winwood even remembers Hendrix changing the string himself in the studio. (These two takes were later edited—with a snippet of Take 3—to create the track "Voodoo Chile Blues" that appears on 1993's *Blues*.) Take 2 did not immediately stop with the broken string but became another opportunity for Winwood and Casady to familiarize themselves with the arrangement, and if you get a chance to hear it, Casady's bass is much more prominent than in the final mix. Take 3 became the master take.

When you read the lyrics of "Voodoo Chile," they don't add up to much—one of Hendrix's weakest actually on the album—but you don't notice because the verses are separated by dueling organ and guitar and drum interludes. (Although thematically "Voodoo Chile" is important as it introduces many images found elsewhere on *Electric Ladyland*. For example, the fire-red moon hints at the fire-red night in "House Burning Down"; when Hendrix mentions the frowning portrait in "The Burning of the Midnight Lamp," you remember he's "right here in your picture frame" in "Voodoo Chile.")

"Voodoo Chile" was one my rediscoveries while writing this book. Over the years, posthumous live recordings of "Red House" and "Hear My Train A Comin'" had become my preferred blues numbers from the Experience Maker and "Voodoo Chile" had no chance to compete because after its recording, it was never played again, probably because of Steve Winwood's significant contributions to the track. Winwood's is a superior performance drawn out by the caliber of the musicians he is playing with. It is disappointing therefore, that Winwood never played on a regular basis with Hendrix and Mitchell as both would've liked to.

This then is the best way to listen to "Voodoo Chile": this is the Jimi Hendrix Experience reimagined with an organist in the lineup. Winwood's playing is distinctly British—he reminds you of Led Zeppelin's John Paul Jones and Deep Purple's Jon Lord at times—so he would've meshed perfectly with the Experience's rhythm section. The only other examples of this would be the TTG Studios version of "Red House" with Lee Michaels (but Buddy Miles is present) and Herbie Rich's performances at Winterland at the late show on October 11, 2012, but his contributions are mixed down.

"Come On (Part 1)"

In the Experience oeuvre, "Come On (Part 1)" is comparable to Dali's *Figure at a Window* in the Spanish artist's oeuvre. This painting of Dali's sister demonstrates his command of what the average person considers to be a good painting: it represents the subject realistically. The same can be said for the Experience's version of Earl King's "Come On (Part 1)." Noel Redding may have dismissed the recording as "just a jam in E," but for others who previously considered Hendrix nothing more than a mere sonic trickster, it proved he could let the good old rock 'n' roll roll. The only other comparable song in Hendrix's catalog is the live version of Chuck Berry's "Johnny B. Goode" on *Hendrix in the West* that was recorded at the Berkeley Community Theatre featuring the Cry of Love band, not the Experience.

Plumb in the center of Side Two's five tracks, "Come On (Part 1)" draws on Hendrix's many years on the chitlin' circuit as a sideman. Earl King was a New Orleans–based rhythm and bluesman whose hero was Guitar Slim, whose own "Things I Used to Do" was also covered by Jimi Hendrix during jam sessions, a copy of which can be found on *Lifelines* with Johnny Winter on rhythm guitar.

King first recorded the song for an Ace Records subsidiary in 1960 as "Darling Honey Angel Child" and then rerecorded it with new lyrics and title the same year for Imperial Records, which released it on both sides of a 45, a common practice for rhythm and blues labels. This explains the "Part 1" in the song's title. King's song is also commonly known as "Let the Good Times Roll."

The Experience session for "Come On (Part 1)" was held on August 27, 1968. It was the last song recorded for *Electric Ladyland* and only because another track was needed to ensure that all four sides of the double album would be comparable in length. There were fourteen takes, and it was recorded live in the studio with little concern for studio manners. It is a guitar workout extraordinaire and one of the few tracks from the Experience's double album to be played live.

"Gypsy Eyes"

This is the track that broke Chas Chandler's back. Forty-one takes by the Experience sans Redding on April 29, 1968, failed to yield a master basic track. Mitchell on occasion could be rhythmically challenged (this is why a studio version of "Like a Rolling Stone" was never completed), but on this occasion Hendrix also had difficulty. Not that this hampered Hendrix's fun at being in the studio as he asked his drummer if he had "ever done this many tracks before." Chandler, on the other hand, sat in the recording booth wondering what was going on. He would tender his resignation within the week.

It's a shame that such a rhythmically joyful song was the result of so much friction. Phased drumbeats are joined by Hendrix's rhythm guitar with its hints of the "chika chika" rhythm from "Voodoo Child (Slight Return)" (and innumerable Johnny Cash recordings). Hendrix's vocal then begins as he uses his guitar lead to mirror his voice, a favored mannerism that can also be heard at the beginning of "Voodoo Chile" and live versions of "Rock Me. Baby" and "Red House." Hendrix's bass track jumps in on the second verse. Lyrically, this is one of Hendrix's songs about his idealized mother. Symbolically it ties in with the jacket Hendrix is wearing on the back of the American cover.

"Rainy Day, Dream Away" and "Still Raining, Still Dreaming"

The two tracks that open Sides 3 and 4 of the double album are actually from the same performance recorded on June 10, 1968. It was strategically spliced during mixing sessions by Hendrix and Kramer to create two separate tracks. By strategic I mean that it occurs just as Hendrix takes his peak wah-wah solo, which must be an overdub. It's too perfect. On "Rainy Day, Dream Away" the wah-wah solo functions as an ideal fade-out—comparable only to Eric Clapton's wah-wah solo on Cream's "White Room"—and then— as an unexpected treat, this same solo is used to introduce "Still Raining, Still Dreaming." Only this time you get to hear the continuation of what was faded out. A master stroke!

The remixed tracks are unique in that Mitchell is not present, possibly because Hendrix knew exactly what type of sound he was reaching for. He told organist Mike Finnigan—recruited by producer Tom Wilson for the session—that he'd be Kenny Burrell to Finnigan's Jimmy Smith because Hendrix was trying to duplicate Smith's early 1960s recordings. Hendrix wasn't even playing through his typical Marshall stacks but instead, according to Finnigan, was using a Fender Showman amplifier.

Finnigan was joined by Larry Faucette on percussion, Freddie Smith on saxophone and Buddy Miles on drums, making this the Band of Gypsys drummer's first session with Hendrix to make it to vinyl. Miles's fatback drumming is such a contrast to Mitchell that one can hear why Hendrix could entertain the idea of playing with him on a more regular basis.

The third verse with its "wet creatures" and "carnival traffic" and "ducks" is so Central Park to me that I find it difficult to believe Hendrix wrote them in the back seat of a car when bad weather forced the Experience's second performance at the 1968 Miami Pop Festival to be cancelled. This concise verse is Hendrix the lyricist at his best.

"1983 . . . (A Merman I Should Turn to Be)"

The finer points of this lyrical epic are discussed in Chapter 10, so let's focus on the music here since Hendrix did refer to the completed piece—the Experience's second longest—as a "sound painting." While the song was not as controversial as " . . . And the Gods Made Love," some critics have objected to the lengthy musical interlude as reeking of self-indulgence. The aforementioned Tony Glover review even went so far as to say Hendrix had created " . . . a beautiful undersea mood — only to destroy it with some heavy handed guitar. My first reaction was, why did he have to do that? Then I thought that he created a beautiful thing, but lost faith it, and so destroyed it before anybody else could — in several ways, a bummer."

I first read that review in the 1970s, and that perception still strikes me as so wrong. I'll give it its due as I've never forgotten the review, but only because I didn't agree with Glover. Without *Electric Ladyland*'s "sound painting," we'd never have Side One of Santana's *Abraxas* or "He Loved Him Madly," Miles Davis's melancholy tribute to Duke Ellington on *Get Up with It*.

Similar to John Lennon's "A Day in the Life," the vocals on the demo versions Hendrix recorded in his room at the Drake Hotel in March 1968 already have nailed the lyrics. The mood cannot be improved upon, so it is the instrumentation that had to be worked on. The basic track was recorded on April 22, 1968, with Hendrix on guitar, bass, and percussion; Mitchell on drums; and Traffic's Chris Wood on flute. Overdubs and mixing were done on May 8, 1968, and June 10, 1968.

Jimi wrote the lyrics for "Rainy Day, Dream Away" at the very wet Miami Pop Festival.

Author's collection

"Voodoo Child (Slight Return)"

Electric Ladyland's closing track is Exhibit A that Jimi Hendrix's preferred method of endless retakes was a creative cul-de-sac and that Chandler's production approach served the guitarist far better. Ranked as #101 in *Rolling Stone*'s list of 500 greatest songs of all time, this song was the result of a jam for a television crew and recorded and completed in one day except for the final mix. (The guitar solo was also ranked as #11 in *Guitar World*.)

This is not to say there weren't many takes—twenty in all—but Chandler didn't object to multiple takes on other songs such as "Can You See Me" from 1966 so long as the takes served a purpose. "Voodoo Child (Slight Return)" was the Experience's attempt to record a new song in front of a television crew from ABC-TV, an attempt that had far greater success than when the Beatles tried to do the same with *Let It Be*. Hendrix drew on the framework of "Voodoo Chile" recorded that same morning.

According to Hendrix, the camera crew asked the Experience to make it appear that they were working on a song, Hendrix told Redding to play in E, and the rest is a vital part of the Hendrixian canon and a fitting closer to *Electric Ladyland* with Hendrix interjecting "Let me say this last thing" before singing the album's final verse about not being late when we meet him in the next world . . . chilling words given that this was the last studio-album track released during his lifetime.

Cover Art Controversy

Album cover art rarely changes over time. (I hesitate to use the word "rarely," but the MCA reissue of the Jimi Hendrix Experience's *Are You Experienced* in 1997 is actually one of the rare instances.) Even when new formats such as 8-track, cassettes, and compact discs are brought to market, an album's original cover art is used for the new product. This art is also used to sell other items such as posters and clothing and items you'd never dream of. A quick click onto the Experience Hendrix website offers you the American version of the *Electric Ladyland* cover as a collector tin, guitar picks, keychain, magnet, even air freshener! So for recording artists and their legacy, it is important to get the cover art they can look at for the rest of their lives.

Jimi Hendrix, however, was more often than not unhappy with the way his music was packaged. He thought Bruce Fleming's cover art for the British version of *Are You Experienced* made him look like a "fairy." He thought the *Axis: Bold as Love* portrayed him as the wrong kind of Indian.

THE JIMI HENDRIX EXPERIENCE ELECTRIC LADY LAND

Although Jimi Hendrix hated the cover that Track Records selected for the British edition of *Electric Ladyland*, it is a fan favorite.   *Courtesy of Robert Rodriguez*

He was aghast at the naked ladies that adorned the British version of *Electric Ladyland* and immediately distanced himself from Track Records' artwork.

On stationary from the Cosmopolitan, a hotel he was staying at in Denver, Colorado, Hendrix went so far as to write Warner Brothers' art department in America in hopes of having some control over the double album's artwork. But while they did use, for the American version, the recommended photos taken by Linda Eastman (later to be Linda McCartney) and a trippy note to the "Room Full of Mirrors" penned by Hendrix, they ignored Hendrix's request that a shot of the Experience sitting atop Central Park's Alice in Wonderland statue surrounded by children be used for the cover.

While some have wondered why Hendrix's estate Experience Hendrix has not reissued *Electric Ladyland* with the cover Jimi wanted, it has at least been included it in the CD's booklet, and the 2010 edition (with a bonus DVD) includes it in the CD sleeve. While I usually side with an artist's wishes, in this case I think the Warner Brothers art department was right in using Karl Ferris's fiery headshot of Jimi. The central park shots by Linda McCartney are sweet but too subdued for the music contained within the borders of *Electric Ladyland*.

16

You Say You Want Me to Take You for a Drive

Original Rock Composers

n *Rock and Other Four Letter Words*, a book written by J. Marks and Linda Eastman and published by Bantam Books in 1968, Frank Zappa is quoted as saying about rock music that: "If you want to come up with a singular, most important trend in this new music, I think it has to be something like: it is original, composed by the people who perform it, created by them even if they have to fight the record companies to do it."

When you look back over the heyday of rock music, there are truly few American musicians who changed the course of the rock art form in the 1960s. Apart from Jimi Hendrix, there's Bob Dylan, Lou Reed, Frank Zappa, Sly Stone, and Miles Davis. (I admit it: beginning with 1969's *In a Silent Way*, Miles played rock, not jazz.) These musicians performed original music they composed because nobody else could and often fought their record companies to ensure it was properly heard. Of these musicians all intersected with Jimi Hendrix except for Lou Reed, who, like a dark star, is an entity unto his own.

Bob Dylan

The *New York Times* called Jimi Hendrix "the black Elvis," but what he really aspired to be was the black Dylan. He even traveled with a copy of the *Blonde on Blonde* songbook so he could study Dylan's lyrics. "Dylan was his all time favorite," said Kathy Etchingham, "as far as lyrics were concerned." This view was seconded by Paul Caruso, who said, "That's one of the reasons he got into Dylan, because it was very literate rock and roll."

Bob Dylan was the only contemporary Jimi Hendrix appears to have been in awe of. He knew he was a better blues guitarist than Eric Clapton.

Thought he could play "Sgt. Pepper's Lonely Hearts Club Band" better than the Beatles. But Dylan? Bob Dylan was his mentor. By the time Hendrix had flown into London, he had been buying Dylan's records for long time . . . and in the first week of release, too.

The earliest Dylan he is known to have owned is *The Freewheelin' Bob Dylan*. He even asked for a DJ to play "Blowin' in the Wind" in a Harlem club with a less than pleasant result. In a *UniVibes* interview, "King George" Clemons, a vocalist who played in rhythm and blues bands in Harlem and later crossed paths with Hendrix in Sweden, said that "to many blacks back then Dylan sounded like a hillbilly, a redneck. And Jimi didn't care about this, so he played that record. So this guy told him, 'I'm gonna cut your throat.' So I said, 'Stop! We take the record off.' And I took Jimi into this other room, and I said, 'Why are you doing that? You know there is gonna be trouble about that.' He said 'These people in Harlem have to learn. They can't go around like this without knowing what's going on.'"

In 1965, Hendrix spent his last pennies on *Highway 61 Revisited*, then Bob Dylan's latest album. Fayne Pridgeon, his girlfriend at the time, wasn't too happy about it but admitted in *A Film About Jimi Hendrix* that "he just loved it to death." On August 8, 1966, Hendrix wrote his father a letter saying he knew he was going to be successful because "nowadays people don't want you to sing good. They want you to sing sloppy and have a good beat to your songs. That's what angle I'm going to shoot for. That's where the money is." He learned that from listening to Bob Dylan.

Hendrix is quoted in *Becoming Jimi Hendrix* that "when I first heard (Dylan) I thought, 'You must admire the guy for having that nerve to sing out of key.' But then I started listening to the words. He is giving me inspiration. Not that I want to sound like him. I just wanted to sound like Jimi Hendrix." But hearing Dylan, he knew they were both trying to strike the same chord. There was a bit of Dylan in him. And wanting to reach that union with Dylan, he started to look a little like him, too. You can even attribute Hendrix's hairstyle circa 1967 to Dylan's circa 1965-1966.

It was around this time that Hendrix and Dylan actually crossed paths. In a *Rolling Stone* interview from November 1969, he told Sheila Weller as they listened to *John Wesley Harding*: "I love Dylan. I only met him once, about three years ago, back at The Kettle of Fish [a folk-rock era hangout] on MacDougal Street. That was before I went to England. I think both of us were pretty drunk at the time, so he probably doesn't remember it."

In 1966, on the night he first hung out with Linda Keith, they spent some of it listening to *Blonde on Blonde*, then Bob Dylan's latest album. Hendrix was already playing "Like a Rolling Stone" with his Blue Flames and would make it part of early Experience sets, culminating in the definitive Monterey version. (Definitive because several studio attempts were undermined by drummer Mitch Mitchell's inability to master the song's carousel time, and the live version mentioned by Chas Chandler as being readied for a live 1967 EP has never surfaced.) The Experience also recorded Dylan's 1965 single "Can You Please Crawl out Your Window?" for a BBC radio broadcast and occasionally played it in concert in late 1967 and the first half of 1968.

In January 1968, as Hendrix was beginning work on what would become *Electric Ladyland*, he had a copy of *John Wesley Harding*, then Bob Dylan's latest album. It appears to have been given to him by his publicist Michael Goldstein, who also worked for Albert Grossman, Bob Dylan's manager. According to one story, Grossman was so concerned about how unrock *John Wesley Harding* was that maybe if Jimi Hendrix recorded something from it, it would give a stamp of approval to rock fans. If that's true, Grossman's hopes were more fully realized than he ever could have hoped.

So impressed was Hendrix with the austere album that he was determined to include a song from it on his next album. Initially he wanted to do "I Dreamed I Saw St. Augustine," but Kathy Etchingham talked him out of it, saying it was "too personal to Dylan." He then settled on recording "All Along the Watchtower." Sessions began in London on January 21, 1968, with Brian Jones and Dave Mason fleshing out the Experience and then continued in New York City between April and July as Hendrix constantly revisited the guitar solos because he felt they could be a little bit better. (He also completely erased the bass work of Noel Redding and Dave Mason and laid down his own bass track.) It wasn't until July 3, 1968, that Hendrix finally stopped tinkering with "All Along the Watchtower." On this date he was unable to mix the song to his satisfaction and decided that a previous mix by Eddie Kramer would have to do.

It did well enough. Jimi Hendrix's version of "All Along the Watchtower" was his only Top 40 hit in America, and since his death it has been named the greatest cover of all time by *Total Guitar* in 2000. And that guitar solo he labored over for months on end? *Guitar World* gave it the fifth spot on their list of 100 Greatest Guitar Solos.

Hendrix's rendition would also affect the song's composer. Dylan told the Fort Lauderdale *Sun Sentinel* in 1995 that "it overwhelmed me, really. He had such talent, he could find things inside a song and vigorously develop them. He found things that other people wouldn't think of finding in there. He probably improved upon it by the spaces he was using. I took license with the song from his version, actually, and continue to do it to this day."

Just as Hendrix continued recording Dylan's compositions. Over two years later he recorded a version of "Drifter's Escape," also from *John Wesley*

Harding. He planned on including it on a double album he was working on at the time of his death.

And on the 2011 box set *West Coast Seattle Boy*, a sixth song associated with Bob Dylan would surface. Written by Dylan and the Band's Richard Manuel, the box set contains a hotel recording of "Tears of Rage" that first surfaced on the legendary *Music from Big Pink* in 1968 and seven years later on Dylan's *The Basement Tapes*.

By the way, Dylan is rumored to have recorded a studio version of "Hey Joe" in January 1992, although it has never been released. He definitely played the Billy Roberts composition that is as identified with Hendrix as is "All Along the Watchtower" on July 12, 1992, in Juan-les-Pins, France. But despite the fact that he opened his set with "Hey Joe," Dylan is not known to have ever played it again.

Frank Zappa

Just as the Butthole Surfers' Paul Leary and Minutemen's D. Boon were the stellar guitarists of the "Our Band Could Be Your Life" era, so too were Jimi Hendrix and Frank Zappa, the stellar guitarists of the hippie era. Embraced by the hippie community that both musicians were suspicious of, these West Coast guitarists—Hendrix, Seattle; Zappa, LA—brandished feedback as a musical tool and were masters of the wah-wah guitar (check out Zappa's "Willie the Pimp" on the Mothers of Invention's *Fillmore East—June 1971* for proof).

It was in fact Zappa who turned Hendrix on to the wah-wah pedal. It was Zappa who told Steve Rosen in *Guitar Player*: "I think I was one of the first people to use (one), I'd never even heard of Jimi Hendrix at the time I bought mine." Hendrix and Zappa met during the Mothers' infamous six-month residency at the Garrick Theatre in Greenwich Village. Noel Redding accompanied Hendrix to the theater on July 7, 1967.

Zappa said of the meeting that "Hendrix came over and sat in with us . . . and was using all the stuff we had on stage." Hendrix was allegedly so fascinated by Zappa's use of the foot controlled wah-wah pedal that Hendrix used the same type of pedal that same night during the Mayfair Studios sessions for "Burning of the Midnight Lamp." (Hendrix had previously used a hand-operated model.) And during "The Stars That Play with Laughing Sam's Dice" recording sessions a few weeks later, Zappa was in attendance. Who knows, Zappa's voice might be among those on the Milky Way Express.

Zappa also attended an Experience performance at Café Au Go Go on July 21, 1967. Of this experience Zappa said "the very first time I saw (Hendrix) I had the incredible misfortune to be sitting close . . . . I was

That really is Jimi Hendrix standing next to Gail Zappa on the cover of the Mothers of Invention's *We're Only in It for the Money*, Frank Zappa's best album.

Courtesy of Robert Rodriguez

physically ill. It was so packed I couldn't escape. And, although it was great, I didn't see how anybody could inflict that kind of volume on himself, let alone other people."

Zappa revisited this aspect of Hendrix's live performances in *Life*: "The sound of his music is extremely symbolic: orgasmic grunts, tortured squeals, lascivious moans, electric disasters and innumerable other audial curiosities are delivered to the sense mechanisms of the audience at an extremely high decibel level. In a live performance environment, it is impossible to merely listen to what Hendrix does . . . it eats you alive."

Zappa paid homage to Hendrix in 1967 by playing "Hey Joe" in concert, and "Flower Punk" on the Mothers of Invention's masterpiece *We're Only in It for the Money* is a parody of the same song (so maybe it wasn't a homage). Speaking of *We're Only in It for the Money*, that is Jimi Hendrix and not a cut-out on the intended cover of *We're Only in It for the Money*, itself a parody of art work for the Beatles' *Sgt. Pepper's Lonely Hearts Club Band*. Just as the Beatles had surrounded themselves on the cover, so too did Frank Zappa, and so Jimi Hendrix was invited to the photo shoot for the cover. The cover was shot in New York City on July 18, 1967, and Hendrix is standing to the right of Zappa. Zappa's pregnant wife Gail is standing between the two guitarists/producers/band leaders. Zappa's record company later insisted the intended cover be in the gatefold to avoid a legal showdown with Beatles management.

Zappa also came into possession of one of the only three Fender Strats that Hendrix actually burnt onstage. He gave his son Dweezil the third one, a sunburst-colored guitar that Hendrix burned at the Miami Pop Festival in 1968. It was his guitar technician Howard Parker who gave the guitar to Zappa.

That same rain-soaked weekend Zappa and Hendrix jammed away together at the Wreck Bar at the Castaways, a hotel on a beach in Hallandale, Miami. Along with the jams with Janis Joplin, the unrecorded jams of Hendrix with Zappa have to be among greatest missed musical opportunities of the century. Even Trixie Sullivan, Mike Jeffery's assistant, thought that jam session that night with Arthur Brown and John Lee Hooker and Frank Zappa was "music like you never heard. Everyone played each other's instruments. Brilliant."

Of course in the name of accuracy, I must admit that after a jealous fan pushed Zappa off of the Rainbow Theatre's stage in London stage in December 1971, breaking one of Zappa's legs and a rib, his mean-spiritedness began dragging down his music. A low point for the Hendrix fan is Ike Willis's attack on Hendrix during "We're Turning Again" on Zappa's *Mothers of Prevention*.

Sly Stone

Sly is one of those musicians whose music changed the direction of Hendrix's music. It's hard to imagine the Band of Gypsys' songbook without the hits Sly and the Family Stone were cranking out in the latter half of the 1960s. You can even hear Hendrix referencing Sly's "Sing a Simple Song" during Buddy Miles's "We Got to Live Together" on *Band of Gypsys*. Robert Wyatt of Soft Machine said Sly's music was what Hendrix liked to listen to in his hotel room when he was on the road.

Then again it was the Experience's singles that fell into the hands of Stone when he was a deejay, thoroughly affecting the ambitious bandleader who, like Jimi Hendrix, was one of the few black musicians to be accepted by a white audience. In fact, according to Charles Shaar Murray, it was Sly Stone, not Hendrix, who represented "the euphoric optimism of the brief liaison between black and white youth. The ironic difference between the two musicians is that it was the outgoing Sly Stone who blended in with his band, while the shy Hendrix towered over his sidemen."

Sly Stone was waiting to jam with Hendrix at the Speakeasy in London the night Hendrix died . . . or so Mitch Mitchell's story of the night goes. Eric Clapton also claims he was supposed to meet Hendrix at Sly and the Family Stone's concert at the Lyceum earlier the same evening. In both stories, Hendrix failed to show.

Miles Davis

Few musicians have affected music—let alone American music—as profoundly as Miles Davis. "Sound. I changed sound," I remember him rasping to a television interviewer when asked his greatest accomplishment. He played trumpet with the legendary Charlie Parker and then went on and changed the direction of jazz at least four times. His bands were classrooms for other musicians who also changed the course of music, including the mighty John Coltrane, the only bandleader of Miles's era who rivals him.

And yet it was Jimi Hendrix who changed the direction of Miles Davis's music and not the other way around; a fact even acknowledged by Miles Davis in his autobiography published in 1989.

Twenty years earlier, beginning with *In A Silent Way* released on July 30, 1969, Davis's albums were labeled "New Directions in Music," perhaps an acknowledgment of the growing presence of electric instrumentation. As controversial as Bob Dylan going electric in 1965, Miles was also considered a "Judas" by jazz traditionalists in 1969. As Bill Milkowski wrote in *Downbeat* in October 1982: "Before Hendrix, the lines were more clearly drawn—there was rock on one side and jazz on the other, with blues straddling the fence. After Hendrix, nothing would ever be quite cut-and-died." And Davis knew it.

Davis had been tinkering with the electric guitar on his recordings before 1969. Joe Beck played on "Circle in the Round" and "Water on the Pond" in December 1967 (unfortunately neither track was released for years) and George Benson played on "Paraphernalia" from 1968's *Miles in the Sky*. But 1969 saw the instrument take on a more prominent role as Columbia Records' president Clive Davis encouraged Miles to follow his muse—who could be said to be Betty Mabry, Miles's future wife, who turned Miles onto Hendrix's music—and go electric.

At the end of 1969, Davis attended one of the Band of Gypsys performances at the Fillmore East where Hendrix unveiled "Machine Gun," which was known to be a favorite of the bandleader around this period. Davis was making the rounds of the rock hot spots to see what new direction he wanted to take his music. Or as Charles Shaar Murray put it: "the Zen *brujo* of the trumpet picks up on some Sly, Hendrix and James Brown records and—bingo!—a genre is born."

That genre is fusion. And no, Miles Davis did not invent it—Tony Williams's Lifetime truly deserves that credit—but Davis perfected and popularized fusion and put out its best albums. And the effect that Jimi Hendrix's sound had on Miles Davis's best recordings of the 1970s is unmistakable. Davis could not have made *A Tribute to Jack Johnson*, *Agharta*, *Pangaea*, and *Dark Magus* without Jimi Hendrix's influence. Those last three are live albums that were made when Davis's band featured Pete Cosey and Reggie Lucas on electric guitar. (Dominique Gaumont joined the duo on *Dark Magus*.) This is Miles Davis at his most electric just before a hip injury forced him off the road and out of the studio for six years. The music on these live recordings is the aural equivalent to *Apocalypse Now!* Collectively, they are a musical outpost that no musician has ventured past.

It was as jazz guitarist Mike Stern, who played with Miles in the early 1980s, told Bill Milkowski in the aforementioned *Downbeat* article: "[Miles] is always saying things to me like 'Play some Hendrix! Turn it up or turn it off!' Miles love Hendrix. Jimi and Charlie Christian are his favorite cats as guitarists are concerned."

It's another one of those missed musical opportunities. As wonderful as it is to dream of the possibilities of Janis Joplin belting the blues while backed by Hendrix or Frank Zappa trading leads with Hendrix, collaboration between Miles Davis and Jimi Hendrix is really the one that might have happened had Hendrix lived. Even though a recording session in late 1969 was squelched when Davis demanded $50,000 just to turn up, plans were still being made for the two to record together. Plans were being made for Hendrix to record with Gil Evans. Miles's friend and collaborator, and even Jimi Hendrix in the weeks before his death told the press that a recording with Miles Davis was likely.

17

We Gotta Stand Side by Side

Guest Appearances

lectric Ladyland is not the first album on which musicians other than the Experience contributed their talents. The Hollies' Graham Nash and the Move's Roy Wood and Trevor Burton can be heard in the backing vocals to "You Got Me Floatin'." In the spiritual musical community that Hendrix envisioned and even labeled Electric Sky Church, the guest appearance of other musicians at his sessions was one that Hendrix encouraged, and it flowered fully on *Electric Ladyland.*

Some of these performances such as Brian Jones's percussion and piano and Dave Mason's bass playing on "All Along the Watchtower" went unused, but a greater number made the final cut and are featured throughout Hendrix's only double album released during his lifetime. It is hard to imagine "Voodoo Chile" without Steve Winwood's organ or "Rainy Day, Dream Away" and "Still Raining, Still Dreaming," without Mike Finnigan's.

Other "help from . . . friends and passengers" includes Jack Casady on bass on "Voodoo Chile"; Al Kooper on piano on "Long Hot Summer Night"; Chris Wood on "1983 . . . (A Merman I Should Turn to Be)"; Freddie Smith (saxophone, although described as "horn" in the album liner notes), and Larry Faucette (congas) on "Rainy Day, Dream Away" and "Still Raining, Still Dreaming." There may even be an uncredited performance or two by Chris Wood's wife Jeanette Jacobs, a vocalist who knew the prestardom Jimmy James in New York City.

Jack Casady

Jefferson Airplane's bassist was not only one of the best in the late 1960s but also one of the coolest looking. He was rail thin and had long long long hair held back by his ears. I was never one of Jefferson Airplane's biggest backers, but it was always pictures of Jack seen in *Rolling Stone* and *Circus* that made me give the Airplane's latest release another try. Some have stood the test of time—*Surrealistic Pillow* and *Volunteers*—and you have to give them their due for the "Somebody to Love" and "White Rabbit" singles.

And just as Jimi Hendrix benefited from a judicious edit on the *Woodstock* soundtrack triple album, so did Jefferson Airplane, whose performance of "Volunteers" was prefaced with Grace Slick's introduction to the performance of "3/5 of a Mile in 10 Seconds" that actually opened the band's delayed set: "Alright friends, you have seen the heavy groups, now you will see morning maniac music, believe me, yeah. It's a new dawn . . . good morning people!" The chords to "Volunteers" ring out in that new, Sunday dawn, and it is a truly moving, if fabricated, live performance.

By the time Jack Casady sat in on the early morning session for "Voodoo Chile" on May 3, 1968, he must've put behind whatever hard feelings there were about the Jimi Hendrix Experience blowing the Jefferson Airplane off of not only the Fillmore West stage, but the bill, the first time the two bands shared a stage on June 20, 1967. It is the stuff of legend.

Rock promoters quickly booked the Jimi Hendrix Experience as an opening act after the Monterey International Pop Festival. Along with Gábor Szabó, a Hungarian jazz guitarist, the Experience was booked as an opening act to the Jefferson Airplane's five-night stand at the hippie hot spot the Fillmore West in San Francisco. After one night, the Jefferson Airplane begged off, saying they had to finish their album.

Boz Scaggs, then playing with the Steve Miller Band, has been quoted as saying what had happened at Monterey "was a wake-up call to all of the San Francisco and LA bands. To see the power of Jimi Hendrix and The Who— what those guys were doing was leaps and bounds ahead of anything in San Francisco." This is what had happened to the Jefferson Airplane. Graham said the Airplane asked him to book Hendrix but then couldn't match the Experience's powerful musical onslaught. The Airplane begged off the bill and Big Brother and Holding Company featuring Janis Joplin was brought on board to open for the Experience. Graham gave each member of the Experience a gold watch for filling the Airplane's void.

Casady's appearance on "Voodoo Chile" came about as the result of another flare-up between Noel Redding and Jimi Hendrix. Redding objected to the overwhelming number of friends and hangers-on at the Record Plant during a session for "Three Little Bears." According to Redding, the nonconfrontational Hendrix told him to "Relax, man," but as Redding recollected in his autobiography: "I relaxed my way right out of the place, not caring if I ever saw him again."

Later that evening, after further work on "Three Little Bears" and "Cherokee Mist," Hendrix and his entourage moved to the Scene club, as he customarily did after recording sessions. Uncustomarily, Kramer joined

Hendrix and Mitchell at the club on West Forty-Sixth Street where they encountered Steve Winwood and Casady. This is how Kramer, who rarely kept unbusinesslike hours in London, was available to engineer three takes of "Voodoo Chile" at 7 a.m. on a Friday morning. The engineer has admitted that "the bass tone wasn't the best it could have been," and of the four musicians on "Voodoo Chile," it is Casady's performance that is the least striking because of this.

Casady also appeared with the Experience in concert twice but not on "Voodoo Chile," a number that, while a centerpiece track of *Electric Ladyland*, was never played live, perhaps because Hendrix thought it wouldn't be the same without Winwood or someone else playing organ. On opening night of the six-show, three-night stand at Bill Graham's Winterland in October 1968, Casady joined the Experience for Howlin' Wolf's "Killing Floor," and then approximately six months later, on April 29, 1969, at the Oakland Coliseum he played bass on the longest live version of "Voodoo Child (Slight Return)." Noel Redding played electric guitar. (The Jefferson Airplane had opened for the Experience.)

A rumored take of Casady on "Room Full of Mirrors" recorded at TTG Studios in October 1968 has never surfaced.

Mitch Mitchell also suggested inviting Casady to replace Redding for the spring 1970 tour when he saw that Hendrix was opposed to resurrecting the Experience again. Hendrix instead opted for his friend Billy Cox.

Steve Winwood

During Jimi Hendrix's first published interview in the January 28, 1967, issue of *Melody Maker*, he observed that the Spencer Davis Group was the shining light of the London music scene. That the eighteen-year-old Steve Winwood was the group's vocalist and keyboardist indicates that Hendrix had quickly taken notice of the musician later to be featured prominently in the Experience's longest studio track, "Voodoo Chile."

Circumstances surrounding the recording date are described in Jack Casady's bio above, but Winwood has such a prominent role in the recording as he duels with Hendrix throughout the epic blues number that it is unsurprising to hear that both Hendrix and his drummer spoke of working with Winwood again or that his involvement in Band of Gypsys was also discussed. The closest the two musicians got to working together again was a jam session on June 15, 1970, that took place after Hendrix showed Winwood and Chris Wood around Electric Lady, his new recording studios. It is our loss that the two musicians did not record together more often. As Kramer says in McDermott's *Ultimate Experience*, "Steve was the perfect

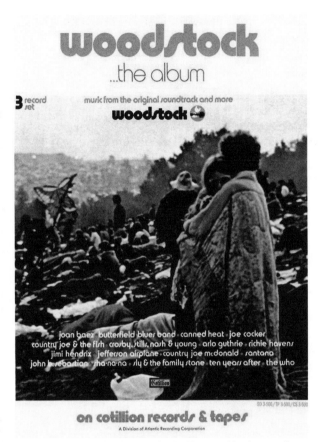

woodstock
...the album

3 record set

music from the original soundtrack and more

woodstock

joan baez · butterfield blues band · canned heat · joe cocker
country joe & the fish · crosby, stills, nash & young · arlo guthrie · richie havens
jimi hendrix · jefferson airplane · country joe mcdonald · santana
john sebastian · sha-na-na · sly & the family stone · ten years after · the who

[Cotillion]

SD 3-500/TP 3-500/CS 3-500

on cotillion records & tapes
A Division of Atlantic Recording Corporation

Jack Casady was the bassist for Jefferson Airplane, whose live version of "Volunteers" on the *Woodstock* LP was enhanced by some judicious editing.

Courtesy of Robert Rodriguez

foil for Jimi and one of the very few musicians who could have kept up with him."

You can find clips on YouTube of Winwood and Eric Clapton playing their interpretation of Hendrix's most personal blues number. Winwood handles the vocals, and Eric Clapton does an admirable job of building upon Hendrix's recorded solo as he pays homage to the Robert Johnson of his era. I particularly recommend the May 12, 2011, performance at the Royal Albert Hall, which must have been a moving experience for the musicians. At fifteen minutes it rivals in length Hendrix's studio version. The only drawback is the lack of drum solos. On "Voodoo Chile" you gotta give the drummer some.

Al Kooper

The virtuoso Al Kooper, who plays acoustic piano on "Long Hot Summer Night"—which, like "Burning of the Midnight Lamp," was a B-side before appearing on *Electric Ladyland*—had known Hendrix when he was struggling Jimmy James in New York City. Kooper's piano was an integral part of the recording session on April 18, 1968, Hendrix's initial session at the Record Plant, co-owned by Gary Kellgren—who had recorded the Experience's fourth single at Mayfair Studios—and Chris Stone. Contrary to other published reports, Kooper was present at the recording of the basic track for "Long Hot Summer Night," and his contribution was not an overdub.

It must have been satisfying for Hendrix to have playing on one of his tracks the same musician who played organ so brilliantly on Dylan's "Like a Rolling Stone." Al Kooper, who was also a member of the Blues Project with guitarist Mike Bloomfield, played a significant role in the formation of Blood, Sweat, and Tears, and is a featured played on one of the first famous rock jam albums: *Super Session* with Bloomfield and Stephen Stills.

Al Kooper has played with a who's who of major rock acts including Alice Cooper, the Rolling Stones, and the Who over the course of hundreds of albums. He helped discover one Rock and Roll Hall of Fame inductee, Lynyrd Skynyrd, and produced their first three albums, including the rock standards "Free Bird" and "Sweet Home Alabama."

Dave Mason

The legendary Hendrix track "Little One" finally saw the light of day on Disc Two of the 2010 box set *West Coast Seattle Boy*. You can imagine Hendrix and his studio friends calling the track "A Little One While He's Away" (paraphrasing a well-known Who track) amongst themselves because this instrumental track from sessions held on December 28–29, 1967, was recorded while producer Chas Chandler "was away" and represents the first time Hendrix asserted himself as producer of one of his own recordings.

"Little One" is also legendary because it features a sitar, and the identity of the sitar player had been a subject of debate for some time. He was originally thought to be Brian Jones of the Rolling Stones, and there are mp3 files online that claim this is true. (Jones's turn on the sitar on "Paint It, Black" rivals that of George Harrison on "Norwegian Wood" as the most popular in pop history.) The sitar, however, was played by Dave Mason, guitarist and bassist with Traffic. See Chapter 18 for what Chas Chandler and the surviving Experience Makers did with the basic track in 1987.

With *Axis: Bold as Love* in the can, sessions had begun on the Experience's third album, and Mason was heavily involved at first. He contributed backing vocals to "Crosstown Traffic" on December 20, 1967, and early in the New Year he would contribute acoustic guitar and lay down bass tracks for "All Along the Watchtower" when Noel Redding had a rift with Hendrix. Although Mason's contributions on bass were subsequently erased by Hendrix, he was strongly considered for the bassist role in the Experience.

According to Mason, in early 1969 Hendrix had discussed with him the possibility of Mason replacing Redding, whose quarrelsomeness Hendrix had tired of. It was no secret that Redding was frustrated with the lack of attention his compositions were receiving by Hendrix and that he harbored high hopes for Fat Mattress, the band he was laying down tracks with. "When I left Traffic," Mason said, "I was gonna join the band on bass, but that kinda got squashed by Chas Chandler and Mike Jeffery."

Mason's post-Traffic band Mason, Capaldi, Wood and Frog, featuring three ex-Trafficers, opened for the Jimi Hendrix Experience at the Royal Albert Hall concerts in February 1969 and explains Mason's presence (along with flutist Chris Wood and percussionist Rocky Dzidzornu) on rhythm guitar on "Room Full of Mirrors" during the second of the Royal Albert Hall concerts. (Still in embryonic form, this seven-plus-minute version of "Room Full of Mirrors" features a Bo Diddley rhythm and is one of the better versions of one of Hendrix's signature posthumous recordings.) These London concerts were filmed as being the final Experience concerts, and so Hendrix would have been looking around for a new bassist.

And why not Mason, whom Hendrix knew as far back as October 24, 1966, when they jammed together? Hendrix played bass on that occasion with Deep Feeling, a forerunner of Traffic, at the Knuckles club. Mason remembers Chandler bringing Hendrix around to London clubs frequented by musicians and industry insiders in those pre–*Are You Experienced* days so Hendrix could get their attention.

And he did. As Mason said: "Jimi would get up in—jeans, suede jacket, big electric hairdo—and just blow everybody away. I remember thinking I might as well take up another instrument."

Mike Finnigan

Keyboardist Mike Finnigan was introduced to Jimi Hendrix by producer Tom Wilson, who was producing the Serfs' 1969 LP *The Early Bird Cafe*. The Serfs was Finnigan's band, and both they and the Experience were recording at the Record Plant in May, 1968, when Hendrix was looking for a musical lineup unlike that of the Experience to give him a Jimmy Smith-like environment in which he could use some lyrics written one rainy day at the Miami Pop Festival the previous weekend. The result was a jam session sometimes called the "Rainy Day Shuffle" that was then edited and remixed in the studio to create two distinct tracks: "Rainy Day, Dream Away" and "Still Raining, Still Dreaming."

It was the only session where Finnigan played his Hammond B3 organ on with Hendrix. The same musical lineup (Hendrix, Finnigan, Freddie

Smith [saxophone], Larry Faucette [congas], and Buddy Miles [drums]) also took a shot at "Have You Ever Been (to Electric Ladyland)," but anything that may have been recorded was not used on the track that was released. His name has been misspelt on *Electric Ladyland* liner notes for over forty years.

Finnigan later played with other recording artists, including Joe Cocker, Crosby Stills and Nash, Dave Mason, Taj Mahal, Rod Stewart, Tracy Chapman, and Jane's Addiction.

Larry Faucette and Freddie Smith

Let's face it, some sidemen just vanish. Percussionist Larry Faucette and tenor saxophonist Freddie Smith have. Their only mention in Hendrix biographies and treatises is their role in the 8:06 jam that was spliced into "Rainy Day, Dream Away" and "Still Raining, Still Dreaming," a gig they only got because they were playing in Mike Finnigan's combo the Serfs at the time. According to legend, the Serfs "ruled Lawrence, Kansas and the Midwest much the same way Bruce Springsteen dominated in New Jersey." Having heard Finnigan playing his Hammond B3 organ, Hendrix invited the organist to play on *Electric Ladyland*, and as a courtesy must have invited these two Serfs along.

Chris Wood

The Jimi Hendrix Experience was the only band other than Jethro Tull and Chicago and Joe Strummer's Mescaleros to use the flute effectively, and, whenever they did, it was Traffic's Chris Wood they called on. In fact, Traffic's members were so close to Hendrix—with three of them appearing on Experience recordings and the Experience having played "Dear Mr. Fantasy" from Traffic's 1967 album *Mr. Fantasy* in concert—that it is somewhat surprising that Hendrix never returned the favor. Traffic was even at the Record Plant recording *Traffic* with engineer Eddie Kramer and producer Jimmy Miller at the same time Hendrix was recording *Electric Ladyland*, which is how Wood wound up contributing to "1983 . . . (A Merman I Should Turn to Be)," Hendrix's masterpiece.

Wood later partook in the "Room Full of Mirrors" jam at the Royal Albert Hall on February 24, 1969, and married Jeanette Jacobs in 1969. Jacobs has also been tied romantically to Jimi Hendrix, but they did not meet through their Hendrix connection. They met while both were playing in Dr. John's band and continued playing together in Ginger Baker's Air Force.

Bookending these gigs was Wood's involvement with Traffic. He was a founding member of the band and played flute, saxophone, and keyboards. When Steve Winwood quit and the band broke up in 1969, the remaining members, including Wood, formed the short-lived Mason, Capaldi, Wood, and Frog with Mick Weaver. (This band opened for the Experience at Royal Albert Hall.) Winwood then invited his former bandmates to contribute to a solo effort, which led to the reformation of Traffic and Wood remained with the band until its breakup in 1975. Traffic was inducted into the Rock and Roll Hall of Fame on March 15, 2004.

But by then it was too late for Chris Wood, who battled alcohol and drug addiction most of his professional life. Wood died of pneumonia in Birmingham, England, on July 12, 1983. His wife had died the previous year.

18

I Can Hear Atlantis

The Jimi Hendrix Experience's Best Unheard Music

Many bands fall apart as they're creating their signature work, but what was surprising about the Jimi Hendrix Experience was that their multiple efforts at recording a fourth studio album would go unheard for so long. It was not until 1987 that selected performances from October 1968 would appear on the *Live at Winterland* CD and three-sided double LP (exactly like that of Hendrix's jazz favorite Rahsaan Roland Kirk's *The Case of the 3 Sided Dream in Audio Color*).

Meanwhile, the recordings at the TTG Studio sessions from the same month have only been released in dribs and drabs over a myriad of post-humous releases, but taken together they also comprise an impressive collection of music that would have served as a satisfying fourth album.

Add in recording sessions as the Experience rehearsed in February 1969 for the filming of the Royal Albert Hall performance and in April 1969 for their forthcoming American tour, and you have many Experience record-ings that the average rock fan is unaware of. Here are the nine best that the Experience Makers made in the order that they finally reached our ears.

"Look over Yonder"

This Experience chestnut's presence on Hendrix's second posthumously released album *Rainbow Bridge* was the first clue that there were Experience recordings hidden in recording studios that cried out to be heard. It opened Side Two, and in addition to the musician credits, it was simply stated that it was "RECORDED TTG STUDIOS • DATE: OCTOBER 22, 1968."

Unbeknownst to most of us was that "Look over Yonder" was an Experience number first attempted as "Mr. Bad Luck" at Olympic Studios on May 5, 1967, during the *Axis: Bold as Love* sessions. It never got beyond laying down the basic track and mixing and so was never a true candidate for the Experience's second album.

Revisited as "Mr. Lost Soul," the song's name was changed to "Look over Yonder" after the seventeenth take on October 22, 1968, which served as the master. The song may also have been attempted in November 1969 by Band of Gypsys, but if it was, those recordings are unavailable.

Lyrically, "Look over Yonder" is about a drug bust, but since Hendrix's arrest in Toronto would not occur until May 3, 1969, it is not autobiographical. He may have been imagining himself in the shoes of other British rock stars who were being arrested in Swinging London. If he is, he is having a good time as his humor is in abundance equating "the blues" with the police and joking that the policeman "even bust my guitar string."

The reason you should hear "Look over Yonder" is that it's an uncomplicated rocker from the Experience from a complicated era and a fine example of Hendrix's noisier side, with a feedback outro thrashing about that is similar to that of "House Burning Down" perhaps an allusion to the fact that his "house is crumbling down."

With *Rainbow Bridge* out of print you can now find "Look over Yonder" leading off 1997's *South Saturn Delta*. "Mr. Bad Luck" can be found on *Valleys of Neptune* and all versions of *West Coast Seattle Boy*.

"The Stars That Play with Laughing Sam's Dice"

"Wait, wait, wait," I can hear you saying. Isn't this the Experience's fourth B-side? And wasn't it included on *Smash Hits*? Yes, it was, but not the remixed version originally intended for Hendrix's third posthumously released album, *War Heroes*. It went unused and surfaced on *Loose Ends* issued by Polydor in England and Germany and Barclay in France in 1974.

The remixing was done by Eddie Kramer and John Jansen in January 1972 and brought forward Hendrix's intergalactic guitar playing previously buried beneath Hendrix's humorous description of tripping aboard the Milky Way Express. The song was one of his first done in an 8-track recording studio, and it shows. The solo is among Hendrix's best and the fact that he chose to bury it speaks to his confidence.

With *Loose Ends* never released in America, you can also find the second version of "The Stars That Play with Laughing Sam's Dice" on 1997's *South Saturn Delta*.

"Peace in Mississippi"

Another TTG Studios outtake—this one from October 24, 1968—had been hidden away by the Hendrix estate until its release as the "Valleys of

Barclay Record's *Loose Ends* included the best mix of "Stars That Play with Laughing Sam's Dice."   *Courtesy of Robert Rodriguez*

Neptune" B-Side on the 2010 CD single. Fans first heard it on *Crash Landing*, Alan Douglas's first posthumous release of Hendrix material. Redding and Mitchell's contributions were controversially removed and replaced with session musicians.

"Peace in Mississippi" is Hendrix's buzziest instrumental, a full-force sonic assault said to have been a political statement because the title stems from a stray visit from some friends he knew from his chitlin' circuit days. They got around to talking about Mississippi, and after a black kid sent out to pick up lunch was brought back by a racist sheriff who thought the kid had stolen the red convertible he was driving, Hendrix changed the title, which had originally been called "Peace."

Recording engineer Angel Balestier says that during the session Hendrix was striving for a "certain sound" that was "bouncing off the glass separating the studio from the control room."

The first version retaining Hendrix's fellow Experience Makers was, fittingly, on *Voodoo Soup*, the final posthumous album that Alan Douglas had a hand producing. In Michael Fairchild's booklet notes he states that this instrumental "has roots in blues in the sense that Hendrix was reconstructing harmonic/melodic riffs mainly from the 12-bar chord statement." It was also the closest Hendrix ever came to making a heavy metal recording, a genre then in its infancy and one that, despite its roots in Hendrix, he did not care for.

"Trash Man"

First appearing on *Midnight Lightning*, the second posthumous album Alan Douglas would release (but last with session musicians replacing the sidemen who actually played at Hendrix's recording sessions), "Trash Man" is the Experience at their best during a period when they were in disarray.

Recorded on April 3, 1969, at Olmstead Studios in New York City, "Trash Man" is built upon the theme of another instrumental, "Midnight," that was recorded two days earlier. "Trash Man" trashes "Midnight." It is the Experience's best instrumental. It is puzzling how elusive the recording of good instrumentals was for the Experience. Despite countless efforts at recording "Tax Free," "Sunshine of Your Love," and "Midnight," they never nailed them.

The full 7:23 minute version featuring the Experience was finally released in 2004 on Dagger's *Hear My Music*. (The Douglas version at 3:18 lopped off the first run-through of the arrangement leading up to Hendrix's solo.) As John McDermott notes in the booklet accompanying *Hear My Music*: "A malfunctioning microphone gives Mitch's snare drum a distorted, thrashing character and provides a perfect complement to Redding's 8-string bass and Hendrix's strident guitar tone."

An alternate version was also issued on an extended version of 2010's *Valleys of Neptune* that was only available in Target stores.

"Gloria"

Another TTG Studios outtake—can you tell how much I love the Experience's work that October week?—was a cover of the classic that Van Morrison recorded with Them. It was first released as a bonus 7″ one-sided EP single with *The Essential Jimi Hendrix* in Britain in 1978 and then again as a bonus single with *The Essential Jimi Hendrix* Vol. 2 when released in America in 1979.

The fact that eight takes were made attests to the fact that this was more than the Experience just jamming and having fun in the studio, although Hendrix's spoken vocal track indicates they were having fun. The spoken vocal track makes it a relative of "The Stars That Play with Laughing Sam's Dice" as Jimi describes life on the road and a groupie named Gloria.

According to Gary Geldeart and Steve Rotham's *From the Benjamin Franklin Studios*—a three-part labor of love that is essential for any Hendrix collector—this version can only be found on hard-to-find CDs. An alternate version is available on *The Jimi Hendrix* box set issued in 2000.

"There Ain't Nothing Wrong"

This one's a bit of a cheat as Redding wasn't at the original session, which featured Mitch Mitchell and Dave Mason on sitar at the first session Hendrix recorded without Chas Chandler. But the formerly titled "Little One" was revisited in 1988 as part of the Chandler Tapes Project by Mitchell, Redding, and Chandler.

The Chandler Tapes Project came about when tapes Chandler had placed in storage eighteen years later were reclaimed by him when the storage company that held them was going out of business. At the time, many of the recordings were unreleased, and so Chandler invited the surviving members of the Experience to overdub on the surviving basic tracks. (Similar to what Paul, George, and Ringo did with John's "Free as a Bird" and "Real Love" for the Beatles' *Anthology* series in the mid-1990s.) The recordings were never issued because Chandler could not reach an agreement with Douglas. (Perhaps Douglas was wary of getting burned again after using session musicians in the mid-'70s.) The estate finally acquired the revisited recordings after Chandler's death in 1996.

Geldeart and Rodham correctly comment that "very little remains of the original track apart from the sitar and Hendrix's guitar," but the overdubs

RON DELSENER PRESENTS

AN ELECTRONIC THANKSGIVING

JIMI HENDRIX EXPERIENCE

EXTRA ATTRACTION

Fernando Valenti
HARPSICHORD

THANKSGIVING NIGHT
THURSDAY, NOVEMBER 28—11 PM ONLY
TICKETS: $4, $5, $6, $7

AT PHILHARMONIC HALL BOX OFFICE, BLOOMINGDALE'S; 59TH ST. & LEX.
AVE.; A&S; BROOKLYN & HUNTINGTON. Mail orders payable to Philharmonic
Hall, 64th St. & 8'way. Phone TR 4-2424.

An ad for An Electric Thanksgiving with the Jimi Hendrix Experience at the Philharmonic Hall in New York City a month after the Experience tried repeatedly to record live concerts and studio sessions for their fourth album.   *Courtesy of Robert Rodriguez*

improve the instrumental recording of "Little One," especially Noel Redding's vocal and bassline, which may be why it's the lead-off track on *Noel Redding: The Experience Sessions*.

"Fire"

What could have been a borefest in less imaginative hands, the live arrangement of "Fire," recorded on February 17, 1969, as the Experience rehearsed for the Royal Albert Hall concerts, is better recorded and superior to the *Are You Experienced* version. You can tell this band's been playing the shit out of this for three years. They really are on fire. Mitchell's drums are given a prominent place in the mix, and Redding's basswork under Hendrix's solo rolls like a subway train. Redding's snide backing vocals are a real kick too.

This version is available on 2010's *Valleys of Neptune*, an album all fans of the Experience *must* own. Why? Because despite the estate's seeming effort to downplay the Experience by opening with three tracks featuring Billy Cox on bass, the remaining nine tracks—75 percent of the release—are of the Jimi Hendrix Experience.

"Hear My Train A Comin'"

This doesn't date to February 1969 but April as the Experience rehearsed for its upcoming tour of America; the final tour of not only America but the Experience. It is a truncated version of the live arrangement. With its striding rhythm, it's not rolling like a locomotive but imitating the singer's plight—he's one of those poor souls who believe he'll find better luck and success further along the train track. He can only hear his train coming:

he's walking to the station. With references to being a Voodoo Chile and coming back to buy the town he's leaving, this song's always felt the most personal of Hendrix's blues originals too. Also available on *Valleys of Neptune.*

"Room Full of Mirrors"

All versions of 2010's West *Coast Seattle Boy* include this version, which is also from the Chandler Tapes Project. Recorded on February 16, 1969, "Room Full of Mirrors" was the only new song played at Royal Albert Hall by the Jimi Hendrix Experience. Retooled later by Band of Gypsys, this version is more primitive thanks to the presence of percussionist Kwasi "Rocky" Dzidzornu (you won't recognize the name but that's him playing the percussion on the Rolling Stones' studio version of "Sympathy for the Devil") and the song's Bo Diddley rhythm.

19

There's a Red House over Yonder

Remodeling "Red House"

J ust about every music fan likes "blues changes" even if they don't like the blues. They may not know that the changes are rooted in the I-IV-V chords of a key, but these three chords often serve as the chassis for the vast majority of popular music: jazz, country, rock, punk. Just about every infamous Ramones song is based on the I-IV-V chords.

Yet these changes are most commonly associated with blues singers and guitarists, having been popularized by the likes of the legendary devil dealer Robert Johnson; the inventive John Lee Hooker; and the father of the Chicago Blues, Muddy Waters, whose "Mannish Boy," "I'm Your Hootchie Cootchie Man," and "Catfish Blues" were recorded by Jimi Hendrix. ("Catfish Blues" is in fact Waters's "Rollin' Stone," best known as the basis of the name of one of the most notable rock bands of all time and an American magazine that has been publishing for over four decades.) Waters was singularly instructive to Hendrix, who—due to his lack of confidence in his vocals—learned from Waters to compensate for this self-perceived deficiency by mastering his hands' innate communion with electric guitars just as Muddy Waters stretched his voice.

Though there are many variations, the basic 12-bar blues has an easily recognizable form, and examples are endless. Two of the first published blues songs, "Dallas Blues" (1912) and "St. Louis Blues" (1914), were 12-bar blues featuring the AAB structure. Robert Johnson's "Me and the Devil Blues" is an example from the classic 1930s Mississippi Delta blues era. Many later blues-influenced songs also follow this structure, including hit recordings that most music fans don't know are 12-bar blues, including these nine examples:

- "Folsom Prison Blues"—Johnny Cash
- "Good Golly Miss Molly"—Little Richard

- "Can't Buy Me Love"—the Beatles
- "Green Onions"—Booker T. and the MGs
- "Riders on the Storm"—the Doors
- "Rock and Roll"—Led Zeppelin
- "Ca Plan Pour Moi"—Plastic Bertrand
- "Still Haven't Found What I'm Looking For"—U2
- "Because I Got High"—Afroman

Hendrix's "Red House" is a standard 12-bar blues progression. He uses this progression in several other compositions such as "Voodoo Child (Slight Return)" and "Who Knows," but "Red House" is his most traditional workout of the progression.

Being an early composition by Hendrix, it shares the autobiographical air found in "Stone Free" and "Highway Chile": all three songs reflect Hendrix's life as a musician. In "Red House" it's implied he's returning to his baby's house after "ninety-nine and one half days" on the road only to find that she's moved away.

The lyrical pattern Hendrix employs is boilerplate 12-bar blues where across three lines a statement is made, repeated (usually with some variation), and then a summation or turn of phrase. For example, here is the pivotal, second verse of "Red House" that he sings after approaching his baby's red house:

> Wait a minute, something's wrong. The key won't unlock the door
> Wait a minute, something's wrong, baby. The key won't unlock the door.
> I got a bad, bad feeling that my baby don't live here no more.

But Hendrix still has his guitar (slung across his back?) and consoles himself outside his baby's door by taking a solo, which he extended in concert deo99spite the fact that Reprise omitted it from the American release of *Are You Experienced?* . . . and then compounded the problem by using an alternate recording on *Smash Hits*. Over the course of less than three years, this three-and-a-half-minute studio recording was stretched out to thirteen-plus minutes. (At one of two shows performed on May 10, 1968, at Bill Graham's Fillmore East in New York City, the longest known version—seventeen minutes—was performed. It must have been some concert since Sly and the Family Stone was the opening act!) Of Hendrix's concerts, Robert Wyatt—Soft Machine's founding member—is quoted as saying, "Night after night, after he had thrown everything at everybody, the high spot of the night where everybody would hold their breath would be 'Red House.'"

So with two studio and approximately two dozen live versions readily available, the following are the ones you should seek.

Takes 1–4

"Red House" is a song that predated Hendrix's arrival in England in September 1966. He played it in New York City with Jimmy James and the Blue Flames, although the lyrics were still in flux. It was inspired by Hendrix's first love, Betty Jean Morgan, who did have a sister (named Maddy) if not a red house. In actuality she lived in a brown house with her parents. A New York City, Fifty-Seventh Street apartment where two friends of Keith Richard's then-girlfriend Linda Keith lived was, however, known as the Red House and may be the source of the title.

When the financially strapped Experience had fifteen minutes remaining on the time booked for the December 13, 1966, CBS Studios session, Hendrix reached for "Red House." Two versions were recorded. Noel Redding's comment in his autobiography "three songs in three hours" is inaccurate, as four songs were taped: the focus was on "Foxy Lady," but "Can You See Me?" and "3rd Stone from the Sun" were done as well as "Red House."

Two months later in February 1967, another attempt was made to capture "Red House" on tape at De Lane Lea Studios because the CBS version was declared inadequate due to flubbed notes. The exact date is unknown, but one can speculate it was around February 6th since that is the date of the first known live recording at the Star Hotel in Croydon, Surrey. It seems likely that the Experience was playing it either in anticipation of taping or because they were pleased to have a performance in the can.

The four extant takes from the February session are fascinating even if only the fourth one is complete.

The first take breaks down not due to Hendrix missing the first line or flubbing the vocals but because he is unhappy with Redding's playing. A sign of things to come, Hendrix can be heard instructing Redding. This is the version referenced by Chas Chandler in *Sessions* and can be found on eBay.

The Studio Versions

As mentioned previously, two studio versions of "Red House" have been officially released:

1. The CBS version released by Track Records (612 001) in the United Kingdom as part of *Are You Experienced* on May 12, 1967; and
2. The Olympic version released by Reprise Records (MS 2025) in the United States as part of *Smash Hits* on July 7, 1969.

On the face of it, the Olympic version is superior. It is the approved version inexplicably unused for the Experience's debut album in the United Kingdom. This is the version recorded at the De Lane Lea Studios in February 1967 and on March 29, 1967 (along with "Teddy Bears Live Forever," an unreleased track). This version was remixed at Olympic Studios in April 1967 (hence the reason it is known as the Olympic Version and not the De Lane Lea Version) and includes premix guitar overdubs.

This version sounds more polished and warmer, possibly because Redding is playing a bass guitar and not the tuned-down electric guitar heard on the CBS version. Hendrix's vocal asides are kept to a minimum. His guitar playing is more assured, more controlled, but there is less risk too. This version ends with grumbling guitar strings, subtly undermining the narrator's boast "if my baby don't love me no more/I know her sister will!" The grumbling guitar notes hint he's still displeased with the turn of events.

So then, how to explain that the CBS version is superior? It as the French author Marcel Proust writes in *The Fugitive*, the sixth volume of the twentieth century's greatest novel, *In Search of Lost Time*: "Let us leave pretty women to men with no imagination."

Let us leave the Olympic Version to fans with no imagination. The CBS version is the one you want hear. It's the mistakes and off-the-cuff flourishes that make it more honest. First it sounds brittle and colder . . . just like a man stuck outside a locked door. On the guitar intro, Hendrix misses and plays a note behind the beat, which was the secret to Frank Sinatra's singing. Then the narrator's anger is suggested by two chopped chords.

Noel Redding's bassline has more swing, more saunter, and sounds different, as it should since he played his basslines on a hollow-body electric guitar tuned half a step down to sound like a bass guitar.

But what really sets the song apart are Hendrix's vocal asides. He'll make little comments, such as just before his solo when he says "My baby didn't say she was leaving. That's okay, I still got my guitar." It sounds so natural. You can picture him standing outside the locked door, sitting on the doorstep, reaching for his guitar.

This version also ends differently. Instead of the grumbling guitar, the song comes to a complete halt with a Mitch Mitchell drum roll.

You can compare this version for yourself. The Olympic version is included on *Smash Hits*, rereleased in 1969. It is also available on the 1993 MCA edition of *Are You Experienced*. The CBS version can be found on *Blues* (although some of the studio chatter has been clipped). It is also available on the 1997 MCA rerelease of *Are You Experienced*, but without the chatter.

A much later studio date of "Red House" was released in 2010 as part of *Valleys of Neptune*. Recorded while the Experience was preparing for the filming of the Royal Albert Hall concerts in February 1969, for all the plusses of being professionally recorded in a controlled setting, it is, for all intents and purposes, the trio just playing the then-current live arrangement. It does not surpass readily available live performances recorded below. It also never makes it to the third verse, making it an incomplete take.

Paris, France—October 9, 1967, at L'Olympia

The Experience always strived to give a top-notch performance at L'Olympia, site of their first major concert success, to the band anyway. Their fourth performance at this concert hall had assured the new group that what was clicking in rehearsals could wow audiences, too.

And because the Parisians had responded so enthusiastically to the then-unknown group's three-song set (comprised of "Killing Floor," "Hey Joe," and "Wild Thing"), the Experience always loved playing L'Olympia, and, to make shows there an event, even went so far as to have Redding play his bass parts on electric guitar during a performance of "Red House" at the second show on January 29, 1968, thereby recreating the instrumentation used for the song's initial recording session.

But that's not the performance I want to praise here.

What is to be recommended about this version on *Paris 1967/San Francisco 1968* on Dagger Records is that it is a good, fast-paced version (for a blues song anyway) and a sterling example of the Experience's early edgy energy. Riding a high from "Rock Me Baby," the previous number, "Red House" on this October night begins aggressively without the quiet rippling riff the guitarist would use later. The Experience is just as aggressive, and the sound of Mitchell's drumming is captured well for an early live performance.

When they head into the solo section, Hendrix's playing style almost turns Coltranean because his solo is a sheet of amplified sound, wailing and tugging. It's the earliest readily available live version; the shortest too, which is what is unColtranean about it. Mitchell's jazzy rolls—like Coltrane's drummer Elvin Jones now that I think about it—spur Hendrix on, culminating in churning, combustible chords.

San Francisco, California—February 4, 1968, at the Fillmore West

Hendrix's embarrassment over his vocal prowess is emphasized when he sings the blues. An admirer of Muddy Waters's powerful verbal delivery, Hendrix, when playing the blues, compensates for his self-perceived vocal limitations by bellowing via his guitar. But this version recorded at Bill Graham's Fillmore West is the rare exhibit of Hendrix—for whatever reason: maybe he really was feeling the blues—letting his guitar take a backseat to his singing. It's a throaty performance, guttural; Hendrix's guitar tone on the winter dates in 1968 can be quite harsh, which is pleasing to the ears on blues numbers.

Ottawa, Canada—March 19, 1968, at the Capitol Theater

Lyrically, the key to "Red House" are the punch lines concluding each verse and the fact that the singer is not really all that upset that his girlfriend has moved: he knows her sister will give him good loving in her stead. But the emotional highpoint comes in the second verse when "something is wrong . . . the key won't unlock this door." I've already pointed out how on early takes Hendrix's guitar in response to this realization is to sound like a man desperately trying the key again and jimmying with the lock. (No pun intended.) Less than fifteen months after his first attempt at recording his blues signature piece, when Hendrix comes to this point it's become a vocal tour de force with falsetto eruptions and guitar mimicking the distraught man, what has come to be known as Hendrix scatting.

What is notable about this version is that instead of saying "I still got my guitar!" at the conclusion of the second version, Hendrix instead says: "My baby didn't tell me she was leaving." It was not uncommon for Hendrix to change lyrics in concert. For example, on the live version of "Purple Haze" included on *West Coast Seattle Boy*, it's not a girl who puts a spell on him but "that headache." (I wonder if he was thinking of Devon Wilson at that moment.) Hendrix then takes an extended workout but relies more on chords than he normally did during the solo and has a smooth, Wes Montgomery vibe to his performance.

San Francisco, California—October 11, 1968, at Winterland, First Show

To give credit where credit is due, the Jimi Hendrix Experience played "Red House" at three of the six shows over three nights at Winterland, and Alan

Douglas picked the choicest one for *Live at Winterland*, a CD-only release. It was rereleased in 2011 as part of *Winterland*, a four-CD box set that presents what the estate has deemed the choicest cuts. Still, I prefer the *3 Nights at Winterland* box set that was "manufactured under license from the Michael Jeffery Estate in 2006. It sounds more . . . well, live. It is also presents the complete six shows, warts and all. Excitement and all. By rarely rehearsing, the Experience live was always the "Tightrope Ride" that the Doors sans Morrison once sang of. Here I just want to talk about this magnificently brooding version of "Red House" no matter what release you find it on.

By this evening's performance, Redding's bassline has lost all of its swing . . . saunter . . . swagger . . . whatever you want to call it. By now it sounds like the heavy steps of a jilted lover, which is in complete contrast to the lyrics. This may be the prime example of Redding not pushing the 4-stringed envelope. But give Hendrix credit because his guitar here broods just as sullenly as Redding's bassline.

The key to this performance is only 1:04 in length. By this point the Experience arrangement of "Red House" had a set structure: intro, verse, verse, lead solo, with the rhythm stepping up the tempo throughout and then a "1983"-esque interlude before the final verse. It is this interlude that makes this performance. It is so tuneful, but unlike any other tune Hendrix ever committed to tape; a perfect example of him soloing via his guitar's toggle switch that guitarist Mike Bloomfield once marveled over.

Hendrix ends this version with what even he in 1968 must have considered to be "politically incorrect" before the phrase was even coined:

> If my baby won't love me no more
> Lord I know good and well her big fat sister will.

Electric Church Red House

In the wake of the Winterland shows, the Experience made Los Angeles their home base for the end of the month. They rented a house in Benedict Canyon, partied with friends, and spent most nights recording at TTG (Two Terrible Guys) Studios (aka Sunset-Highland Studios) in Hollywood. On October 29, 1968, what is now known as the "Electric Church Red House"—chiefly for Hendrix's intro rap—was recorded. Over an extended trill invoking the recently released "Voodoo Chile," Hendrix announces:

"Yeah, about this time I'd like to present you to the Electric Church. Mitch Mitchell on drums. Buddy Miles on another set of drums. We got Noel Redding on bass. We got a whole lotta friends beating tambourine.

We got Lee Michaels on organ. Not rehearsing; just gonna jam right now. We feel very free. We'd like you all to have, yeah." He strikes some notes on his guitar. "We'd like all of you have peace of mind. Too many things are happening now. Everybody grasping too. We don't want the light to be lost. And maybe you all listening to our notes . . . yeah . . . now I see . . . you know playing, instead of rapping, hanging our heads down. Maybe this will be good enough for a rainy day. A stupid song. It's all freedom."

Then with a flourish of Stratocaster guitar and Hammond organ— courtesy no doubt of mixing magic—we are into what is a fairly standard rendition of the latest live Experience arrangement *except* it is also the most fully realized recording of the Electric Church conceit defined in Chapter 23. Although never stated, the Electric Church conceit was an expansion of sound: implicitly a choir of instruments centered on organ. Hendrix had previously and constructively incorporated the organic talents of Steve Winwood and Mike Finnigan on *Electric Ladyland* tracks (on "Voodoo Chile" and "Rainy Day, Dream Away" respectively), and so adding organ to his sound was already proven to be a natural outgrowth.

(Hendrix had jammed with Lee Michaels at the Whiskey A Go Go on October 19th and presumably invited him to participate in the TTG sessions begun the previous day. The Electric Church format was not only a new one for Hendrix; it would have been an atypical one for Lee Michaels too. He was known chiefly for duet performances with a drummer, usually the Grassroots' Joel Larson or the Sweathogs' Bartholomew Eugene Smith-Frost. [He is unusually linked with drummers: Johny Barbata, later of Jefferson Airplane among other bands, was in Michaels's first band, the Sentinels.] His session with Hendrix predates his only Top Ten hit, "Do You Know What I Mean," by approximately three years. Michaels semiretired from the music business in 1979.)

The success of this recording rests largely on the contributions of the other Experience members, especially Noel Redding and what author Dave Henderson rightly calls his "adventurism." When the jam gets going after the second verse, its Redding's fills spurring on Hendrix's ascending guitar with his long sustained, guttural B. B. King notes that makes this performance reach for the cathedral apse. The performance, unfortunately, is cut short at the 7:40 mark, and we never get the third verse with its humorous (or chauvinistic) punch line. It's hardly noticed. I recommend you search this one out. An edited version with Hendrix's spiel trimmed can be found on *Blues*. The complete version can be found on the hard-to-find *Variations on an Instrument*.

San Diego, California—May 24, 1969, at San Diego Sports Arena

The 1969 performances of "Red House" are consistently recommendable, and it's hard to direct you to just one. The two versions from the Stockholm, Sweden, concerts in January are the bluest this song ever got with Redding's sustained bass notes. The version at the Royal Albert Hall on February 24, 1969, is one of Hendrix's noisiest, as if he was were trying to atone for what was a legendarily poor performance at the same venue just a few days before. You should check out the April 27th mono recording at Oakland Coliseum for Hendrix's vocals and the way he alters the lyrics, saying that he hasn't seen his "nappy haired baby." Redding's bassline after February 1969 also regains some half-steps to his step.

Recorded at San Diego Sports Arena on May 24, 1969, this "Red House," according to noted Hendrix historian John McDermott, is "arguably Hendrix's best recorded version." It is the typical structure of the live arrangement, but features Hendrix using chords a trifle more, perhaps to guide his bandmates as he knew the performance was being recorded for possible inclusion in a live recording for Reprise.

After the second verse, however, Hendrix sidesteps the standard torrid blues solo, strikes a few chords, and uses them to sheepdog Redding and Mitchell into upping the tempo. The "1983"-esque interlude is more rhythmic too before the band comes to a full stop for a totally atypical wah-wah solo.

Then, when it seems as if Hendrix is reaching for the third verse, Mitchell unleashes a few rolls, and Redding prods Hendrix into another high-spirited jam. If I didn't know better, I'd suspect engineer Eddie Kramer of splicing the tapes and editing in a piece of another performance. (Redding is particularly good on this performance, giving Hendrix the drive he needs.) They rock on before abruptly pulling up the reins for the final verse, punch line, and quick conclusion.

The easiest place to find this version is on *Hendrix in the West*, reissued in 2011 but with track substitution, additional tracks, and a new sequencing. The original *Hendrix in the West* album, for example, had placed "Red House" after "Little Wing," which worked much better than the 2011 sequencing. This version is also available on Disc Three of *The Jimi Hendrix Experience* box set and the *Stages* box set. (Avoid *Stages* at all costs because to my ears, the San Diego disc sounds as if it was mastered at the incorrect speed, which may explain why it was discontinued and has not been reissued by Authentic Hendrix, although one would think Eddie Kramer could remix at the proper speed. The Paris concert has also since been rereleased on Dagger records.)

By the time the Jimi Hendrix Experience played Jimi's hometown of Seattle on May 23, 1969, "Red House" had quadrupled in length. The following night in San Diego they would play what is considered the definitive version of Jimi's best known blues number. *Author's collection*

"Red House" on Film (*Woodstock* and *Wild Blue Angel* Versions)

Legal red tape prevents the best cinematically preserved performance of "Red House" from being viewed. This is the February 24, 1969, performance by the Jimi Hendrix Experience at London's Royal Albert Hall. (And seeing that more than four decades have passed, that's strong tape!) Determined to salvage Michael Jeffery's film project after a disastrous performance six nights earlier, the Experience regrouped and delivered a top-notch performance that is not as immobile as reported elsewhere. Hendrix considered blues to be "holy music" and as such was reverential when playing a blues number. You won't see any flashy stage antics when he plays the blues. He stands there, not immobile but rooted. Footage of this concert is available on a bootleg DVD, but "Red House" is not. Only an audio version is accessible.

So, sadly, what footage we do have of Hendrix's signature blues piece are four performances that range from abysmal to mediocre. The earliest performance is from the first show at Konserthus in Stockholm, Sweden, on January 9, 1969, and it looks eerily similar to the February 18th performance that Chas Chandler witnessed and characterized as "a lousy show" and "if I had still be in charge, [the rhythm section] would have been sacked the next day." Of most interest is the fact that Hendrix is playing a white Gibson SG.

Returning to white Fender Strats at the Woodstock (August 18, 1969) and Atlanta Pop (July 4, 1970) Festivals does little to improve the renditions. "Red House" is actually one of the better numbers by Gypsy Sun and Rainbows, his overjammed but underrehearsed band at Woodstock, because it is a traditional 12-bar blues that practically every 1960s musician could passably perform.

There is considerable debate about the quality of the final filmed version at the Isle of Wight. According to McDermott's *Hendrix: Setting the Record Straight*, this is a good performance, but Charles Shaar Murray in *Crosstown Traffic* remarks: "Even on his slow blues 'Red House,' the musical refuge to which he could always retreat for shelter when things weren't going right, the guitar fought him, betrayed him; strings tauntingly slipping from beneath unaccountably numb fingers." So who is right? A little of both. Not to be wishy-washy but watching the performance—Hendrix by the way uses his Gibson Flying V with a black finish—you agree with Murray. You can see Hendrix struggling. But if you just listen to the performance available on *Blue Wild Angel: Jimi Hendrix at the Isle of Wight Festival*, it sounds fine.

Other Renditions

Bluesmen and jazz musicians pay homage to their heroes or departed contemporaries by playing their songs. Hendrix, for example, played blues numbers by B. B. King, Elmore James, and Muddy Waters. Stevie Ray Vaughan, in honoring Hendrix, played "Little Wing" and "Voodoo Child

(Slight Return)." Jeff Beck, Eric Clapton and Carlos Santana have each praised Hendrix the best way they can: by playing his songs.

And if "Red House" is Hendrix's signature piece, it stands to reason that it has been covered by such singular bluesmen as Buddy Guy, John Lee Hooker, Albert King, and the albino, tattooed Texan Johnny Winter. Even Mick Taylor, formerly of the Rolling Stones, has been known to play it as part of his set lists as far back as 1986. Taylor crossed Hendrix's path a few times in the late 1960s, as is demonstrated in Chapter 22.

20

Let the Drummer Play

The Experience's Evolutionary Drummer: Mitch Mitchell

The more I learned about Mitch Mitchell, the Experience's evolutionary drummer, the more I began to believe that the cliché "he marches to the beat of his own drum" was coined for him.

In the early haze of the Experience, Mitchell was standoffish; spoke with a posh, fabricated, accent to make himself sound higher class; and was always late for rehearsals, even though he was the Experience's drummer only because a coin toss went his way. Mitchell clearly thought himself too good for the group prior to their quick ascension as one of London's best bands.

It's not difficult to understand how Mitchell could have seen things this way. By the time he was selected as the Experience's drummer over Aynsley Dunbar, John "Mitch" Mitchell had starred as the lead child character in *Jennings at School*, a BBC-TV series; played drums on recording sessions for the likes of Petula Clark and Brenda Lee; and worked with Georgie Fame and the Blue Fames for a year and a half. He had known tangible success. With Hendrix virtually unknown at the time of his hiring, Mitchell only agreed to play drums for the Experience for two weeks so that Hendrix could tour in France with Johnny Hallyday and probably expected to latch onto a better-paying gig afterwards.

Management probably would have liked that because with his tardiness and complaining about playing cover tunes at early rehearsals, Mitchell was soon known as "The Troublemaker." (At least until Redding started asking about where the money was going a few years later.) Mitchell's tardiness was soon curtailed after management fined him, but they did explore the possibility of replacing him, possibly with Dunbar.

By this time, however, Mitchell wanted to keep his spot in the Experience. Not only was "Hey Joe" the success Chas Chandler had envisioned, but he relished the freedom Hendrix was giving behind the kit. The Blue Fames had been a rhythm and blues band playing songs with horn charts and tight arrangements, an experience he compared to prison after being set free in the Experience.

Or as the Animals' Alan Price said to *Melody Maker* about Mitchell's playing with Hendrix after the time spent with Georgie Fame: "It's rather like a civil servant becoming a demolition worker."

Relationship with Hendrix

According to Chas Chandler, when it came to Mitch Mitchell, the Experience's drummer, Hendrix "loved Mitch's drumming, but he didn't love Mitch."

And according to girlfriend Kathy Etchingham, in her autobiography *Through Gypsy Eyes*, Jimi sometimes banged on Mitchell's drums with his guitar's head or neck when his drummer's innovations were getting out of hand and undermining the music.

And yet Hendrix knew he couldn't lose Mitchell if he didn't want his music to suffer. The fact that Mitchell was Hendrix's drummer of choice for all of the musical projects he undertook after October 1966, except for Band of Gypsys, confirms the guitarist's statement to *Melody Maker* in July 1968 that "Mitch is becoming a little monster on the drums . . . . He's the one I'd worry about losing."

No wonder, because in describing the combined playing technique of the guitarist and drummer in crafting the majority of *Electric Ladyland*'s final songs after exasperating Redding and causing Chandler to depart, Keith Shadwick in *Musician* astutely observes that it is the "sudden breaks and pauses" of the Hendrix-Mitchell performances "that give the music its grammar and punctuation."

More self-reliant than Redding, Mitchell adjusted better to the twists Hendrix's lifestyle took—the aborted concerts, the constant retakes, the after-hours jams—and so found himself outside looking in at the Hendrix-Redding skirmishes. When Hendrix announced to *Melody Maker* in November 1968 that the band was taking what bands nowadays label a hiatus, it was an effort at easing the friction of the two Experience Makers who flanked him onstage. Mitchell would go with the flow.

Of the many futures Hendrix announced for the Experience around this time—the separate band projects, the elusive fourth studio album, the mega concerts where each member would play with a band before playing together as the Experience—was just "a figment of imaginations" as Mitchell told Harry Shapiro. Whereas Redding felt as constrained in the Experience as Mitchell had felt with Georgie Fame, within the Experience Mitchell had all the freedom he needed.

Best Performances

In my introductory paragraph to this section, I described Mitch Mitchell as an evolutionary drummer because it's hard to imagine the evolution of rock drumming without him, and, sadly, he doesn't get his proper due possibly because his work has been obscured by that of his guitarist. This was well stated by Keith Shadwick, who noted Hendrix's luck in finding a drummer "who fused the alert responses of a jazz drummer with the heavy stressing of the snare beat that was at the core of every competent rock drummer's repertoire."

Listen to live recordings of an Experience concert circa 1968 or 1969, and Mitchell solos almost as much as Hendrix. He kicks off live versions of "I Don't Live Today," controls "Fire," and solos on "Catfish Blues" and "Tax Free" and "Spanish Castle Magic." More than any rock drummer, he brought jazz drumming to rock (and maybe that's why Miles Davis used Mitchell on the *Bitches Brew* demos.)

Mitchell was a softer drummer than most, but what could be a disadvantage onstage was an asset in the studio. Much like Ringo Starr's performances on Beatles recordings, you rarely question Mitchell's choices whether it be the drum brushes on "Up from the Skies," the mallets on "Cherokee Mist" or the bass drums underpinning "Voodoo Child (Slight Return)."

In many ways Mitchell was as much a soloist as Hendrix. You could even call him a lead drummer as is evidenced by the following studio tracks—in chronological order—where Mitchell solos:

- "Fire"
- "If 6 Was 9"
- "Bold as Love"
- "Tax Free"
- "Voodoo Chile"
- "1983 . . . (A Merman I Should Turn to Be)"

The following are the best of his readily available performances.

"Fire"

This live concert staple was the first Experience number recorded at Olympic Studios. But while Jimi declares "Move over Rover and let Jimi take over," "Fire" is more accurately a showcase for ever-inventive Mitchell. The black holes in the riff would collapse if not for the intergalactic drumming provided by Mitchell. These mini-solos stand apart from the riff while completing it at the same time.

The inventiveness continued in concert where Mitchell did not simply mirror the recording but took the fills further each time out, much like Keith Moon's principle of drumming, which, according to the *New Yorker*'s James Wood "was that the drummer does not exist to keep the beat." (This may be why Mitchell is not present on the beat-driven "Rainy Day. Dream Away" or "Still Raining, Still Dreaming" and Buddy Miles is.)

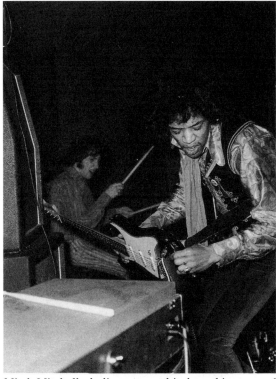

Mitch Mitchell whaling away at his drum kit at one of the Experience's earliest performances. *Author's collection*

Compare any live performance of Mitchell to that of Buddy Miles on the Band of Gypsys version of "Fire" on the box set *West Coast Seattle Boy* and you'll hear what I mean. At first the Miles version sounds exciting—almost like Chubby Checker's "The Twist" with the constant accentuating of the backbeat—but the excitement is doused when Miles can only resort to tricks to fill the gaping holes in the riff. (Though in fairness to Miles, he only played the song once in concert. Given more opportunities he might have come up with an approach that made the most of his fatback drumming style when playing "Fire.")

"I Don't Live Today"

Not many Experience songs begin with Mitchell, but the closing track to Side One of *Are You Experienced* does, It is also one of the highlights of live recordings of Mitchell because he extended the introduction. His tribal drumming musically reinforced Hendrix's explanation to critics that "I

Don't Live Today" wasn't autobiographical but a comment on the dire lives led by American Indians.

"I Don't Live Today" was as carefully crafted by Chandler and Hendrix as was the Beatles' "A Day in the Life" and has two distinct parts. The first part clocks in at 2:15. Another take is then welded onto the first. This instrumental take, however, is faster paced but jazzier, not rockier, with Hendrix pushing himself into atonal territory accompanied by what Keith Shadwick characterized as "tumultuous drumming by Mitchell."

"She's So Fine"

This is the best example of Mitchell mimicking Keith Moon. Americans forget (or never knew) that the Who was primarily considered a singles band before *Tommy*, and so Moon often retained his composure long enough to turn in a pop performance. On Noel Redding's first song for the Experience, both Hendrix and Mitchell are clearly mining the Who songbook when playing. Mitchell also mimics Moon on the version of "Mr. Bad Luck" recorded in May 1967.

"If 6 Was 9"

Mitchell's dexterity with the hi-hat is on display on what some characterize as Hendrix's manifesto in which he castigates not only the "white collared conservative" but hippies too, saying he doesn't care if they "cut off all their hair." This is his paean to personal freedom. This is also the song where Hendrix says, "play on, drummer," as the song shifts into an instrumental passage that was known separately as "Symphony of the Experience" at early recording sessions. It feels just that as Redding's basslines walk the walk, Hendrix lays on several guitar lines, and Mitchell provides another example of his dexterity.

"Bold as Love"

Hendrix and his engineering team of Eddie Kramer and especially George Chkiantz took phasing to an entirely new level with the title and concluding track of the Experience's sophomore album *Axis: Bold as Love* in the way they treated Mitchell's drum track. After Hendrix puts the verses in their boxes, there's a pause, a smattering of drums, and then a roll into the song's instrumental coda. The drum track is then clearly treated, and it is Hendrix's guitar that mirrors the sound of Mitchell's drums.

"Catfish Blues/Voodoo Chile"

The earliest version of the Muddy Waters cover that became the catalyst for "If 6 Was 9" and "Voodoo Chile" dates to February 4, 1967, at London's Flamingo Club. It was first recorded for BBC radio's *Top Gear* on October 6, 1967, and filmed a month later during a November 10, 1967, performance on Danish TV. Even at this early stage Mitchell's solo is an integral part of the arrangement and became the first vehicle for Mitchell to solo and show his stuff.

Luckily the Danish TV performance has been preserved. Luckily because if you are a student of Mitchell's drumming, it's instructive to hear how his role is transformed over BBC and bootleg recordings into what should be his most renowned solo: "Voodoo Chile." The eruption of percussion that allows Hendrix and Winwood to pause and regroup following their dueling solos is actually an integral part of the song's structure as live versions of "Catfish Blues" from 1968 attest to. The easiest place to compare the two arrangements is on *Blues*, where the November 10, 1967, performance of "Catfish Blues" is followed immediately by "Voodoo Chile Blues."

"Voodoo Child (Slight Return)"

Mitchell's incisive instincts are showcased on the recording session that birthed "Voodoo Child (Slight Return)" in a single day. Asked by his publicist, Michael Goldstein, to act like the Experience were recording a new song for a television crew, Hendrix took the riff from the previous day's recording of "Voodoo Chile" and wah-wahed the hell out of it with Mitchell tagging on the hi-hat snap that is a signature feature of the song's riff on his very first hearing. I think this is the finest example of the musical telepathy that existed between Hendrix and his drummer. Without the hi-hat snap, the riff is missing its exclamation point.

Producing *The Cry of Love*

In Mitchell, Hendrix had found a kindred spirit. Whereas, according to Chris Barber, Noel Redding "didn't seem to be particularly interested in music one way or another, Jimi was very interested in music, and so was Mitch." This was seconded by Hendrix, who told a journalist from *Beat Instrumental* in May 1968 that: "Mitch has this 'feel' for sounds, like knowing exactly what instruments to use."

This is why when a desperate Michael Jeffery reached out to Mitchell to coproduce Hendrix's first posthumous album, he had unwittingly tapped the perfect source. Jeffery was simply looking to salvage eighteen months' worth of recordings and maximize the public's desire to purchase what Lenny Kaye called "Hendrix's final effort" in his *Rolling Stone* review of *The Cry of Love.*

But it was Mitchell with his "'feel' for sounds" who suggested overdubbing drums on "Angel" and having Buzzy Linhart add vibes on "Drifting" when challenged with fleshing out a bare track that, while featuring all the members of Hendrix's Cry of Love lineup, was essentially a melody held in place by mirroring guitar lines and Hendrix's backwards guitar track. Recalling in his autobiography that one of the guitar lines "had gone through a univerb 'leslie' effect"—an effect favored by George Harrison during his *All Things Must Pass* phase—Mitchell thought vibes would complement the guitar line nicely and that was "what Jimi would have wanted."

Buzzy Linhart was a former member of Seventh Sons at the start of a solo recording career that would stretch to the mid-1970s and include coauthorship for Bette Midler's theme song, "Friends." Known for his expertise on vibraphone, he was asked to come to Electric Lady Studios and add the vibes track. Of this experience Linhart is quoted in John McDermott's *Hendrix*: "It was just so touching to be in the studio he built, playing back this tape and hearing Jimi's beautiful voice."

In interviews with John Platt that form the basis of his autobiography *Inside the Experience*, Mitchell revealed that, aside from still grieving for Hendrix, what made the effort of the coproducers more daunting was that Warner Brothers had tapes in addition to the tapes stored at Electric Lady Studios, but they weren't allowing their usage. (Mitchell didn't know the reason behind this lack of cooperation, but we know now that Jeffery owed Warner Brothers a substantial amount of money.) They weren't working with all the best material Hendrix left behind.

And what was left behind "was a real jigsaw puzzle to put together" because the pieces weren't always in the same key or the recording was inferior. Mitchell told Platt that during the piecing together of *The Cry of Love* he kept "getting these incredibly vivid dreams and conversations. 'What do you think of this mix?' And he'd tell me." So according to Mitchell at least, Hendrix did have a say in what was presented to the world as Hendrix's swan song. As Kaye wrote, it was "something to savor slowly because there'll be no others."

Little did Lenny know that it would only be the foundation for a cottage industry: in September 2011, *Forbes* announced Jimi Hendrix was one of the top fifteen dead celebrities along with the likes of Michael Jackson,

Charles Schulz, and Albert Einstein. His estate had brought in over seven million dollars thanks to reissues and new box sets between October 2010 and October 2011, which made Hendrix #9 on the list, a number he would have approved of since many of those who knew him, including Sharon Lawrence, have recalled Hendrix discussing numerology and his fascination with the number 9.

Post-Experience Lawsuits

Mitchell along with Redding had signed a production contract with Mike Jeffery and Chas Chandler in October 1966. Although initially hired to merely be Hendrix's backing band, the contract stipulated that the drummer and bassist were part of the Jimi Hendrix Experience. The band would split 2.5 percent of record sales royalties and each member put on a weekly salary. The sidemen each took in £15 weekly. When Hendrix signed a management contract with Yameta—basically a Bahamian tax dodge—the sidemen were not asked to sign, and they were never employees of Yameta. A sizeable portion of the Experience's income, however, was funneled into Yameta's accounts and never made it back to the pockets of the rhythm section that earned it.

Redding had been asking questions as early as 1967 about the Experience's finances, but now that Hendrix was dead, Mitchell too was concerned. Attorney Leo Branton had been hired by Al Hendrix to straighten out the financial mess left in the wake of his son's passing, and the surviving Experience Makers sought a settlement according to the oral agreement between the three Experience Makers to split everything on a 50-25-25 basis. Leo Branton argued, however, that this oral agreement had no basis in law, and without a signed contract to substantiate their claim, the sidemen had to settle for a sum in 1972 far less than what they had earned and did not take into account what the estate was to earn in subsequent years from record sales, CD sales, videos, mp3s, and so on. Mitchell settled for $300,000 in 1973.

Another Hendrix-related lawsuit that Mitchell was involved with concerned the British publication of David Henderson's *'Scuse Me While I Kiss the Sky*. Many members of Hendrix's London entourage were upset with Henderson, a black journalist, casting Mitchell and Redding as racists. Kathy Etchingham was also upset as being portrayed as a white, spaced-out party girl who caused Hendrix's drug addiction and eventual death. Redding owned up to calling Hendrix a "coon" but said it was said affectionately and that Hendrix had laughed about it.

Jimi Hendrix knew that Mitch Mitchell (center) was his partner in time.   *Author's collection*

The Black Gold Suite

An autobiographical suite of songs known as the *Black Gold Suite* was on a cassette tape Hendrix gave to Mitchell with five other tapes while in Maui, Hawaii, for the filming of what would become *Rainbow Bridge*. According to Mitchell, he was returning to England and the tape was given to him so he could develop drum parts for the acoustically recorded suite before meeting up with Hendrix and Cox to play the Isle of Wight Festival.

Upon Hendrix's death, the tape became the stuff of legend and was rumored to be owned by a disgruntled Electric Lady employee who had stolen it until Hendrix historian Tony Brown innocently asked Mitchell about the tape, which was in his possession twenty-two years later. Mitchell didn't know that Hendrix collectors all over the world were searching for it. Mitchell eventually sold it to Experience Hendrix.

Some of the fourteen songs on the cassette ("Here Comes Black Gold" is on both cassette sides, and "Astro Man" is presented in two parts) have been previously issued although with full instrumentation. These songs are "Drifting," "Stepping Stone," "Machine Gun," and "Astro Man." Another song, "Send My Love to the Joan of Arc," has the same chord progression as "Send My Love to Linda."

In a 1969 interview, Hendrix described his autobiographical work-in-progress and the characters such as Astro Man and Captain Coconut and said "I was all these people." The song titles on the tape do sketch out a story's arc.

The first song from *The Black Gold Suite* cassette to be issued by the estate was "Suddenly November Morning," the closing track on *West Coast Seattle*

Boy. (The estate has indicated that it intends to issue the suite in its entirety sometime in the coming decade.) It's a poignant song, quite moving, with the reference to a November morning possibly referring to Hendrix's birth and hence the reason it was the first song in the autobiographical suite.

The Guitar That Made Woodstock Famous

Having received insufficient compensation for his contributions to Hendrix's music, Mitchell in 1990 sold the guitar that made Woodstock famous: the white Fender Stratocaster used to play "Star Spangled Banner."

In an article written for musicradar.com, Neville Marten said that when Mitchell brought the guitar in to be repaired, he studied the guitar he had seen in the movie *Woodstock*: "The nut had been switched around in its slot to accommodate Hendrix's upside-down stringing method; . . . cigarette burns were evident on the headstock (Jimi would secure his cigarette under the sixth string, and when he went off on an extended solo it would burn down to the stub); and there was staining from his shirt on the creamy-white finish." It was the real McCoy.

Sotheby's sold the guitar in London for £198,000 (approximately $340,000 at the time). It has since been resold privately and is owned EMP Museum in Seattle. It is rumored to have been bought by Microsoft's Paul Allen for $2,000,000.

Death

Mitch Mitchell died in his sleep from natural causes at the Benson Hotel in Portland, Oregon, on November 12, 2008. He was sixty-one years old and had been on tour as part of the eighteen-city 2008 Experience Hendrix All Star Tour, a semiannual tour that he had taken part in previously. He had played at the Arlene Schnitzer Concert Hall five days earlier, although according to reports his appearance had been limited to one song and he was seen by fans being assisted as he entered the auditorium. Mitchell and others on the tour thought he was suffering from the flu. The show in Portland was the final show of the tour, and Mitchell had decided to rest up at the Benson—the Portland hotel where every U.S. president since William Taft has stayed—before returning home to England.

He is said to be buried in Seattle, Washington. Since Jimi Hendrix is also said to be buried in Seattle, one thinks immediately that the two musicians must be buried near one another, but this is not the case. Hendrix is actually buried in Greenwood Memorial Park in Renton, Washington, eleven miles away from Seattle.

The cover of *Cry of Love*, one of two posthumous albums that Mitch Mitchell co-produced.   *Courtesy of Robert Rodriguez*

21

By the Time We Got to Woodstock

Gypsy Sun and Rainbows

One has only to hear the Electric Church version of "Red House" (described in Chapter 20) to understand why Hendrix believed the concept of adding musicians and expanding the sounds around him would work and enrich the music he was creating. It was this desire for expanded lineups and the revelation that Billy Cox would be his future bassist expressed to *Rolling Stone* journalist Jerry Hopkins that led to Noel Redding quitting the Experience before the final planned concert of the 1969 tour of America at the Denver Pop Festival and flying home the following morning.

Hendrix's publicist Michael Goldstein correctly observes in *Jimi Hendrix: Live at Woodstock* that "the one thing you have to know about an act is that they have a direction that they're going in musically. And when they reach the summit of their life, when they are creatively on top of the mountain, they don't know where to go next and start looking around." With Redding gone back to England, Hendrix had no recourse but to follow through on his often-stated vision of musical expansion, which he began to do with Billy Cox, the bassist he knew from back in his army days. As Cox says in *Jimi Hendrix: Live at Woodstock*, "We knew it would take getting away, concentrating on getting the right people together to form this group that he had desires in forming."

This group would be Gypsy Sun and Rainbows.

Woodstock Music and Art Fair

Hendrix and Cox were in the process of forming the lineup that would become Gypsy Sun and Rainbows when management informed the guitarist that he'd been signed to headline the Woodstock Music and Art Fair for $32,000. Hendrix was already living in the Woodstock area and jamming with the men who would form the basis of Gypsy Sun and Rainbows—the band incorrectly identified as the Jimi Hendrix Experience by the stage emcee—and the one featured in the Woodstock movie. Billy Cox had reached out to Larry Lee, another Nashville musician just back from a stint in Vietnam, to play rhythm guitar, and Hendrix hired Jerry Velez and Juma Sultan, two percussionists he knew from New York City. The omission of a keyboardist in Gypsy Sun and Rainbows is baffling. With the musical rewards that playing with Steve Winwood, Lee Michaels, and Herbie Rich had demonstrated on previous occasions, it's strange that Hendrix failed to find a spot for a keyboardist in his new band.

Up in the air in July was whether or not the drummer at the festival would be Mitch Mitchell or Buddy Miles, who had met Larry Lee at the airport with Hendrix. Mitchell had arrived back in London on July 13th and was known to be reluctant to be in a band of minorities. This wasn't a racist thing. He just wasn't sure if he would fit in. But as expressed elsewhere, Hendrix did not want to lose Mitchell: he knew his drummer was his partner catalyst.

In the end, Mitchell—probably through the intervention of manager Michael Jeffery—returned to play Woodstock, but the drummer sensed trouble with Hendrix's new lineup immediately. He couldn't understand why there was a need for a rhythm guitarist—hadn't that idea already been nixed in December 1966?—and, as he stated in *Inside the Experience*: "There's always a problem with two or more drummers or percussionists—either it works well or it gets competitive. It's all right having competition if you can count, if you can't, you're fucked. They couldn't count. The band was a shambles."

Worst of all, Mitchell knew Hendrix knew it. Heck, even Billy Cox knew it and approached Larry Lee about trading in his Gibson Les Paul for a Fender Stratocaster and a sound that suited Hendrix's music. Lee stuck to his guns, however, and so when you see any footage from Woodstock—one of Gypsy Sun and Rainbows' three appearances—Lee's up there playing his Gibson. He's wearing a white outfit similar to Hendrix's. That is where any resemblance between the two guitarists ends.

When Michael Jeffery had signed the contract for Jimi Hendrix to headline the festival that is now simply referred to as Woodstock, he did not envision it would be the defining concert of a generation. Jeffery already lived in the area ninety miles away from New York City and could not envision hundreds of thousands of young people trekking to a nearby rock concert festival where they would close down roads, drop acid, and dance naked in the rain.

By the time Hendrix and his ramshackle band of Rainbows made it to Woodstock, it was no longer "half a million strong." Tens of thousands had begun to make their way home. For the musicians still arriving, the helicopters made them feel as if they were in a military zone, as Mitch Mitchell says in the DVD *Jimi Hendrix: Live at Woodstock*, and not a peace festival.

Bands had trouble getting to the site—legend has it that Neil Young and Jimi Hendrix stole a jeep to get there after missing their helicopter connection—and so the schedule slipped. Jefferson Airplane was the first band signed for the now historic festival and so slotted in as headliners for the second night, but Saturday night came and went without them. They wouldn't go on until Sunday morning, and when you hear Grace Slick refer to "the heavy groups" on the movie soundtrack, she is referring to the Who and Ten Years After, the bands who actually wound up headlining Saturday's lineup.

A similar fate awaited Jimi Hendrix. Concert promoter Michael Lang suggested reconfiguring the schedule to ensure Hendrix's appearance came on Sunday night but Hendrix's management team nixed that idea, and so Sunday night's headliner waited all night in a cottage with no heat before going on Monday morning at approximately 8 a.m. By then the crowd had dwindled to approximately 30,000. (Nineteen-fifties revivalists Sha-Na-Na went on just before Hendrix.)

A legendary performance was caught on film and record (Hendrix's engineer Eddie Kramer was behind the boards), but that is only because of judicious editing, as evidenced by the 1999 release of the *Live at Woodstock* two-CD set (Hendrix's entire set except for the two numbers sung by rhythm guitarist Larry Lee; the studio version of "Mastermind" on *West Seattle Country Boy* demonstrates why) and the DVD *Jimi Hendrix: Live at Woodstock* (missing the Lee numbers and "Hear My Train A Comin'").

During the first two-thirds of the 140-minute set there are flashes of brilliance, especially during the heavily percussive sequence of "Spanish Castle Magic," "Lover Man," and "Foxy Lady." The crowd is really into "Jam Back at the House" as surviving footage proves. It is not the unmitigated disaster some would have you believe. Yes, Hendrix apologizes frequently for the ramshackle lineup behind him, but he is often smiling and even dances, something I've never seen him do elsewhere.

The set suddenly catches fire during an almost fourteen-minute rendition of "Voodoo Child (Slight Return)" as the core of the group—Hendrix, Mitchell, and Cox—free themselves of the fellow musicians hobbling them and forge ahead, split apart for Hendrix's iconic version of "Star Spangled Banner" (which was not on Hendrix's handwritten set list) and then segue into "Purple Haze" as the Experience had done during shows on their final tour of America.

Concert poster for what would be the final Jimi Hendrix Experience appearance ever.
Courtesy of Robert Rodriguez

The Harlem United Block Association Benefit

One of the refrains you pick up from fellow musicians, old girlfriends, even business associates is that Jimi Hendrix's downfall can be attributed to his inability at forming close ties with those around him. It's a fair enough observation but begs the following question: "If he didn't care about friends, why did he reach out to pre-stardom friends when he returned to America and in the years afterwards?"

Running back to Harlem in July 1967 to tell of his "overnight success" in London to old flame Fayne Pridgeon and the twins he had befriended named Arthur and Albert Allen, they received Hendrix as real friends would: they didn't believe him.

Pridgeon told Hendrix that the empty album sleeve bearing his likeness was a fake and something he had printed up in Times Square to fool them. If he really made a record, where was the vinyl evidence? It was only after he took them downtown to Central Park where the Jimi Hendrix Experience was opening for the Rascals at Wollman Skating Rink that they believed him.

And being a friend, Hendrix stayed in touch, and it was the Allen twins who helped arrange his appearance benefiting Harlem's United Block Association on September 5, 1969. Jeffery agreed reluctantly to the appearance, which his star hoped would be the beginning of making inroads with the black community absent at his concerts. Only on the day of the event, it was clear the locals were more interested in Big Maybelle, a rhythm and blues vocalist who, according to DJ Eddie O'Jay, "was a household name in most of Harlem."

Hendrix and his entourage didn't help matters by arriving late, which forced a rearrangement of the scheduled acts, and many left after Big Maybelle's performance. Even the cameraman hired by the Allen twins to document the event for posterity used most of the film shooting Big Maybelle, and all that was left of Hendrix that September day is footage of him taking the stage, which was after a couple of kids had stolen his guitar. It was only retrieved through connections that the Allen twins had with the community.

The event didn't do much to kindle Hendrix's ties to the black community, but it did help his friends the Allen twins. They said they could deliver a big star to headline the benefit and they had. Hendrix continued to nurture his friendship with the twins, and in 1970 he not only allowed the twins, rechristened as the Ghetto Fighters, to contribute background vocals on four tracks ("Dolly Dagger," "Freedom," "Izabella," and "Stepping Stone") but was producing their album at Electric Lady Studios when he died. The Ghetto Fighters album died with him.

Dick Cavett

An exhausted Hendrix missed the appearance on *The Dick Cavett Show* featuring other musicians who had played Woodstock. Cavett's show was broadcast live, and according to Bob Levine, the talk show host "kept saying 'Hendrix should be here anytime now,'" but that "Hendrix had thought his appearance had been cancelled as a result of his own delay getting on stage at Woodstock." Hendrix was forced to placate ABC's talk show host by appearing on September 9, 1969.

It was Hendrix's second appearance on the show, and the television host called upon the guitarist to defend his performance of the national anthem, which was already creating a storm in the press. Hendrix seemed bemused by the reaction. He had been slipping the "Star Spangled Banner" into sets since August 23, 1968, where he played it at the Singer Bowl in Flushing Meadow Park in New York City. But his near solo performance at Woodstock—only Mitchell accompanied him, and according to the drummer he only did so to keep his hands warm—had now brought national attention and discussion to his battle-strewn arrangement. It was as if many citizens had never read Francis Scott Key's lyrics, which describe . . . a battle scene.

Although some bootleg performances of "The Star Spangled Banner" do include derogatory asides from Hendrix—for example, after playing the passage where the flag still stands, Hendrix would say "Yeah, big deal!"—it is best to view Hendrix's arrangement as the voice of the loyal opposition. The bombastic complaints overlook the beauty inherent in Hendrix's performance at Woodstock and elsewhere. (Although it must be said the Woodstock performance is the peak live version; also highly recommended, however, is the studio version recorded at the Record Plant on March 18, 1969, that is available on the essential *The Jimi Hendrix Experience* box set released in 2000.) And Hendrix himself told Cavett that he thought his arrangement was beautiful. Cavett then let the viewing audience know that Hendrix had been a paratrooper and served his country. In his commentary to the DVD of Hendrix's Cavett appearances, Cavett says he shared this part of Hendrix's bio so the rednecks (and hardhats) out there in television land would understand that the guitarist was a loyal American.

For the performances of "Izabella" and "Machine Gun" on *The Dick Cavett Show*, Hendrix limited his supporting lineup to Cox, Mitchell, and Juma Sultan, although Sultan said even on this occasion Jeffery had tried to prevent the percussionist from appearing. Jerry Velez has said he was prevented from appearing on *The Tonight Show* in July and that the same thing almost happened to Juma, who, although asked by Jimi to accompany

Jimi Hendrix at the Woodstock Music and Art Fair.   *Author's collection*

him, arrived at *The Dick Cavett Show* only to find his drums had not been delivered by Hendrix's roadies. He had to borrow a conga from a friend. "It was supposed to be Mitch, Jimmy and Billy, so that (Gypsy Sun and Rainbows) wouldn't be publicized," said Larry Lee.

The Salvation Club

On the evening following the second Cavett appearance, Gypsy Sun and Rainbows played their final concert at the Salvation Club, a performance that was reviewed better by the local press than it has been remembered historically. Hendrix only agreed to the concert at the small club because it was a press party, and the club's owner, Bobby Woods, was a friend who often scored cocaine for Jimi. Woods was later found murdered, the victim of a gangland rubout.

The appearance of a rock superstar went unadvertised, but a mention in the *Village Voice* brought in a lucky crowd that appears to have been disappointed when the set did not feature Experience numbers. They started playing at 12:15, and, according to the review that appeared in *Rock*: "Jimi

Jimi leads Gypsy Sun and Rainbows at Woodstock. Larry Lee is in the foreground.
Author's collection

began the set with an untitled instrumental that quickly turned into a jam. . . . Mitch Mitchell sat, mouth wide open, flailing away at his drums, taking a solo, receiving well-deserved applause, the African drummer kept a frantic beat, and the bass player, sadly, could barely be heard above the din. Alternating with Jimi, the second lead guitarist took half the leads and he was wonderful, providing a good foil for Jimi who did his spectacular thing, often with the help of his trusty wah-wah pedal. When Jimi was allowed to take over, the room simply rocked with sound."

Sounds like a good show to me and a hint of the Band of Gypsys that was to come.

Dissolution

Hendrix's roadie Eric Barrett told Chris Welch that Hendrix "realized (Gypsy Sun and Rainbows) was not the right formula. The other guys were just jamming, and not playing properly." And so between recording tracks such as "Valleys of Neptune" and "Sky Blues Today" in late September, Hendrix informed percussionists Sultan and Velez that he was disbanding Gypsy Sun and Rainbows. Larry Lee had already returned to Memphis fed up with interference from Michael Jeffery. Of these three musicians, only Sultan was to play with Hendrix again.

Cox, however, was held over to form Band of Gypsys and would be Hendrix's bassist for the rest of his life, including the Alan Douglas sessions.

22

Have You Heard About the Midnight Rambler?

The Rolling Stones Meet Jimi Hendrix

I had a chick run off with Jimi Hendrix once," Keith Richards is quoted as saying in *The Ultimate Experience*, Johnny Black's oral history of the life and times of Hendrix, flippantly adding: "I think he's a nice cat, actually." The "chick" he was referring to was British model Linda Keith, his girlfriend of a little over two years when she flew in May 1966 to New York City in advance of the Richards, who was scheduled to arrive with the other Stones on June 23rd for a thirty-show summer tour, which sometimes included two shows in two cities on the same day. Little did either Keith know it was just the beginning of the complicated relationship between Jimi Hendrix and the Rolling Stones.

Keith Richards and Linda Keith

The couple was already drifting apart over drug abuse—believe it or not, Linda Keith's, not Richards's—but this is not why Linda Keith did not accompany the Stones' lead guitarist on the tour. Touring in 1966 was strictly for the boys; girlfriends were not invited because both management and the press were eager to make rock stars appear available to female fans.

The boys in the band were also eager to take advantage of this feminine attention. It was as John Lennon told Jann Wenner in his infamous *Rolling Stone* interview conducted shortly after the Beatles' breakup: "The Beatles tours were like Fellini's *Satyricon*." With the Rolling Stones' sharpened bad boy image, one could only expect the same from Mick and company. So try to imagine Richards's surprise when he returned to Manhattan after nine nights on the road only to find his girlfriend infatuated—and probably involved with—an unknown black guitarist. And had been for weeks.

Accompanied by her friends Roberta Goldstein and Mark Kaufman, Keith had walked into the Cheetah Club at Fifty-Third Street and Broadway in May 1966 for one of Hendrix's final performances with Curtis Knight and the Squires. The club, which could hold 2,000, was holding considerably less. The lead singer wasn't holding Keith's interest either when she met the Squires' guitarist "and from that moment I just became completely involved."

Keith asked the "shy and nervous" performer over for a drink. He told her his name was Jimmy James and he was ditching Knight and clubs in Times Square and even Harlem for the scene further downtown in Greenwich Village. He told her that another singer-guitarist named Ritchie Havens had told him a few nights earlier that the Village crowds would be more receptive to what he was trying to do musically.

James took Keith up on her offer to accompany her to her friends' apartment on Sixty-Third Street that was known as the Red House because of its mostly red interior, including red velvet walls. (It was also possibly the inspiration for the song titles of Hendrix's best-known blues number; a possibility given credence when Hendrix sang "My girlfriend Linda don't live here no more" during his infamous Isle of Wight performance in August 1970, just weeks before his death.)

According to Charles R. Cross's *Room Full of Mirrors*, Hendrix was asked if he'd like to try some acid, only to answer "No . . . but I'd love to try to some of that LSD stuff." Hendrix's new friends laughed, unaware that acid was known as a white person's drug at the time and not used by Hendrix's Harlem friends, which explains his unfamiliarity with the slang term even if he was a musician.

Hendrix's first acid trip may have begun at the so-called Red House, but it wound up in Keith Richards's room in the Hotel Hilton on Sixth Avenue. Linda Keith's love of the blues was deep—it was one of the things that had drawn her to Richards—and Hendrix welcomed the rare opportunity to discuss his deep feelings for this music with a white woman. Keith played rare blues 45s she had in her collection as well as Bob Dylan's *Blonde on Blonde*. The recording artist who would go on to be Dylan's finest interpreter revealed his love of Dylan—something else ostracizing him from his Harlem friends—and grabbed a guitar and played along. "It was the most special concert you could imagine," Keith told Cross.

Keith insists her relationship with Hendrix was strictly the meeting of two minds over music and not sexual because "I was going out with Keith and I was a middle class girl with middle class values." This portrayal of their relationship is challenged by the recollections of Andrew Loog Oldham and Seymour Stein, two established rock managers she lured to Hendrix's performances at the Café Wha? in Greenwich Village in hopes of finding him representation.

Oldham was the obvious first choice. Not only was he the Rolling Stones manager and record producer at the time, he was also in town helping with the promotion of *Aftermath*. It was through Oldham that Keith had met Richards—Keith was best friends with Oldham's wife Sheila—and she hoped this connection could work to Jimmy's advantage. But when Oldham went to see Hendrix, all he saw was "trouble with a capital T" as Robert Preston sings in the musical *The Music Man*. He quickly questioned the nature of the relationship between his lead guitarist's girlfriend and the black performer addressing her from the Café Wha?'s stage. "I had enough trouble already with the Stones," Oldham told Cross and decided to pass on signing Hendrix.

The second manager Keith persuaded to have a look at Jimmy James was Seymour Stein, who was still a decade from being the renowned squire of Sire Records who had signed the Ramones and Talking Heads and renamed punk music as "New Wave" because he disliked the term "punk." But in 1966 he was just founding Sire Productions with record producer Richard Gottehrer and looking for acts. Stein sensed Hendrix's potential, but he too was put off as he watched Hendrix smash his guitar. Still, Stein did like Hendrix's original material and gave him a second look, only to walk away for good after witnessing a violent argument between Keith and Hendrix.

Having failed with Oldham and Stein and running out of options, Keith decided to play her remaining ace: the Rolling Stones.

Bill Wyman

The Rolling Stones were a little over a week into their summer tour of America tour on July 2, 1966, when they helicoptered into Forest Hills Tennis Stadium in Queens, New York, to kick off the 1966 Music Festival before "9,400 listeners and 375 policemen" according to the *New York Times'* less than flattering review the following morning.

The ten-song set at Forest Hills was ample evidence that the rhythm and blues band now fully embraced rock 'n' roll music as they closed with "19th Nervous Breakdown," "Paint It, Black," and "(I Can't Get No) Satisfaction." The band planned to celebrate wowing New York City afterwards by partying at Ondine's, on East Fifty-Ninth Street, where a black guitarist championed by Richards's girlfriend was playing. The Stones' love of the blues was at the core of their collective identity, and, according to Linda Keith, nobody played blues guitar the way Jimmy James did.

This is the night that bassist Bill Wyman leaves so many details out of in his foreword to Gared Mankowitz's *The Experience*, a superb collection of two

photo sessions Mankowitz shot with the Jimi Hendrix Experience before their debut album, *Are You Experienced*, catapulted the band to fame. Wyman misrepresents the Stones' role in bringing "Jimmy James" to the attention of the Animals and their bassist Chas Chandler, who would go on to manage Hendrix since it was Linda Keith and not the Rolling Stones who brought Chandler and Hendrix together. But inside Ondine's that summer night, Wyman and Brian Jones were the most supportive Stones of the unknown guitarist. While Mick Jagger was decidedly unimpressed (and left underestimating his future rival in London), Keith Richards nervously assessed Hendrix's relationship with *his* girlfriend. Wyman and Jones offered their support, but there was little they could do for Jimmy while in the middle of a tour.

But when Jimmy James—now fully metamorphosed as Jimi Hendrix—stepped off of a Pan Am Airways flight at Heathrow Airport in London on September 24, 1966, Wyman was more than willing to abet the American's rise.

On November 16th, Hendrix ironically attended the "Ruby Tuesday" recording session inside Olympic Studios. (Ironically, because the Stones' future #1 hit in America was written by Keith Richards and an uncredited Brian Jones for Linda Keith, who was now involved with Jones because Richards and Keith had broken up over her affair with Hendrix in Manhattan. Jagger, though credited, played no role in the song's composition.) It was Hendrix's first visit to Olympic, the Stones' studio of preference. Wyman later urged both the chief Experience Maker and his manager Chas Chandler to book time at the same recording studio the Stones were using.

Chandler at the time, however, was calling all the shots and, because cash was tight, said they couldn't afford Olympic; he was selling off his bass guitars as it was to fund the band's recording sessions! Wyman was adamant that Olympic with its 60 feet by 40 feet by 28 feet dimensions was the only recording studio adequate for recording Hendrix, who taped his sessions as loud as he performed. When a dispute over unpaid bills at De Lane Lea studios, where "Hey Joe" and the initial tracks for *Are You Experienced* had been recorded, forced the Experience to move to Olympic a few months later, Chandler and Hendrix found out Wyman's advice had been sound: every English Experience recording session thereafter was held at Olympic Studios.

Bill Wyman also crossed paths with Hendrix on January 29, 1968, and contributed to a special event in Paris's most prestigious music hall. L'Olympia was in the Ninth Arrondissement, and since its opening in 1888, it has survived two World Wars and hosted legendary concerts by a wide range of performers from local (Edith Piaf) to international (Grateful Dead). One of those performers was Jimi Hendrix, whose Experience gave their fourth concert ever there, opening for Johnny Hallyday. Hendrix was forever grateful for the warm reception the Parisians gave him and his unknown group, and for this reason he always tried to have something special up his multicolored sleeve when he played Paris.

So when the Experience returned to L'Olympia for their third appearance, their fortunes had changed considerably. They had four hit singles and two hit albums and were the headliners when they took the Olympia stage for the second time that night. Within their nine-song blues-heavy set, Hendrix told the audience as he introduced "Red House" that "Noel Redding's going to play guitar now." The only problem was that Redding's guitar was back at his hotel. No problem. Bill Wyman was on hand and lent Redding his electric guitar.

Brian Jones

Of all Swinging London's reigning lead guitarists, Brian Jones of the Rolling Stones was the most gleeful at the dismay the newly arrived American guitarist was causing his colleagues. "It's all wet down in the front," Brian Jones said to vocalist Terry Reid in the Bag O' Nails, a Dickensian club on Kingly Street, during one of the Experience's earliest performances. "It's wet from all of the guitar players crying."

And it was true. Hearing Hendrix the first time forced Jeff Beck to fully reassess his approach to playing electric guitar. Pete Townshend, who like Jagger had been unimpressed when Chandler first introduced him to Hendrix at a Who recording session, quickly saw past Beck's complaint that Hendrix had stolen Townshend's act. Here was a guitarist combining the rock 'n' roll of Townshend with the blues of Eric Clapton. Clapton said Hendrix, more than anyone else, was responsible for his getting to know Pete Townshend. The two guitarists both felt weak at the knees hearing this American and often attended Hendrix's earliest performances around London together.

Brian Jones's best friend, Guinness heir Tara Browne, had just died in the December 18th car accident that would be immortalized not by Jones but by John Lennon in "A Day in the Life," and so the time was ripe for Hendrix to step into this void. The guarded Hendrix, who, because of a childhood of hurt and abandonment, was wary of forming close ties with men and women, was to become friendlier with Jones than any other musician in London.

Jones and Hendrix spent countless nights together at the Cool Elephant Club, a blues club not frequented by the rock elite of London, but older music aficionados. Hendrix and Jones bonded initially over the blues but

found they enjoyed each other's company and shared a penchant for self-indulgence in drugs and flashy clothing and sleeping with their guitars.

Both musicians may have also sensed in one another the mean streak their gentle demeanors cloaked. Kathy Etchingham, who dated Jones before meeting Hendrix on his first night in London and "lived" with Hendrix for nearly three years says in *Stone Alone*, Bill Wyman's biography of the Rolling Stones: "We went to this party together and (Brian) told me the drinks were in the garage. He didn't tell me there was a big hole in the floor. I went marching in there and went straight into it. I had no skin on my knees and elbows. He was behind me and brought a few friends to watch. He thought it was very, very funny."

Jones went more out his way than the other Stones in aiding Hendrix's meteoric rise. He spoke about Jimi in interviews, talked about producing this new recording artist someday, and played on at the original stab at Dylan's "All Along the Watchtower," although Jones's piano work was never used in the final mix.

Jones hung out so often with Hendrix during the first half of 1967 that he seemed more part of the Experience camp than the Rolling Stones, and it was no surprise to those involved that he willingly introduced the Experience at the Monterey International Pop Festival.

Indirectly, Hendrix's success in his home country contributed to Jones's downfall. Within half a year, Hendrix had relocated to New York City, and so the two friends saw little of each other before Jones's death the evening of July 2, 1969. Though some suspect murder, it is officially accepted that Jones, dismissed a month earlier from the Stones, drowned in his swimming pool, the property having formerly been owned by *Winnie the Pooh* author A. A. Milne.

According to Experience drummer Mitchell: "Brian Jones' death hit Jimi very hard." Jones was the first rock superstar to die in his prime, and one wishes Jones's death had hit Jimi harder; one wishes it had made him reevaluate his own self-destructive lifestyle. As it was, Hendrix himself was dead within fifteen months, and a second rock superstar entered into the infamous 27 Club, of which, at the time of this writing, Amy Winehouse is the latest inductee.

Keith Richards and Linda Keith (Slight Return)

But we get ahead of ourselves.

Back in New York City in July 1966 the transit fare was raised to twenty cents, former Yankees and current Mets manager Casey Stengel was elected to baseball's Hall of Fame, and Linda Keith of the United Kingdom was running out of options that might help Jimi James. (Hendrix had changed the spelling of his name, thus beginning his metamorphosis into Jimi Hendrix.) Andrew Loog Oldham and Seymour Stein had both passed on managing Hendrix, and the Rolling Stones had left town and Hendrix with no more than encouraging words.

Linda Keith was also running out of time. The Rolling Stones tour would end at the Hawaii International Center in Honolulu on July 28th, and she'd soon be going back to merry ol' England and her modeling career. Then she ran into Chas Chandler of the Animals, an acquaintance from London, in Ondine's one evening. Chandler let Keith know that he was on a farewell tour of sorts. Front man Eric Burdon would be soldiering on with a new lineup of Animals, but Chandler was leaving to try his hand at the more lucrative profession of managing; Animals manager Michael Jeffery had agreed to split management duties for acts that Chandler found.

Keith urged Chandler to make Jimi James and his band the Blue Flames his first signing and suggested he come round the Café Wha? before the Animals' performance at Wollman Skating Rink in Central Park the following afternoon. Chandler agreed, arrangements were made, and Keith hurried to find Hendrix with a little inside info: Chandler had revealed he was looking for a singer or a band he could use as a vehicle to release "Hey Joe" as a single in the United Kingdom. The Leaves had already recorded and released Billy Roberts's only composition as a single in the U.S. after hearing the Byrds perform the song in concert. Their version, as well as the Byrds version on their album *Fifth Dimension,* was sprightly, and Chandler was convinced a slower rendition would chart back home.

As Keith Richards wrote in his best-selling autobiography *Life,* Keith "picked up a copy of a demo I had of Tim Rose singing a song called 'Hey Joe.' And took that round to Roberta Goldstein's, where Jimi was, and played it to him. This is rock-and-roll history. So he got the song from me, apparently." This is just the latest fuel to the debate as to whether Hendrix was already familiar with "Hey Joe" before Keith mentioned Chandler's intentions, but there's no doubt the version Hendrix played for a flabbergasted Chandler inside Café Wha? convinced the new manager that he had to sign the black, left-handed guitarist he was listening to.

Hendrix also got a white Fender Stratocaster from Richards as well, a point confirmed by both Keiths. Linda Keith had lifted it from Richards's hotel room and gave it to Hendrix, who was in desperate need of a guitar. This was the same guitar—the only guitar—that Hendrix brought with him when he landed at Heathrow Airport after he had agreed to go with Chandler to England.

Keith found Hendrix in the Scotch of St. James in Mayfair in central London, a club done up like a Scottish hunting lodge that rock's elite frequented. Hendrix was drinking with friends of Chandler and talking to Kathy Etchingham, the aforementioned party girl who would go on to become Hendrix's steadiest flame in England. On this November night, however, Etchingham did not know who Keith was or of her relationship with Hendrix and was surprised when a row broke out that involved pulled hair, an overturned table, and a broken whiskey bottle being held up to Keith's pretty neck by one of Etchingham's girlfriends.

The next morning Keith burst into the hotel room where Hendrix and Etchingham were sleeping and stole back Richard's white Fender Strat from Hendrix. As quoted by Hendrix historian Tony Brown, Etchingham said, "Later, after we were up, she came back, took off all her clothes, and climbed into bed. She said Jimi could have his guitar back on condition that he got into bed with her. For once he refused such an offer and sent her on her way."

Still, Hendrix did need that Fender Strat and told Etchingham he'd have to pay Keith a visit and convince her to give it back. Little is known of what was said or done (or undone), but Hendrix, as he did with so many women, somehow charmingly disarmed Keith and returned with the guitar he would use on his earliest recordings, including his first single "Hey Joe." Chandler was right: the song was a hit in England, rising to #6 and spending ten weeks on the charts.

Mick Jagger

Jimi Hendrix's relationship with Mick Jagger was the most complicated with a Rolling Stone.

When Sharon Lawrence quotes Jagger in *Jimi Hendrix: The Intimate Story of a Betrayed Musical Legend* as having expressed to a British journalist in early 1967 that "Hendrix is the most exciting, sexual, and sensual performer I have ever seen," Jagger was speaking from firsthand experience. Not only had he seen Hendrix swoop in and steal Keith Richards's "bird," he'd sat beside his own girlfriend Marianne Faithfull in London's 7½ Club in January 1967 and watched Hendrix charm Faithfull: a sexual competition that would span two continents was on.

Faithfull wrote later that Jimi Hendrix was the only performer Jagger felt threatened his position as Swinging London's leading satyr, which accounted for his often cavalier behavior toward Hendrix.

Faithfull writes in her autobiography of her regret that she never went off with Hendrix. Devon Wilson, however, *did* go off with Jagger when he made similar advances to Hendrix's American soul mate, the inspiration for "Dolly Dagger," the surname's deliberate rhyme being one of several digs at Jagger in the song's lyrics.

A beautiful black super groupie from Ohio, in the wake of Hendrix's Monterey triumph, Wilson latched on to him and became his *personal* secretary, the person who would secure drugs and even girls for Hendrix's pleasure, increasing her hold over him as she did. He saw an evil twin in her, and she welded great influence over him. Hendrix's heroin addiction—the depth of which is a subject of much debate—can be traced directly back to her and may have been something she used to keep him addicted to her.

Jealousy was another means of manipulation, and it was her involvement with Mick Jagger whenever he came to New York City that led to Hendrix hiding behind Keith Richards's amp on the evening of November 27, 1969, the first of two shows at Madison Square Garden. The Stones were in the middle of their first tour of America since the 1966 tour where they first encountered Jimi James, and their first with Mick Taylor, the replacement for Hendrix's dead friend Brian Jones. This didn't prevent Hendrix from being friendly with Taylor prior to the show.

Taylor had jammed previously with Hendrix in 1968 when, as one of John Mayall's Bluesbreakers, he'd opened for the Experience. As Stanley Booth recalls in *The Ultimate Experience*: "Mick Taylor handed his guitar to Hendrix and asked him to play. 'Oh I can't,' he said. 'I have to string it different.' Hendrix was left-handed but he went ahead and played guitar upside down, a wizard he was." (Footage of this can be seen in the 40th Anniversary Deluxe Box Set edition of *Get Yer Ya-Yas Out!*, the Stones' first great live album.)

November 27, 1969, was also the occasion of Hendrix's twenty-seventh (and final) birthday, and Devon threw a big party for him at Monte Kay's Upper East Side apartment that many of the Stones attended, including Jagger. In the June 1970 issue of *Rags*, an interview with Wilson appeared in which she recounted to Daphne Davis how she met the Stones: as is usually the case she went out first with Brian Jones, "the true Rolling Stone." (The Rolling Stones were rather incestuous with their Lady Janes!)

When she heard the Stones were coming back to the United States in 1969, she "knew I would hear from Mick. He called me and asked me to come to Philadelphia for their concert. Then we spent a week together in New York. Six beautiful days and nights." The interviewer asked what Hendrix thought, possibly because the interview was conducted in his apartment and he was only a bedroom away. "What did Jimi think? Oh he loved it but he was jealous, too."

Mick Taylor was playing with John Mayall's Bluesbreakers when he first met Jimi Hendrix. *Courtesy of Robert Rodriguez*

Jagger sought Hendrix out at the party, and the two disappeared for a while, a disappearance that has been the subject of many rumors, including fisticuffs over Devon Wilson. Sharon Lawrence, who was close to both Hendrix and Jagger, says Wilson played no part in what the two rock stars discussed. Instead, Jagger, who had faced trumped-up drug charges in London in 1967, met with Hendrix to offer support and words of advice over similar phony charges facing Hendrix in Toronto in less than a fortnight's time.

Aftermath

In September 1970, both Hendrix and the Rolling Stones toured Europe. Hendrix's tour took him through Sweden, Denmark, and West Germany before canceling dates in Austria, France, and the Netherlands due to the lingering, mentally bewildering effects bassist Billy Cox was experiencing after ingesting some bad acid in Gothenburg, Sweden. There was talk of carrying on with former Experience bassist Noel Redding or ex-Blind Faith bassist Ric Grech, but Hendrix chose to return to London, where he could keep an eye on Cox.

The Rolling Stones tour was going far better as they blazed through the many of the same countries on Hendrix's tour itinerary. Mutual friend Sharon Lawrence was recruited personally as the Stones' press representative for the tour, their first of Europe since 1967. Hendrix had warned Lawrence about working for the Stones, especially with rumors of Richards's increased drug intake. But once on the road, it was rumors of the mishaps affecting the Hendrix tour that was upsetting to Lawrence, so upsetting that Jagger—displaying a sensitivity he is not often given credit for—urged Lawrence to seek Hendrix out and determine for herself the truth behind the rumors she was hearing about his erratic behavior.

Lawrence caught up with Hendrix in Copenhagen, only to find him in good spirits backstage and surrounded by fans and musicians. This was not the man rumored to have been unable to perform at a concert in Arhus, Denmark, the previous night. Hendrix assured her he was alright and that he'd "be good tonight!"

A fortnight later, her friend was dead. The most widely accepted explanation was death by misadventure. According to the coroner's statement: "The cause of death was clearly inhalation of vomit due to barbiturate intoxication, but there is no evidence as to intention to commit suicide."

Quashed by Hendrix's death was his possible signing onto the Rolling Stones' new label. Hendrix's contract with his manager Michael Jeffery was due to lapse soon, and Hendrix had expressed an interest to several people in acquiring a new agent as well as a new label. It's unlikely such a plan would have come to fruition since he contractually owed Warner Brothers multiple recordings as repayment for loans to build Electric Lady Studios, his new recording studio on Eighth Street in New York's Greenwich Village, but it's fun to imagine what might have been. If Hendrix had signed with Rolling Stones Records, the label just might have become something more than the Stones' private label.

With Hendrix deceased, the mythmaking began and the victors began rewriting history. Jagger agreed to be interviewed for *Jimi Hendrix*, Joe Boyd's documentary. In it, a disheveled Jagger can be found sitting cross-legged on a bed, describing his interactions with Hendrix in Swinging London: "I thought he had just come out of nowhere and, like, we had just adopted him. We felt in England, like, 'cause he was great and, like, he wasn't big in America and he'd come here. I mean he'd come to England and we were there and, like, he had his first big record in England and he was ours, you know?"

No mention of seeing Hendrix as an unknown in Manhattan or of Hendrix stealing Richards's "bird" and flirting with Marianne Faithfull or Jagger's worries in 1967 that the Experience might replace the Rolling Stones as the bad boys of England as more than one rock journalist hinted. Nope, Hendrix was buried in Seattle, Washington, and Jagger rewrote the history to suit him.

23

Gonna Be a Lotta Rearrangin'

The Band of Gypsys

In the predigital age, many photographers commented that they hoped to get one good photograph for every roll of film they shot. Perhaps the same dictum should be applied to the Band of Gypsys. Together less than two months, the only artifact Jimi Hendrix's short-lived outfit officially left behind after rehearsals and five concerts was a live album issued to settle a contract dispute. We should consider that one live album—a snapshot of a time and place—to be a roll of film that left behind one great shot: "Machine Gun."

Alan Douglas

Key to the rearranging going on in Jimi Hendrix's life in 1969 was his new circle of Manhattanite friends. Devon Wilson had struck up a friendship with Collette Mimram, owner of a clothing boutique a stone's throw from the Fillmore East. Stella Douglas worked with her sister-in-law in Collette's boutique, and her husband was Alan Douglas, a producer of jazz and spoken-word records, including commercially successful recordings of Lenny Bruce and Malcolm X that were posthumously repackaged (which, unfortunately, became a blueprint for Douglas's handling of Hendrix's tapes for two decades and hence the reason some Hendrix aficionados view him as a villain).

Back in 1969, however, Douglas's role in Jimi Hendrix's life was uncontroversial. Hendrix was introduced to Douglas at Collette's boutique and thereafter they met occasionally at parties or get-togethers hosted by Stella. A stray invitation to attend an autumn recording session led, according to Douglas, to Hendrix asking Douglas's aid in imposing some structure on what Douglas saw as nothing more than jam sessions. There was a strain in the Hendrix-Jeffery relationship following the breakup of Gypsy Sun and Rainbows, and Douglas Records' offices on Fifty-fifth Street became a refuge for Hendrix during the fall of 1969.

The first session that Douglas formally produced involving Hendrix was a jam session involving Stephen Stills, John Sebastian, and Buddy Miles. Seeing that Stills had brought his guitar, Hendrix played bass. Among the takes recorded were four of Joni Mitchell's as-yet-unheard "Woodstock," and this jam was later used as the backing for "Live and Let Live," a track on Timothy Leary's *You Can Be Anyone This Time Around* that coupled Leary's voice from a press conference with "Take 5." According to Stefan Bright, who was a staff engineer with Douglas Records, Mitch Mitchell later replaced Miles at the session for some demos that Stills recorded.

The next session Hendrix did with Douglas was backing a spoken vocalist named Lightning Rod from the Last Poets, a Harlem act that had released what is arguably the first rap record on Douglas's label. Hendrix played guitar and Buddy Miles played drums, and then they dubbed bass and organ to flesh out a funky groove that would become "Doriella Du Fontaine" when Lightning Rod added his words. Unreleased in Hendrix's lifetime, it is a curiosity item with some shocking lyrics about a prostitute.

Legend has it that Band of Gypsys were formed to provide the live recording that Hendrix owed PPX and Capitol Records as part of the settlement of Ed Chalpin's lawsuit in America, but Buddy Miles had already broached the idea of forming a band to Hendrix at Douglas Records' offices. This is how Douglas got involved in producing Hendrix's own compositions. Only this version of Band of Gypsys were to include Billy Rich, Miles's bassist from the Buddy Miles Express, and it was only after Rich was unavailable that Billy Cox came on board.

There was, however, tension in the studio as Bright was not entirely supportive of using Cox as the bassist, and this ruffled the otherwise mild-mannered bassist from Nashville. The two had words, and, after a session on November 21, 1969, at the Record Plant, Cox returned to Nashville.

It was around this time that Douglas put into motion plans for a recording session that would involve Hendrix, jazz legend Miles Davis, and Davis's former drummer Tony Williams. According to Douglas, the idea originated with Davis and Hendrix was agreeable. It seemed a timely match. Davis was moving toward fully embracing electricity and production techniques used by rock bands and was in the middle of mixing the music that would become the pivotal fusion double album *Bitches Brew*. Tony Williams had already one-upped his former leader by issuing *Emergency!* with his band Lifetime in 1969. (Lifetime included Larry Young, who had jammed with Hendrix in May.)

Everything seemed settled. Reprise would issue the record. Davis, Hendrix, and Williams would each write three songs for the record. Unfortunately on the eve of the recording session Davis demanded $50,000 just to show up, and when Williams heard, asked his manager to do the same. Douglas could not meet this demand and could not approach Jeffery for the cash as Jeffery viewed Douglas as a threat. The recording session was canceled, and a dream lineup remained a dream.

In the early 1970s, Buddy Miles was a headliner in his own right.

Courtesy of Robert Rodriguez

Via a letter, on December 4, 1969, Douglas officially removed himself from having any role in Hendrix's current projects, and so Band of Gypsys progressed without his involvement.

I Hear a Caravan A Comin'

The foundation of Band of Gypsys was to be found in Gypsy Sun and Rainbows. Look at the Woodstock set and you'll find "Message to Love" and "Izabella." "Machine Gun" was first attempted in the studio on August 29, 1969, not long after Woodstock and played publicly for the first time on *The Dick Cavett Show*. Although initially performed by Gypsy Sun and Rainbows, these are all songs we associate with Band of Gypsys.

This is fair enough given that at Woodstock, when emcee Chip Monck incorrectly announced the Jimi Hendrix Experience, Hendrix said: "Dig, we'd like to get something straight. We got tired of the Experience . . . . It was blowing our minds. So we decided to change the whole thing around, and call it Gypsy Sun and Rainbows. Or short, it's nothin' but Band of Gypsys." So, fittingly, Hendrix's next band was Band of Gypsys.

Hendrix was changing the whole thing around. The lineup had reverted to the Experience blueprint (guitar, bass, and drums), but the white rhythm section was now black, and this heralded a shift. His lyrics had darkened and centered on conflict (leavened occasionally with appeals for messages and the power of love), and the new music was rooted in genres associated with black musicians.

This was the direction first indicated at Woodstock. David Fricke in his notes to *Jimi Hendrix: Live at Woodstock* says the music played that August morning "was a rough prototype for a new black-rock futurism, the missing link between Sly Stone's taut, rainbow party R&B and George Clinton's blown-mind, ghetto army funk." With the white guys now gone, that "black-rock futurism" was allowed to fully flower in Band of Gypsys, which is where many black musicians, such as Vernon Reid of Living Colour, first heard Jimi Hendrix.

Billy Cox

I'll confess that I have never been a huge fan of Billy Cox. In fact, I've had a hard time pinpointing the source of my underwhelming appreciation of Cox because I do think his playing a plus at times. He gave Hendrix some of his best basslines, especially on "Machine Gun," but while his playing on *Live at Fillmore East* is top-notch, I also find his performances to be so predictable. His style of play to me amounts to someone dotting i's and crossing t's: it's risk free, which Redding's playing was anything but.

As I watched him in *Jimi Hendrix: Voodoo Chile*, the documentary by Bill Smeaton that is available as part of the *West Coast Seattle Boy* box set, it came to me why I found him unappealing when I saw him at midnight showings of Hendrix films in the 1970s: Billy Cox was not rock enough, certainly not hippie enough, to be in Jimi Hendrix's band. He looks like the R&B player he was. He looks like he accidentally stepped on Hendrix's stage and is gaming his way through before anyone notices.

Which I know is not the case.

Billy Cox had been patiently waiting in the wings ever since an April 21, 1969, Record Plant recording session devoted to takes of "Room Full of Mirrors" while Jimi found a way to ease Noel Redding out of the Experience's live appearances. This would take some time as the Experience had a two-month tour of America lined up, and Michael Jeffery was resistant to any changes to his cash cow. It was only when Redding quit in Denver that Cox became Hendrix's full-time bassist, although it is important to note that after the aforementioned April 21st recording session, Redding only worked with Hendrix in the studio on one more occasion: March 23, 1970, on Noel Redding's "My Friend," which was intended for Redding's unreleased *Nervous Breakdown* album (perhaps a reference to Redding's nervous breakdown before a Fat Mattress concert the previous December).

Hendrix had gone and done what Redding himself had done when frustrated that the trappings of stardom didn't provide any friends: he reached into his past for Billy Cox, who wasn't only a bassist but an old army buddy.

It was in Nashville in November 1961 that Cox first heard Hendrix practicing. The sound of the guitar coming out of a serviceman's club was "somewhere between Beethoven and John Lee Hooker." Coming from a musical family—Cox's mother had played with Duke Ellington—Cox introduced himself, told the guitarist that he played bass, and soon the two had partnered and formed the King Kasuals, the beginning of a musical relationship that continued after both men were discharged and was only interrupted in spring 1963 when Hendrix—uncertain of what musical horizon he wanted but knew that unlike Cox he wasn't going to find it in Nashville—left to tour with Gorgeous George Odell.

Six years later in the spring of 1969, Hendrix telephoned Cox, who was still living in Nashville. The Experience's American tour was taking them to Memphis on April 18th, and the two arranged a meeting backstage. This was when Jimi expressed his dissatisfaction with Redding's involvement with his solo project Fat Mattress and was looking for a new bassist. Cox was agreeable and went back to Nashville with $500 from Hendrix to wait for a call that came quickly since the two were recording in New York City three days later.

Following the implosion of Gypsy Sun and Rainbows, Cox also fell out of Hendrix's orbit. He's on the only recording session Hendrix did in October, but otherwise, between September 24th and November 17th, Cox was not at any recording session until his return to form a third of the Band of Gypsys with Hendrix and Buddy Miles, the only drummer Hendrix played with in the interim.

Buddy Miles

Like Jimi Hendrix, Buddy Miles was an anomaly in the 1960s rock scene: he was a black musician in an otherwise white band. True, they had met in 1964 in Canada when the Isley Brothers shared a bill with Ruby and the Romantics that Miles was drumming for, but when they remet at the Monterey International Pop Festival, Hendrix was fronting the Experience and Miles was manning the beats for another band making its own debut: the Electric Flag.

In some ways you could classify Buddy Miles as "the difficult drummer," a characterization substantiated by Hendrix's hardware technician Eric Barrett, who commented to British journalist Chris Welch that "I think Buddy Miles and Jimi Hendrix were both front line men. Buddy played guitar as well as drums and there was a personality clash that made the [Band of Gypsys] impossible."

Like Billy Cox, Buddy Miles came from a musical family; his father played acoustic bass for several legendary jazz band leaders including Charlie Parker, Count Basie, even Duke Ellington. (You have to wonder if Cox's mother played in Ellington's band when Miles's father did.) The nickname that was to stick a lifetime came from an aunt because her nephew played drums like Buddy Rich did only Buddy Rich was a jazz drummer and Buddy Miles a fatback drummer.

Fatback drumming is a more elusive term than you'd think and not found even in music dictionaries, which is fitting as it is street slang given to drumming slang. According to www.drumdrums.com, the phrase was coined by black soul musicians in the mid-60s, which was when Miles was flitting from touring band to touring band just like Hendrix. It is said that fatback rhythms create a sound that is similar to "pork rinds cooking in deep fat," hence the name. It describes Miles's drumming perfectly as it was centered on "8th-note rock variations, and syncopations."

Photographs confirm that Hendrix and Miles renewed their friendship at Monterey, and the oft-talked-about jam session at Stephen Stills's house where everybody tripped and jammed for twenty hours straight in Stills's estimation. The friendship further flowered as the Electric Flag faded and Miles's subsequent band the Buddy Miles Express met only moderate success. Roadies spoke of Miles mooching off of Hendrix, but whenever Hendrix was on the West Coast the two men hung out and jammed, so it was only natural that they would play together someday. Or was it?

Buddy Miles told author Charles R. Cross that Hendrix "wanted a black band with a black drummer," but this has been refuted by Sharon Lawrence, who says that Hendrix told her he "'got himself talked into agreeing' that Buddy would be part of the trio." One can easily imagine Miles pressuring Hendrix to give him the slot, especially after Mitchell had turned it down, according to Cox because he wanted to spend that December back home in England. (The name Band of Gypsys originated with Mitch Mitchell, who—upon seeing Hendrix surrounded by hangers-on—commented to roadie Neville Chesters, "It's like a fuckin' band of gypsies in there.") One can easily imagine Hendrix giving in because already announced concerts at the Fillmore East were crucial to moving forward, and Miles, his session drummer for two months now, at least knew Hendrix's latest music.

Why was it crucial for the concerts to happen if Hendrix was to move forward? Because as part of the settlement (in America at least) in the summer of 1968 with Ed Chalpin (see Chapter 12) over the dollar contract signed in 1965, Hendrix owed Chalpin and Capitol Records his next album. Michael Jeffery had come up with the ingenious idea of meeting this obligation with a live album, and that's why it was essential that the New Year's Eve and New Year's Day shows at the Fillmore East occur. Even Jeffery was probably happy to know that Chalpin would not be getting an Experience album.

Band rehearsals at Baggy's Studio near Chinatown commenced. Cheaper than the Record Plant, Baggy's was run by Tom Edmonston, Soft Machine's former road manager, and it had a two-track reel-to-reel tape machine so Hendrix could "measure the group's progress throughout the rehearsals," as John McDermott states in his liner notes to *Jimi Hendrix: The Baggy's Rehearsal Sessions*, Dagger Records' fifth release. Building on Gypsy Sun and Rainbows material and a few of Miles's own compositions, Band of Gypsys' repertoire was whipped into shape in a matter of weeks.

One of Miles's songs—"Them Changes"—would go on to be his de facto theme song after Band of Gypsys met an inglorious end in the wake of a disastrous appearance at a benefit concert in Madison Square Garden. The song became the title track of his 1970 solo album and even featured Billy Cox on bass. Miles was recording his next solo album, *We Got to Live Together*, when news of Hendrix's death in London reached him. He attended the funeral in Seattle and even partook in the jam session Hendrix said he would have wanted at his funeral.

JIMI HENDRIX:
LIVE AT THE FILLMORE EAST

1999
M·C·A
MUSIC CORPORATION
AMERICA

© JAN BLOM / AUTHENTIC HENDRIX, LLC

This publicity shot for the *Live at the Fillmore East* posthumous album shows Jimi Hendrix during his Band of Gypsys phase.   *Author's collection*

Although he would go on to record with Carlos Santana, appear on Cheech and Chong comedy songs, and sing lead vocals on "I Heard It Through the Grapevine" on the California Raisins claymation ad that ran in 1986, Miles's career had peaked with his association with Jimi Hendrix as the headline to his *New York Times* obituary on February 29, 2008, attests: "Buddy Miles, 60, Hendrix Drummer, Dies." Death was due to congestive heart disease.

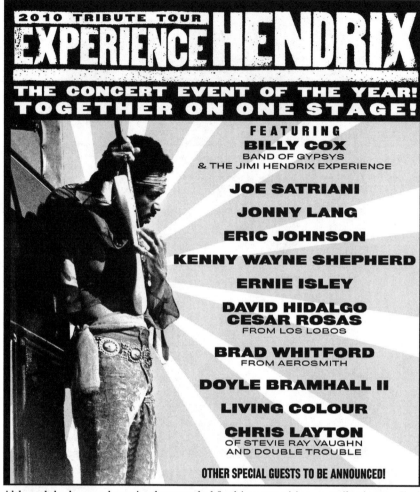

2010 TRIBUTE TOUR
EXPERIENCE HENDRIX

THE CONCERT EVENT OF THE YEAR!
TOGETHER ON ONE STAGE!

FEATURING
BILLY COX
BAND OF GYPSYS
& THE JIMI HENDRIX EXPERIENCE

JOE SATRIANI

JONNY LANG

ERIC JOHNSON

KENNY WAYNE SHEPHERD

ERNIE ISLEY

DAVID HIDALGO
CESAR ROSAS
FROM LOS LOBOS

BRAD WHITFORD
FROM AEROSMITH

DOYLE BRAMHALL II

LIVING COLOUR

CHRIS LAYTON
OF STEVIE RAY VAUGHN
AND DOUBLE TROUBLE

OTHER SPECIAL GUESTS TO BE ANNOUNCED!

Although he has not been justly rewarded for his songwriting contributions to Jimi Hendrix's material from 1969 and 1970, Billy Cox has been the main draw of the All-Star Tribute Tours organized by Experience Hendrix LLC.

Courtesy of Robert Rodriguez

The Fillmore East Performances

"Happy New Year, first of all," Hendrix said, stepping up to introduce "Machine Gun" at the first show on January 1, 1970. "I hope we have a million or two million of them . . . if we can get over this summer." Hearing that has always saddened me because Hendrix didn't get "over the summer." By the time autumn came he had been dead three days.

The four shows were sold out. The Voices of East Harlem were the opening act. Joshua White's Joshua Light Show provided the psychedelically lit backdrop behind the Band of Gypsys, whose stage setup was the same as the Jimi Hendrix Experience with Hendrix stage right, Miles center stage, and Cox stage left.

When asked his opinion after the first set on December 31st, Bill Graham told Hendrix he was coasting and getting by on his stage antics and not his musicianship. It certainly wasn't his Experience hits because *2 Nights at the Fillmore East*, a mini box set released on Voodoo Chile Records in 2007 that contains all four complete shows, reveals that Hendrix didn't play any. Yes, he did play "Lover Man" and "Hear My Train A Comin'," but neither of those songs played by the Experience were familiar to fans at the time.

According to Graham's telling, Hendrix was shocked. And pissed off. Being called out, he was immovable during the evening's second set and focused on proving Graham wrong. Maybe that's why Graham was a legendary promoter, because what he heard during that second set, "with respect to Carlos and Eric and all those others, that the most brilliant, emotional display of virtuoso guitar playing I have ever heard." Graham said Hendrix walked over to the impressed impresario standing by the side of the stage and asked, "You satisfied, motherfucker?," and then gave the audience all the stage antics. And the second show's set does end on a trio of Experience favorites, including a thirteen-minute workout of "Foxy Lady."

Dissolution

Beginning in mid-January, Band of Gypsys returned to the studio on dates that Hendrix and Eddie Kramer weren't mixing the live album. Songs they were working on included "Power of Soul," "Burning Desire," "Ezy Rider," and "Earth Blues." Around the same time, Peter Yarrow of Peter, Paul, and Mary reached out to Alan Douglas to see if Jimi Hendrix would appear at the Winter Festival for Peace at Madison Square Garden on January 29, 1970. Others slated to appear included Dave Brubeck, Harry Belafonte, Judy Collins, and Blood, Sweat, and Tears, among others. What followed was an unmitigated, but perhaps not unintentional, disaster.

Band of Gypsys went on at 3 a.m. but only made it through "Who Knows" and an aborted "Earth Blues" before an obviously ill Jimi Hendrix was forced to leave the stage. He had already insulted a woman who called out for "Foxy Lady." The question remains what made him ill. Buddy Miles said he witnessed manager Michael Jeffery slip Hendrix two hits of acid before he took the stage because he wanted Band of Gypsys to look bad so he could persuade Hendrix to disband his black band. Texas blues guitarist Johnny Winter, however, said Hendrix told him he was ill from something Devon Wilson had put in his drink.

Whatever the cause, Jeffery won out. A few days later he called Buddy Miles and told him, "The trip's over." Band of Gypsys were no more.

Over the years, Buddy Miles continued to emphasize Jeffery's role in his ouster. While it is certainly true that Jeffery actively maneuvered behind the scenes for the re-formation of the Experience and must have been gladdened to enact Miles's dismissal, it's equally true, as Jeffery's assistant Trixie Sullivan said in the *Live at the Fillmore East* DVD, that Hendrix was "totally in charge of the artistic side" and that Jeffery "would not interfere with the music side of things."

As Billy Cox has related in conversation with John McDermott, Hendrix felt Miles did not know his place in the band, that Miles did not "render unto Caesar the things which are Caesar's." This is understandable. Buddy Miles had led his own band previously and was used to being the center of attention. According to Cox, Hendrix felt Miles was grabbing too much of the spotlight, and others were not happy with the bills he was running up.

24

Evil Men Make Me

Band of Gypsys' Musical Legacy

When Jimi Hendrix sings "Evil men make me kill you" in "Machine Gun," he could have just as easily been thinking "evil men make me make this album." The guitarist abhorred the thought of giving any of his work to Ed Chalpin and never believed his management or the record executives and lawyers at Warner Brothers/Reprise had adequately defended him against Chalpin's lawsuit. This was reflected in the product he delivered to Capitol Records, because, with all of the singing Buddy Miles does on it, *Band of Gypsys* could be considered Buddy Miles's record, not Hendrix's.

Because it was short-lived, Band of Gypsys were long considered a wrong turn, but with the posthumously released Hendrix recordings centered on Band of Gypsys (as well as the DVD *Live at the Fillmore East*), it is now clear this trio was on a new path.

One has to wonder what fans expected when they bought tickets to see Jimi Hendrix (as advertised in the newspapers) and arrived at Bill Graham's Fillmore East and found "JIMI HENDRIX AND THE BAND OF GYPSYS" on the marquee. Clearly, they were not getting the Experience, so what were they expecting that evening? Ironically, they got a jazz band without Hendrix's jazz-inclined drummer.

Jimi, throughout mid-1969–early 1970, was flirting with jazz. In May 1969, he jammed with Larry Young, who later formed part of Lifetime with Tony Williams and John McLaughlin. (McLaughlin also jammed with Hendrix on one occasion, but he considers the session so inferior that he has never sanctioned the release of even one jam, which is regrettable because it's better than the jam with Larry Young that keeps being released.) Tony Williams almost took part in a session that would have brought about a Hendrix and Miles Davis collaboration (Davis, by the way, attended one of the Band of Gypsys performances at the Fillmore East), but that never occurred over last-minute demands for money by both Davis and Williams.

And so the Band of Gypsys' music is the best representation of Hendrix's jazz leanings during this time period. You could almost use the title of Frank Zappa's *Make a Jazz Sound Here* for *Band of Gypsys*. The songs performed by Band of Gypsys feature extended guitar solos, frequent time changes that Buddy Miles implied in an interview Noel Redding was incapable of, and explorations of musical scales John Coltrane would have been proud of.

Band of Gypsys

Hendrix was judicious in the selection of songs he felt he was unfairly forced into giving away. Although he did record studio versions of "Power of Soul" and "Message to Love," he never returned to them after the album was released. Band of Gypsys inexplicably never undertook "Machine Gun" in the studio, but Hendrix may have felt it was too long a track for a studio album and fit better on the live offering. Of the three songs that were Buddy Miles vehicles, only "Them Changes" was recorded in the studio, but even that was only at one session. As Eddie Kramer, who mixed the live

"Stepping Stone" was the last single released in Jimi Hendrix's lifetime. Credited to Hendrix Band of Gypsys, it was quickly withdrawn from market by Reprise Records because of issues with the mix.

Courtesy of Robert Rodriguez

album with Jimi, said: "He didn't want to include new songs that he wanted to finish at Electric Lady."

Even though much of the featured vocals are by Buddy Miles, the album tracks were radically truncated from what had transpired at the concerts. Take, for example, the closing track "We Gotta Live Together." On the album it is 5:45; live it was 16:43. (Even worse, it was a medley with "Voodoo Child (Slight Return)," a coupling that is grating.) According to Kramer, Miles's vocal showboating really troubled Hendrix during the mixing and editing of *Band of Gypsys*, and this shows in the final product. As producer, Hendrix had final say on just how much of Buddy Miles was released.

This is not to say that Hendrix did not put a substantial amount of consideration into what songs made the album. "Hear My Train A Comin'" and "Izabella" were considered but rejected only because the vocals were not adequately recorded.

Some critics are dismissive of "Who Knows," but it has Cox's catchiest bassline (as Digital Underground revealed to the world when they sampled it for their "The Way We Swing" and the title track of their hit rap album *Sex Packets*), the best example of the potential for Hendrix and Miles vocal interplay, and a fine guitar solo. Lyrically I prefer the shorter version on *Live at the Fillmore East* where Hendrix ad-libs about 1969.

"Machine Gun" is discussed below, but in addition to the two Miles tracks, Hendrix included on *Band of Gypsys* two of his best compositions from 1969. Both "Power to Love" (better known as "Power of Soul") and "Message of Love" belong to the type of missionary lyric that Hendrix explored in 1969 when not singing about war or evil women (as in "Who Knows") and fits in nicely with Miles's "We Gotta Live Together."

Best Band of Gypsys' Songs

Over two nights at the Fillmore East, Band of Gypsys played twenty-three different songs. Eliminating the Experience-era compositions, they played eleven new songs and two covers (if you include the traditional "Auld Lang Syne" Hendrix arranged to open the second show on New Year's Eve and adequately honor the ushering in of not only a new year, but a new decade). A review of the set lists offer some surprises: only three songs were aired at all four concerts, "Izabella," the next single (and warmly received by the audience), only once; and "Room Full of Mirrors" not at all.

It's a strong collection of original material, with only "Burning Desire" never gelling. Even "Stepping Stone," with its hoedown drumming and cartoonish pace, has lyrics that save it. When Hendrix sings "I'm a man, at least I'm trying to be" or "You're a woman, at least you say that you are," the song is given a depth of confusion missing in the music.

The fact remains that no other band that played together sporadically over a two-month period and only played four full concerts together have as much to show for it as Band of Gypsys. Here then are Band of Gypsys' six best live songs.

"Machine Gun"

Played at all four shows, the version on *Band of Gypsys* is only considered the definitive version because it was released. With three now readily available, it is clear that you can make an argument that each released Band of Gypsys version is the best. (The unreleased version from the first show is marred by Miles's scat singing, which is only appropriate if you think the chicken sounds he is making are supposed to bring to mind the farm.) The two live versions from *Live at the Fillmore East* quote Francis Scott Key's "Star Spangled Banner," and it may be for this reason that Hendrix did not choose them. The absence of the national anthem from the *Band of Gypsys* version makes the song a universal condemnation of war rather than anti-American dogma.

The rhythm section's cohesion—a word favored by the military—provides the firm support Hendrix needs to properly execute all of "Machine Gun's" ideas. This is one of their best performances with Miles's rat-a-tat-tat drumming; Cox's menacing bassline; and the rhythm section's mournful harmonies.

Referencing his friend's mastery of the boxes he used, Cox recalled, "You could hear all of it kicking in on 'Machine Gun.' It was incredible. There were people in the audience with their mouths open." Supporting Cox's statement, Keith Shadwick in his fine book on Hendrix (*Musician*) says Hendrix utilizes "his pedals and effects, just as other instrumentalists . . . use different tonal characteristics of their instruments to express different approaches to each part of the song." Here Hendrix uses them to recreate the missile sounds associated with the Woodstock version of "Star Spangled Banner" in an original Hendrixian composition.

"Earth Blues"

It's hard to believe Hendrix omitted "Earth Blues" from *Band of Gypsys* (or that it never made it onto any of the posthumous albums that Kramer produced in the 1970s). The line that you "better hope (love) comes before the summer" would have tied in nicely with Hendrix's introduction to "Machine

Gun." It was played three times during the Fillmore East shows, which leads me to suspect that Hendrix did strongly consider its inclusion but ultimately didn't because he felt "Earth Blues" was still a work in progress. Studio versions include Ronnie Spector on background vocals.

"Stone Free"

Band of Gypsys expanded on the Experience's first B-side twice during the Fillmore East shows, and both are readily available. The longer version (17:21) features digressions into "Nutcracker Suite," "Outside Woman Blues," "Cherokee Mist," and Cream's "Sunshine of Your Love" but it is the somewhat shorter version (12:52) that opened the second show on January 1st that you have to own.

Available on *Live at the Fillmore East*, Buddy Miles's drive perfectly powers this song about a musician on the road who will not be caged. Miles's drive allows Hendrix to jam so effortlessly that you forget this was originally cut for 45. Cox and Miles's background vocals are more harmonious than those of the Experience and—except for some Miles scatting—an asset.

"Power of Love"

One of Band of Gypsys' oldest songs, it dates back to a May 1969 recording session, and by December Hendrix had fully worked out the arrangement. A long instrumental opening with a compounding riff, it is beloved by Hendrix's fans. The lyrics are elusive but the line in the chorus stating that "with the power of soul anything is possible" is one of Hendrix's most enduring philosophical statements.

"Auld Lang Syne"

The live version of "Auld Lang Syne" that appropriately opened Band of Gypsys' second show on December 31, 1969 (and opens Disc Two of *Live at the Fillmore East*) sends shivers down my spine every time I hear the Fillmore East's emcee (Kip Cohen) ushering in 1970 and wishing everyone "a Happy New Year, a very Happy New Year" to the strains of Guy Lombardo. And then Hendrix takes over.

(At Baggy's Studios in downtown Manhattan on December 19, 1969, Band of Gypsys rehearsed three holiday songs—"Little Drummer Boy," "Silent Night," and "Auld Lang Syne"—so they'd have something to play at the Fillmore East. Two versions of this three-song medley have since been released on the *Merry Christmas and Happy New Year* EP. You might call this double dipping, but despite some sonic dropout in the extended version, I highly recommend this recording.)

"Them Changes"

We gotta give Buddy Miles one even if Hendrix tired of him and didn't appear to think much of his compositions. His signature song has a catchy riff, and it's probably Hendrix's best vehicle as a sideman after stardom hit him. Coming from an album with titles such as "Message of Love" (with its Beatlesque background vocals) and "We Got to Live Together," I remembered this song as being about social change and a sign of the tumultuous '60s, but it's not. It's just a song about a guy whose baby has "stepped out on me," and that mars the song's impact somewhat. Except there's no more significant social change a man can go through than his baby stepping out on him, so I guess it is about social change after all.

As happened with the original mix of Side One of *Axis: Bold as Love,* the mix for *Band of Gypsys* went missing after the record was pressed. Some suspect Hendrix deliberately lost the tapes because he resented having to give his music away to Ed Chalpin.

25

You Gotta Practice What They Preach

American Artist, Not Revolutionary

P art of the Beatles' enduring appeal is that by breaking up in 1969, they remain tethered, and therefore representative, of the twentieth century's most tumultuous and progressive decade. The '60s are "the '60s" in large part due to that decade's artists, none more significantly than the decade's rock musicians who—because they had the good sense to die young and die pretty—are often the faces of the '60s. What was it that Jimi Hendrix said of dying? "Once you're dead, you're made for life." He was right. And of America's musicians from the 1960s, no one has it made more than Jimi Hendrix. You'll find his T-shirts in Target stores, footage of his Monterey performance promoting Apple products, his silhouette in storefronts across cities in Europe and Asia.

But one place where Jimi Hendrix's image won't appear is on an American stamp, and that's to our national shame because the man was a patriot. More importantly he was an American artist, a troubadour who through his recordings and performances spread the American notion of freedom throughout the world.

I think of Hendrix whenever I hear Patti Smith proclaiming in "Babelogue" that she is "an American artist" and that she has "no guilt" and seeks "the nerves under your skin." She says this just as the musicians behind her, the sublime Patti Smith Group, are kicking into gear "Rock N Roll Nigger"—a song that even names Hendrix. "Jimi Hendrix was a nigger," she says controversially, meaning that artists are viewed as "niggers" by society, none more so perhaps than Jimi Hendrix, the American artist. He struck the nerves under America's skin. This is why our nation's leaders continue to at best misunderstand and at worst manipulate his contributions to our society. These politicians still believe Jimi Hendrix to be a radical and a probable supporter of the Black Panthers and violent revolution, when he was only attempting to provide answers and solutions through his music.

A little-known quote given to Danish reporter Jorn Rossing Jensen before a performance on September 1st in Gothenburg, Sweden, drives the point home. Jensen, referencing the Rolling Stones' support of revolution in the lyrics to "Street Fighting Man," asked Hendrix if he was on the front line.

And Jimi Hendrix, American artist, replied with his obscure common sense: "No, I'm not. At one point you have to choose: Revolution or Frank Sinatra. For me it was Frank Sinatra . . . . I want to show people a lot of things—with t-h-i-s." Jensen says Hendrix then picked up his guitar and played it. In other words, Jimi Hendrix believed he could affect and change society for the better only through his music, not revolution. He had said something similar to the *Charleston Gazette* in spring 1969: "Music is stronger than politics. I think the answer lies in music." Jimi Hendrix when confronted by the Black Panthers, and the yippies, chose Frank Sinatra as is evident by how he reacted to some of the most divisive American issues of the decade.

The Vietnam War

Swinging London's elite rockers were taken aback by Jimi Hendrix's view of American involvement in Vietnam. According to a 1967 Hendrix interview in *Kink*, a Dutch magazine that quotes Hendrix as saying, "The Americans are fighting in Vietnam for the complete free world. As soon as they move out, [Vietnam]'ll be at the mercy of the communists. For that matter, the yellow danger [China] should not be underestimated. Of course war is terrible, but at present it's still the only guarantee to maintain peace."

But what else would you expect a former paratrooper to believe? Even one who only joined the military to avoid prison. Hendrix's views of military intervention and violence may have morphed over time to provide antiwar perspectives in "Izabella" and "Machine Gun," but the sentiment is still not anti-American or even antimilitary. In addition to being above racism, Jimi Hendrix was apolitical.

In New York City in July 1969, he said that "politics is really an evil scene, you know. That's the way I look at it anyway." Why would a man who views politics as evil want to change the world through politics? It's as he says further in the same interview: "You have to rely on a more of an earthier substance. Like music . . . ."

Racism

When it comes to racism, Hendrix gets it from all sides. A man who traveled the chitlin' circuit could not have been unaffected by racism. He probably endured untold slights, and yet some white journalists of the era took him to task for being color-blind in London or for being an "electric Uncle Tom." Blacks took him to task for playing with two whites, not two brothers, ignoring the fact that it was the musical telepathy that Hendrix shared with Redding and Mitchell that helped make his music successful. (Miles Davis, the Prince of Darkness, was also often criticized by black journalists for having white musicians in his bands.)

Hendrix's point of view, however, as expressed in Berlin in 1967, was that "I think we can live quietly, side by side. With violence, a problem like that is never solved." That explains his reaction to the Black Panthers.

Black Panthers

Hendrix may have said on occasion that "Voodoo Child (Slight Return)" was the Black Panther national anthem, but he only said this to appease black militants badgering him. What does that mean anyway: "Voodoo Child (Slight Return)" as Black Panther national anthem? There is nothing black or revolutionary in that song's lyrics.

The Black Panthers had touched Jimi Hendrix for money and according to associates tried to play a guilt trip on the guitarist, but according to Kathy Eberth: "[Hendrix] tried to quell them by telling them that 'the only colors I see are in my music.'" That was in Honolulu in May 1969, but the Black Panthers were back at it—"moving in for money" according to Fat Mattress bassist Jimmy Leverton—at the Newport 69 Pop Festival. It was Hendrix's own bassist, Noel Redding, who had them thrown out of the dressing room after seeing "six or seven of them sitting around Hendrix, and Hendrix was looking white." Jimi Hendrix was as fearful of the Black Panthers as any hardhat of the era. He was far from a supporter of the Black Panthers' revolutionary propaganda.

After the Harlem benefit appearance, the Black Panthers spread the word that Hendrix would do a benefit for them. He had been approached, but true to his nature, he left it to manager Michael Jeffery to get him out of ever doing the benefit. He was uncomfortable with becoming the figurehead of their revolution. "I felt like they put me in a box," he said of the Black Panthers in a *New Musical Express* interview published September 11, 1970, a week before his death

Martin Luther King Jr.

The Jimi Hendrix Experience was in Virginia Beach, Virginia, when news of King's assassination reached Hendrix. He was sitting in a bar with members of the Experience and Soft Machine. Men at the bar were toasting the assassin, and Soft Machine's light man, Mark Boyle, thought they were trying to instigate Hendrix into reacting. Years on the chitlin' circuit had taught him not to.

Not known for financial donations, Hendrix did give the Martin Luther King Jr. memorial fund $5,000 in June 1968 and made an appearance at a tribute concert for King at Madison Square Garden, although he did not perform.

Riots

As early as in Berlin in 1967 Jimi Hendrix was decrying the riots in towns across America. "The black riots in American cities . . . are just . . . crazy. What they are doing is irresponsible." On another occasion, he said he had been educated by records, and it was through his records that he tried to point out the foolishness of riots. In "Up from the Skies" he points out "the smell of a world that has burned," and in "House Burning Down" he advises those listening to "learn, not burn, hear what I say."

Hendrix had seen the rioting firsthand in Newark, New Jersey, the day after Martin Luther King Jr. had been assassinated. With the Jimi Hendrix Experience scheduled to play Symphony Hall, Noel Redding had sighted "tanks in the street" as the band arrived. Buildings were burning. There was fear among the roadies that some crackpot might take a shot at Hendrix. Reports vary about concert attendance—some say packed, others say sparse. The latter is probably true as the two shows were combined into one, but the show that was performed was emotional, with Hendrix rising to the occasion again and honoring the slain civil rights leader through his music. The Experience closed the show with "I Don't Live Today," the only time they did so during their touring career.

Peter Doggett in *There's a Riot Going On*, his look at "revolutionaries, rock stars and the rise and fall of the '60s," felt that by not speaking to his mostly white audience that night in Newark Hendrix had "dodged" his black identity, but Hendrix was from all accounts—unless he had liquor—a soft-spoken wallflower by nature. He believed he could get his points across "with t-h-i-s": his guitar.

"The Star Spangled Banner"

If there is any reason that we should honor Jimi Hendrix as an American it is for his live rendition of "The Star Spangled Banner" at Woodstock.

Hendrix wasn't supposed to have played it that Monday morning at Max Yasgur's farm. It wasn't listed in the handwritten set list. Billy Cox played the first five notes before stopping, realizing he didn't know the notes to his nation's national anthem well enough to accompany his old army buddy. This indicates that it had not been played at the jams back at the Shokan house. But Hendrix knew it well enough. He'd already recorded versions in the studio with the Experience as well as by himself, including overdubs, at the Record Plant on March 18, 1969. A Brit, Mitch Mitchell, however, did know "The Star Spangled Banner" because it had been included in Experience sets as far back as September 1968 (and possibly Atlanta in August of that same year), and sometimes Mitchell accompanied Hendrix and sometimes he did not. That Monday morning at Woodstock he did, but only to keep his hands warm.

Other live renditions of Francis Scott Key's tribute to his country before and after Woodstock pale by comparison. These versions are included on box sets, and I often wish they weren't. Not to fan the mystique or the often-believed myth that Jimi Hendrix only performed "The Star Spangled Banner" once in his career. They simply are not as good. There's often a rushed feel, sometimes a sense of embarrassment or a wonderment of what must the fans be thinking. Maybe it would have worked better as the opening number, especially at concerts held in the sports stadiums he sometimes played.

But from any objective perspective, the ability to take a nation's anthem and transform as if it is heard for the first time in decades, to restore its dignity that millions of out-of-tune singings have buried is a valuable contribution to the social fabric, and the musician should be honored by his country.

The criticism is of course that Hendrix's arrangement suggests bombs and warfare and it a criticism itself of the Vietnam War because surely the hippie must hate his country. Such criticisms overlook Francis Scott Key's lyrics themselves, which mention a "perilous fight" and "the rockets' red glare, the bombs bursting in air," and that Hendrix's arrangement merely reflects the lyrics.

Peter Doggett, for example, states that "Jimi Hendrix subverted the tune at Woodstock." But even Billy Idol's guitarist Steven Stevens, who saw Jimi on *The Dick Cavett Show* in September 1969 said that, in responding to questioning from the television host, "Hendrix tried to clarify that he thought it was a real compliment the way he did it, not derogatory."

"I thought it was beautiful," Hendrix told Dick Cavett.

A better line of questioning from Cavett may have been what drew the guitarist to national anthems. If you remember, as a gift to the generous reception given to him at Monterey, Hendrix prefaced his performance of "Wild Thing" with "the combined British and American anthem" (even then he warned the audience to not get mad), recorded a rendition of "La Marseillaise" for French Radio (never broadcast and presumed lost), and began his Isle of Wight performance with "God Save the Queen."

So it may be more than simple coincidence that the lyrics to "1983 . . . (A Merman I Should Turn to Be)" echo Francis Scott Key's lyrics to the national anthem. Written in 1968 before "The Star Spangled Banner" was ever performed in concert, the second verse opens with "Oh say, can you see": the same five words that begin the national anthem.

You might say then that since "1983 . . . (A Merman I Should Turn to Be)" describes a world torn apart by war, his arrangement of "The Star Spangled Banner" is criticism of America involvement in Vietnam: both ask us to see a battle scene. But the intent behind Hendrix's playing of "The Star Spangled Banner" is closer to what he told journalists after Woodstock. As quoted to Charles R. Cross, Hendrix said: "We're all Americans . . . it was like 'Go America!' . . . We play it the way the air is in American today. The air is slightly static, see."

26

Here Come the Bad Side

Realism in Jimi Hendrix's Later Lyrics

urchasers of *Band of Gypsys* when it was released in America on March 25, 1970, (and nearly three months later in the United Kingdom with another controversial cover featuring rock star dolls), would have noticed a not so subtle shift in Jimi Hendrix's lyrics. Science fiction was a thing of the past; the chief Experience Maker had embraced realism. This was a turn in Hendrix's lyrics that was even more palpable with the posthumous releases.

"Who Knows" features the first truly evil woman in Hendrix's lyrics since the women wanting to trap him in a plastic cage in "Stone Free." (It's probably no coincidence that "Stone Free" was revisited at the same concerts at which "Who Knows" made its debut.) This evil woman named Sally was soon joined by Dolly Dagger, and both are no doubt based on Devon Wilson, the super groupie cum super druggie. The person being addressed in "Crash Landing" could only be Devon, as is reinforced by Jimi asking the woman to "take out your *dagger* and cut me free."

"Message to Love" could also be construed as a message to Devon. The woman "wrapped up in chain" is likely an allusion to the hold drugs had upon her. And in Hendrix's plea to "find yourself first and then your talent," his hope that she could save herself is shown. (And she did try to right herself and prove herself to Hendrix by getting a bit part in an off-Broadway theatre production, only the part was that of a whore.) Drugs abound in Hendrix's lyrics, but, like that of the Clash, latter-era references to drugs are darker. Drug use in Hendrix's later lyrics is destructive, not mind-expanding. There's no kissing the sky anymore. In "Crash Landing" Jimi tells the woman that he's "gonna throw away your stupid needle," and in "Freedom," he's "tryin' to slap it out of her hand."

But, as if in a word of caution to himself, he says in "Earth Blues," "don't get too stoned, please remember you're a man." In "Stepping Stone," he says that "I'm a man, at least I'm trying to be," and, in the realistic lyrics of

1969 and 1970, we find Hendrix confronting lyrically the mess he was in, the mess the world was in and trying to be a man. Even the outro on "Astro Man" musically echoes "I'm a Man," a song that was written by his friend and sometime studio cohort Steve Winwood.

Battle imagery had been present in "1983 . . . (A Merman I Should Turn to Be)," but in "Machine Gun" there isn't any underwater paradise to escape to. As is evident by his dedication of the song to not only the soldiers in Vietnam, which he mentions last, but also "Chicago, Milwaukee and New York," "Machine Gun" is not about war but civil strife and another comment on the riots in America and the soldiers called out to contain them.

Shooting and guns are referenced in "Crash Landing," "Freedom," and "Power of Soul." Originally titled "Paper Aeroplanes" because of the song's opening verse, in "Power of Soul," Hendrix asks the woman to "shoot down some of those airplanes you been drivin'," probably another request to Devon Wilson to give up drugs.

Religion also is a force in the lyrics from 1969 and 1970. In "Message to Love," Hendrix thanks God for being "what I am" and then asks God to bring understanding to people, the same people who in "Earth Blues" are

"Freedom" featured Jimi's latter period realistic approach to lyricism.   *Courtesy of Robert Rodriguez*

"reachin' up, but not quite touchin' the promised land." What is the light he references in "Earth Blues" but that of God?

Children were also on Hendrix's mind. Where the devil's children were called forth in 1968 and 1969, in June 1970 he was writing about God's children. In "Freedom," he mentions "my children" as he imagines himself being married and a father; in "Izabella," he is "fightin' in this war for the children in you"; in "Belly Button Window"—a song he said was inspired by the baby in Lynn Mitchell's belly—he is the voice of that unborn child.

The use of realistic images was Hendrix's attempt to provide the answers to questions being asked of him. Justifiably believing he could contribute more through music than revolution, he tried to pass lessons along and instruct. In "Earth Blues," he acknowledges that there's "gonna be a whole lotta rearrangin'," but hopes it will not be through violence. He says that "you better hope love is the answer," notes that "they're talkin' about getting together," says that "everybody can hear the sound of freedom's bleedin' heart." Jimi Hendrix believed there were better times ahead.

This is reinforced by the lyrics to "Straight Ahead" where he says that "communication, yeah, is comin' on strong," that "everybody is dancing in the street," that it don't matter "if your hair is short or long" because we "gotta stand side by side." (These are the kind of lyrics that Michael Jeffery was said to roll his eyes up at.)

In "Straight Ahead," Hendrix is talking about "power to the people," "freedom of the soul," and how we "gotta tell the children truth . . . because one of these days, baby, they'll be running things." On the fourth studio album it most likely would have had a prominent spot. Already in concert in 1970, he sometimes played "Straight Ahead"—a still unreleased track—near the end of concerts and even on September 4th, his penultimate concert, as the set opener. Some have said that *First Rays of the New Rising Sun*, the album Hendrix was prepping at the time of his untimely demise was too unwieldy, the product of too long a period to be cohesive. I think this incorrect. In many ways, lyrically it was his most cohesive. The recurrence of images—daggers, freedom, highways—pull the songs together like short stories in a collection.

I Travel at the Speed of a Reborn Man

The Second Experience

With Band of Gypsys quashed after their disastrous appearance at the Winter Festival for Peace at Madison Square Garden— although Buddy Miles did record once more with Hendrix at the Record Plant on February 16, 1970—Michael Jeffery was eager to get the Experience flying all over America again. The purpose was twofold: to generate cash flow for completion of Electric Lady Studios and to put Band of Gypsys behind Jimi.

All he had to do was get the world's greatest guitarist to agree.

With Fat Mattress giving him no support, Redding was eager to tour and Mitchell was on board as well. An interview was arranged with *Rolling Stone* journalist John Burks at Michael Jeffery's apartment on February 4, 1970, to announce plans for the Experience's reunion and the new tour, but Hendrix only participated to avoid arguments with Jeffery. The chief Experience Maker was still uncertain about touring with Redding, whose moodiness, pill addiction, and drinking problems had erased whatever desire Jimi had expressed in an apologetic letter penned to both Redding and Mitchell in spring 1969 that "the Experience wasn't just a skeleton, 'it's three,' a living entity that needed to be reborn."

The *Rolling Stone* interview appeared in issue #54 (March 19, 1970) and is a fascinating read. You can find it online. It's fascinating because being of the time it cannot be tempered by time and you can see even as early as March 1970 that although there was objection among fans and critics to Buddy Miles's extended singing during the Band of Gypsys performances at the Fillmore East, Hendrix's all-black band had still been received favorably. What Burks wants to know then during the interview is what happened? Why the breakup? The fact that he felt the magazine he represented was being manipulated is palpable. Why is Hendrix's manager present? The journalist is even a bit snide, comparing the Experience reunion to Richard Burton and Elizabeth Taylor's remarrying.

The interviewer asks about Hendrix's supposed support of the Black Panthers, which he evades by saying, "Naturally (I) feel part of what they're doing. In certain respects. But everybody has their own way of doing things. They get justified as they justify others, in their attempts to get personal freedom." Hendrix is with them in spirit, "not the aggression or violence or whatever you want to call it. I'm not for guerrilla warfare." In some respects it sounds like a verse from Lennon's "Revolution."

Hendrix goes on to say that he isn't into black-only enterprises and doesn't know much about John and Yoko's sit-ins for peace, but he would go back to Toronto now that he had been cleared of the drug charges against him. He's evasive again about saying at the trial that he had "outgrown dope."

From a creative standpoint he alludes to the cartoon characters from *Black Gold* and that the music he's hearing in his head he "can't get on the guitar," which is used as an explanation (or excuse) for the Experience's reunion. Most of the Experience's compositions had been studio grown between the three Experience Makers, and if Hendrix were to get the music he heard in his head on guitar, he needed to work with Noel and Mitch again. (This was indeed the case, but sadly, Hendrix did not seem to comprehend that.) They cite the composition of "Voodoo Child (Slight Return)" as an example:

> Redding: "Actually, the reason we work everything out in the studio is so everything will get as live and as *actual* as possible."

> Hendrix: "It's like 'Voodoo Child.' Somebody was filming us as we were doing that. It was basically for the filming, we thought. We weren't thinking about what we were playing. We did it like three times."

> Mitchell: "There's like a riff and we were just doing that . . ."

Burks correctly surmises that for all the talk of a new album, none is forthcoming. Not even the Band of Gypsys live album that Kramer and Hendrix were already mixing is discussed. The next album when discussed in veiled terms might not even be entirely comprised of Experience material. It is also said that each side will be continuous—like the Miles Davis live albums of the 1970s that Davis had not even released yet—to avoid the record company releasing singles that the band did not want to see released. Of special interest is mention that Chas Chandler was producing although he hadn't worked with Hendrix in almost a year: not since the Royal Albert Hall concerts.

When asked about the Experience's new direction, Hendrix replies, "We're going to go out somewhere into the hills and woodshed or whatever you call it, to get some new songs and arrangements and stuff together. So we'll have something new to offer, whether it's *different* or not."

It must have been "not" because when the Experience did play the mid-April gig at the LA Forum mentioned in Burks's article, Redding was not on the stage. Billy Cox was.

Billy Cox (Slight Return)

The nicest guy in the Hendrix biography is Billy Cox, the army buddy, resilient bassist, and faithful friend. His contributions to the Hendrix songbook have been basically ignored. He has said in several interviews

that had Hendrix lived, he (Cox) would have received songwriting credits on several songs released posthumously. While he has never stated which songs, this does sound plausible as after Cox teamed up with Hendrix, many compositions are more riff and scale driven: the result of Hendrix and Cox jamming together. (And proof that if Redding had just been more willing to jam in the studio instead of "pulling birds," as he liked to phrase it, he might have held onto his position as the Experience's bassist.) And there's no denying that the basslines on "Machine Gun" and "Who Knows"—two songs created with Cox—are the best-known basslines from the Hendrix canon.

After the breakup of Band of Gypsys, Cox was asked by Buddy Miles to join

Jimi Hendrix during one of *The Cry of Love* weekend tour appearances.   *Author's collection* the revamped Buddy Miles Express on bass, but Cox declined. (He did, however, contribute fuzz bass to the Express's studio recording of "Them Changes.") The city life had little appeal to Cox and so he returned to his obscure yet pleasant lifestyle in Nashville, Tennessee, that Jimi had plucked him from the previous year.

It was the second time he had returned to Nashville in less than a year. A nice guy, but Cox would speak up when he felt mistreated, and in November 1969, he had returned to Nashville when he didn't care for the disregard Alan Douglas and his engineering staff had for his playing. And so he was understandably reluctant to re-enlist for a third stint with his old army buddy. He might not have known that Jefferson Airplane and Hot Tuna bassist Jack Casady had been considered as Redding's replacement for the spring 1970 tour, but he knew Jeffery wouldn't be supportive. But according to Cox: "[Jimi] promised that I would have no hassles, so like a fool, I came back for the third time."

Weekend Tours of America

What Billy Cox was coming back for was the spring tour of 1970 mentioned in John Burks's *Rolling Stone* interview. It was Hendrix's first scheduled tour in nearly a year and one he did not want to make but was forced to undertake to meet financial commitments. (In retrospect it's difficult to comprehend how three of the most creative, influential musical forces of their generation—the Beatles, the Rolling Stones, the Jimi Hendrix Experience—were able to avoid the road for extended periods in the 1960s.) Hendrix was much more interested in making sense out of the music committed to reels and reels of tape since the *Electric Ladyland* sessions.

A compromise therefore was reached between the musician and his management team: tour dates would be restricted to weekends. In between, Hendrix and the second Experience lineup of Billy Cox and Mitch Mitchell—since dubbed the Cry of Love band after the tour of the same name—would retreat to New York City to remix, overdub, and record music.

Other oft-stated reasons by Hendrix for his lack of enthusiasm for touring were the demands of his audiences to play his "hits" and to hump his amplifier and burn his guitar. While I'm sure there was truth to the latter—who could not after having seen D. A. Pennebaker's *Monterey Pop* have hoped to see Hendrix set his guitar aflame?—a review of set lists gleaned from bootleg albums and tapes and CDs makes the former complaint laughable.

Experience set lists were often studded with long jams and blues numbers such as "Tax Free" and "Catfish Blues" that no one in the audience had heard before. Even the April 25, 1970, set list at the LA Forum included "Lover Man," "Hear My Train A Comin'," "Ezy Ryder," "Room Full of Mirrors," "Hey Baby," "Villanova Junction," and "Freedom": seven of the fourteen songs on the set list were new. (And two of the seven known songs—"Message to Love" and "Machine Gun"—were from *Band of Gypsys*, which was selling better than any Hendrix recording since *Are You Experienced*.) Hendrix's audience was an incredibly tolerant one for a major recording artist.

The weekend tours of America took Hendrix, Cox and Mitchell through California (thrice), Wisconsin, Minnesota, Oklahoma (twice), Texas (twice), Pennsylvania, Ohio, Missouri, Indiana, Tennessee, Maryland, New Mexico, Massachusetts, Georgia, and Florida. It wasn't until July 17th that the lineup played New York City, where they were spending so much of their "free time" on weekdays. Unfortunately Hendrix's final performance in his adopted hometown at the New York Pop Festival on Randall's Island was subpar and combative.

Two weeks after, the Cry of Love lineup played a well-received concert at the Sports Arena in San Diego—making it the fourth weekend in California—and a rain-drenched show at Sicks Stadium in his hometown before flying to Hawaii for Hendrix's participation in the movie Mike Jeffery was making with director Chuck Wein.

The less said about the film project that became *Rainbow Bridge*, the better; this is why I have avoided writing about it or even watching it since pot-enhanced viewings at midnight screenings way back in the 1970s. The 17 minutes Hendrix and his band are on the screen are worthwhile, but unfortunately the original running time of the film is 74 minutes and the footage without Jimi and given over to hippie propaganda that drags on interminably. The 57 minutes seems like 57 hours. Unbelievably, there is a director's cut that runs 125 minutes.

Since Jeffery had received funding from Warner Brothers for his pet film project, however, he had been trying to persuade Hendrix to make an appearance in the movie. Hendrix was already on the hook for the soundtrack, and so what was supposed to be a vacation in Hawaii snowballed into two shows filmed on July 30th in front of a sparse, yet obviously stoned, crowd. Ever the showman, Hendrix was able to surmount windy conditions in the middle of nowhere and turn in a decent performance.

The Isle of Wight Festival

As much as Jimi Hendrix's legacy has benefited from filmed performances at Monterey and Woodstock, so too has it been damaged by what is seen of him at the Isle of Wight. His haggard appearance, his lack of command, his wardrobe malfunctions have all contributed to the posthumous impression that he was suffering from drug addiction, creatively spent, embarrassing himself. Powerful performances and recording sessions from the previous months issued posthumously have done nothing to erase that perception by the public.

Hendrix did little to ensure his first appearance in England since the Royal Albert Hall concerts in February 1969 would be a success. He is said to have worried aloud if England even remembered him and surely must have wondered how the absence of Noel Redding might be received, but he never even rehearsed for the show. He had not played with Cox and Mitchell since the International Center in Honolulu, Hawaii, on August 1, 1970, almost a month earlier. Normally, lack of rehearsal had served Hendrix well in concert and lent performances a dangerous edge, but at the Isle of Wight the only thing evident was rust. Couple this with lack of sleep and temperamental equipment and you have the recipe for a legendarily bad performance that unfortunately has also been repeatedly reissued in the ensuing decades.

The estate may have hoped that *Blue Wild Angel*, the DVD released in 2004 and reissued in 2011, might have led to a reassessment of this performance. But while there are high moments such as the British national anthem and the twenty-minute version of "Machine Gun" that is enhanced by unintentional security transmissions broadcast over the Marshall amps, the film only displays a situation beyond Hendrix's control.

September Tour of Europe

Hendrix's Isle of Wight appearance continues to be remembered in the public's collective consciousness as his last concert, as if he returned to his London hotel and died the next day, but this was not the case. As was common at festivals, his Isle of Wight appearance started at 1 a.m. on August 31st, and on the evening of that same date he was stepping onto another stage in Gröna Lund, an amusement park in Stockholm, Sweden. The concert was the beginning of a two-week tour that would take him through Sweden, Denmark, West Germany, Austria, France, and the Netherlands. That the tour was not completed has been attributed to the unstable mental condition of bassist Billy Cox.

At a party following the gig at the Liseburg amusement park in Gothenburg, Sweden, on September 1, 1970, Cox was handed a drink that was laced with a drug that, rather than giving a psychedelic reaction, gave him a psychotic reaction. Hendrix was able to calm his army buddy down, and the tour continued for a few days—bootleg recordings for the show in

Berlin on September 4th attest that Jimi Hendrix still had many memorable notes in him—before reaching another festival on the Isle of Fehrman. It was perhaps the way that events unfolded at what was to be Jimi Hendrix's final performance that caused Billy Cox to relapse.

Ironically, the Isle of Fehrman was supposed to be a Love and Peace festival, but as had happened at the Rolling Stones' performance at Altamont Speedway the previous winter, bikers caused mayhem and a wretched time was had by all. The bikers robbed the box office, threatened car park attendants, and shot a stagehand.

Torrential rains postponed Hendrix's performance for a day, and when he did take the stage, he was greeted by a surly audience who actually booed him and told him to go home. They were upset that he had not appeared the previous night. Hendrix tried reasoning with them, asking them to "boo in key." This performance is available on Dagger Records but is more important to completists and historians than the casual fan. After the performance Hendrix and his band fled the Isle of Fehrman via helicopter as the bikers burned down the stage.

While at the Isle of Fehrman, Cox had become increasingly paranoid and told those around him that they would never get off the island alive. Hendrix was genuinely concerned about the fragile mental state of his bassist and felt responsible for him. The Hendrix entourage returned to London, and a doctor was hired to treat Cox, who returned shortly thereafter to the United States to recuperate with his parents in Pennsylvania. Some discussion was held about carrying on the remaining dates with Noel Redding or Ric Grech, formerly of Blind Faith, but the tour was cancelled instead.

Attributing cancellation of the tour entirely to Cox's condition in hindsight is not completely honest. Hendrix's behavior in Sweden and Denmark was increasingly erratic—probably due to heroin withdrawal—and he may have used his old army buddy's illness as an excuse to cancel a tour he was not physically up to continuing.

What is clear is that if Hendrix had survived, Cox's presence at least in concert was a thing of the past, and so when just arriving at a turning point that might have boded well for his future, Jimi Hendrix died.

28

If I Don't See You No More in This World

The Death of Jimi Hendrix

The last days of Jimi Hendrix read like something out of a *Thin Man* script where all the suspects are gathered by Nick and Nora for identification of the murderer.

Women he had been romantically linked with in 1966 saw him again in London. He had sought out Linda Keith at the Speakeasy. He had bumped into Kathy Etchingham. He proposed to the Danish actress Kirsten Nefer (and possibly Monika Dannemann). Upon hearing rumors of the engagement to Nefer that had been reported in the Danish press, Devon Wilson had flown into London against Hendrix's wishes to see him.

Old and potential new managers had been approached. Hendrix reached out to Chas Chandler about the possibility of helping produce and putting to bed the tracks he was working on with Eddie Kramer at Electric Lady. He had asked for Alan Douglas's help in getting out from under his legal entanglements with Michael Jeffery and together they spent the night of September 15th evaluating Hendrix's projects they could undertake together once Jeffery was out of the picture. Still, he called Jeffery in Spain on September 17th, but they missed one another.

Legally, Hendrix had called Henry Steingarten (also on the 17th) and told his lawyer he wanted to leave Jeffery. It is not known if during this phone call they discussed the paternity suit brought forth by Diane Carpenter, a prostitute Hendrix had befriended in 1966. (The first of two paternity suits facing Hendrix, who had been confronted backstage two weeks earlier in Stockholm by Eva Sundquist, who said he had fathered her son.) Nor is it known if they discussed Ed Chalpin's lawsuit against Hendrix and Track Records. Chalpin was in London and depositions were to be taken on the same day that Jimi Hendrix died.

It would make for a suspenseful scene: what really happened to Jimi Hendrix the evening of September 17th? Because four decades after the death of King Guitar—as rock journalist Keith Altham called him in a September 11, 1970, interview (to which Hendrix responded: "King Guitar, now? That's a bit heavy.")—we are no closer and presumably never will be to knowing why Jimi Hendrix died. Was it death by misadventure? Was it murder? Was it suicide? Noel Redding mentioned all three scenarios to Chris Welch shortly after Hendrix's death, and four decades later all remain plausible . . . until you weigh the facts.

Hendrix's Last Days in London

Back in London for the first time since a weeklong visit in March in a fruitless effort at patching up differences with Kathy Etchingham (who had already married someone without his knowledge), Hendrix began having second thoughts about returning to New York City. As he admitted to journalists and people he met, he was entertaining the idea of righting himself by relocating back to London, the scene of what must have now seemed to him happier times.

The timing seemed propitious. He had been forced to cancel the mini European tour to ensure Billy Cox's health. Once his friend had departed for America, Hendrix could see new horizons opening for him. Cox clearly did not have the constitution for the rock 'n' roll lifestyle and was no longer a suitable choice to be Hendrix's bassist. A new bassist would mean a new direction. In a September 4th interview in Berlin with American Forces BFBS's Chris Romburg, he had spoken enthusiastically of the "bass and guitar unison things" he had been doing, but these riff-driven songs of the previous eighteen months written with Cox (which Hendrix confirmed in a Swedish radio interview with Kals Burling) would now give way to something new: presumably the autobiographical *Black Gold*.

Staying in London was also his way to be rid of Devon Wilson, the super groupie who was now a super junkie probably not only using heroin but using heroin to keep Hendrix close. Hendrix's addiction to heroin has been hotly disputed. His fear of needles is often trotted out as proof that he would never shoot up heroin and therefore never be addicted, but he was known to snort heroin. His appearance at Isle of Wight and inexplicable behavior in Sweden, Denmark, and Germany—missing flights and breaking into railway compartments to sleep—has all the earmarks of a man going through heroin withdrawal. Hendrix was even turned away from a jam at Ronnie Scott's with Eric Burdon's new band War; Tony Brown in *The Final Days of Jimi Hendrix* quotes War's musicians as saying the reason was that Hendrix looked "smacked out."

His insistence that Wilson stay behind in New York City and not accompany him to London and on the European tour was probably an attempt on his part to go cold turkey. A show on September 2nd had been as bad as the Madison Square Garden appearance that is always written about. On that evening in Vejlby Risskov Hall in Aarhus, Denmark, only three songs were played before Hendrix terminated the set after twenty-four minutes—disappearing from the stage during an extended Mitch Mitchell drum solo—and a bad reaction to drugs has been given as one of the reasons. The following night in Copenhagen, a shaky and sweaty Jimi had been sighted before the concert. The CD booklet that accompanies UniVibe's *Jimi in Denmark* notes that someone from the Rolling Stones had called, inquiring about Hendrix's health, and this could only have been Sharon Lawrence, one of the few people in his life who seems to have cared more about the man than his music or the money he could generate.

When Lawrence had seen him in London on September 11th at Ronnie Scott's, she found a friend whose appearance was "ashen." He didn't even recognize her. Before being pulled away by a "foreign-looking woman" (who could only have been Monika Dannemann), Lawrence has written in her book that Hendrix said to her, "I'm almost gone." Whether this is a reference to how high he felt or hints at thoughts of suicide is open to interpretation, but death was clearly on his mind.

It is a matter of record that in early September Hendrix spoke to two Danish journalists about the possibility of dying. When asked, Hendrix told Jorn Rossing Jensen that the book he was writing would be published after his death, and had told Anne Bjørndal he was "not sure I will live to be twenty-eight years old. I mean, the moment I feel I have got nothing more to give musically, I will not be around on this planet any more, unless I have a wife and children. Otherwise I have got nothing to live for . . . ."

When Lawrence spoke to him on the telephone the following morning, the chance meeting in Ronnie Scott's was not mentioned. Instead Hendrix sounded to her like a man under a tremendous amount of stress. He complained about Jeffery and Alan Douglas, but it was the ongoing legal skirmishes with Chalpin that were taking a real toll. Leo Branton—an attorney from Los Angeles who had represented several black entertainers and controlled Hendrix's estate for several decades—according to Sharon Lawrence, has said that Chalpin appeared to "get a sexual vicarious thrill out of litigating." Hendrix was the direct opposite. Although Chalpin's lawsuit in America had been resolved, it was still ongoing in Great Britain and Europe, and Hendrix complained to Lawrence about being forced to hand over to Chalpin more of the one possession he prized: his music.

Jimi Hendrix at one of his final concerts.   *Author's collection*

Chas Chandler (Slight Return)

Hendrix's former manager Chas Chandler was in Gothenburg, Sweden, visiting his wife Lotte's parents when Hendrix played Liseburg amusement park on September 1, 1970, and Chandler caught the concert. By all accounts it was one of the three best shows Hendrix played on the shortened tour of Europe. By all accounts, that is, except for Chandler's; he is quoted in Tony Brown's *The Final Days of Jimi Hendrix* as saying "it was a disastrous concert, it was really awful to watch . . . I mean, no discipline at all."

Chandler said, "I told him exactly what I thought," so he must have been shocked when two weeks later on September 16th Hendrix came calling at Chandler's apartment in London and expressed an interest in having

Chandler produce him again. According to Chandler, Hendrix wanted his former manager to return with him to Electric Lady Studios in New York City and put the finishing touches on the songs he was mixing for his next album. When Chandler balked due to a prior commitment to visit his parents, Hendrix offered to have the tapes flown over to London to be mixed at Olympic Studios. "He wanted to use that studio again," Chandler said, "because [Hendrix] really felt that's the way to put it right."

By putting it right, Chandler implies that Hendrix wanted to make amends for letting Chandler walk away in May 1968. Unable to tolerate the hangers-on in the studio and lack of discipline during the *Electric Ladyland* sessions in New York City, it had been Chandler's suggestion to leave and sell his stake in Hendrix to Mike Jeffery, but Chandler had been hurt that Hendrix hadn't made any effort to keep the manager who had plucked him out of obscurity and made him a star. But what Chandler didn't realize was that it was difficult for Hendrix to form close ties with anybody and that, according to Kathy Etchingham, "their relationship lasted longer than any other Jimi had with a male friend." Now back in London, maybe Hendrix realized just how much Chandler contributed not only to his success, but to the quality of his music.

Chandler told British journalist Chris Welch that he even discussed the design for the next album cover with Hendrix and was looking forward to seeing him the following week in London but wasn't totally surprised to hear upon meeting his father at the train station that Hendrix was dead. "Something had to happen and there was no way of stopping it. You just get a feeling sometimes. It was as if the last couple of years had prepared us for it. It was like a message I had been waiting for."

Chandler went on to manage and produce the best glam rock band ever: Slade. (That is, if you discount David Bowie's Ziggy Stardust and the Spiders from Mars.) Certainly the best selling. Slade never broke big in America, but in the UK they outsold every other British band in the United Kingdom in the 1970s in terms of singles. (I also believe that singer Noddy Holder, an atypical front man, paved the way for the acceptance of Joe Strummer as a rock star.) In addition to managing Slade for twelve years, Chandler produced their records through 1977's *Whatever Happened to Slade* (again without the question mark!), owned a recording studio for four years, published music, and operated several record labels. These business enterprises worked out very well for Chandler and—despite having made no money during his chart-breaking years in the Animals—he found himself successful. In 1983 he sold his businesses and resumed a career in music. In the 1990s, he was the prime mover behind the development of Newcastle Arena in Newcastle upon Tyne, his hometown.

When Chas Chandler died on July 17, 1996, from a heart condition he was a wealthy man, but you can imagine him wondering from time to time what might have been had Jimi Hendrix showed up that following week with his unfinished tapes.

The Facts Surrounding Jimi Hendrix's Death

Kathy Etchingham says Hendrix's fellow Experience Makers had told her of his habit of picking up "the worst possible dogs" or "crazies," taking them back to the hotel he was staying at after the concert, having sex, and then tossing them out of his hotel room. For nearly four years Jimi Hendrix had gotten away with this habit, but on the night of his death, the irresponsible behavior of the "crazy" he had paired up with may have been a contributing cause of his death.

And it is because of Monika Dannemann's conflicting statements to the authorities and journalists and in her book, the abysmal *The Inner World of Jimi Hendrix* (credited to "his fiancée" no less), that presenting the facts surrounding Hendrix's death on September 18, 1970, is difficult. The Hendrix historian has to sift through Dannemann's tall tales, newspaper accounts, inquest statements, biographies and autobiographies, and a reinvestigation by British authorities into the death in the 1990s and make some judgment calls.

Monika Dannemann had met Hendrix in a hotel bar in Dusseldorf, Germany, on January 13, 1969. The tall, German blonde who described herself as a "former ice skating champion" had attended the Experience's second show the previous night. Wary of Hendrix's reputation, she was won over nevertheless by his shy, reserved manner and accompanied him to Cologne, where she watched the Experience from the side of the stage. The extent of their relationship over the course of the following twenty-one months has been disputed (and likely exaggerated by Dannemann), but the two hooked up one last time at the Speakeasy in London on September 15, 1970. Another former girlfriend of Hendrix, a black woman named Alvinia Bridges who would go on to work for the Rolling Stones, arranged the meeting at Dannemann's request.

Dannemann said that their meeting was prearranged and that Hendrix asked her to rent the basement apartment at the Samarkand Hotel in Notting Hill she was staying at for the two of them, the same basement apartment Jimi Hendrix was found dead in. It appears unlikely, however, that he ever asked Dannemann to rent the apartment for the two of them because during the same time he was seeing her in London, he never checked out of his suite at the Cumberland Hotel, where he'd been staying after the aborted European tour. The Cumberland Hotel was where Jimi Hendrix kept his clothing and continued to make and receive messages related to his business matters, just as he did on the afternoon of September 17th.

We know this fact because while caught in a traffic jam, two girls in a car recognized Jimi Hendrix, began waving to him, and one of them told the driver of the car, Phillip Harvey, the identity of the man they were waving to. Harvey was the son of a well-known conservative member of Parliament but still told the girls to invite the rock star for tea. Hendrix agreed but said he had to stop off at the Cumberland Hotel first. Harvey followed the blue car Dannemann was driving, parked outside of the hotel while she and Hendrix went inside and was surprised when the two returned. This was approximately at 4:30 in the afternoon, and while at the Cumberland, Hendrix spoke to Gerry Stickells about signing a contract for a German tour in October. He also spoke with Mitch Mitchell about jamming with Sly Stone at the Speakeasy that night, a jam that never occurred although they waited for Hendrix until closing time, which was 4 a.m.

At Harvey's house, a pleasant night smoking hash, drinking French wine, and eating vegetarian food was ruined when Dannemann suddenly stood up, announced she was leaving, and walked out. Harvey thought she was jealous of the attention Hendrix was receiving from the two girls he knew. After Hendrix followed her outside, Harvey heard her berate Hendrix for at least thirty minutes. He tried to invite them back inside, mostly because he was fearful that the police would be summoned, but she refused. Hendrix eventually went back inside, apologized to his host, and said that Dannemann had had too much to drink. According to Harvey, she was still yelling at Hendrix as they drove away at approximately 10:40 p.m.

Prior to meeting Harvey and the two girls, Hendrix had made Dannemann stop the car when he had seen Devon Wilson with Collette Mimram and Stella Douglas. According to music agent Daniel Secunda, Hendrix had spent the evening of September 14th dining with Wilson and Stella and Alan Douglas and that "Jimi and the girls were so smacked out . . . they barely ate anything or even said a word." More talkative this early afternoon, the three women invited Hendrix to a party later that evening at the residence of Track Records cofounder Pete Kameron. It is likely that after leaving Harvey's house, Hendrix had had enough of Dannemann and asked her to drop him off at the party, because he arrived alone and in an agitated state.

Hendrix stayed at the party for several hours; long enough to eat Chinese food and take an amphetamine capsule with the street name of Black Bomber that Devon Wilson gave him. The two also took some LSD that made Wilson pass out. Dannemann returned and, using the intercom, asked to speak to Hendrix. Stella Douglas at Hendrix's request told her to go away. When Dannemann returned some time later, this time he told her he wasn't ready to leave the party yet. According to a letter that Angie Burdon, Eric Burdon's ex-wife, wrote to Kathy Etchingham, her ex-roommate, when Dannemann came back a third time, Hendrix "got angry because she wouldn't leave him alone for long enough . . . in fact she was bugging him . . . in fact I felt everything was bugging him period." He tried to get Stella Douglas to make Dannemann go away again, but after finally talking to her on the intercom, he decided to leave. It was the last time anyone other than Dannemann saw Jimi Hendrix alive.

As early as 9:30 a.m. (and possibly much earlier, as dawn was breaking), Dannemann called the residence she thought Alvinia Bridges was staying at trying to find the number of Hendrix's doctor in London. Another woman answered and told her that Bridges was staying at the Russell Hotel where Eric Burdon and the musicians in War were living while playing their dates at Ronnie Scott's.

Dannemann then called Bridges in Eric Burdon's room, waking them. This is confirmed in Eric Burdon's biography *I Used to Be an Animal But I'm Alright Now*. Bridges said she was upset and told Burdon that Hendrix was "so stoned he won't wake up." Still half-asleep, Burdon suggested Dannemann get him coffee and slap him awake. Burdon then went back to sleep, but when he woke up again, he immediately called her and repeatedly tried to convince her to call for an ambulance. Dannemann, however, was worried about the narcotics that were in the basement apartment. Burdon yelled at her and told her to flush the drugs down the toilet but not before calling an ambulance. He said he'd be right over.

What Eric Burdon found upon arrival was a dead friend in bed. Both Burdon and Dannemann claimed to have called the ambulance at 11:18 a.m. Burdon said he "got the guitars out" as well as the drugs and themselves. He insists that Dannemann "didn't leave in the ambulance, she was with me and Alvinia."

This is indirectly confirmed by statements taken from the ambulance crew that arrived at the Samarkand Hotel at 11:27 a.m. Both members of the two-man crew had decades of experience responding to emergency calls, and both the attendant, Reginald Jones, and the driver, John Saua, said nobody responded when they called into the darkened apartment. Jones said that "the door was flung wide open, nobody about, just the body on the bed." They entered the room and, upon opening the curtains, Saua said "we knew he was gone."

Whoever called the ambulance had not mentioned Jimi Hendrix's name. Saua said "I did not recognize him, don't know anybody would have recognized him, his mother wouldn't have recognized him. He was in a pool of vomit, it was everywhere." The crew followed procedures even though they knew it was futile. The police were summoned, and after they arrived, the ambulance crew removed the body. "The gases were gurgling," remembered Saua, "you get that when someone has died, it wasn't too pleasant. The vomit was all the way down, we couldn't have got an airway down. He was flat on his back, it's a shame he wasn't on his side because he probably would have pulled through."

The ambulance arrived at St. Mary Abbotts Hospital at 11:45 a.m. According to Dr. John Bannister's letter to biographer Harry Shapiro in 1992, the Surgical Registrar reported to "Casualty" to attend to an unconscious man, but Jimi Hendrix "was obviously dead. He had no pulse, no heart beat and the attempt to resuscitate him was merely a formality . . . ." He also noted "the very large amounts of red wine that oozed from his stomach and his lungs, and in my opinion there was no question that Jimi Hendrix had drowned . . . ." and that "I can quite clearly recall large amounts of red wine causing his hair and clothes to be matted."

This is a crucial fact because as Tony Brown wrote in *The Final Days of Jimi Hendrix*: "It is curious that despite the copious amounts of red wine that Jimi had in his body, his blood level was low." He was the first to note that from Dr. Bannister's letter one could surmise that the red wine "had been poured over [Jimi] and left to dry. He could have been soaked in wine for hours."

Up to now you are probably wondering why I have labeled Monika Dannemann a "crazy." At the time of Jimi Hendrix's death she was only twenty-five years old, and not unreasonable for a young woman in her situation to panic: after all, in all likelihood she was a white woman in a foreign country who woke up next to a world-famous black musician who was dying or dead. It was her behavior after Jimi Hendrix's death that makes one question her sanity and motives.

When Sharon Lawrence met Monika Dannemann on September 19th in Eric Burdon's hotel room, she wanted some answers as to what had happened to her friend. The death had not overly surprised her—she had a foreboding that something bad was going to happen to Hendrix—but she wanted to understand the circumstances. Dannemann was already dressed in the black garb of a widow. After Dannemann misrepresented events of the night he died, Sharon was shocked when she started talking about her artwork and how much Hendrix liked it. Sharon didn't want to talk to her about Monika's artwork. She wanted to know what had happened to her friend.

Dannemann repeated what she had already told authorities and would be confirmed in the coroner's reports: Hendrix had taken nine Vesparax pills. The normal dosage is half a pill. The pills had been prescribed for Dannemann for pain after a skating accident. She said that she had not given him the pills, but it was likely that, unable to sleep from the drugs taken at Pete Kameron's party, he had taken the pills himself. Others confirmed that Hendrix often took barbiturates to help sleep. Only he probably underestimated the strength of the Vesparax pills. Later when he had a choking fit, the pills made him too incapacitated to sit up or even roll on his side, and he choked on his vomit.

It was Dannemann's behavior in the weeks and decades after Hendrix's death that made her seem like a "crazy" to others. The inquest was scheduled on September 28th, and before it was held, Dannemann flew back to her hometown of Dusseldorf and, in a photograph accompanying a local newspaper article, was posed smiling in front of her artwork. At the inquest, she was no longer a skating instructor but called herself an artist. It was apparent that she would try to use her connection to Jimi Hendrix's death to further her artistic career.

Dannemann's statements at the inquest contradicted those given to authorities immediately after Hendrix's death, beginning a pattern that would continue until her death in 1996. And the contradictions served two purposes. First, she wanted to absolve herself of any blame in his death, and so over time, her story changed, and according to Dannemann, Hendrix died due to drugs that Devon Wilson gave him, Michael Jeffery killed him, the ambulance attendants' actions caused Hendrix's death, the doctors at the hospital were racist and neglectful. Secondly, she wanted to convince people that her relationship with Hendrix was more substantial than it really was. It was true that during those four September days he was with Dannemann, she was wearing what might have been an engagement ring and that she was telling anyone who would listen that she was his fiancée, but it's unlikely that they had an engagement that lasted several years. As Eric Burdon said, he didn't realize until later that Dannemann was a stalker.

Over time, she used litigation against anybody who doubted her conflicting statements and directed the blame for Jimi's death at her basement door. When Kathy Etchingham and the surviving Experience Makers took issue with their portrayals in David Henderson's 'Scuse Me While I Kiss the Sky, they invited Dannemann—who none of them knew—to discuss what sort of actions they should take. Nothing came of this and subsequent meetings, except the dawning upon Hendrix's intimate friends that Dannemann's versions of events were untruthful and she was mentally unstable.

One thing she did do with Kathy Etchingham (and Sharon Lawrence too) over time was pepper them with personal questions about Hendrix—"What did he like to eat?" and "What did Jimi say about the number nine?"—so that she could then use the same personal details in interviews and her manuscript to convince people that she and Hendrix were kindred spirits. Even after his death, she said that on nights when the moon was full, "Jimi and I are in communication. We go together travelling on the astral plane."

Etchingham was disturbed enough about Dannemann's claims that the ambulance attendants and doctors were responsible for Hendrix's death and that there might have been a cover-up that she petitioned successfully in the 1990s for a reinvestigation that not only brought about many of the facts reported above but the realization that it was Dannemann who was covering something up, and Etchingham said so. Then when she was informed in 1995 that Dannemann's just-published *The Inner World of Jimi Hendrix* stated that Etchingham's accusations against her had been unsubstantiated, Etchingham considered filing a lawsuit.

Nearly a quarter of a century after Hendrix's death, Kathy Page Etchingham was happily married to a medical professional, and the mother of two boys. She wasn't pleased about things Dannemann had written about her in the book but was still willing to ignore her until in a *Musician* interview, Dannemann said Etchingham was a middle-aged party girl who had met her husband in a hospital after nearly overdosing on heroin. In order to defend her husband as well as herself, Etchingham filed a suit against Dannemann, who committed suicide by asphyxiation on April 5, 1996, two days after a magistrate ruled in favor of Kathy Page. There is evidence that at the last minute she tried to prevent the act by turning off her Mercedes-Benz's motor but was too late.

Are You Suicidal?

After returning with Eric Burdon and Alvinia Bridges and checking into the Lincoln House Hotel, the hotel Burdon was staying at, Dannemann went with Gerry Stickells and Eric Barrett to retrieve some of her belongings and Hendrix's possessions. According to her, Barrett convinced Stickells to let Dannemann keep Hendrix's favorite black Fender Stratocaster that he called "Black Beauty," which was last seen in 1995.

Dannemann said the next day she remembered the allegedly last poem Hendrix had written had been left behind at the Samarkand Hotel, and she snuck out and retrieved the pages it was written on. This poem, "The Story of Life," had been seen by Burdon the previous day, and he told friends and members of the press that the poem was Hendrix's suicide note because it contained references to Jesus and death and life being "quicker than the wink of an eye." It was during an incoherent BBC interview given by an obviously stoned Burdon that flames of the story of Jimi Hendrix's suicide were fanned. As Burdon said of Hendrix's demise: "His death was deliberate. He was happy dying. He died happily and he used the drug to phase himself out of this life and go someplace else. Because he realized that for him to stop off and correct what was wrong with his organization . . . ."

Burdon's theory of Hendrix's death was based on conversations he'd had with Jimi who often spoke of death as a way out. It was also based on Burdon's own experiences of being managed by Michael Jeffery and having nothing to show for it financially. Burdon said he tried to warn Hendrix early on about Jeffery, who would make him a penniless star. Everyone sensed the stress Hendrix was under his final weeks, and Burdon naturally thought Jeffery the cause and suicide as his way of correcting what was "wrong with his organization." Burdon has since changed his opinion of Hendrix's death now that Dannemann's initial statements have been discredited.

The strongest, most persuasive case, however, for the idea that Jimi Hendrix did make a suicide attempt is Sharon Lawrence's *The Intimate Story of a Betrayed Musical Legend*. Lawrence is one of the more mature people you come across in accounts of Jimi Hendrix's life and death. An American who had just acted as publicist for a short Rolling Stones tour, she found herself in London the day Hendrix died and was determined to understand how her friend died. After meeting the woman who had been with him, Lawrence was the first person to harbor suspicions about Monika Dannemann's version of events.

The meeting took place in the small hotel room of Eric Burdon, who had made the arrangements. Taken aback by Dannemann's unemotional demeanor and desire to be friends, Lawrence questioned her. The questions came easily. Lawrence worked for United Press International. When Dannemann told Lawrence that Hendrix had taken nine Vesparax pills, Lawrence said the number aloud. Dannemann wanted to know why. "It was Jimi's number," Lawrence said, recalling a conversation she had had with her deceased friend.

Numerology was one of Jimi Hendrix's interests, and he had given Lawrence a book on the subject that he said he had read "dozens of times." It was when handing her this book that he had said "I'm a nine" and that

DRUG OVERDOSE KILLS ROCK IDOL HENDRIX

Newspapers were quick to incorrectly attribute Jimi's demise to drugs.
Courtesy of Robert Rodriguez

"It's a powerful number, and it can be very good or very bad. Nines are meant to accomplish things in this world."

When Dannemann showed Lawrence "The Story of Life," she too took the words to be Jimi Hendrix's suicide note. Lawrence knew he kept completed lyrics in a leather portfolio for safekeeping. If these three pages were left atop a bedside table, then Hendrix "must have wanted these particular pages to be seen." To Lawrence, the fact that her friend had taken nine pills was proof of his intent to commit suicide.

Murder, He Wrote

Ed Chalpin immediately suspected murder upon seeing the headlines in London's newspapers proclaiming Jimi Hendrix's death, and the rumors have persisted ever since. Some have suspected the FBI due to Hendrix's alleged support of the Back Panthers, and Monika Dannemann said Devon Wilson gave him pills that he died from.

A former business associate of Michael Jeffery's, however, made Hendrix's "murder" the centerpiece of a memoir. James "Tappy" Wright's *Rock Roadie: Backstage and Confidential with Hendrix, Elvis, the Animals, Tina Turner, and an All-Star Cast* was published in May 2009. Eric Burdon says in his first autobiography that Wright was one of the best rock managers in the business, and his role in the Animals' affairs attests to a relationship with their rock manager Michael Jeffery. But would Jeffery, whose life was not only a room but a house full of mirrors, have revealed to Wright that he had Jimi Hendrix murdered?

Because that's Wright claim in *Rock Roadie*. According to Wright, a few months before his death in a fiery airplane crash, Jeffery admitted in a Spanish bar to having had his most famous client murdered. Jeffery was suspected by many—including musicians he managed—as having ties to organized crime on two continents, and allegedly he hired a gang of thugs who entered Dannemann's basement hotel apartment and forced down

Hendrix's throat nine Vesparax pills and the red wine later found matted in his hair and clothing by the ambulance attendants. Wright's book also claims that Dannemann was complicit in the murder.

Jeffery's motivation according to Wright was debt. Fearful that Hendrix would drop him as his manager when his contract lapsed in a few months, Jeffery was desperate that he would be unable to pay off his debts. So he took out a life insurance policy on Hendrix that was worth $2,000,000 and that named Jeffery as the beneficiary.

In a *National* article published in July 2009, Dr. Bannister, the Surgical Registrar who attended to Jimi Hendrix the morning of September 18th, admitted that murder was "'plausible' from a medical perspective at least." You'll find that quoted often online as well as other details. What is often omitted, however, is Bannister's opinion that "I'd never thought of it as being murder." What is also left out is the fact that Bannister, an Australian who relocated to Sydney in 1972, where he "worked as an orthopedic surgeon until 1992 when he was deregistered in NSW for fraudulent conduct."

Wright's accusation against Jeffery is probably as authentic as the two guitars he said belonged to Hendrix that were sold at a Sotheby's auction but that Noel Redding—in his only mention of Wright in his autobiography—says he didn't recognize.

Spill the Wine

But the question of the copious amounts of wine that contributed to Jimi Hendrix's death needs to be answered, does it not? The "couple of bottles of red wine" referenced in Phillip Harvey's affidavit and consumed by five people does not account for the amount of wine found in and around Hendrix's corpse. According to Tony Brown's account of the medical investigation following the death, "his blood alcohol level was fairly low," and he must have drunk the red wine just before he died.

In the intervening decades, Sharon Lawrence wondered about this aspect of her friend's demise, but on the advice of friends and even Hendrix's own lawyer, she avoided the woman in his company when he died. She had been so upset during her questioning of Dannemann in Eric Burdon's hotel room to learn that the German blonde had been more worried about what the press would say while Hendrix lay dying than calling for medical help that she wanted no further contact with her.

This is what Lawrence remembered when Dannemann telephoned her twenty years later asking if she could visit Lawrence in Los Angeles. When that was rebuffed, Dannemann invited Lawrence to East Sussex in England, where she lived. This, too, Lawrence rejected, suspecting that Dannemann wanted to talk to her to glean more personal information about Hendrix for her manuscript (just as she would use Lawrence's mentioning of his interest in numerology in *The Inner World of Jimi Hendrix*). Lawrence even refrained from contacting Dannemann when the so-called ice skating champion's lawyers sent her a letter warning her not to write anything that incriminated their client in the death of Jimi Hendrix.

Lawrence's frustrations with Dannemann's lies and litigation against friends, however, forced her to confront Dannemann in 1996 with a question she had wanted to ask for years. Once again Dannemann had telephoned Lawrence to invite her to England. Only this time, Lawrence says in her autobiography that she "let loose." Finally accusing Dannemann of not helping Hendrix in his hour of need, Lawrence asked something she already knew the answer to: was it Dannemann who in a state of panic forced him to drink the red wine?

"I thought it would help," Lawrence says Dannemann admitted.

29

Not Quite Touching the Promised Land

Electric Lady Studios

Whereas most famous musicians of the 1960s founded vanity labels—e.g., the Beach Boys with Brother Records, the Moody Blues with Threshold Records, Jefferson Airplane with Grunt Records—Jimi Hendrix was the only one to open his own recording studio. It may be the only wise business decision Hendrix made in his career as Electric Lady Studios is still in use over forty years after its opening. (Kanye West, Coldplay, and the Strokes are just a few names to use Hendrix's studio in 2010 and 2011. It was also featured in the film *Nick and Nora's Infinite Playlist.*) Unfortunately for Hendrix, he never lived to use his studio after its opening party on August 26, 1970.

Abstract Artist Hans Hofmann

Jimi Hendrix wasn't the first artist of note to work at 52 West Eighth Street in New York City's Greenwich Village: that would be abstract expressionist Hans Hofmann, who established the Hans Hofmann School of Fine Arts at the address in 1938, thirty years before Hendrix leased space there. Some critics suggest that Jackson Pollock's drip paintings were influenced by Hofmann's works, including *Spring* from 1940. Hoffman's artwork gained notoriety and acclaim throughout the 1940s and 1950s and in 1958 he gave up teaching to concentrate on his artwork and converted the location of his school into his studio. He continued working in his studio on Eighth Street until his death on February 17, 1966.

The Generation Club

Fifty-two West Eighth Street is a split-level dwelling, so I'm being a little facetious if I've led you to believe that Hans Hofmann and later Jimi Hendrix actually created within the same space. Being a painter, Hans Hofmann would have required the light that the upper level could provide. His studio became the Eighth Street Playhouse, which was where the midnight weekend screenings of *The Rocky Horror Show* ran for fifteen years. It was later the site of TLA Video.

Electric Lady Studios is actually in the basement of 52 West Eighth Street. Previously it had been the Generation Club, an old club purchased by Hendrix's manager Michael Jeffery who had relocated his base of operations from London to New York City. Jeffery's success began with the operations of clubs in Newcastle, and throughout his management career he continued to operate clubs: Sergeant Pepper's in Majorca, Spain, and now the Generation Club in New York City.

Opening night featured the likes of Joni Mitchell, Janis Joplin, Buddy Guy, and B. B. King. There's nothing original to this: defunct clubs often become new clubs, and before it was the Generation Club the space had housed the Village Barn, which was owned by crooner Rudy Vallee and—despite its "hick" name and atmosphere—hosted big band concerts.

What was original about the original plans was the intent to build a small recording studio on the club's premises. Two bootleg performances have survived of Hendrix playing the Generation Club—both from April 1968, the latter legendary because it features B. B. King—and Hendrix, notorious for taping everything he could, wanted to have a space where his after-hours jams could be recorded and sifted through for ideas afterwards.

You can find selections from this appearance on Radioactive Records' *Blues at Midnight* (minus B. B. King), and you can see grainy footage of Hendrix playing at the Generation Club with Roy Buchanan on YouTube.

Design, Delays, and Overruns

Architect and acoustician John Storyk was twenty-two years old when he drew up plans for the club and small studio. But before construction could begin, he was told to draw up a new set of plans for the layout of just a recording studio.

Accountant Jim Marron had been asked by Jeffery to audit the money Hendrix was spending on round-the-clock recording sessions at the Record Plant, and when it was discovered to have been $300,000, it was reasoned that money could be saved if Hendrix owned his own studio. Eddie Kramer flew over from England in early 1969 to assist Storyk with the planning and purchase of equipment that would make Jimi Hendrix the first musician to own his own studio. Little did Storyk know at the time that he would one day be the recording studio designer of choice for the likes of Bruce Springsteen, Jay-Z, Alicia Keys, and others.

Construction of Electric Lady Studios took longer than originally estimated. The ceiling required more layers than normal so that the sound could not be heard in the Eighth Street Playhouse. Contractors discovered that the basement studio was to be built over Minetta Brook, an underground stream, but not before it flooded the premises.

Acquiring the best recording equipment and designing a studio where Hendrix could feel at home and let his creative flag fly also ran up costs, and after spending $369,000, Hendrix and Jeffery had to borrow an additional $300,000 from Warner Brothers Records to finance completion of the project.

By this time Hendrix had reservations about building a studio in a leased space and being forced to perform in order to meet financial payments. Hendrix and Jeffery were now financially obligated to pay Warner Brothers $50,000 every six months for the next three years. He also could see how splitting ownership of the studio with Jeffery would make it an impediment to signing with a new manager.

On top of all this, Jeffery had managed to sign a second contract with Warner Brothers to fund a movie called *Wave*, which is the original title of the awful movie *Rainbow Bridge*. Before signing the contract, Warner Brothers insisted that Hendrix provide original material for the soundtrack for the movie and his appearance in the film as well. It was understood that there would be enough music for an album to be released.

A postcard for Jimi's studio on East 8th Street.

Courtesy of Robert Rodriguez

Hendrix's Recording Sessions

Hendrix's regret about owning a studio dissipated as he was finally able to enjoy the benefits. The round windows he had requested were in place as well as curved walls and multicolored lighting that could be adjusted to fit and feed his mood. Hendrix had also insisted that the control booths be large enough for the recording artists to work with the engineers when mixing music.

(It has been written that he hated the 100-foot-long cosmic mural leading from the entrance throughout Electric Lady, but that seems unlikely as it wasn't until Hendrix had been dead for three months that California artist Lance Jost finally arrived in New York City to begin researching the mural. Hendrix himself had asked Jost to paint the mural after seeing artwork Jost had done for an album cover for Moon, a European band that Jeffery managed. Research for the mural took three months, and then it was painted over six months in a Fourth Avenue loft before being assembled in Electric Lady Studios. According to Jost, Eddie Kramer shook his hand after seeing the completed mural.)

Although Studio A was used earlier by Hendrix and Kramer for revisiting recordings made by Gypsy Sun and Rainbows and Band of Gypsys, it wasn't until after June 8, 1970, that Hendrix began work on new material at the studio he owned. Everyone was impressed by the studio and began to believe that the thirteen months that construction had taken were worth it. Hendrix himself noticed immediately what an improvement the studio was over what he was accustomed to, and this spurred him to finally shape the jams of the previous year into songs. He even began showing up at the studio on time.

Another significant change was the installation of a closed-circuit television system that helped minimize the presence of the hangers-on that had plagued the *Electric Ladyland* and other subsequent recording sessions. Eddie Kramer had been as dismayed as Chas Chandler at this unwanted element, and it, too, had caused a rupture between the artist and his favored recording engineer. The construction of the studio and the stricter rules about attendance helped repair their relationship, and during the few months Hendrix was able to record at Electric Lady, Kramer acted as a coproducer during the sessions, determined to achieve the results that Jimi wanted.

According to Billy Cox, the first song revisited inside Electric Lady once it was operational was "Ezy Ryder," a song originally recorded by the Band of Gypsys lineup. Other previously recorded music that was revamped through overdubbed tracks included "Bleeding Heart," "Earth Blues," "Stepping Stone," "Angel," and "Room Full of Mirrors."

The first session to involve all three members of the Cry of Love lineup was held on June 15, 1970, when they did an instrumental called "All God's Children" that Hendrix apparently never was able to return to and add lead vocals.

In addition to jams with Ritchie Havens and Traffic's Steve Winwood and Chris Wood, between June and August 1970, Hendrix also recorded (chronologically) "Night Bird Flying," "Straight Ahead," "Messing Around," "Beginnings," "Freedom," "Drifter's Escape," "Astro Man," "Cherokee Mist," "Hey Baby (New Rising Sun)," "Valleys of Neptune," "Drifting," "Dolly Dagger," "Bolero," "Slow Part" (an excerpt of which would be released as the Jeffery-titled "Pali Gap"), "Midnight Lightning," "Belly Button Window," "Coming Down Hard on Me," "Lover Man," and "In from the Storm."

Percussionist Juma Sultan also participated in some of these recording sessions but says Hendrix's management team ran interference and tried to prevent his participation. They even offered him a contract so he could not attend Hendrix's sessions.

Several demos were also committed to 4-track tape, but except for "Belly Button Window," the demos to "Locomotion," "Electric Lady—Slow," and "This Little Boy" are lost to posterity.

The last new recording at Electric Lady was "Slow Blues."

I list the above to indicate that, contrary to Hendrix's physical appearance and musical performance at the Isle of Wight Festival, he was not in the summer of 1970 in a state of creative decline. Yes, there were conflicts with Devon Wilson and management, and I believe a slight heroin addiction, but there was also a concerted effort by Hendrix, Eddie Kramer, Mitch Mitchell, and Billy Cox to get the next album completed. On the date of the opening party for Electric Lady Studios, Hendrix and Kramer even booked time at Sterling Sound so they could cut masters for "Dolly Dagger" and "Night Bird Flying," the two songs Hendrix wanted to use for his next single.

Glenn Gould

You wouldn't think that a rock star and classical pianist would have much in common, but this is not the case when one considers Jimi Hendrix and Glenn Gould, both left-handed musicians known for unusual body movement onstage and for being temperamental if equipment and instruments were not working properly.

The unreleased sessions at Electric Lady Studios have resulted in hundreds of bootleg recordings.   *Courtesy of Robert Rodriguez*

Both men died relatively young, of course, but Gould, who lived nine days past his fiftieth birthday, was able to demonstrate what might have been the trajectory of Hendrix's life had he lived long enough to properly utilize his own private recording studio.

Both men were unorthodox. Both were criticized in their lifetimes for their radical arrangements of beloved pieces and known for canceling concerts on whims: two factors that played into the controversy surrounding Glenn Gould's scheduled performance of Brahms's *Concerto for Piano and Orchestra No. 1 in D Minor* on April 6, 1962, at Carnegie Hall in New York City. When conductor Leonard Bernstein took the unusual liberty of addressing the audience from the podium, his first words were to reassure them that Glenn Gould was indeed present. No, what Bernstein wanted to share with the audience was his objection to how slowly Gould intended to play certain passages of the piece:

> You are about to hear a rather, shall we say, unorthodox performance of the *Brahms D Minor Concerto*, a performance distinctly different from any I've ever heard, or even dreamt of for that matter, in its remarkably broad tempi and its frequent departures from Brahms's dynamic indications. I cannot say I am in total agreement with Mr. Gould's conception and this raises the interesting question: "What am I doing conducting it?" I'm conducting it because Mr. Gould is so valid and serious an artist that I must take seriously anything he conceives in good faith and his conception is interesting enough so that I feel you should hear it, too.

One can easily imagine Arthur Fiedler making a similar statement if asked to conduct Jimi Hendrix playing "The Star Spangled Banner," a song that the Boston Pops had released as a 45 single on RCA Victor label in 1965. It is not as far-fetched as it sounds. The Jimi Hendrix Experience did play two concerts at Philharmonic Hall in New York City on Thanksgiving 1968, which had harpsichordist Fernando Valenti and the New York Brass Quartet as the opening act. Mitch Mitchell even sat in with the orchestra.

Both Hendrix and Gould's lives were shortened by substance abuse and have led to the observation that both men might have accomplished so much more had they not. Gould is faulted for not composing much and leaving a multitude of projects unfinished. The same could be said of Hendrix, who spoke frequently in interviews of albums and projects that never came to fruition.

But where Hendrix and Gould are most alike is the spell that the recording studio cast upon them. Both men were bewitched with perfection. Glenn Gould gave up touring at the age of thirty-two and approximately 200 concert performances. (Hendrix, too, during his last interview with Keith Altham talked of "less personal appearances.") The reason he gave up live performances was his "love affair with the microphone" as was stated in *Piano Quarterly* in 1974. Gould relished the ability to manipulate tape and create perfect performances. Does this not sound like the same proclivity that drove both Chas Chandler and Noel Redding mad with Jimi Hendrix? Didn't Michael Jeffery suggest building Electric Lady Studios because Hendrix was spending all of his midnight hours pursuing perfect muses?

Gould, however, was able to spend the last twenty-eight years of his life—longer than Jimi Hendrix's entire life—working in recording studios, tweaking tapes and releasing radio and television broadcasts on the Canadian Broadcasting Company.

That last point is critical. During Hendrix's final interview conducted a week before his death, Keith Altham asked him about "the importance of having film with your music" and Hendrix's was like that of an inventor. He foresees virtual reality and imagines "this whole room (that) can be like the total audiovisual type of thing. Like you go in there and . . . the whole thing just blossoms out with this color and sound type of scene." You can hear his enthusiasm in the printed word as he continues: "You put in your favorite star and all of a sudden this music and the audio, I mean the visual scene comes on."

Hendrix then was at the forefront of whole new form of artistic expression. He clearly saw the possibilities in audiovisual equipment before other performers and went so far as having portions of the Band of Gypsys appearances at the Fillmore East taped. Just imagine the body of work that Jimi Hendrix—the proud owner of a recording studio who was interested in creating audiovisual productions—might have left behind had he lived to the ripe old age of fifty.

The Party

The studio's opening party was held on August 26, 1970, just before Hendrix's departure for the Isle of Wight headlining performance and a tour of Europe. In attendance at the party were Noel Redding, Yoko Ono, and Mick Fleetwood. Music recorded at Electric Lady by Hendrix and other artists was piped in. In addition to the two songs for his next single, "Ezy Ryder" and "Straight Ahead" comprised the four songs played repeatedly that evening.

By all accounts, Hendrix kept a low profile, hanging with friends and speaking of his upcoming trip to England, from which some of those in attendance received the impression that it was a trip he did not want to make. He was much more interested in finishing his next album.

Unfortunately, destruction seemed to follow in his wake—he owed over $35,000 in damages to the house in Slokan, New York—and a food fight broke out at the party, which upset Hendrix because what was being destroyed was the first tangible piece of property that he owned. He left the party early, never to return to his studio, never quite reaching his promised land.

Famous Recordings Made at Electric Lady Studios

Little did John Storyk and Eddie Kramer know when they were designing and ordering equipment for Electric Lady Studios that they were building what was to be one of the most successful recording studios ever. Built exclusively as a refuge and creative laboratory for Jimi Hendrix, soon after his death his studio was very much in demand. Hendrix is that rare artist—on par with Alfred Hitchcock and Charles Schulz—whose work appeals not only to the public but their artistic brethren as well. Hoping to mine a creative spirit in the space where Hendrix found his, other recording artists began flocking to Electric Lady.

The first important album partially recorded at Electric Lady was *Music of My Mind* by Stevie Wonder. Only twenty years of age when released, it was his fourteenth studio album and heralded what is considered his peak period. Songs for his following album *Talking Book* as well as *Fulfillingness' First Finale* were also recorded at Electric Lady.

By the end of the decade, a who's who of 1960s and 1970s rock artists had recorded or mixed there, including AC/DC (*Back in Black*), David Bowie (*David Live*), Led Zeppelin (*Led Zeppelin III, Houses of the Holy*, and *Physical Graffiti*), Lou Reed (*Sally Can't Dance* and *Coney Island Baby*), and the Rolling Stones (*Some Girls*).

It was also used by many recording artists associated with punk, hardcore, and new wave over the years, including Patti Smith (*Horses* and *Gone Again*), the Clash (*Sandinista!* and *Combat Rock*), the Dead Boys (*Young Loud and Snotty*), Blondie (*Eat to the Beat*), the Cars (*Heartbeat City*), the Bad Brains (*God of Love*), and Rancid (*. . . And Out Come the Wolves*).

In the early 2000s, Electric Lady Studios began losing clientele, but whereas Hendrix's favorite recording haunt the Record Plant was forced to close its doors in 1987, his "promised land" has survived. There was a change in management, equipment renovated, and an effort made to reach out to artists who had created there previously. Eddie Kramer in a *New York Times* article commemorating the studio's fortieth anniversary says another reason Hendrix's studio survived was: "In a word: vibe. We wanted to create an environment where Jimi could feel really happy, and feel that he could create anything." And other recording artists have fed off that vibe ever since, including many not alive when Hendrix died, including members of the White Stripes, the Strokes, the Magnetic Fields, and the Roots, and solo recording artists such as Kanye West, Erykah Badu, and Rhianna.

30

May You Never Hear Surf Music Again

Hendrix in the Culture

While touring with his underrated band the Mescaleros at the beginning of the aughts, Joe Strummer was asked how he knew the Clash had made their mark. "The culture, we're in the culture," Strummer answered. "Like CCR and the Doors." Reading that, I knew what the singer/rhythm guitarist meant. No matter your record sales, no matter your level of stardom, what matters most, what says the most about your body of work is its effect on the generations that follow. Are the kids who never saw you playing your records? Are they wearing your T-shirts? And more importantly, are you inspiring the musicians who come after you?

Jimi Hendrix is certainly "in the culture" forty years after his premature death; his impact so pervasive it is taken for granted and underacknowledged. You can make the argument that of all American musicians, it is Louis Armstrong and Jimi Hendrix who changed the course of Western music the most. Like Armstrong, the path music took in Hendrix's aftermath is unimaginable. Like Armstrong, his influence was immediate. Unlike Louis, Hendrix's influence is felt further afield. Armstrong affected jazz for sure, but beyond challenging his contemporaries, Hendrix laid the groundwork for heavy metal, moved Miles Davis to go electric and create fusion jazz, let glam rockers and funksters know it was alright to be flamboyant, intimidated wannabe guitarists into creating punk, and left behind samples as the springboard for hip-hop and rap.

When Derek and the Dominoes' *Layla and Other Assorted Love Songs* was released in December 1970, Hendrix's "Little Wing" was one of the assorted love songs. It was seen as a tribute from the greatest guitarist who ever lived and survived to the greatest guitarist who had ever lived and died (even though Eric Clapton actually recorded "Little Wing" nine days before Hendrix's death). Hendrix's presence has continued to be heard in the works of other musicians ever since. The following is an assortment of important musicians—all influential in their own right—whose music have been touched by Hendrix's aura.

David Bowie

The only rocker David Bowie has owned up to inspiring Ziggy Stardust is Vince Taylor, so the song "Ziggy Stardust" can't be about Jimi Hendrix, can it?

But if most rock critics and fans believe "Ziggy Stardust" is about Jimi Hendrix, then it can be about Jimi Hendrix, can't it?

Let's look at some facts.

When Vince Taylor is remembered nowadays, it is for having written "Brand New Cadillac," the first song recorded by the Clash for *London Calling*. But back in the 1960s in France and other European nations, Taylor was considered on par with Elvis, his forte being the same type of rockabilly that would put Presley on a stamp one day. Taylor's fame came to a crashing halt, however, when after one drug too many he proclaimed to his fans that he was Matthew—one of Jesus's twelve Apostles. This Bowie admits formed the basis for the rise and fall of Ziggy Stardust that is recounted on Side Two of the album of the same name.

When fleshing out the character, Bowie pieced Ziggy Stardust together like the Edgar Winter Group's "Frankenstein" from remnants of other musicians. The name was inspired by Iggy Pop, the "screwed down hairdo" was fellow glam rocker Marc Bolan's locks, when "Ziggy sucked up into his mind" Bowie was referencing the mental distress that forced Syd Barrett to quit Pink Floyd. The only reference that is unmistakably Taylor is that of the "leper messiah." (In Bowie's telling, Taylor allegedly proclaimed he was Jesus Christ.)

But whereas these musicians can be said to have contributed one of the lyrical Ziggy Stardust's traits, Jimi Hendrix reflects multiple traits, and the song "Ziggy Stardust" can be interpreted as being about the rise and fall of the Jimi Hendrix Experience. Let's take a close look at the lyrics.

Even if is admitted that "Ziggy really sang," it is his ability on guitar that gets repeatedly mentioned. The opening line states that "Ziggy played guitar," we find out that "boy, could he play guitar," that "he played it left hand" (other than a famous bassist from Liverpool, no other guitarist was as well known for being left-handed as Jimi Hendrix). The pissed-off narrator wonders "should we crush his sweet hands?" Even the song's closing line repeats the point: "Ziggy played guitar." (Also quite possibly the final line of Bowie's concert career: he suffered a minor heart attack during a Berlin concert in 2004 and has not toured since, as of this writing. The set's last song? "Ziggy Stardust.")

It has been said by Bowie that "Weird and Gilly"—Bowie bandmates in the Spiders from Mars—were named for Trevor Bolder (bass) and Woody Woodmansey (drums), but the fact remains most fans imagine "Jamming good Weird and Gilly" as being "Mitch and Noel," the drummer and bassist of the Jimi Hendrix Experience: what band other than Cream were as well known for their jamming capabilities? And in fact, the complaint that they "made it too far," and that Ziggy "became the special man, then we were Ziggy's band" sounds an awful lot like Noel Redding bitching about his subservient role in the Experience.

Other Hendrixian references abound:

- The name of the backup band "the Spiders from Mars" may be a homage to Hendrix's frequent usage of science fiction imagery.
- "Screwed up eyes" can be a drug reference to Hendrix's legendary fondness for drugs.
- The "screwed down hairdo" can describe Hendrix's hair circa 1967 as well as it does Bolan's.
- "Like some cat from Japan" is admittedly a stretch, but I've always taken it to mean Hendrix's light skin color and almond-shaped eyes. (I'm not the only one to do so as there is a Hendrix tribute band that goes the name of Some Cat from Japan.)
- That Ziggy "could lick 'em by smiling" captures Hendrix's infectious, disarming smile.
- "Came on so loaded man" can be read as an allusion to that the fact Jimi Hendrix performed many concerts while high.
- "Well hung": his penis dimension, as Frank Zappa might say. (Groupie Cynthia Plaster Caster is infamous for her plaster casts of rock star hard-ons, and Hendrix "posed" for his at Chicago's Hilton Hotel while in town in 1967 to play the Civic Opera House. Of the modeling session, and Hendrix, she is quoted as saying "and he has this really big, honkin'—it's true what they say about black men.")
- "Snow white tan" could be taken as another reference to the light tone of Hendrix's black skin.
- "He took it all too far" has been said to be of Hendrix getting trapped by his rock stardom.

And do you know of another musician that "played for time, jiving us that we was voodoo?" Do you know another musician who sang about voodoo as often as Jimi did? Do you?

The Rise and Fall of Ziggy Stardust and the Spiders from Mars can only very loosely be considered a concept album, unlike say Lou Reed's *Berlin*, to cite a recording by one of Bowie's more obvious musical heroes. According to David Buckley's liner notes for the thirtieth anniversary two-CD edition, it was through mistaking Doug Yule for Lou Reed that Bowie came to believe "that the fake, the contrived, the artificial could be more 'true' than the original" and that this "powered the Ziggy myth." This is also why I believe the public's perception of "Ziggy Stardust" being Jimi Hendrix is the right one. The artificial is truer than the original. Or as Senator "Rance" Stoddard is told by newspaper editor Maxwell Scott in John Ford's *The Man Who Shot Liberty Valance*: "When the legend becomes fact, print the legend."

Patti Smith

When Jimi Hendrix bumped into a girl sitting on the steps outside his Electric Lady Studios on August 26, 1970, little did he know she would one day make him the centerpiece of an album that is consistently in the Top 10 of All Time lists. How could he? Even Patti Smith couldn't know: in 1970 she was a fledgling poet with more desire than ability, and, although her rawness had already been noticed by the likes of Bobby Neuwirth (Bob Dylan's sometime cohort) and Janis Joplin, her first poetry reading at St. Mark's Church on February 12, 1971, was still more than five months away.

Smith already had a thing for heroes since touching Brian Jones's ankle at a Philly Stones concert in November 1965, but at this point was more infatuated with French symbolists such as Rimbaud and Baudelaire, female screen icons such as Maria Falconetti and Edie Sedgwick (later the subject of "Poppies"), and Rolling Stone lovers such as Anita Pallenberg. (It is said Smith adopted her Keith Richards look so she could seduce Pallenberg, whom Smith's book of poetry *Seventh Heaven* is half-dedicated to.) Even she would have been unable to tell you that she would make an album called *Horses* that celebrated her rock heroes such as Jim Morrison in "Break It Up." Sure, Patti had thought while seeing the Doors perform at the Fillmore East in 1968 that "watching Jim Morrison, I could do that . . . ," but she wisely kept this opinion to herself. At this point, she had no idea she would one day front a band that heralded the third generation of rock 'n' roll.

She had seen Hendrix before inside El Quixote restaurant, next door to West Twenty-Third Street's Chelsea Hotel where she roomed with the then equally unknown photographer Robert Mapplethorpe, but this was the first—and only—time she and Hendrix would speak. Smith had secured an invitation through Jane Friedman, whose Wartoke Concern was handling the press for the new studio and the party celebrating the opening of

Electric Lady Studios, but she was too embarrassed to step inside and join the likes of Yoko Ono and Johnny Winter. Hendrix—who was extremely generous of his time with fans—stopped and chatted with her even though he was leaving to catch a flight. He sat down on the steps and shared thoughts on his own shyness. He also talked of his plans for Electric Lady Studios, plans for musicians to come together and play and, as Patti writes in her book *Just Kids*, make "the language of peace, you dig?" Those plans never would come to fruition because the flight he was catching took him to the Isle of Wight Festival, a short European tour, and his death in London.

And so when she returned to Electric Lady Studios on June 5, 1974, to record her debut single—the first CBGBs act to record—Smith felt an obligation to Hendrix to commit to tape a recording that would fulfill the hopes he expressed for the studio. She felt "a real sense of duty. I was very conscious of getting to do something that he didn't." The song she had chosen for her A-side was a cover she had already performed in her cabaret act: "Hey Joe." Stepping up to the Studio B mic, she whispered, "Hi Jimi," acknowledging his presence.

Assisted by guitarists Lenny Kaye and Television's Tom Verlaine and pianist extraordinaire Richard (DNV) Sohl, Smith subverted and feminized the song that had first made Hendrix famous by making it about Patty Hearst, then a captive of the Symbionese Liberation Army. An infamous bank surveillance photo of Hearst toting a machine gun during a robbery was celebrated in Smith's retelling of "Hey Joe," and so it wasn't a man now "with that gun in your hands" but a woman.

(It would be "Piss Factory," the "B-side" of the double A-side single, that became the more infamous song from Smith's debut single, 5:05 full of lyrics about fame and desire and based on her job at a toy factory, Sohl's throbbing piano fueling the single's 5/4 rhythm and success. The song is about leaving South Jersey and making it in New York City. And then she closes with "Watch me now!" Who else ends a song this way? David Bowie in his Ziggy Stardust persona on "Star.")

The 1,500 copies of the only single pressed by Mer Records sold out and quickly became a coveted collector's item. It was a DIY affair produced by Lenny Kaye, paid for by Robert Mapplethorpe, and publicized by Jane Friedman chiefly to further Smith's trajectory.

Although she would achieve greater chart satisfaction, it has been rightly said that 1975 was probably the height of her initial success. Her performances were the talk of Manhattan. She headlined CBGBs for seven straight weeks. Artists as diverse and acclaimed as Andy Warhol and William Burroughs attended. Bob Dylan came to check out the androgynous singer (with the Modigliani neck) being compared to him. Lou Reed brought

3 Chord Rock Merged With
The Power Of The Word

"Patti Smith's first album 'Horses' is an extraordinary disk and every minute of it is worth repeated rehearings. Devotees of Miss Smith will want to know how honestly and accurately this record captures the feeling of her club performances and the answer is—marvelously! The songs are infused with discreet, subtle touches that enhance them, and the vocal over-dubbing is handled brilliantly. 'Horses' may be an eccentricity, but in a way that anything new is eccentric. If you are responsive to its mystical energy, it will shake you and move you as little else can do!"
—John Rockwell/THE NEW YORK TIMES

"The first album from Patti Smith justifies all the incredible things that have already been said about her!" —Noe Goldwasser/CRAWDADDY

ARISTA

Patti Smith's iconic album *Horses* was recorded at Electric Lady Studios.
Courtesy of Robert Rodriguez

around Clive Davis, the former honcho at Columbia Records. Davis was looking for a new star to generate interest in Arista Records, the new label he was starting. He signed Patti Smith for $750,000.

Smith and her band—now fleshed out with Ivan Kral on guitar and Jay Dee Daugherty on drums—reconvened in Electric Lady Studios in late August 1975 in Studio A. The sessions for what would become known as "a Sgt. Pepper for the pre-punk generation" did not go smoothly. For five weeks Smith repeatedly butted heads with John Cale of Velvet Underground heritage. (Cale had also produced the Stooges' debut album.) His challenge was channeling her spirited live performance onto tape.

Smith is that rare poet whose hero worship became fodder for important poetry and lyrics. "I've always been in love with heroes," she admitted to biographer Victor Bockris. "That's what seduced me into art." The lyrics of *Horses* are largely concerned with heroes. Even the words "horses" and "heroes" are strikingly similar.

Since Smith is on the record as saying "my motivation for doing *Horses* was part to thank and remember people like Jimi Hendrix" and that she was aware of his ghostly presence, let's consider all the Hendrixian connections to *Horses*. The most obvious is the studio: it being Jimi's Promised Land. Beyond that, the lead song, "Gloria"—reimagined as a lesbian conquest— was a song the Jimi Hendrix Experience had taken a stab at. Hendrix too had taken an untraditional approach and penned his own lyrics for it, although penned might be a stretch. Ad-libbed is probably closer to the truth. His version first saw the light of day as a bonus 7″ single included with *The Essential Jimi Hendrix Vol. 2* issued in 1979, so truthfully Smith might not have been aware of this connection, although it's hard to believe that Lenny Kaye, with his extensive rock knowledge, did not know of its existence. It's not an unbelievable stretch of the imagination to believe Hendrix's "Gloria" was already available in Greenwich Village on a bootleg.

"Birdland" is about William Reich, the controversial psychoanalyst whose work on the orgasm was burned by the Food and Drug Administration after his trial and imprisonment. Smith's version was based on a dream of Reich's son Peter of his father in a UFO, and the song ends with the arrival of a UFO as so many of Hendrix's songs do.

But it is on "Land" and "Elegie," the album's closing tracks, that Hendrix takes center stage.

"Land" can be traced back to live performances at Max's Kansas City during a ten-night stand in August-September 1974. In a year's time it had morphed into a song as much about a boy named Johnny—a rock 'n' roll archetype as old as Chuck Berry's riffs—as it was about Jimi Hendrix, whom Smith claimed inspired it. Built onto "Land of 1,000 Dances" (a song the Experience had rehearsed in its earliest days), it is a long song with three parts: 9:25 and 1,070 words. After the first take it was "decided that the instrumental track was just what they wanted." It was Patti's improvisational poetry that had come up short. She took another stab. Felt closer. Took a third take. Cale encouraged her to mix the three, to let the words bob and sink and leap in "the sea of possibilities" that had surfaced during the second take. "On that last take it was obvious that I was being told what I wanted to know about Hendrix's death," Smith has said. And so when the waves of words subside and Smith says "In the sheets . . . there was a man . . . everything unraveling like some long Fender whine," there's no mistaking that it is a vision of Hendrix dying in his London hotel room a little more than three weeks after she had met him.

"Elegie" recaptures his final moments. It was recorded on the fifth anniversary of Hendrix's death, and the final four lines mournfully compile couplets from two of Hendrix's own songs: "1983 . . . (A Merman I Should Turn to Be)" and "Are You Experienced." (In *Patti Smith Complete*, the lyrics are facing a smiling portrait of Hendrix.) It is a quiet song, the quietest of *Horses*. "Patti in her piano bar–Chris Connors persona" is perfectly perched atop Sohl's piano keys and moaning guitar courtesy of Blue Öyster Cult's Alan Lanier, then Smith's boyfriend, to commemorate her hero's passing . . . and the passing of the torch.

Patti Smith would not record at Electric Lady Studios again until sessions for *Gone Again* twenty years later. Speaking for her group in 1976 she said, "We love the studio, man, but it kept breaking down." It is not known if she was speaking of the studio equipment or the traumatic recording sessions with Cale. What is known is that Hendrix has continued appearing in Smith's songs. During the title track of *Radio Ethiopia*—a twelve-minute Led Zeppelin–like romp—Smith sings that "With a little soul anything is possible," echoing the same line from the Band of Gypsys–era song "The Power of Soul."

According to her, "legend has it" that "Jimi Hendrix had played" her 1957 black and white Fender Duo-Sonic. This guitar is familiar to Patti Smith fans. Whenever she straps it on, the energy in the concert hall lifts because her fans know they're about to hear one of her noisier rockers, usually "25th Floor" or the liberating "Rock N Roll Nigger" another song that mentions her fallen hero ("Jimi Hendrix was a nigger!") and regularly closes her sets decades after its release on *Easter*, her third album.

In 2005, Patti Smith was asked to curate the Meltdown Festival in London, a weeklong celebration of song held annually in June that had previously been curated by the likes of Elvis Costello, Nick Cave, and Morrissey. As curator, Smith was allowed to invite performers she admired to stage shows as well as participate in theme-related concerts. In addition to shows honoring Kurt Weill and Robert Mapplethorpe, on June 26, 2005, she presented *Songs of Experience*, a celebration of the music of Jimi Hendrix. Performances that night featured a wide range of musicians: rising (Joanna Newsom) as well as established (Jeff Beck and James "Blood" Ulmer). The evening climaxed with a Patti Smith–led riveting rendition of

"1983 . . . (A Merman I Should Turn to Be)"; and Smith's rap-like delivery of the lyrics was wholly original.

Opening the tribute that night, she had performed "Are You Experienced." She would later record it for *Twelve*, her album of covers, complete with sampling from Hendrix's own "Moon, Turn the Tides . . . Gently, Gently Away" and incorporating "1983 . . . (A Merman I Should Turn to Be)" as if referencing their inclusion in "Elegie." Unfortunately, it's a mediocre version, disappointing to anyone who's seen her perform the Hendrix composition in concert. In the studio, it is just short of the five-minute mark, whereas in concert, it's never shorter than eight. (And has devolved or exploded with snatches of other songs of Hendrix's such as "Who Knows" or "Machine Gun.") It's a shame she chose not to record it with the expanded lineup that recorded the live version of *Horses*, also during the Meltdown Festival festivities. This lineup featured Tom Verlaine and the Red Hot Chili Peppers' Flea. This same lineup regrouped for two more performances of *Horses* at the Brooklyn Academy of Music on November 30, 2005, and December 1, 2005. If you want to hear a really exemplary version of Patti Smith and Her Band playing "Are You Experienced," it's worth your while finding a bootleg recording of one of those performances.

Neil Young

As he had done for the Everly Brothers (1986) and Woody Guthrie (1988), and would do for Paul McCartney (1999) and the Pretenders (2005), Neil Young gave the induction speech for the Jimi Hendrix Experience into the Rock and Roll Hall of Fame, on January 15, 1992. Admitting he hadn't written anything down, Young then went on to say: "You know, when you play guitar, you can play, or you can transcend, and you can go as far—there's no boundaries, how far you can go in your own body and how far your mind can expand when you're playing it. Jimi showed me that; I learned that from Jimi. And he was at one with his instrument."

Young also gave the other members of the Experience their due: "But you can't make it there by yourself, so lucky for me, I had Crazy Horse, and lucky for Jimi, he had the Jimi Hendrix Experience. Because without Noel and without Mitch, it's hard to say what would have happened, even though Jimi is a legend, and a ground-breaker, and everything everyone says and more, it's hard to say whether he could have done that without these other two guys." So it must have been a thrill for Young later that same evening when—in addition to playing "Purple Haze" with Rolling Stone Keith

Richards—he also got to lead the surviving members of the Experience through Bob Dylan's "All Along the Watchtower."

(One wonders how Redding felt about this as he is the only person on the planet to state a preference for Bob Dylan's original version. Even Bob Dylan is on the record as saying that "Hendrix's is the definitive version.")

By 1992, Neil Young had played as prominent a role as any contemporary in keeping rock fans aware of Hendrix through his own music and performances. But to anyone who knew Young from his hippie days, to Stephen Stills say, it must have seemed a like a long, strange trip seeing him playing with Hendrix's band, because, although Young had met Hendrix a few times and even jammed with him once at his fellow Buffalo Springfield-er's house in California, Young had initially been wary of Hendrix's effect on Stills and other guitarists. He had been heard to complain, "What did we have to be like Hendrix for?"

This could simply have been due to a sense of rivalry. Though long they may have run today, back in 1967 when Stills was something of a Hendrix devotee (Hendrix is even rumored to have laid down a lead guitar track on the acoustic demo version of Stills's "Love the One You're With" that Stills erased while laying down overdubs), Young just might have been jealous of how much time the two were spending together, a jealousy that was long gone by the time he recounted how he flew into the wrong airport with Hendrix on their way to the Woodstock Music and Art Fair in August 1969.

As interviewed on Mary Turner's *On the Record* ten years after, Young said that what he remembered most about the generation-defining concert was that "The roads were jammed and there was nobody at the airport, so we had no way to get to the concert. So we're standing at the airport with [attorney] Melvin Belli trying to figure out what to do. And Melvin Belli steals this pickup truck parked at the airport. So it's the three of us in this stolen pickup truck trying to get to the Woodstock concert to play—Jimi, Melvin and me." (Almost sounds like the basis for Young's line from "Pocahontas" on *Rust Never Sleeps*: "Marlon Brando, Pocahontas and me.")

Young had come around by then. He even wore a Jimi Hendrix badge on his peace sign guitar strap throughout the *Rust Never Sleeps* tour in 1978. Not only can it be seen throughout the Neil Young–directed film of the same name, it is also featured prominently in a close-up shot on *Live Rust's* back cover art. I was not yet a big fan of Young's solo work when I saw the live album on a King Karol shelf, but the round, green image of Hendrix's face was the reason I bought *Live Rust*.

In the '70s, my friends and I often argued over joints and White Castle hamburgers over who was the best guitarist. By then nobody was calling Clapton "God." It was Jerry Garcia who had his advocates, while others in the bar bands that played interminable versions of "Southern Man" always argued that Young was the man. Seeing Hendrix's face on the back cover assured me there'd be some good electric guitaring inside. Side Four with "Like a Hurricane," "Hey Hey My My (Into the Black)," and "Tonight's the Night," is one of the best live sides ever.

A later and greater reference from Neil Young to the departed guitarist is found in "From Hank to Hendrix," *Harvest Moon*'s second track. Rockers had already rebonded with Young over *Freedom* (1989) and *Ragged Glory* (1990) after a pretty dreadful decade, but it was the platinum-selling *Harvest Moon*—his long-desired follow-up to 1973's *Harvest*—that righted Young's career with those who prefer his mellow, acoustic, Nashville side. Acknowledging it was the follow-up, he even lined up any member of the Stray Gators he could get. After all, they had participated in the original sessions for *Harvest*.

Recorded and mixed at Redwood Digital in Woodside, California, "From Hank to Hendrix" is a plaintive song full of hurt harmonica. Using pop references such as Hank Marvin (of the Shadows and not Hank Williams as many have mistaken), Jimi Hendrix, Marilyn Monroe, and Madonna to mark the passage of time, Young sings of a relationship "headed for the big divorce California style," one of the song's "sublime turns of phrase" according to Young's unauthorized biographer Jimmy McDonough. And yet the narrator is stubbornly hopeful, asking, "Can we still get it together?" Young said that a central theme of *Harvest Moon* was "How can you keep an old relationship new? How do you make love last? How can you bring the past with you?" He uses Hendrix and the others to recall that past.

A similar version can also be found on the CD (released June 15, 1993) and DVD of Young's appearance on MTV's *Unplugged*, possibly the last hurrah for musicians from the Golden Age of Rock 'n' Roll. (Eric Clapton, Bob Dylan, Paul McCartney, and Rod Stewart all made memorable appearances, and in many cases it was the last collection that topped the charts.) Acknowledging how the song struck a chord with his fans, Young closes his *Unplugged* performance with "From Hank to Hendrix."

Chuck D.

Rockers and rappers have been sampling Hendrix tracks for a long time. Some examples of rockers sampling Hendrix include the Cure, Jesus Jones, Pearl Jam, and the Queens of the Stone Age. The more notable rappers who have sampled Hendrix are the Beastie Boys, DJ Shadow, NWA, and A Tribe Called Quest.

You can add to that list Public Enemy. When lead rapper Chuck D. declaims "Most of my heroes don't appear on no stamps!" during "Fight the Power"—the lynchpin to Spike Lee's best movie, *Do The Right Thing*—one of those heroes is Jimi Hendrix. He has sampled "Foxy Lady" on his solo song "Dr. No," and Public Enemy has sampled Hendrix on one track.

(It is sometimes thought that "Aintnuttin Buttersong" from *Muse Sick-N-Hour Mess Age* uses Hendrix's Woodstock version of "Star Spangled Banner" as a sample to decimate the national anthem and attack American pride for its hypocritical values, but that is not the case. Hearing the track, it obviously is an imitator.)

But the Public Enemy track that does use a Hendrix sample for its chassis does not appear when you search the Internet for "use of Hendrix samples." The track is "Long and Whining Road" from 2007's *How Do You Sell Soul to a Soulless People Who Sold Their Soul?*, and it samples the opening guitar flourish from "Hey Baby (New Rising Sun)." The reason this does not appear when looking for Hendrix samples is because on the Public Enemy liner notes the usage is uncredited, perhaps because they never secured the rights. Burned when AC/DC would not let them sample "Back in Black" for the same album, forcing them to rerecord new backing tracks that sounded like "Back in Black," Public Enemy may never have asked Hendrix's estate for permission.

But Hendrix's "Hey Baby (New Rising Sun)" is one of my favorite posthumous releases, so I know it when I hear it. First released on the out-of-print *Rainbow Bridge* and available on *First Rays of the New Rising Sun*, it was recorded on July 1, 1970, at Electric Lady Studios. While the song had surfaced at recent live performances such as the shows filmed and recorded at the Berkeley Community Theatre in May of that year, a studio version had yet to be attempted. When the recording of "Dolly Dagger" was proving to be as difficult as Hendrix's girlfriend Devon Wilson, who inspired the composition, Hendrix switched gears and started working on "Hey Baby (New Rising Sun)." It is the second take—with Hendrix asking Eddie Kramer, his producer, "Is the microphone on?" after the first lead guitar break—that fans are familiar with.

Prior to this Hendrix begins by playing unaccompanied. Billy Cox on bass shadows the guitar run on the second go-round. Mitch Mitchell rushes in on the third pass, and the trio plays in unison until the 1:05 mark. The rhythm section pauses, and Hendrix plays unaccompanied again for five seconds and slackens the tempo for the first guitar solo and verse. It is over this five seconds of solo guitar—looped and fleshed out with other instrumentation from Public Enemy's backing band—that Chuck D. gives a quick history of pop music by the usage of puns (the title "Long and

Whining Road" an obvious play on the Beatles' "The Long and Winding Road") and naming the likes of Johnny Cash and alluding to others such as Bob Dylan by referencing song titles associated with them—although by saying "All along the watchtower," Chuck D. could be said to be adding Hendrix to the mix. He then recounts the bumpy history of Public Enemy from the Def Jam years onward.

But it is not only through the use of samples that Hendrix has influenced Public Enemy. As stated in the October 2000 issue of *Vibe* magazine, directed at a black audience: "Public Enemy embraced Hendrix's aesthetic of sonic collision, their crosscutting slabs of corrosive sound echoing Hendrix's use of colliding guitar parts and darting production heard in the more gorgeous moments of *Axis: Bold as Love* and *Electric Ladyland*."

Lastly, the overlooked political content of Hendrix's lyrics has informed the work of Chuck D. Hendrix's lyrics were constant evolving. While they always retained an undercurrent of naturalism, Hendrix's words were rooted in the traditional symbols found in the blues and rhythm and blues numbers he loved. From there they morphed into psychedelia . . . flew off with science fiction and fantasy . . . delved back into rhythm and blues . . . before finding realism. As if to be heard by the black community that had largely turned their backs on his music, Hendrix in his final years wrote of war and riots and the damage drugs was doing to their community.

Chuck D. picked up on this strain of Hendrixian lyrics and carried it forth as he criticized the white American government holding blacks down (hence the album titles *It Takes a Nation of Millions to Hold Us Back*) and white paranoia (*Fear of a Black Planet*). Ironically, it is whites that embraced Public Enemy, and the black community has been as cool to Public Enemy as they were to Hendrix. This may be because Public Enemy often samples white acts such as the Who, but more likely, it is the group's stinging criticism of blacks and other rap bands that caused this. Chuck D. calls them as he sees them and has decried the drug abuse of the 1980s that destroyed black families, called out black men on their mistreatment of women and abandonment of children, and targeted other hip-hop and rap acts for only being in it for the money and being derelict in their obligation to educate their fans.

31

I Used to Live in a Room Full of Mirrors

The Posthumous Years

Stateless author Roberto Bolaño strikes me as the literary world's equivalent of Hendrix. The body of work published before his death due to liver failure in Blanes, Catalunya, Spain, at fifty-four on July 15, 2003, has been burnished internationally by the novels, short stories, poems, newspaper columns, even interviews that have been translated and published posthumously. Two novels published after his death—*2666* and *The Third Reich*—are as good as, if not superior to, the work published during Bolano's lifetime. He is simply the Jimi Hendrix of the literary world.

Why? Because not only has an incredible bounty of Hendrix's music been only released and heard posthumously, but the quality of the previously unreleased music has polished his reputation. If anything, his songwriting abilities are more appreciated. He is no longer known for his guitar mastery and showmanship alone. Dozens of the posthumously released songs—not just outtakes but new songs—are equal to the work of the Jimi Hendrix Experience. And the Band of Gypsys material reveals a missed opportunity.

Some critics theorize that Hendrix's enduring fame and sales stem solely from *Are You Experienced*, *Axis: Bold as Love*, and *Electric Ladyland*. I beg to differ. They form a formidable bedrock, but interest in Hendrix—as in Bolano—continued to grow because there was a treasure trove of unheard music to keep old fans listening while new generations of fans grew up. With each new release fulfilling great expectations, admiration of and affection for and allegiance to Hendrix has continued to grow.

For this, proper due must be given to the guardians who have steered Hendrix's work through three stages since his death . . . even those whose decisions we sometimes did—and still do—have issues with.

The Funeral

Road manager Gerry Stickells identified Jimi Hendrix's body at St. Mary Abbotts Hospital, and after the autopsy he made the arrangements and accompanied the body—dressed in a lumberjack's shirt and blue jeans by the undertakers—back to Seattle, Washington, for burial.

The funeral was not the jam session Jimi Hendrix had said he wanted. Nor was it the all-star wake in Madison Square Garden wanted by Buddy Miles. Instead, it was a modest affair (if you consider a funeral service attended by Miles Davis to be modest). The service held at Dunlap Baptist Church in Renton, Seattle, on October 1, 1970, was attended not only by friends and family and fellow musicians. It was attended by three men and a woman who would have considerable sway over the music released under Jimi Hendrix's name over the next four decades: Michael Jeffery, Eddie Kramer, Alan Douglas, and Janie Hendrix, then just the nine-year-old step sister of the deceased.

These would be the key players in the three regimes that have managed Hendrix's music since September 18, 1970, and each tackled the thorny question of exactly what his fifth album would have sounded like.

Using the same pool of approximately forty songs, they released collections as varied as the names Hendrix gave to the unreleased albums; titles as varied as the favored *First Rays of the New Rising Sun*; *People, Hell and Angels*; *Strate Ahead*; and *Between Here and Horizon*. Truman Capote's novel *Answered Prayers* may be the only posthumously released work that was as fervently awaited by the public as that of Jimi Hendrix's fifth album. That may be because Hendrix, like Capote, kept referring to his future work in interviews.

As early as in a 1969 BBC interview, he "announced" to Tony Norman that there would be "two forthcoming albums—the first called *Little Band of Gypsies* and the second *First Rays of the New Rising Sun*." Probably unexpected by Hendrix, his next album did have "Band of Gypsies" in the title, and posthumously his next work took the title of *First Rays of the New Rising Sun*. It was to be an ambitious work. Hendrix was quoted as saying to Norman that "the Americans are looking for a leader in their music. *First Rays of the New Rising Sun* will be about what we have seen. If you give deeper thoughts in your music, then the masses will buy them."

The Cry of Love and *Rainbow Bridge*

Reviewing *The Cry of Love* for *Rolling Stone* in April 1971, Lenny Kaye had no idea how far off he would be when he concluded Hendrix's first posthumous release "has become that much more precious, something to savor slowly because there'll be no others."

Apparently the boxes and boxes containing hundreds of Hendrix's takes and retakes were not yet street knowledge because between March 1971 and February 1974, four studio albums, two live albums, and one double album soundtrack were released by legitimate labels in America and/or Europe. All were issued with Michael Jeffery's approval. Warner Brothers refused to release the final studio album, *Loose Ends*, in America, claiming it was subpar, but it is more worthy than the third studio album, *War Heroes*. But generally they were worthy recordings and should not have been discontinued in America by Warner Brothers for reasons detailed in Chapter 32. *Rainbow Bridge* and *Hendrix in the West* are the finest, the latter so good that even Experience Hendrix rereleased it in expanded form in 2011 with uneven results.

Michael Jeffery never approved of Jimi Hendrix's next release being a double album, let alone the triple album the chief Experience Maker spoke of in interviews, and now in control of the bulk of Hendrix's unreleased recordings, he was determined to make the single album he thought would not only maximize Hendrix's commercial potential but honor the contract he had signed in order to get money from Warner Brothers to finish construction of Electric Lady Studios and bankroll the movie he made with Chuck Wein. This is why, whereas Alan Douglas (*Voodoo Soup*) and Janie Hendrix (*First Rays of the New Rising Sun*) tried to honor Hendrix's wishes by releasing the unreleased music in a way that Hendrix would have approved of, Michael Jeffery chose to split the best material between two single albums (*The Cry of Love* and *Rainbow Bridge*).

Interestingly, none of the three regimes have used the track selection that Jimi Hendrix himself wrote out. First published in November 1994, only three sides were sketched out:

- Side One: "Dolly Dagger," "Night Bird Flying," "Room Full of Mirrors," "Belly Button Window," "Freedom"
- Side Two: "Ezy Ryder," "Astro Man," "Drifting," "Straight Ahead"
- Side Three: "Drifter's Escape," "Come Down Hard on Me," "Beginnings," "Cherokee Mist," "Angel"

It's hard to imagine the fourth side remaining blank, especially considering the only album known to have a blank side—Rahsaan Roland Kirk's *The Case of the 3 Sided Dream in Audio Color*—was not released until May 1975, and probably would have included "Izabella," "Hey Baby (New Rising Sun)," and "Just Came In (aka "In from the Storm") because the first two reference a rising sun and the last two were staples of Hendrix's final concerts.

Another list of Hendrix's dating from sessions at Electric Lady Studios indicates that "Songs for the LP Strate Ahead" would include "Ezy Ryder," "Room Full of Mirrors," "Earth Blues Today," "Valleys of Neptune," "Cherokee Mist," "Freedom," "Stepping Stone," "Izabella," "Astro Man," "Drifter's Escape," "Angel," "Bleeding Heart," "Burning Desire," "Night Bird Flying," "Electric Lady—Slow," "Getting My Heart Back Together Again," "Lover Man," "Midnight Lightning," "Heaven Has No Sorrow—Slow," "Sending My Love—Slow to Medium," "This Little Boy," "Dolly Dagger," and "The New Rising Sun." Interestingly, it doesn't include "Straight Ahead."

So you can see the difficulty Jimi Hendrix was encountering while sorting through the boxes of tapes amassed over the previous two years. This recalls the situation involving his most underrated song from the post-Chandler era: "Room Full of Mirrors." One of the few songs to be played in the studio by the Experience, Band of Gypsys, and Cry of Love lineups, surprisingly it was never named by Hendrix as the title of his next album. Surprising because it is the obvious title, the one Chas Chandler might have suggested he use if Hendrix had ever returned from New York City with all these sonic reflections of himself.

Because having written "Room Full of Mirrors" in 1968 and recorded and rerecorded it, it's hard not to imagine Hendrix searching through his tape recordings of jams and incomplete sessions and not feeling like he was surrounded by confusing sound images of who he had been. There's even a twenty-two-minute home recording known as the "Room Full of Mirrors Poetry Recital" that dates from early to mid-1968, sort of a "Revolution 9" collage with Hendrix speaking about a room full of mirrors over three songs from Eric Burdon and the New Animals' *The Twain Shall Meet*. At one point he says, "the mirrors are beating the hell out of my mind," and I'm sure at times the recording studio full of unfinished tapes must have felt as if they were beating the hell out of his mind.

Charting at #3 in America, *The Cry of Love* enjoyed the greatest success of Hendrix's initial posthumous releases both from the public and the critics—Robert Christgau even rated it an A in his capsule review for the *Village Voice*—but it is a rather aimless collection despite the good intentions of those who compiled it. The problem isn't with the songs: it lies in the presentation, which had never been an issue previously with Jimi Hendrix's albums. For example, "Freedom" is an appropriate opener, but the mood is immediately thwarted with "Drifting." There's nothing wrong with "Drifting," but the third track "Ezy Ryder" would have been a better choice for the second song as it would have sustained the mood established by "Freedom's" drive. Instead, the mood seesaws throughout both sides, and *The Cry of Love* never feels like an album.

It is ironic, then, that *Rainbow Bridge*, the "soundtrack" album to a movie Jimi Hendrix wanted out of, was more satisfying. Christgau only gave this one an A-, but he was on the mark when he wrote that "*The Cry of Love* seems like the verbal/vocal half of the double-LP Hendrix was planning when [he] died." He's right. It was. Years later, you don't listen to "Drifting" or "Angel" or "Belly Button Window" for the guitar playing. If *The Cry of Love* was still commercially available, you'd play it for the vocals.

Rainbow Bridge was, then—to finish Christgau's thought—the guitar half of the double LP Hendrix was planning. Hendrix's own track selection given above belies this intent, but with two instrumentals and a live blues number clocking in at 12:05, this collection does feature his guitar playing.

A perfect example is in the songs that end Side One of each release. Both songs are Experience-era recordings that Jimi Hendrix never ever would have included on his fifth album. "My Friend" and "Star Spangled Banner" are so strong that no one takes issue with producers Eddie Kramer and Mitch Mitchell using them, and each fits the particular mood of the albums they appear on.

"My Friend" is Hendrix at his most Dylanesque and so fits perfectly on *The Cry of Love*. Recorded at Sound Center Studios in New York City on March 13, 1968, it does not include any other members of the Experience as Hendrix was going for a different feel and rounded up Fugs guitarist Ken Pine, who played a 12-string guitar, Village friend Paul Caruso on harmonica, drummer Jimmy Mayes, and Stephen Stills, who contributed the opening piano bit. It was recorded in three takes (one incomplete), and Jimi added a lead vocal and mixed it the following day. It was then forgotten; maybe because it is *too* Dylanesque. But it fits the wordy atmosphere of *The Cry of Love*. It's even wordier than "Straight Ahead," which opens Side Two.

The studio version of "Star Spangled Banner" is the other extreme. Recorded almost one year later on March 18, 1969, at the Record Plant in New York City, it is an instrumental, and the only musician on the recording is Hendrix. "Star Spangled Banner" also took three takes and is a far battle cry from the infamous Woodstock version. This is a pristine, stately version featuring guitar overdubs, perfect for inclusion on the guitar-dominated *Rainbow Bridge*.

It's surprising that "Dolly Dagger" was left off of *The Cry of Love* because it was one of the few songs finished prior to Hendrix's death, and he had spoken of the track as being the A-side of his next single in interviews. The song is similar in structure and narrative to the autobiographical "Highway Chile" even down to the guitar solo. This was probably intentional on

Hendrix's part, considering the song is about Devon Wilson, his feminine alter ego.

It has been rightly said that Hendrix's latter rockers such as "Dolly Dagger" better show off their blackness. This is possibly due to the success of Sly and the Family Stone, one of the bands he championed along with Chicago (inviting them to open concerts for him) and Pink Floyd during 1970. Sly's commercial success perhaps emboldened Hendrix, and he displayed a little more prominently in the mix genres normally associated with the chitlin' circuit. "Earth Blues" features the singing of the Ronettes and follows "Dolly Dagger" beautifully, sustaining the rhythm and blues mood.

"Pali Gap" is the first instrumental on *Rainbow Bridge*. As lovely as the music is, it was the result of a jam instigated by Billy Cox playing the Spencer Davis Group's "Gimme Some Loving" bassline at the end of Take 6 of nineteen takes of "Dolly Dagger" committed to tape on July 1, 1970. (The version of "Hey Baby (New Rising Sun)" that closes the "soundtrack" so well was also recorded on July 1, 1970, at Electric Lady, one of Hendrix's most fruitful recording sessions in years.) Also known as "Slow Part," when the "Gimme Some Loving" jam ended, Hendrix improvised over Cox's riff and then sensing the improvisation's potential added another guitar line. It was then shelved and rediscovered when Eddie Kramer was searching through the reels of tapes. It was Michael Jeffery who named the piece after the Pali Gap on the island of Oahu, Hawaii, so it sounded like Jimi wrote the instrumental specifically for the soundtrack owed to Warner Brothers.

Tastefully edited by Eddie Kramer, "Pali Gap" ends and "Room Full of Mirrors" comes crashing in. Of the songs ultimately chosen for the various versions of Hendrix's fifth album, only "Angel," "Look over Yonder," and "My Friend" are older compositions, and none were subjected to the rigorous rearrangement that "Room Full of Mirrors" was.

The best Jimi Hendrix box set, 2000's *The Jimi Hendrix Experience*, contains the earliest known version albeit a short demo. Only 1:25 in length, "Room Full of Mirrors" as of August 12, 1968, has a standard 12-bar blues structure and features Paul Caruso on harmonica. It's our loss that a longer version of the song at this tempo does not exist. By the next time it's heard in February 1969 at rehearsal sessions for the Royal Albert Hall concerts and in the hall itself, it has a Bo Diddley shuffle to go with the reworked lyrics.

A long, long, long session on the evening of April 21, 1969, yielded thirty-one frustrating takes as Cherry People drummer Rocky Isaac was unable to master the rhythm Hendrix wanted. It was also Billy Cox's first studio session with Hendrix since his old paratrooper buddy had become King Guitar. Take 31 can be found on the aforementioned box set from 2000. At 7:55, it's the longest known version, too.

In between the dissolution of Gypsy Sun and Rainbows and the formation of the Band of Gypsys, Hendrix made another attempt at recording
"Room Full of Mirrors." This Record Plant recording from September 25,
1969, can be found on *Morning Symphony Ideas*, although percussionist Juma
Sultan's contributions cannot. Accompanied only by Buddy Miles, this version interpolates "Message of Love" and features a catchy guitar lead that's
very Tony Iommi, if you catch my drift.

Billy Cox is back for the November 17th session, and this Band of Gypsys
version yielded the basic track that Hendrix and others have tinkered with
ever since. Tom Erdelyi—later known as Tommy Ramone, drummer and
co-producer of five Ramones' albums—was the second engineer on this
date, assisting Tony Bongiovi, and he has said that for this "Room Full of
Mirrors" session Hendrix focused on getting the slide guitar sound right,
the sound that is a signature of the finished track as the echoing slide
aurally reflects all the images he is seeing of himself in the room. Hendrix
added overdubs and mixed the track at Electric Lady on August 20, 1970,
and this is the version used on *Rainbow Bridge*.

The November 17th session led to a spat between Hendrix and Alan
Douglas's associate Stefan Bright, who, according to Erdelyi, was producing
the session. Bright didn't know that the musician who had sung in front of
tens of thousands of people at a time was uncomfortable singing in front of
studio personnel when laying down his vocal tracks. His request for studio
baffles left his producer incredulous. Of course, he got his way, but the lack
of sensitivity on Bright's part contributed to Hendrix's feelings that he was
not the right producer for him.

And yet the vocal on "Room Full of Mirrors" from this session is Jimi
Hendrix at his best. The ease belies the tension in the studio, the music
perfectly setting the scene. I disagree with Keith Shadwick about the effec-
tiveness of the vocals, but he has it right when he says the November 17th
recording "sounds as if the scene is taking place within the maelstrom, as
slide-guitar parts fly around . . . ." Because that's what happening: Hendrix
is in his room full of mirrors, uses his spirit to smash them, chuckles as
he says "making love was strange in my bed," and then finds sunshine all
around and shining over mountains and the sea. The promising resolution
makes this the ideal closer for what should have been Hendrix's fifth album.
Instead, the aforementioned, graceful studio version of "The Star Spangled
Banner" closes out the side.

The only unreleased Jimi Hendrix Experience song to surface in the
1970s—"Look over Yonder"—gets Side Two off to a good start; its feedback
fumes reminding the listener of "House Burning Down" and an ideal spot
for Hendrix's scatting intro to a live version of "Hear My Train A Comin'"

from the first Berkeley Community Theatre concert filmed by Peter Pilafian on May 30, 1970. This elephantine version is simply the peak performance of the Cry of Love lineup and one of Hendrix's top five blues recordings.

Mitch Mitchell and Eddie Kramer preferred quieter pieces for concluding the two albums they coproduced, and for *Rainbow Bridge* they close with a six-minute studio version of "Hey Baby (New Rising Sun)" that again features Hendrix's guitar playing, albeit tapping his Wes Montgomery vein. Recorded in one take on July 1, 1970, it was never meant to be the version heard by the world. Hendrix can even be heard asking Eddie Kramer, "Is the microphone on?" (While it helps sustain the illusion that it may be another live recording, I've never understood why his query has never been edited out of this or subsequent releases.)

Lyrically, "Hey Baby (New Rising Sun)" has much in common with "Angel": a feminine, unworldly creature comes to Hendrix and takes him to a better place. In "Angel," he is rescued (like in "Long Hot Summer Night"); in "Hey Baby (New Rising Sun)," she is spreading peace of mind and when Hendrix asks to "come along" with her, he does, closing what is arguably the best posthumous recording put out in his name.

As Harry Shapiro says in his outdated yet invaluable discography in *Jimi Hendrix: Electric Gypsy*, it is "unforgivable" that Reprise Records saw fit to discontinue this title, but the resourceful Hendrix aficionado can recreate this release in its entirety from mp3 files gleaned from *First Rays of the New Rising Sun*, *South Saturn Delta*, *The Jimi Hendrix Experience*, and *Blues* released between 1994 and 2000.

Voodoo Soup

The legal maneuverings surrounding Jimi Hendrix's musical legacy are sketched out in Chapter 32, but to suffice it for this chapter, the controversial, two-decades-long musical stewardship of Alan Douglas ended in 1995 with *Voodoo Soup*, his own take on what Hendrix's work-in-progress would have sounded like had he lived.

Hendrix's track listing for the *Strate Ahead* LP ends with "The New Rising Sun," but it's a stroke of genius on Alan Douglas's part to use it to begin the poorly titled *Voodoo Soup*. This severely edited instrumental—less than half the length of the completed second take—was not only Hendrix's first recorded use of the rising sun concept, it also fulfilled his penchant for opening with the most controversial track and getting it over with. Recorded at TTG Studios on October 23, 1968, while recording the Experience's fourth studio album that never was to be, it is a solo performance.

Featuring Hendrix playing through a Leslie speaker, the song has him not only adding a lead guitar overdub and backwards guitar tracks but manning Mitch Mitchell's drum kit and adding drumbeats that were slowed down in the mix a la ". . . And the Gods Made Love." It's possible Hendrix himself considered it a candidate to begin the Experience's fourth album. Douglas edited the track so that it segues into "Belly Button Window," another solo Hendrix performance. On the face of it, the two tracks are incompatible, but the mix works, and when you consider the narrator of "Belly Button Window"—a baby in his mother's womb contemplating a troubled world—it's perfectly placed.

If only Douglas had gone with "Freedom" as the third track and not the fourth. It's not much of a stretch to see the characters in "Freedom" as the troubled parents of "Belly Button Window." Instead, we get a controversial mix of "Stepping Stone." Make no bones about it, Alan Douglas was a producer who took complete artistic license. He freely remixed Hendrix's recordings and used session musicians to perfect tracks that he thought subpar on the part of Hendrix's original accompanists. Not pleased with Mitch Mitchell's drumming, he enlisted the Knack's drummer, Bruce Gary, to lay down a new drumbeat, hence the controversy. It's undeniably tighter. Whether it's better is questionable.

Controversy aside, "Stepping Stone" would have worked better on *Voodoo Soup* as the fourth track following "Freedom" and not the other way around. The song after all at one stage had been called "Trying to Be a Man," and that's what the protagonist in "Freedom" is trying to be, too. "Room Full of Mirrors" would have followed "Freedom" better than "Angel," but overall, Douglas's vision of Hendrix's unfinished album works better than the others. In addition to "The New Rising Sun" there are two instrumentals ("Midnight" and "Peace in Mississippi") and a nice pairing of "Night Bird Flying" with "Drifting." The album closer, "In from the Storm," contains the sense of personal triumph that Hendrix probably would have approved of, only I think he would have inserted "Hey Baby (New Rising Sun)" before it as he did in concert. The vocal cousin of "The New Rising Sun" would have fit perfectly, and it's downright weird that the estate-approved *First Rays of the New Rising Sun*, released two years after *Voodoo Soup*, does not include both versions. A tremendously missed opportunity.

First Rays of the New Rising Sun

Michael Fairchild's liner notes for *Voodoo Soup* give the clearest explanation of what exactly Hendrix's "new rising sun" meant, attributing its influence to science fiction author Arthur C. Clarke's first novel, *The Sands of Mars*, published in 1951. Hendrix's love of science fiction is well known, as is its influence on his songs (e.g., "Purple Haze" and Philip José Farmer's *Night of Light*), so Fairchild's hypothesis has validity. Clarke's novel contains a description of a sky "aglow with the *first light of the rising sun*," which is a Martian moon detonated to create a life-giving sun, and Fairchild believes this is where Hendrix's concept of *The First Rays of the New Rising Sun* originates.

In Fairchild's same liner notes, Mitch Mitchell is quoted as saying "there were various titles that would be floating around, just like various riffs . . . but I think [Jimi] would have used *First Rays of the New Rising Sun* at some point in time."

And that's what Experience Hendrix—the Hendrix family–operated estate that won control over his musical legacy in 1995—named their first release in 1997. The family, led by Janie Hendrix, wisely brought recording engineer Eddie Kramer back into the fold, and he has played a role in the production of all albums released by Experience Hendrix as of this writing. Having helped design Electric Lady Studios and participated in all of Jimi Hendrix's Electric Lady sessions, Kramer's stamp of approval ensures that the music released under Hendrix's name sounds as Hendrix would have wished.

This also means, however, that *First Rays of the New Rising Sun* is nothing more than an expanded version of *The Cry of Love* album. It still begins with "Freedom," ends with "Belly Button Window," and includes all ten tracks found on the 1971 release. The seven "new" songs all appeared on *Rainbow Bridge* or *War Heroes*. The only difference is the sequencing of songs. "My Friend" still precedes "Straight Ahead," and "In from the Storm" still precedes "Belly Button Window," but "Izabella" now follows "Freedom" and "Night Bird Flying" (named for New York City DJ Allison Steele) serves as a better intro to "Angel." It's better than *The Cry of Love* but isn't really a fresh attempt.

32

They May Even Wrap Me in Cellophane and Sell Me

The Best Alan Douglas Productions

One of the two men approached as potential producers by Jimi Hendrix during his last week on earth parlayed the conversation into management of King Guitar's musical legacy over a span of twenty controversial years. It didn't happen immediately, but by 1975 the legal team handling affairs for Al Hendrix had gained control from Michael Jeffery's estate, and Warner Brother tapped Alan Douglas to produce Hendrix's unheard music from Record Plant sessions, the rights to which were transferred to a Panamanian corporation. Douglas had a unique vision for this material, and he would use some unorthodox methods in his productions.

Many Hendrix aficionados consider Alan Douglas's production methods to be unsound. He had the audacity to erase tapes, he created songs from multiple takes, replaced the backing performances of bassists Noel Redding and Billy Cox and drummers Mitch Mitchell and Buddy Miles with bassist Bob Babbitt and drummer Allan Schwartzberg: musicians who had never even met Jimi Hendrix let alone recorded with him. This rhythm section would play along with guitarist Jeff Mironov to tape recordings of Hendrix playing. Douglas even gave himself co-songwriting credit on five of the eight songs on some releases of *Crash Landing*.

(This need not have happened, as a version of *Crash Landing* in largely the same sequence but with the original sidemen was readied for release by Alan Douglas but abandoned. This album is readily available on eBay but missing the "Scat Vocal-Lead 1-Scat Vocal 2-Lead Vocal 2" track.)

Douglas's unsound methods also gave Jimi Hendrix his second posthumous top ten album and first in four years; "Stone Free Again" was an

FM staple in the mid-'70s; *Crash Landing* brought to the public's attention such gems as the title track, "Crash Landing," "Peace in Mississippi," "Trash Man," and "Once I Had a Woman"; rescued the Jimi Hendrix Experience's "lost" BBC recordings from obscurity; released the Monterey performance in its entirety; and ended his stewardship with two worthy releases, *Blues* and *Voodoo Soup*, the former so good that even Experience Hendrix has recognized its merits and rereleased it.

In between he released some terrible collections—the instrumental *Nine to the Universe* and *Band of Gypsys 2* (which inexplicably contained several Experience performances) are particularly putrid. But while I'm not condoning Douglas's methods, even the purist in me recognizes that some of his productions of Jimi's unreleased music were successful. I was teenager when *Crash Landing* and *Midnight Lightning* were released in 1975 and I enjoyed them and they made me want to hear more of Hendrix's music; decades later I still enjoy them. Whether we like it or not, we cannot erase Douglas's role in sustaining Hendrix's celebrity and artistry. Jimi Hendrix's estate is one of the most profitable in the world, and the eleven "original" albums and one box set Douglas had a hand in helped create that empire.

Crash Landing

Alan Douglas's first Hendrix entrée was coproduced with Tony Bongiovi, who had engineered previous Hendrix sessions and would go on to produce Talking Heads (*Talking Heads: 77*), the Ramones (*Leave Home* and *Rocket to Russia*), and Ozzy Osbourne (*Bark at the Moon*). *Crash Landing* was a commercial success, peaking at #5 on the U.S. charts, a mark not to be surpassed by a Jimi Hendrix collection until 2010's *Valleys of Neptune*. The commercial success of *Crash Landing* caused Warner Brothers Recordings president Mo Ostin to declare that his record company was "recalling all previously issued posthumous Hendrix albums from distributors and retail stores." Thus Warner Brother discontinued all the prior posthumous releases with the exception of *The Cry of Love*.

Lyrically, the eight songs on *Crash Landing* mesh very well. The majority are from Hendrix's realistic period as most of the Hendrix rhythm, lead, and vocal tracks that Douglas added to the songs stem from 1969 and 1970. Even "Somewhere over the Rainbow," an Experience-era track, fits in because Hendrix later used the lyrics as the starting point for "Earth Blues." The instrumental "Peace in Mississippi" is so harsh, it sounds realistic.

The four stand-out tracks are "Somewhere over the Rainbow," the title track, "Stone Free Again," and the composite "Captain Coconut." Even if

Alan Douglas' first posthumous release of Jimi Hendrix's music was controversial because studio musicians rerecorded backing tracks.   *Courtesy of Robert Rodriguez*

the lyrics in "Somewhere over the Rainbow" were later modified, they fit the purgatorial moodiness on this version better. Similarly, some of the lyrics for "Crash Landing" were later used for "Freedom" (i.e., the first verse in "Crash Landing" becoming the third verse in "Freedom"), but the Douglas version based on the same April 1969 lineup that had recorded "Room Full of Mirrors" has a completely different feel.

"Stone Free" was rerecorded by the Jimi Hendrix Experience in April 1969 as a possible single but was scrapped when the original B-side appeared on *Smash Hits*. Douglas took this unreleased track, scrubbed it clean of the Experience rhythm section's contributions as well as the harmony vocals of Andy Fairweather and Roger Chapman, added the contributions of session musicians, and compressed Hendrix's lead vocals.

The key sin is the drummer providing typical session type drumming and reducing the drummer's role to that of a time keeper, thereby violating a cardinal rule of Hendrix's musical theory: it is the bassist's function—not the drummer's—to hold down the fort.

But the argument for not erasing "Stone Free Again" from the Hendrix catalog are Hendrix's lead vocals. They are the same as on the later released versions, except Douglas heavily treated them with studio gimmickry; you could almost say he poured cologne over the mixing board because the end result was a sexier vocal, one that trumps other versions. The panning makes it trippier, and Hendrix's asides (e.g., "Listen to this baby") and laughs are much more effective. (This is a feature of his earliest recordings that Hendrix largely avoided on *Axis: Bold as Love* and *Electric Ladyland*). And the sexy treatment enhances the persona, the free spirit of this piece. I suspect that Hendrix wanted to revisit this song because it was very personal to him. You could almost call this his signature recording if his arrangement of Dylan's "All Along the Watchtower" wasn't such an FM staple. The lyrics are half freak flag flyin' high/half hootchie cootchie man.

A primary feature of the reworked arrangement is the intro. Guitar notes ring out with hints of U2, sort of in the manner that Turner's late paintings hint at Monet.

You usually find the instrumental "Captain Coconut" relegated to "how dare they" footnotes because it is not a musical piece conceived by Jimi Hendrix. Rather it is the result of splicing together three excerpts: Hendrix playing a solo flamenco piece at Electric Lady Studios between June and August 1970 (possibly "Bolero"); a January 23, 1969, Band of Gypsys jam; and "The New Rising Sun." The three passages were originally spliced together by Electric Lady engineer John Jansen for possible inclusion on *War Heroes*. Eddie Kramer was aghast that someone would do this, so it was never attempted again. (Captain Coconut was one of the cartoon characters Hendrix referenced in interviews along with Astro Man and Captain Midnite.)

A few years later when Douglas was searching through boxes of tapes, he found Jansen's tape and reworked it by adding Allan Schwartzberg on drums and Jimmy Maeulen on slinky and created the illusion of more than one lead guitar track by Hendrix by adding heavy echo delay. "Captain Coconut" as the closing track was—and still is—one of my favorite recordings on *Crash Landing*.

John Jansen's manipulation of Hendrix recordings from different eras is no different from what Miles Davis and producer Teo Macero had done to create the studio recordings that appear on such masterpieces as *In a*

Silent Way and *Bitches Brew*. They would take parts of various takes and then splice them together to create the finished piece. The caveat is that it was Miles Davis who made the decision to have Macero manipulate his recorded sessions in this fashion. But Hendrix, like Davis, saw the recording studio as a laboratory—this was what differentiated Hendrix from his hero Bob Dylan—and it is unlikely he would have objected as strongly as the purists have. It is common practice nowadays to have DJs and others remix recordings by Radiohead or Mogwai with finished results that in no way resembles the original.

Actually, it's mildly surprising that *Crash Landing* has not been rereleased by Experience Hendrix. Long before he took to calling the mid-'70s Douglas-Bongiovi productions "controversial" in the liner notes of the booklets he's authored for all estate releases since 1997, John McDermott presented the most evenhanded recount of how *Crash Landing* and *Midnight Lightning* came about in *Setting the Record Straight*. (McDermott's booklet notes for estate-approved releases are factual but a little dry, whereas Fairchild's booklet notes for Douglas-approved releases are scholarly and visionary. You won't agree with every idea Fairchild throws out there, but he gets you thinking.) Those "controversial" recordings required a lot of painstaking work and the assemblage of songs from bits of tape. (Just releasing the original recordings with the Experience and Band of Gypsys would have been the easier route for both Douglas and Bongiovi). Experience Hendrix should reissue *Crash Landing* as a double disc and include the unreleased version. They only have to look on page 311 of McDermott's first book on Hendrix for the details.

Radio One/BBC Sessions

With the release of *Radio One* in 1988, the long-awaited fourth Jimi Hendrix Experience finally arrived. The awful cover really makes Hendrix look like rock 'n' roll's Wild Man of Borneo, but thankfully the music within is everything the fan could want. All seventeen tracks were recorded for BBC radio in 1967, including a jingle for Radio 1. This is the Experience at their peak before America rended them asunder. You get alternate versions of Experience hits and album tracks, blues covers, a Hendrix original never officially released ("Driving South"), and the Experience's take on two pop classics: the Beatles' "Day Tripper" and Elvis Presley's "Hound Dog."

Ten years later, Experience Hendrix released an expanded version called *BBC Sessions* with two discs and fourteen more tracks (nineteen if you count host introductions). Whereas *Radio One* only included one version per song, on *BBC Sessions* there are three versions of "Hey Joe" and "Driving South," and two times Hendrix hears his train a comin'. Of special interest is Bob Dylan's "Can You Please Crawl out Your Window," two tracks with seventeen-year-old Stevie Wonder, and the entire Lulu BBC television appearance from January 1969. So essential that I wonder "what were they thinking?" whenever I see a copy in a used CD store.

Blues

On his way out, Douglas released two worthy additions to the Hendrix discography, with the penultimate release *Blues* the best. The conceit is simple: Jimi Hendrix always identified with the blues. When speaking of the Experience's chemistry, he would talk of being into the blues while Mitchell did his jazz thing and Redding was into a rock bag. Although blues numbers were a staple of his live performances, only two were released in his lifetime: "Red House" and "Voodoo Chile." And even Reprise balked at the inclusion of "Red House" on the American version of *Are You Experienced*.

Why not then release an album comprised completely of blues numbers? There are dozens of versions of "Red House" and "Hear My Train A Comin'" to choose from. There are live versions of "Catfish Blues" and an unheard take of "Voodoo Chile," the song it spawned. There are worthy jam sessions no one has heard. Hendrix was a blues master, one of the few to transcend the genre and make the blues palatable to those music lovers who don't get the hubbub about Robert Johnson or Muddy Waters.

The cover of *Blues* resurrects the classic illustration from *Crash Landing*, only now with photos of blues musicians such as Albert King, Albert Collins, and Son House alongside. (The inclusion of Curtis Mayfield is a stretch. Some think Chuck Berry shouldn't be there, but Berry's compositions are based on the blues, so he merits inclusion.) Michael Fairchild provides copious notes, testaments on Hendrix from bluesmen such as B. B. King and Buddy Guy, and Hendrix's own thoughts on how the blues shaped his music. "The background of [the Experience's] music is a spiritual blues thing."

Blues has eleven tracks. Not all are original. The acoustic version of "Hear My Train A Comin'" was on the *Jimi Hendrix* double-album soundtrack, "Red House" is the CBS Studios version heard on the British version of *Are You Experienced*, "Electric Church Red House" had been on *Red House: Variations on a Theme* (a collection of six versions of "Red House" plus a rendition by John Lee Hooker), and the electric version of "Hear My Train A Comin'" was the same one heard on the discontinued *Rainbow Bridge*.

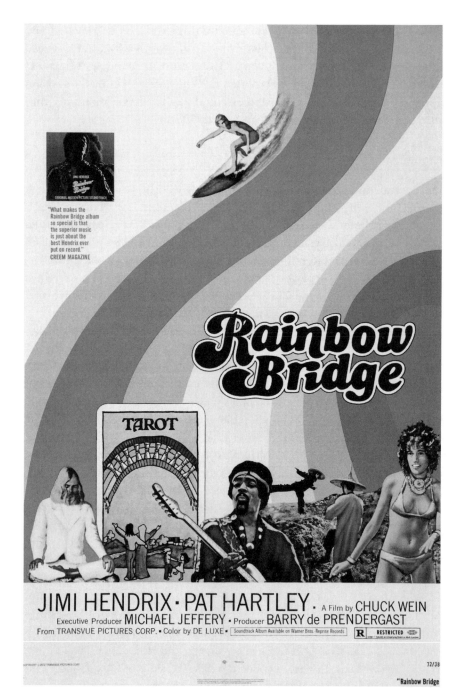

"Hear My Train A Comin'" appears on both the *Blues* and *Rainbow Bridge* posthumous recordings.

Author's collection

But the two versions of "Hear My Train A Comin'" appeared together for the first time and frame the collection well. Among the new tracks were "Born Under a Bad Sign," "Voodoo Chile Blues" (created by Douglas splicing together the first vocal take and second instrumental take), "Mannish Boy" (another composite), "Jelly 292," and "Once I Had a Woman" with the contribution of the Band of Gypsys rhythm section restored.

33

Can'tcha Tell I'm Doing Fine?

The Best Estate Releases

I n his capsule review of Experience Hendrix's expanded rerelease of *Radio One*, rechristened *BBC Sessions* and bearing a much better cover of the Jimi Hendrix Experience at their permed peak, Robert Christgau observed that "the good guys (now) control the catalogue . . . ." And that was—and is to this day—the general consensus. After finally wresting control of their relative's legacy in 1995, the Hendrix family—a small portion anyway—went about providing "a whiff of completism coming off the definitive Hendrix reissue program."

The first order of business now that the production triumvirate of Janie Hendrix, Eddie Kramer, and John McDermott was in place was to reissue on April 22, 1997, remastered releases with their original covers of the Jimi Hendrix Experience albums. These would replace the 1993 editions Alan Douglas had supervised and audaciously approved new album covers for.

(As much as I disagree with replacing the covers, the 1993 MCA release of *Are You Experienced?*—this time with the "?"—has some justification as it was expanded to include the first three British singles—A-sides and B-sides—and then the Experience's first album—with the British track sequencing—in order of release so you can truly hear the band's growth as the British rock public did way back in 1966 and 1967. It is, as the back cover advertises, "a key to the union of ancient and futuristic urges. Each song meets essential requirements for a comprehensive rock education.")

On the same date, Experience Hendrix delivered Jimi's unfinished fourth studio album. Six months later, *South Saturn Delta* was issued. This collection certainly does have a whiff of completism about it. It collects almost all of the material that appeared on the initial Jeffery-approved posthumous releases but didn't make it onto *First Rays of the New Rising Sun;* supplementing those with unreleased recordings such as "Angel" (incorrectly identified as "Little Wing") and the jazzy "South Saturn Delta" and alternate mixes and recordings, including the initial version of "All Along the Watchtower" with Dave Mason on 12-string guitar and Brian Jones on percussion. It's a nice collection of songs that is curiously unsatisfying.

In 1998, Experience Hendrix began a new label, Dagger Records, to release professionally recorded live performances and other hard-to-get recordings to the die-hard fans. The first release on February 27, 1998, was *Live at the Oakland Coliseum*. It is a mono recording that was made by fan Ken Koga. The highlights of the two-disc set are "Foxy Lady" at three times the studio length and the set closer "Voodoo Child (Slight Return)" featuring Jefferson Airplane bassist Jack Casady and thus freeing Noel Redding to play rhythm guitar. Between 1998 and 2009, Dagger Records released eleven titles, most featuring Jimi Hendrix Experience performances.

Experience Hendrix's first truly significant release was *Live at the Fillmore East*, another double-disc offering that arrived in stores on February 23, 1999, and featured unheard tracks from the Band of Gypsys' short stint at the Fillmore East that closed out 1969. The opening track, "Stone Free," clocks in at 12:56 and by time it's over, you've given Hendrix's black band the Bands of Gypsys a major reassessment. You've got to give the "good guys" their due. You can be disappointed that family members such as Hendrix's brother Leon have been cut out of his inheritance, but that's "a family affair" as Sly Stone once sang. (More questionable is their treatment of Hendrix's sidemen.) But as fans, we're only entitled to judge how the estate is managing his legacy and making it available. And on that scale the "good guys" are making sure Hendrix is doing fine. The following are the half dozen Experience Hendrix and Dagger Records releases since 1999 that you should own.

Live at the Fillmore East (1999)

It's a shame we couldn't have had the best of both worlds and have two bands, one white (the Jimi Hendrix Experience) and one black (the BOG (the acronym you'll find for Band of Gypsys in some books), because each have their own merits. Buddy Miles can't do "Fire" justice, but Mitch Mitchell can't do "Machine Gun" either. That high point of *Band of Gypsys* gets two airings here, and each is as good as the original.

Another highlight is the best performance of "Izabella," perhaps the only Hendrix composition addressed to a woman that often lacks passion. You get it here, and the crowd sounds really into the performance. You can understand why Hendrix considered it 45 worthy. "Voodoo Child (Slight Return)" is marred by segueing into Buddy Miles's "We Gotta Live

Together"—I mean, after all, there's a reason Experience concerts ended with *Electric Ladyland*'s closing track: you can't top it. But that's practically the only wrong move made on this collection. Even "Who Knows" is worth checking out.

The Jimi Hendrix Experience (2000)

There are more than a half dozen Jimi Hendrix box sets in the marketplace, but this four-disc, fifty-six-song collection is the best. Not an anthology per se—you'll have to pick up *West Coast Seattle Boy* if you want to hear Hendrix's years of apprenticeship with the likes of the Isley Brothers and Little Richard—*The Jimi Hendrix Experience* presents the "experience" of Hendrix's four short years in the spotlight: from the band's first live recordings in Paris at their fourth show ever through a short track (1:45) called "Slow Blues" recorded at Electric Lady Studios on August 25, 1970, the day before he reluctantly flew to England for his Isle of Wight headlining appearance.

Paris 1967/San Francisco 1968 (2003)

A little over eight months before the Winterland concerts discussed below, the Experience during the first of two American tours in 1968, played San Francisco's Fillmore West. That evening's entire set of six songs is presented on this CD. All are well played, but two are essential recordings. "Catfish Blues" is given its definitive reading, including one of Mitch Mitchell's finest drum solos, and Traffic's "Dear Mr. Fantasy" with Buddy Miles guesting appears as two parts. The songs were not often played by the Experience, and Hendrix takes them to the limit.

Hear My Music (2004)

The majority of Dagger Records releases are live concerts but not 2004's *Hear My Music*. Vastly superior to some of the widely distributed collections (e.g., *South Saturn Delta* and *Valleys of Neptune*), it is a mixed bag of Experience recordings, impromptu studio recordings, jams, and solo performances that really should be more widely distributed.

There's an early yet lengthy run-through of "Ezy Ryder" by the Experience in London as they rehearsed for the Royal Albert Hall shows that incorporates the earliest studio version of "Star Spangled Banner"; a remixed "Jam 292" that demonstrates Billy Cox's strengths; and the Experience's complete performance of "Trash Man" that Alan Douglas stripped Redding and Mitchell's performances from and then halved before adding studio musicians for *Midnight Lightning*.

"Trash Man" is the Experience's best instrumental, and *Hear My Music* is worth having for that track alone. (An alternate version was released in an expanded version of *Valleys of Neptune* sold only in Target stores but now readily available on eBay.)

In the West (2011)

In the West was Jimi Hendrix's first posthumous live release in the United States when Reprise Records issued it in February 1972. Reissued in 2011 in an expanded format, the Experience Hendrix version of *In the West* attempts to rectify the fact that not all of the recordings were really recorded "in the west" and in doing so diminishes its power.

Among the five new songs are four from what is arguably the best Experience concert ever (May 25, 1969, at San Diego Sports Arena), but what's missing from the 1972 release is the Royal Albert Hall performance *in the east* of "Little Wing" in full flight. By this I mean that many believe the studio version had its wings clipped due to a rush to complete the Experience's second album and only in live settings was its potential achieved. The fleshed-out instrumental ending is much more satisfying than the studio version. "Little Wing" was a rarity in concert, and so unfortunately Experience Hendrix had to resort to using a slightly inferior version from Winterland *in the west* on October 12, 1968. What's also lost is the segue with "Red House" from the original album, which was a perfect pairing.

Winterland (2011)

The recordings of the Jimi Hendrix Experience's six-show, three-night stint at Bill Graham's Winterland on October 10–12, 1968, have had a checkered past. Intended as the Experience's elusive fourth album, the project was given a thumbs down by the Experience themselves and remained in the vaults for nearly two decades until Alan Douglas melted the shows down into the CD-only release, *Live at Winterland*, the first such Hendrix release not to be issued on vinyl. (A few tracks from Winterland had already appeared on 1982's *The Jimi Hendrix Concerts*.)

Except for one show five nights earlier in Honolulu, the Experience had been off the road for almost a month and did not rehearse for the shows. This was standard modus operandi for Jimi Hendrix who did not like to rehearse, preferring each show to be unique. Even set lists were drawn up minutes before showtime. He is sometimes faulted for this lack of professionalism, but this lack of preparation made Jimi Hendrix concerts exciting events, and he is not the only performer to eschew rehearsal. Miles Davis also avoided over-rehearsing his band, and on one occasion even hired two sidemen whose first rehearsal with Davis was live in concert.

The comparison to Davis is particularly apt for these recordings as this is the Experience at their jazziest and most expansive. Being in San Francisco, a city known to have embraced the loose jam concept, rarely are any of the forty-eight songs played under the five-minute mark. There were five versions of "Foxy Lady," and none are identical. Hendrix supplemented the Experience with other musicians such as flautist Virgil Gonsalves and organist Herbie Rich of the Buddy Miles Express (one of the opening acts) and bassist Jack Casady of the hometown band Jefferson Airplane, perhaps the best band other than the Dead Kennedys to have come out of San Francisco.

The audience was treated to rare performances of "Are You Experienced," "Little Wing" and "Manic Depression"; drum and bass jams; and several covers such as "Tax Free," "Like a Rolling Stone," Lover Man," "Sunshine of Your Love," "Hear My Train A Comin'," and the national anthem that had not yet been released.

The professionally recorded shows at Winterland are an exciting example of the Experience at their peak as a live act even if Redding thought otherwise. He let his personal frustrations with the Experience color his critique. His emotional response was the opposite of the recording engineers, who instead of hearing daring performances only heard out-of-tune instruments or distorted amplifiers, a common ailment of the Experience's concerts where Hendrix pushed the volume to the max every night on Sunn amplifiers he did not care for but was given to his management team for free. The aforementioned drum and bass solos were actually band-aids to cover the fact the roadies were fixing Hendrix's amps

Experience Hendrix's four-CD box set *Winterland* seems to have been released to compete with a six-CD bootlegged box set from the Michel Jeffery Estate (*3 Nights at Winterland*) that presents each show in its original running order. In fact much of the estate's new releases from 2009 onwards seem to be driven by a need to provide "official," sonically improved versions of performances already available on eBay and so the Hendrix aficionado can be thankful for their illegal existences. But there are trade-offs. The October 10th disc on the Experience Hendrix's box set is the closest-to-a-complete Experience set, but the second show's rendition of "Foxy Lady" is added. Discs Two and Three for October 11th and 12th blatantly merge each night's two shows. What would you rather have: full shows or professionally mixed sound?

At the very least, let the collection open with "Are You Experienced?" if you're going to include it on the bonus disc anyway. Substituting "Are You Experienced" and "Voodoo Child (Slight Return)" for the fifteen-minute "Tax Free" that opens Disc One really makes you feel like you've climbed on a dragonfly.

34

Taking for Granted

Greek Classical Elements in Hendrix's Lyrics

I don't hang much with the classicists. Greek and Roman gods hold no sway with me. But I do place stock in the four roots identified by Empedocies, later classified as elements by Plato and expanded to include a fifth in Aristotle's *On Generation and Corruption*. The four classical Greek elements are Air, Fire, Earth, and Water. It is because of the recurrent presence of these classical elements that the work of Jimi Hendrix remains vital to later generations. Air, Fire, Earth, and Water are essential to the worldview of all generations of humankind, so it's not surprising that Hendrix's lyrics also tap into these four Greek classical elements. Repeatedly. Taken for granted, these roots of Hendrix's worldview have contributed to his posthumous success by resonating with his new fans.

Air

In Hendrix's lyrics, angels and hands come from a *heaven* ("Angel" and "Astro Man" and "Ezy Ryder"); Dolly Dagger's riding broomsticks ("Dolly Dagger"); and mobs paint red through the *sky* ("House Burning Down"). Hendrix's head is in the *clouds* ("Earth Blues") that Little Wing's walking through ("Little Wing") and UFOs chuckle in ("Somewhere").

Never mentioned but often implied, "air" is all around. When the sky isn't being kissed ("Purple Haze"), it's something for Hendrix's characters to pass through: Astro Man is *flying* two times higher than Superman ever could ("Astro Man"); a woman can be a "night bird *flying* through the night" ("Night Bird Flying"); the Spanish castle is reached by traveling through air on a dragonfly ("Spanish Castle Magic").

Fire

There's a song called "Fire," of course, but also in Jimi Hendrix's lyrics the sunrise is *burning* his eyes ("Ain't No Telling"), he sits before the "same old *fireplace*" ("Burning of the Midnight Lamp"), tears "*burn* a garden green" ("Castles Made of Sand"), there's *burning* desire ("Fire" and "Burning Desire"), *flaming* hair ("Highway Chile"), and *hell fire* skies ("House Burning Down"). In "Long Hot Summer Night," "everybody's on *fire*"; in "Somewhere," cities are *burning*; in "Voodoo Chile," the moon turns a *fire* red.

Earth

In Hendrix's lyrics, "every inch of *earth* is a fighting nest" ("1983 . . . (A Merman I Should Turn to Be)") where men are shot down ("Machine Gun") on "*battle grounds*, red and brown" ("Spanish Castle Magic"). Queen Jealousy's gowns sneer at *ground* that is grassy ("Bold as Love"), a young Indian plays "war games in the *woods*" ("Castles Made of Sand"), and a gypsy roams the *countryside* ("Gypsy Eyes"). It's not always happy times as lonesome lovers will go back "among the *hills*" ("Red House"), "happiness staggers on down the *street*" ("The Wind Cries Mary") and a sweet darling can be seen digging in the *mud* ("In from the Storm").

But look up and lightning is flashing all around the *trees* ("Midnight Lightning"), the Voodoo Chile chops down a mountain with the edge of his hand ("Voodoo Chile"), and there's a spaceman who wants to know all about Mother Earth ("Up from the Skies"). Maybe he's even the same spaceman circling the third stone from the sun, which is, of course, earth.

Water

In Hendrix's lyrics, "May This Be Love" was originally titled "Waterfall." A gypsy is told she has "*tears* in your eyes" ("Gypsy Eyes"), blue are the life-giving *waters* ("Bold as Love"), and *rain* is crying ("In from the Storm"). In "Somewhere," across the *water* Hendrix sees weapons barking out of the sand. The description of the wet city park and its inhabitants in "Rainy Day, Dream Away" is as vivid as the thunderstorm scene in Woody Allen's *Manhattan*. In fact, *rainy* days abound in his lyrics—you'll even find one in "Fire." You just can't escape the rain in his songs. Rain cuts deep in his mind ("My Friend"), objects are compared to it—"Pencil 'n' lipstick tube shaped things continue to *rain* ("1983 . . . (A Merman I Should Turn to Be)," "bullets fly like *rain*" ("Machine Gun")—and it even bathes in the parkside pool ("Rainy Day, Dream Away").

Rain is one of the most frequently referenced water related images in the Hendrix canon. The other is the sea, which—whether it be love filled or comprised of heartbreak or methane—is something to float your lifeboat on ("Drifting"), fly right over ("Have You Ever Been (to Electric Ladyland)"),

and mountains fall into ("If 6 Was 9"). The sea is someplace you watch the sunrise from the bottom of ("Are You Experienced"). The original lyrics for "Purple Haze" were, according to Hendrix, "all about a dream I had that I was walking under the sea."

Deleted from the completed lyrics of "Purple Haze," the concept of living under sea is one that continued to fascinate Hendrix, and so not only does he mention doing so in "Are You Experienced?" but he built his masterpiece around the very concept of a man fleeing a war-torn world and walking through "the noise to the sea" and living underwater in "1983 . . . (A Merman I Should Turn to Be)."

35

They Were Still Arguin' About Me Then

The Hendrixian Library

For the most part, Hendrix's biographers and historians have been devoted to preserving the departed guitarist's legacy. While it is true that some are self-serving (bios by Monika Dannemann, Al Hendrix, and Curtis Knight flagrantly so), almost every book on Hendrix has a commendable aspect.

Chris Welch's short *Hendrix*, originally published in 1972, is not really a biography per se as half the book consists of black-and-white photographs, and the text is a series of essays and interviews with what passed for Hendrix's confidants, although the back cover clearly states that Hendrix may have "had many friends, but few would claim to be close." The interviews, nevertheless, are invaluable, and, though not explicitly acknowledged in most of the subsequent biographies, their words were heavily requoted in those biographies. The most insightful interviews are with manager Chas Chandler, fellow Experience Maker Noel Redding, roadie Eric Barrett, and lover Jeanette Jacobs. All are still trying to come to terms with the death even if, as Chandler put it: "Something had to happen and there was no way of stopping it. You just get a feeling sometimes. It was as if the last couple of years had prepared us for it. It was like the message I had been waiting for."

Mitch Mitchell is not interviewed in *Hendrix*, but you can find his take on things in *Inside the Experience*, written with John Platt. It is mostly an oral history but valuable nonetheless because Mitchell rarely granted interviews to biographers. It was published in 1990, in what was a watershed decade for books on Jimi Hendrix. Hendrix historian Tony Brown alone published three books on Hendrix that decade, the best of which is *The Final Days*. Seen from a certain perspective, Tony Brown was Hendrix's archeologist. Another book of his, *Jimi Hendrix: A Visual Documentary*, does not only display rare certificates and other family artifacts, it was the first attempt to document day-by-day the activities of Jimi Hendrix

Jerry Hopkins's biography could be dismissed as a hack job meant to cash in on the success of *No One Gets Out of Here Alive*, his biography of Jim Morrison and the Doors that remains the definitive Morrison biography—but is not without insights. For example, his observation that "only *Jimi* was 'home' in the U.S. and the others around him were homesick" cuts to the heart of troubles affecting the psychological well-being of the Jimi Hendrix Experience. Hopkins's biography will be of most interest to those who want to know the nuts and bolts of Hendrix's contractual agreements and the mismanagement of his estate. Building on his 1976 *Rolling Stone* article "A Piece of the Rainbow," the 1996 edition summarizes the legal maneuvering that resulted in the 1995 settlement whereby Hendrix's work was rightfully awarded to his father, half-sister, and a nephew.

All these aforementioned books are recommended, but if you're looking for the cream of the crop, the following are indispensable.

Best Biographies

Reading every Hendrix biography in less than three months was an insightful journey into the art of the biography. None are perfect. All reflect the strengths and weaknesses of the author. One comes away wanting to combine them like Hendrix combining the American and British national anthems during his intro to the Monterey rendition of "Wild Thing" or wishing that an author with Norman Mailer's clout would take all that has been written about Jimi Hendrix, edit, and reissue it as he did with his investigation into the troubled life of Lee Harvey Oswald in *Oswald's Tale: An American Mystery*.

The earliest biography, by British music journalist Chris Welch, was published in 1972. His *Hendrix* is a fairly subjective take on Hendrix's career, which he saw in decline as early as mid-1967, and I think played a large role in many misconceptions that have taken root and have been hard to clear away. Imperfect as they are, the following are the biographies I recommend:

'Scuse Me While I Kiss the Sky

David Henderson's achievement of bringing the first full-blown biography of Jimi Hendrix to market brings drawbacks along with its many assets. Originally published as *Jimi Hendrix: Voodoo Child of the Aquarian Age* in 1978 by Doubleday, it has been in print ever since, possibly because it is the most gossipy. Where else are you going to find Jimi Hendrix telling Marianne Faithfull that Mick Jagger is a cunt?

I am reluctant to recommend it because of the same justifiable racial flaws that Hendrix's inner London circle found—they took Henderson to court for libel in London—and the errors contained within are significant and glaring to someone who is well versed in the facts of Hendrix's life, recording sessions, and concert performances. Not only is the book repetitive and poorly edited with incorrect dates, but if this is the only book on Hendrix that you read, you'll come away with many major and minor misconceptions.

For example, Henderson misrepresents Hendrix's jam with Cream on "Killing Floor" on October 1, 1966, at Central Polytechnic by writing that the "Experience's first gig in London was on the same bill with Cream at Central Polytechnic." (Never mind that this jam occurred three days before Chas Chandler even offered Mitch Mitchell an audition with Hendrix.) That's a minor misrepresentation, but to have Hendrix jamming with B. B. King and Buddy Guy at the Generation Club in New York City minutes after Martin Luther King Jr. was assassinated is just plain wrong. (Hendrix was actually in Virginia Beach with the Experience for two shows that were cancelled.)

On the plus side, Henderson's biography carries a freshness that other biographers can never capture. Written and published less than a decade after Hendrix's death, it benefits considerably from access to press materials published in Hendrix's lifetime, first-generation bootleg recordings, and interviews and conversations with relatives and the musicians and lovers who knew Hendrix and when their memories were the freshest. (Written shortly after Hendrix's times, they best capture those times.)

While Henderson's purple prose can at times be distracting, it also helps capture vividly Hendrix's sound. Concert performances are as thrilling as if you had been in the audience and the writing three-dimensional. His descriptions of studio recordings are stirring and aided with permission to print Hendrix's lyrics, although you sometimes wonder why when airing an album he describes songs out of order.

Jimi Hendrix: Electric Gypsy

Published twenty years after his passing, *Electric Gypsy* is the only biography as epic as Hendrix. At 732 pages it is the *Electric Ladyland* of bios. This labor of love from Harry Shapiro and Caesar Glebbeek (of Amsterdam's now defunct Hendrix Information Centre) touches on as many Hendrixian facts and myths as it can. True, they print some of Hendrix's tall tales as fact, but they tell the story as straight as they could.

Hendrix and others are quoted at length, brief insights into the musicology behind key songs are given without intimidating the average fan, Hendrix's lyrics explained without the purple prose of David Henderson.

There are 165 photos (20 in color), and that's not including reproductions of postcards home, scribbled lyrics, posters (but does include Hendrix's oft-stamped passport). The majority of these illustrations you will not see anywhere else. The end matter is endlessly fascinating with five appendices, including a detailed discography through 1990; a technical file on Hendrix's gear (Noel Redding and Mitch Mitchell's too!), techniques, guitar and studio effects; a chronology; a family tree; and what you can find in print and film (at least through 1991). The only blind spot is the recording sessions themselves, possibly because Eddie Kramer declined to be interviewed.

Hendrix: Setting the Record Straight

Though the back cover of the 1992 Warner Brothers edition claims to be "told completely in firsthand accounts," this is not an oral history along the lines of George Plimpton's *Truman Capote: In Which Various Friends, Enemies, Acquaintances and Detractors Recall His Turbulent Career.*

(Believe it or not, American literature's Tiny Terror crossed paths with Jimi Hendrix at a party at the Waldorf-Astoria on March 15, 1968. Other attendees included Mike Bloomfield, Eric Burdon, producer Tom Wilson, and Bianca Jagger before she was Bianca Jagger. It was through Bianca that Capote made it to Hendrix's party. According to Truman, Hendrix was "very, ah, not like anything that I would subsequently know about him. He was a very subdued rather shy guy." One wishes that when Capote was writing his "Conversations with Capote" feature for Andy Warhol's *Interview*, he had written about the night he partied with Jimi Hendrix.)

What author John McDermott does do is, as advertised on the back cover, take the words of "Jimi's closest friends, associates, and fellow musicians" and less scandalously relate the facts than Henderson. McDermott (with Hendrix's recording engineer Eddie Kramer's input) honestly strives to document Hendrix's rise and fall and explain the handling of his work in the aftermath of his death. Some interviews are put to better use than others. For example, despite acknowledging Crosby, Stills, and Nash's "anecdotes about Jimi" and the fact that Paul and Linda McCartney met with the authors "at home and abroad," these interviews yield little insight. Yes, the book does feature "never-before-published photos from Linda,"

Mitch Mitchell's autobiography features many concert posters although not this one from Flint, Michigan, in 1969.   *Courtesy of Robert Rodriguez*

but you'll learn much more about Stephen Stills's almost monkish devotion to Hendrix in 1967 from *Shakey*, Jimmy McDonough's 2003 biography of Neil Young.

McDermott has more success utilizing interviews with Garry Stickells (Hendrix's road manager), Alan Douglas (Hendrix's controversial posthumous producer), and Linda Keith (a British model only in America because she had accompanied Rolling Stone Keith Richards). Usually relegated to a factual but shadowy role in Hendrix's rise, Keith's comments bring to life meeting Hendrix at the Cheetah, a discothèque at Fifty-Third Street and Broadway, and how she hastily orchestrated the initial movements of Hendrix's rise. She knew she'd only be in America for as long as the Rolling Stones tour was scheduled to last. It is particularly sad to hear her say that Hendrix's death was brought on when his "elaborate double life backfired on him."

This is the bio to read if you want to avoid the gossip. The facts are accurate and include informative recording details even if I disagree with his assessment of some of the posthumous releases. (For example, he underestimates *Rainbow Bridge* and overestimates *War Heroes*.) There is also a particularly good discography for the average buyer, although it only includes up to the four-disc *Stages* box set released in November 1991. I really appreciated seeing the track listing for the Alan Douglas–selected *Crash Landing* and *Mulitcolored Blues* releases that were never issued in the mid-'70s.

An updated version of *Hendrix: Setting the Record Straight* chronicling the court battles and later releases of Hendrix's music has never been published, which is baffling until you consider the role McDermott has played in the Hendrix estate since it was awarded to three Hendrix relatives in June 1995. Along with Janie Hendrix and Eddie Kramer, he has "produced" albums and DVDs issued by the estate and written liner notes for new and reissued recordings. Given the less than forthright manner in which Janie Hendrix has managed her stepbrother's legacy, it is hard to imagine McDermott and Kramer continuing to set the record straight without offending their co-"producer."

Room Full of Mirrors

Given its title, it's surprising that the cover of Charles R. Cross's biography doesn't have the one of the mirrored portraits of Jimi Hendrix that appeared in *Life* magazine's October 3, 1969, issue. Any one of them would have been an ideal cover for what may be the closest we get to the definitive biography of Jimi Hendrix. Having done his research and conducted over 300 interviews, Cross yields new anecdotes, a new paramour (Carmen Borrero), and the Mitchell brick marking the burial spot of Hendrix's mother Lucille in the same Seattle cemetery where her son rests.

Cross recreates Hendrix's latchkey childhood, explores the roots of his violent side, explodes myths surrounding his military service, and—to his credit—does not allow himself to be swayed by self-serving autobiographies. He recounts the legal issues related to the management of the legacy by the estate, which may account for the absences of any interview with Janie Hendrix.

Curiously, Cross does not dwell on recording sessions or attempt to explain the majesty of Hendrix's musical accomplishments, opting instead for a presentation of concrete facts and stories. There is also a lack of focus on the emotional weight that the Ed Chalpin lawsuits and Michael Jeffery management tactics had on Hendrix's final days. Reading *Room Full of Mirrors*, one has the impression that Cross believes that drugs were the principal cause of Hendrix's death rather than a misguided, desperate means of escape.

Best Autobiographies

Autobiographies by those who knew Hendrix abound and usually for two reasons: either to cash in (Al Hendrix, Curtis Knight) or to set the record straight from their point of view (Kathy Etchingham, Sharon Lawrence). Monika Dannemann, Mitch Mitchell and Noel Redding managed to do both. While the autobiographies by Etchingham and Mitchell are worth reading, the following two are indispensable.

The Intimate Story of a Betrayed Musical Legend

In the spirit of *Miracle on 34th Street*, let me say that if you are going to read only one book on Jimi Hendrix, Sharon Lawrence's is the one because it is the closest you'll ever come to reading Hendrix's autobiography. Sharon Lawrence was a reporter for United Press International when she met Hendrix on February 9, 1968, in Los Angeles, where she lived. They struck up an unlikely friendship, and, even if Lawrence gets some major facts wrong (e.g., telling Chas Chandler in New York City in 1966 of his existing contract with Ed Chalpin), her biography rings true. If you are going to read one biography of the left-handed guitar master, Lawrence's is the one.

It is also the saddest because it chronicles the fall of a very sweet man. Lawrence sheds considerable light on Hendrix's unhappy childhood through interviews with neighbors and the man himself. Most importantly, she removes the Vaseline gauze off of the portrait of Al Hendrix, Jimi's father, that's been promoted over the years. In other bios he comes across as befuddled and not the mean-mannered, womanizing father he probably was. It explains why Hendrix sings in Elmore James's "Bleeding Heart" with such conviction and why he was a "rolling stone gathering no moss." After his army stint, there was nothing to return to in Seattle, something Jimi said to Lawrence.

There are several truly dramatic moments in this biography including an intimidating meeting with manager Michael Jeffery prior to Hendrix's trial in Toronto in early December 1968; an encounter with a very stoned Hendrix at Ronnie Scott's less than two nights before he died; and a telephone confrontation in 1996 with Monika Dannemann shortly before Dannemann's suicide. I would be surprised if this biography has not been optioned as a film. It is that dramatic.

Drawing on personal memories, cassette interviews with Hendrix, and court records, Lawrence argues convincingly that Hendrix did commit suicide (that Eric Burdon was correct when he said the three-page poem Hendrix wrote hours before his death was a suicide note) and is not fearful of taking on the Hendrix estate.

This is the only book on Jimi Hendrix that almost reduced me to tears.

Are You Experienced?

Sharon Lawrence's autobiography includes a page or so on Noel Redding's death, including remembrance of a conversation in which Redding finally admitted he wished he'd been more supportive of Hendrix and not "so caught up in myself" during his stint in the Experience. In Redding's autobiography he was still caught up with himself, but it's a good read nonetheless.

First published in the United Kingdom in June 1990, *Are You Experienced?* was coauthored by Carol Appleby, Redding's partner and lover for seventeen years. She died the same week that the book was published. (Redding woke up next to her body in a car following what sounds like a drinking binge. Redding himself would die in 2003 from "shock hemorrhage due to esophageal varices in reaction to cirrhosis of the liver.") A libel lawsuit by Monika Dannemann (who thrived on litigation as much as Ed Chalpin) prevented publication in America until 1996.

It had been turned down by several publishing houses before 1990 because of Redding's focus on the music industry's machinations. But it is because of this very topic that it's the perfect book to be read by any aspiring musician. Redding may have lost millions through signing bad contracts, but he doesn't want you to.

Another topic that may have put off publishers is Redding's griping about not being adequately compensated for his contribution to Hendrix's canon, but some of the drama of the book stems from Redding jousting with legal windmills.

Unlike Mitchell's autobiography, this is not an oral history padded with photos. Redding actually sat down and wrote it, and Appleby whipped it into shape. Redding kept a diary during his Experience days, and he used it and other documents as a basis to recreate the era. (He even still had in his possession the apologetic note Hendrix wrote him and Mitchell in late 1968 saying how important it was to keep the Experience together.) Being a frank autobiography, it reveals many of Redding's blind spots, but that's part of what makes the book so valuable. *Are You Experienced?* isn't a candy-coated account of what happened within the Experience.

For Musicians Only

There are several worthy books out there related to Hendrix that are for musicians only. Michael Heatley's *Jimi Hendrix Gear* is ideal for the guitar nerd. John Perry's *Electric Ladyland*, a 33 1/3 imprint for Continuum, was written ostensibly for the common man, but is more useful for the musician. There's a discourse on feedback, Hendrix's mastery of the wah-wah pedal, how he recorded with guitars tuned down a semi-tone, the Hendrix chord (E7#9), and so on. John McDermott's *Jimi Hendrix: Sessions: The Complete Studio Recording Sessions 1963–1970* might not do for Jimi Hendrix what Mark Lewisohn's *The Beatles Recording Sessions: The Official Abbey Road Session Notes 1962–1970* did for the Beatles, but it's close. It has since been updated to include live concerts and new information in *Ultimate Hendrix* and includes valuable insights from Eddie Kramer and Billy Cox.

Jimi Hendrix: Musician

The best book, however, for a musician is *Jimi Hendrix: Musician* by Keith Shadwick, so don't be put off by the fact that it is a coffee table book. (I say that because I almost was.) This book by Shadwick, a jazz journalist who died in 2008, is the real McCoy for the musician who wants to read something about Hendrix from a purely musical standpoint and not that of a layman like me.

Presented chronologically, *Jimi Hendrix: Musician* goes as far back as Seattle in the 1940s to describe the dance halls and bands that Jimi Hendrix's parents danced to and the music scene that he eventually sprang from. There is a reason that he described himself as a "West Coast Seattle

Boy." He may not have wanted to be buried there, but he could not ignore his roots.

Shadwick's knowledge of jazz is also put to good use here as he details the morphing of swing bands into rock bands as being the sound of rebellion for youths. Shadwick points out how Lionel Hampton recorded a rock 'n' roll album in 1946 that his label would not release because it was considered "a black thing." He highlights the influence of Louis Jordan and the emergence of small rhythm and blues bands led by squawking tenor saxophones. (Maybe that's why during his final tour Hendrix kept saying he was playing "uh, public saxophone.") And Shadwick delves into the roots of the blues, too.

Shadwick gives the Experience their due (he concludes that whereas the Band of Gypsys followed Hendrix, the Experience accompanied him), dissects the songs, compares Hendrix often to John Coltrane and substantiates the comparison. He is the only writer who discusses Hendrix's habit of scaling scales in his latter compositions such as "Message to Love" and "Angel" and ties this back to Coltrane.

But Shadwick was a formidable writer, too. For example, when discussing "House Burning Down," he describes Hendrix's guitar parts as "commentaries" on the lyrics and elucidates how this is so. Ten Years After guitarist Alvin Lee told rock journalist Keith Altham in 1970 that Jimi Hendrix *the songwriter* wasn't sufficiently appreciated, and Shadwick does much in *Jimi Hendrix: Musician* to rectify this. This coffee table book is therefore highly recommended to the musician who truly wants to understand just what Jimi Hendrix, the musician and songwriter, was attempting to achieve.

For Collectors Only

There are several products that are musts for collectors. These items are loaded with rare information.

Black Gold—The Lost Archives of Jimi Hendrix

If *Jimi Hendrix: Musician* is perfect for the living room, Steven Roby's *Black Gold* is ideal for another room in your house, albeit a much smaller one. By this I do not mean to denigrate Roby's contribution to the Hendrixian library. His is an invaluable book to any of us interested in what was recorded and preserved and lost.

Roby was the editor of *Straight Ahead: The International Jimi Hendrix Magazine* from 1989 through 1996, has worked with Hendrix's estate, has published Hendrix-related material in magazines, produced annual radio shows honoring Hendrix, even promoted Hendrix tribute concerts: the man knows his Hendrix!

A little dated because of what has surfaced in the decade since publication, *Black Gold* is still a fun read. Naming the book for the "lost" autobiographical suite that Tony Brown found in Mitch Mitchell's possession, Roby has taken journey into Hendrix's recording past—as far back as the Rocking Kings in 1959—and listed as many recording sessions and concerts and jam sessions as possible and whether or not recordings are preserved or presumed lost. By doing so, he gives you a type of biography that documents Hendrix's activities in ways and stories you won't find in other books.

For example, as much as I consider Frank Zappa the second-greatest lead guitarist ever, I've soured on him over the years; his smugness gets under my skin. But I still admire the first two incarnations of the Mothers of Invention, and *We're Only in It for the Money* is undeniably one of the best rock records ever. I always wondered about Jimi Hendrix's image on what was originally intended to be the cover. It is a parody of the Beatles' *Sgt. Pepper's Lonely Hearts Club Band*. Hendrix couldn't have really been there for the photo shoot, could he? Surely it was a cut-out image. Roby's book set me straight. Not only was Hendrix there, but footage actually exists of Hendrix with the Mothers of Invention posing for the cover!

From the Benjamin Franklin Studios

You only need the three-volume *From the Benjamin Franklin Studios* (and its companion *The Studio Log*) if you are a collector, but you aren't a collector unless you have them. The third edition was published in 2008, and it is the best source for information on official and unofficial recordings. (Another book, *Look over Yonder*, is dedicated to movies, television appearances, fan footage: anything that was filmed of Jimi Hendrix.) It is a labor of love by Gary Geldeart and Steve Rodham.

Part 1 is subtitled "The Complete Guide to the Available Recordings," and it is just that. It contains an alphabetical listing of every song Jimi Hendrix is known to have recorded, a listing of what records and CDs the song has appeared on, and information where warranted. For example, as of 2008 there are seventy-five different known recordings of "Hey Joe," the song that, as Lulu said when introducing the Experience, "absolutely made them." You get brief recording details, details on the mixing, and a number listing of every recording each of the seventy-five versions appears on. There are also Appendices A through O that provides supplemental information to the recordings. For example, Appendix G details the producers and engineers that worked with Hendrix. At 352 pages, it is invaluable.

This numbered listing mentioned above corresponds with Part 2, which is subtitled "The Reference Discography." This part documents official and bootleg releases, provides a picture of the vinyl and CD covers (including singles), and lists the songs on each release. This is continued in Part 3, which just gives you an idea of the multitude of Jimi Hendrix recordings. Taken together, Parts 2 and 3 amount to 526 pages.

Fated unfortunately to becoming dated due to the continual—almost daily—emergence of new recordings, repackagings, books, and so on, this problem faced by *The Benjamin Franklin Studios* is rectified by *Jimpress*, a magazine that since 1991 has been keeping aficionados up-to-date with official and unofficial releases, books, DVDs, anything that has anything to do with Jimi Hendrix. They are also the publishers of *The Benjamin Franklin Studios,* and issues of *Jimpress* since 2008 have included articles relevant to the book such as "mysteries solved" and "embarrassing revelations."

The Studio Log is also compiled by Gary Geldeart and Steve Rodham and details every known recording session by Hendrix, including a list of the contributing musicians, songs recorded, number of takes, and background information. The book concludes with "a brief review of posthumous activity" and information related to Hendrix's "home" recordings. It gives you the basic session info quicker than McDermott's *Ultimate Hendrix.*

Anger, He Smiles, Towering in Shiny Metallic Purple Armor

The Best Jimi Hendrix Recording

To take this full circle, after reading that Jimi Hendrix had died, I remember walking over to King Karol Records the following Saturday and staring at his albums lining the shelf. "Which one is the best?"—or something to that effect—I asked one of the store's employees. I can still picture him: lean, the hint of a five o'clock shadow, *Revolver*-era long hair . . . I don't know if I'm making up the part about bellbottoms.

"None."

I gave him a quizzical look. I used to look at record shop employees with awe: they knew everything there was to know about music, I imagined. I was confused.

"All of them."

He went on to explain—as I've tried to do with this FAQ—that each studio album released in Hendrix's lifetime is the best. So it's funny that *Axis: Bold as Love* has diminished in stature over the years. Of the Experience's three albums, it is the one that isn't the subject of a book. The best comparison is the Clash's *Give 'em Enough Rope* and not just because the two albums are the sophomore effort.

Both were recorded by bands on the dash while touring and consolidating their successes to fortify their position within a startled industry. Both the Jimi Hendrix Experience and the Clash would go on to be wracked by acrimony, but this was not the case when recording their second album. United by their upstart status, both bands were in good spirits for the second go-round. Jimi Hendrix may have been King Guitar, but the world at large did not know yet what the other British lead guitarists knew—that he was a towering musical figure—and with Hendrix's universe still floating around his London entourage, he was in a good spot. The moon had not yet roughly turned the tides on him. It's no wonder that Kathy Etchingham and Noel Redding and Roger Mayer all identify *Axis: Bold as Love* as Jimi Hendrix's best album, Redding going so far as to say it was as raw as the first album "but more refined," according to Sean Egan. The phoenix was still experiencing his initial rise.

Recording Sessions

Unlike *Are You Experienced*, unlike *Electric Ladyland*, all the songs for *Axis: Bold as Love* were recorded and mixed at one place: Olympic Studios. The sessions unofficially began on May 4, 1967, with the recording of the basic track for Noel Redding's "She's So Fine." Beginning with the bassist's song is testimony to the camaraderie the three musicians in the Experience still shared. It was a fun session, with Hendrix and Mitchell providing humorous backing vocals and Hendrix suggesting the solo. Redding was beside himself with the glee that the Experience was actually recording a song he wrote.

Several other tracks were recorded that evening ("Mister Bad Luck," "Taking Care of No Business," and "Cat Talking to Me"), but more importantly, the basic tracks for the two sections of "If 6 Was 9"—perhaps the signature *Axis* track—were laid down.

Section B was later dubbed "Symphony of Experience," and work continued on it the following evening with Hendrix and Mitchell adding overdubs to the rhythm track. Also added on May 5th were Hendrix's lead vocal and flute, background vocals, and the footstomps of guest musicians Graham Nash and Gary Leeds nee Walker to give the track its unique percussion. (Similar percussion can be heard on the Clash's 45 version of "White Riot.") Within a week's time, "If 6 Was 9" was in the can.

And that is where sessions for *Axis: Bold as Love* remained until the Jimi Hendrix Experience returned from its triumphant debut appearance at Monterey, the initial West Coast concerts in America, the recording of the fourth Experience 45, the initial East Coast concerts in America, a European tour, as well as television and radio appearances. It was nearly five months later—October 1, 1967—that the Experience Makers found themselves back inside Olympic Studios recording the basic tracks for "Little Miss Lover," which was intended to be on the second Experience album that management wanted in the shops in time for Christmas.

Two nights later, "You Got Me Floating" and "One Rainy Wish" were recorded, and "Little Miss Lover" was blinged with overdubs and mixed as the Experience warmed up for "Bold as Love," another signature track from *Axis: Bold as Love* that was recorded and perfected on October 4th and 5th.

Radio and television dates prevented further work until October 25th. (Although Hendrix and Mitchell did lay down the earliest known recording of "Angel" on October 14th, albeit at a brisker tempo.) "Little Wing," arguably Hendrix's prettiest composition, was recorded on the 25th, and over the next five nights the Experience recorded "Wait Until Tomorrow," "Spanish Castle Magic," "Up from the Skies," "Bold as Love," "Castles Made of Sand," and "EXP." Mitchell's childhood acting experience came in handy when asked to play the role of the interviewer to Hendrix's spaceman during "EXP." Decades later, "EXP" plays like skits found on rap albums.

Several of those tracks received overdubs, as did Noel Redding's "She's So Fine." In fact, the October 30th overdub session for the first song cut for *Axis: Bold as Love* way back in May was the last song worked on prior to final mixing by Chas Chandler, Jimi Hendrix, and Eddie Kramer.

The Missing *Axis* Mix

Halloween 1967 was a real treat for the Experience mixers, and Hendrix perhaps played a trick on Chandler and Kramer. The threesome spent the day mixing all thirteen tracks for *Axis: Bold as Love*. Then later that evening, after attending a party, Hendrix lost the box containing the tape for A side when he left it behind in a taxi. The story is plausible as he was known to habitually lose things. But some suspect that, unhappy with the mix for Side A as well as being forced to record an album in sixteen days, Hendrix deliberately lost the tape box. (A similar mishap befell the master tapes for *Band of Gypsys*.) Hendrix bemoaned the losing of the original mix to interviewers, but he was known to be happier with the remixed "EXP." The mono mix was made on November 2nd, and the Experience gave *Axis: Bold as Love* a listen and their blessing on November 7th. It was mastered on November 16th and released on December 1st.

Axis Defined

The theory of "Axis" was one of most importance to Jimi Hendrix and one he tried defining with limited success. After all, being a musician, his music spoke for him. But about the Experience's second album, he is quoted by David Henderson as saying, "I just thought about the title. There might be a meaning behind the whole thing: the axis of the Earth turns around and changes the face of the world and . . . if a cat falls in love or a girl falls in

The cover poster for *Axis: Bold as Love*, which is considered by Jimi's London entourage to be the best Jimi Hendrix Experience album.   *Author's collection*

love, it might change his whole complete scene. *Axis: Bold as Love* . . . 1-2-3, rock around the clock."

Signature Tracks

If *Are You Experienced* can be said to have four signature tracks, the tracks that define the album, the same can be said of *Axis: Bold as Love*. Roger Mayer thought that "3rd Stone from the Sun" "kind of set the tone for the next album, *Axis*" and he's right. The success of the experimentation that went into that intergalactic track allowed Hendrix to get away with singing from a spaceman's point of view or singing about flying dragonflies.

"Spanish Castle Magic"

The third track from *Axis* invoked Hendrix's early memories of going to concerts given by the Wailers, the Frantics, and the Dave Lewis Combo at a club named the Spanish Castle in Seattle in 1959 and 1960, hence his declaration that "it's not in Spain." One of the earliest bands he was in—the Rocking Kings—also gigged there. It's unclear if Hendrix knew the Spanish Castle had closed in 1966, but the nostalgic nature of "Spanish Castle Magic" makes it likely that he was.

The song structure is early heavy metal: repetitive, echoing notes crash against chugging chords. The rhythm is similar to "Little Miss Lover." It was the only song from *Axis* to be played with some regularity in concerts, although it was not a staple of set lists except during late 1968 and the Experience's spring tour of America in 1969.

"Little Wing"

The reason the Jimi Hendrix Experience was the power trio of choice in 1967 was that while they could compete with Cream when it came to jams, Cream could not write pop classics. Some credit for this must be given to Chas Chandler for reining Hendrix in, but in 1967 and throughout *Axis: Bold as Love* there are several fully realized pop classics that in 3:30 or less will educate listeners just as records had educated Hendrix. There's "Little Miss Lover" reeking of free love, the exuberant "You Got Me Floatin'," and the romantic "Little Wing." Those three songs honestly depict three aspects of love and tell you more than you'll ever learn in a classroom.

The woman in "Little Wing" is vague because the way she is described in the first verse is a composite of Hendrix's experiences at the Monterey International Pop Festival; she's more spirit than flesh and blood. She is the follow-up to the "waterfall" in "May This Be Love" and the precursor to the angel that will come to him in the song of the same name that first cropped up during the *Axis* sessions, and there's a similarity in 1967 between the two.

Hendrix's guitar playing complements the lyrical, the deft striking of strings in duos and triads suggesting Little Wing's wildly running circus mind. The only flaw to the song is the ending, which dashes off through the clouds. The sense that there was more to be said with Hendrix's guitar was confirmed with the Royal Albert Hall live version that graced the original album version of *In the West*, where he adds a solo coda that finishes the musical thought.

"If 6 Was 9"

This song is Jimi Hendrix's manifesto, which explains the riff's roots in "Experiencing the Blues," a Muddy Waters/John Lee Hooker–derived blues number that the Experience occasionally played. The lyrics were influenced by the *I Ching*, one of China's oldest written works and considered hip reading in Swinging London, where no doubt someone handed it to Hendrix.

The rhythm slithers, and so it's totally appropriate that Mitchell's hi-hat hisses like a snake as Hendrix almost speaks the first two verses about living his own lifestyle. He pointedly says he doesn't care what the hippies do even as the conservatives are "pointin' their plastic finger at me." That Jimi Hendrix was not a hippie is something that has been misconstrued by popular culture, although this confusion is created somewhat by him saying that the conservatives are "hopin' that soon *my kind* will drop and die." Saying "my kind" makes him the spokesman for a youth culture of the late '60s that he was not totally comfortable with.

Hendrix cleverly addresses the falling mountains of the first verse by asking them not to fall on him, and then the Experience strike up their own special brand of symphony as they spiral off and come the closest they ever will to atonal jazz.

"Bold as Love"

Colors were everywhere in Swinging London. The Rolling Stones were singing "She's a Rainbow," and Donovan's "Mellow Yellow" was one of his most successful singles, second only to "Sunshine Superman" in his career. So it was only natural that Hendrix would take a stab at an ode to colors, and the result "Bold as Love" references both hit singles.

His scene, however, is more militaristic and highlights the warfare between the sexes. Clearly, Hendrix the male is angry and sparring with the female, Queen Jealousy. Like many couples caught up in an emotional conflict they don't know the roots of, the male and female are wondering "why the fight is on."

His red—his anger—is so confident, whereas his yellow is not mellow, and Hendrix takes an un-rock star pose by admitting his flagging confidence. It's a very cloaked yet forthright assessment by Hendrix of his inability to be close to anyone due to his difficult childhood with an absent mother and drunken father. Only the bravado-echoing title statement feels a little false. You wish he had ended "Bold as Love" with: "Just ask the Axis, 1-2-3, rock around the clock." It would have been so lyrically Hendrixian: so clear, yet so obscure.

Everybody in the studio was looking for a special way to close the album, and judging from Jim Miller's *Rolling Stone* review, they found the "pomp and circumstance [to] usher [*Axis: Bold as Love*] out" but it didn't come from Chandler or Hendrix or Kramer or even the Experience's rhythm section contributing ideas of their own such as Mitchell's use of brushes on "Up from the Skies." The idea came from second recording engineer George Chkiantz.

Phased guitars peaked in the late '70s, early '80s when acid punk bands such as Siouxsie and the Banshees and PiL brandished the sound, but in 1967 it had never been used on pop records even though a primitive version known as artificial double tracking existed. It was a sound that piqued Chkiantz. It wasn't fully realized. So while working on the Small Faces' eponymous second album, he took a stereo mix of a song named "Green Circles," and the first song with mono phasing was born.

When Kramer played the new sound for Hendrix, the guitarist was ecstatic. It was exactly the sound Hendrix had heard in a dream and previously mentioned to Kramer. Wouldn't it be something if Section II of "Bold as Love" could use that sound? ("Bold as Love," like "If 6 Was 9," had been worked on as two sections.) Kramer enlisted the efforts of Chkiantz producer Glyn Johns, and together the threesome created phasing in stereo. It gave "Bold as Love" the symphonic-sounding outro that *Axis: Bold as Love* needed.

Selected Bibliography

Books

Black, Johnny. *Jimi Hendrix—The Ultimate Experience*. London: Carlton Book, 1999.

Brown, Tony. *The Final Days of Jimi Hendrix*. London: Rogan House, 1997.

Brown, Tony. *Jimi Hendrix—In His Own Words*. London: Omnibus Press, 1994.

Brown, Tony. *Jimi Hendrix—A Visual Documentary*. London: Omnibus Press, 1992.

Cross, Charles R. *Room Full of Mirrors*. New York: Hyperion, 2005.

Egan, Sean. *Not Necessarily Stoned, but Beautiful*. London: Unanimous, 2002.

Etchingham, Kathy. *Through Gypsy Eyes*. London: Orion, 1998.

Geldeart, Gary and Rodham, Steve. From *The Benjamin Franklin Studios, Part 1*. London: Jimpress Publications, 2008.

Geldeart, Gary and Rodham, Steve. From *The Benjamin Franklin Studios, Part 2*. London: Jimpress Publications, 2008.

Geldeart, Gary and Rodham, Steve. From *The Benjamin Franklin Studios, Part 3*. London: Jimpress Publications, 2008.

Geldeart, Gary and Rodham, Steve. *The Studio Log*. London: Jimpress Publications, 2007

Heatley, Michael. *Jimi Hendrix Gear*. London: Voyageur Press, 2009.

Henderson, David. *'Scuse Me While I Kiss The Sky*. New York: Doubleday, 1978.

Hendrix, Janie L. *Jimi Hendrix: The Lyrics*. New York: Hal Leonard, 2003.

Hopkins, Jerry. *The Jimi Hendrix Experience*. Baltimore: Arcade, 1996.

Lawrence, Sharon. *Jimi Hendrix The Intimate Story of a Betrayed Musical Legend*. New York: Harper, 2006.

McDermott, John with Kramer, Eddie. *Hendrix—Setting the Record Straight*. New York: Warner Books, 1992.

McDermott, John with Cox, Billy and Kramer, Eddie. *Jimi Hendrix Sessions*. New York: Little, Brown and Company, 1995.

McDermott, John with Kramer, Eddie and Cox, Billy. *Ultimate Hendrix*. New York: Backbeat Books, 2009.

Mitchell, Mitch with Platt, John. *Jimi Hendrix—Inside the Experience*. New York: St. Martin's Press, 1990.

Murray, Charles Shaar. *Crosstown Traffic—Jimi Hendrix and Post-War Pop*. London: Faber and Faber, 1989.

Perry, John. *Electric Ladyland*. New York: Continuum, 2004.

Potash, Chris. *The Jimi Hendrix Companion—Three Decades of Commentary*. New York: Schirmer Books, 1996.

Redding, Noel and Appleby, Carol. *Are You Experienced*. New York: Da Capo Press, 1996.

Roby, Steven. *Black Gold—The Lost Archives of Jimi Hendrix*. New York: Billboard Books, 2002.

Roby, Steven and Schreiber, Brad. *Becoming Jimi Hendrix* New York: Da Capo Press, 2010.

Saunders, William. *Jimi Hendrix London*. Berkeley, CA: Roaring Forties Press, 2010.

Shadwick, Keith. *Jimi Hendrix—Musician*. New York: Backbeat Books, 2003.

Shapiro, Harry and Glebbeek, Caesar. *Jimi Hendrix—Electric Gypsy*. New York: St. Martin's Press, 1991.

Stubbs, David. *Jimi Hendrix The Stories Behind Every Song*. London: Carlton Books, 2010.

Unterberger, Richie. *The Rough Guide to Jimi Hendrix*. London: Rough Guides, 2009.

Welch, Chris. *Hendrix—A Biography*. London: Omnibus Press, 1982.

Websites

http://crosstowntorrents.org
http://www.jimpress.co.uk

Index